Microsoft Dynamics™ CRM 4

FOR DUMMIES®

Microsoft Dynamics™ CRM 4

FOR DUMMIES®

by Joel Scott, David Lee, and Scott Weiss

WILEY

Wiley Publishing, Inc.

Microsoft Dynamics™ CRM 4 For Dummies®

Published by
Wiley Publishing, Inc.
111 River Street
Hoboken, NJ 07030-5774

www.wiley.com

Copyright © 2008 by Wiley Publishing, Inc., Indianapolis, Indiana

Published by Wiley Publishing, Inc., Indianapolis, Indiana

Published simultaneously in Canada

For general information on our other products and services, please contact our Customer Care Department within the U.S. at 800-762-2974, outside the U.S. at 317-572-3993, or fax 317-572-4002.

For technical support, please visit www.wiley.com/techsupport.

Wiley also publishes its books in a variety of electronic formats. Some content that appears in print may not be available in electronic books.

Library of Congress Control Number: 2008929979

ISBN: 978-0-470-34325-8

Manufactured in the United States of America

10 9 8 7 6 5 4 3 2 1

WILEY

About the Authors

Joel Scott is the president of the Computer Control Corporation, which began focusing on CRM software in 1989. Since the early 1990s, Computer Control has been an elite dealer of GoldMine software, winning many sales and business process awards. Mr. Scott has also written the entire series of *GoldMine For Dummies* books.

With the release of Microsoft CRM 1, Computer Control Corporation made the decision to expand its product line and expertise to Microsoft CRM as well. Mr. Scott has been the lead author for the *Microsoft CRM For Dummies* series. This is now the third book in the series.

In 2007, the Computer Control Corporation merged with a friendly competitor, Core Solutions, Inc. Mr. Scott now handles GoldMine and Microsoft CRM sales and design work for Core Solutions, as well as focusing on client retention consulting, writing, and speaking engagements. Mr. Scott can be reached at `joels@ccc24k.com`.

David Lee is the Chairman of the Board of Trustees for the University of Northern Virginia, Vice Chair of the Board of Trustees of Myers University, on the Board of Advisors to ECPI, and was also adjunct faculty for George Mason University.

He founded Vertical Marketing, Inc., as a home-based business in 1985 and has grown it to a force in the CRM industry, with offices in four cities worldwide. It has won numerous industry awards and certifications and has completed more than 1,000 CRM projects using dozens of CRM applications.

Dr. Lee is a recognized speaker and thought leader in the customer relationship management (CRM) industry. He is a regular contributor to several CRM publications and writes a CRM column for *MSDynamicsWorld*. He is certified in many of the primary mid-market CRM systems.

Before founding Vertical Marketing, Dr. Lee served as Marketing & Support Manager, Vice President of Marketing, Vice President of Sales, and President in such organizations as Rand Teleprocessing, Barrister Microsystems, and Market Wise Inc., and as an officer in the U.S. Army. He is also a karate black belt and a competition-level dancer.

Mr. Lee can be contacted at `dlee@vermar.com`.

Scott Weiss is president and CEO of Core Solutions, Inc., a CRM consulting firm specializing in Microsoft CRM, SalesLogix, and GoldMine. He is a graduate of Rutgers University and earned a MBA from Boston University. With over 20 years marketing and sales expertise, Mr. Weiss is authoring his first *For Dummies* book.

Mr. Weiss founded Core Solutions in 2000. With offices in Newton, Massachusetts, and Rocky Hill, Connecticut, Core Solutions has provided CRM solutions to hundreds of clients. Mr. Weiss hosted a weekly radio show "Winning Business" from 2005–2006. He has guest lectured to graduate business students on entrepreneurship.

Prior to founding Core Solutions, Mr. Weiss spent several years in sales and marketing management in the medical diagnostics industry. He lectured on international marketing for the Massachusetts Port Authority.

Mr. Weiss can be reached at sweiss@consultcore.com.

Authors' Acknowledgments

Joel Scott: No one writes a book alone. Perhaps it's possible for a work of fiction. I plan to find that out shortly. But even then, a collection of editors and technicians all have some say in the appearance of the work. Bob Woerner and Chris Morris, our editors at Wiley, have consistently been there for us working hard and responding quickly.

I also need to thank my co-authors, Dave Lee and Scott Weiss. Our early brainstorming sessions about this book and continuing communications made this writing easier.

I also want to thank everyone at home for taking up the slack while I was so often sitting in my room moaning and groaning over words I had written and rewritten so many times.

David Lee: I would like to thank two of my senior engineers, Benjamin Mwendwa and Patrick Pawlowski, for their help and support in this effort. They spent many hours reviewing and checking the facts, capturing pictures of the screens, and doing technical reviews. Without their help I could not have written this book and still run my company, Vertical Marketing.

I also need to thank my friend, partner, competitor, and co-author, Joel Scott. He risked a friendship spanning more than a decade by asking me to co-author our first Microsoft CRM For Dummies book. Now, after our second round of late nights and deadlines, I still like the guy.

I could not leave out Scott Weiss, the newest member of our little team of co-authors. By taking on one third of the chapters, he cut my workload by 50 percent.

Finally, I would like to thank you, the reader, for your interest in Microsoft CRM. CRM is my passion (I am a pretty dull guy), and it is people like you who allow me to do the work that I love.

Scott Weiss: First and foremost I want to thank my wife, Rachel, and my three children, Zach, Ethan, and Stephanie, for their support and understanding during the writing process. Without them, I never would have completed my work.

I'd also like to thank Umang Vasa of Microsoft, who has been a valuable resource throughout this process. I'd also like to thank the entire Wiley team and, in particular, Chris Morris, senior project editor; Heidi Unger, copy editor; and Bob Woerner, senior acquisitions editor, for their expertise and easygoing style. I'd also like to thank our technical editor, John Straumann, for his help and insights.

Lastly, thank you to Joel Scott and David Lee for adding me to the team of authors. Their guidance and patience were and are very much appreciated.

Publisher's Acknowledgments

We're proud of this book; please send us your comments through our online registration form located at www.dummies.com/register/.

Some of the people who helped bring this book to market include the following:

Acquisitions, Editorial

Sr. Project Editor: Christopher Morris

(Previous Edition: Susan Pink)

Sr. Acquisitions Editor: Bob Woerner

Copy Editor: Heidi Unger

Technical Editor: John Straumann

Editorial Manager: Kevin Kirschner

Editorial Assistant: Amanda Foxworth

Sr. Editorial Assistant: Cherie Case

Cartoons: Rich Tennant
(www.the5thwave.com)

Composition Services

Project Coordinator: Katie Key

Layout and Graphics: Carl Byers, Reuben W. Davis, Melissa K. Jester, Stephanie D. Jumper, Christine Williams

Proofreaders: Broccoli Information Management, Caitie Kelly, Jessica Kramer

Indexer: Lynnzee Elze

Publishing and Editorial for Technology Dummies

    Richard Swadley, Vice President and Executive Group Publisher

    Andy Cummings, Vice President and Publisher

    Mary Bednarek, Executive Acquisitions Director

    Mary C. Corder, Editorial Director

Publishing for Consumer Dummies

    Diane Graves Steele, Vice President and Publisher

    Joyce Pepple, Acquisitions Director

Composition Services

    Gerry Fahey, Vice President of Production Services

    Debbie Stailey, Director of Composition Services

Contents at a Glance

Table of Contents

Introduction

*T*his book is about Microsoft Dynamics CRM version 4, which we refer to as simply Microsoft CRM or just CRM. We assume that Microsoft CRM just showed up on your desktop computer or notebook. Chances are, you already have some experience with one or more of the popular predecessors to CRM — ACT, GoldMine, SalesLogix, or an earlier release of Microsoft CRM. Maybe you thought your Outlook was actually a CRM system. (It isn't.) Or maybe you've never had any kind of CRM system — and never wanted one either. In any event, now you have to get yourself up and running with this new software. If you relate to any of this, *Microsoft CRM 4 For Dummies* is for you.

If you're a technical type looking for help with installation, integration, or serious customization, you'll need more than just this book. You'll need some technical references, an experienced dealer, and some time.

If nothing else, Microsoft CRM is an organizational tool. Whether you're in sales, marketing, customer service, or management, this software will provide a significant return on your investment — whether that investment is money or time. Beyond that, if you've fallen in love with Microsoft Outlook and refuse to relinquish it, relax. Not only can you still use Outlook, it's one of the primary means by which you'll communicate with Microsoft CRM.

How CRM Fits in the Market

Microsoft came to the CRM market seemingly a little late but with a system built on a platform called .NET. With CRM, you work in networked mode or in offline mode. Networked mode doesn't require a direct connection to your office file server. In fact, with .NET technology, *networked* actually means connected to the server through the Internet. *Offline* mode also takes great advantage of the Internet but enables you to work while disconnected by using a tool that Outlook users will find familiar.

And, now, Microsoft has an answer for all those users clamoring for a hosted version of its software. With the release of version 4, Microsoft is also offering CRM Live — a hosted version of essentially the same software you can purchase and install on your own servers.

If you have an IT department that's comfortable with the care and feeding of servers and have Internet connectivity with good firewalls and security, you should consider installing and using CRM. Otherwise, you can have CRM hosted. The third-party hosting company or Microsoft maintains the equipment and software in return for a monthly check.

How to Use This Book

Microsoft CRM is divided into six major sections: Workplace, Sales, Marketing, Service, Settings, and the new Resource Center. This book loosely follows these themes. We describe navigating the workplace and CRM in general in Chapter 3. In Part II, you find out all about setting up the system. Then we jump into sales topics, a little marketing, and some customer service.

You should be able to comfortably read the book from start to finish, but for those of you so caffeinated you can't sit still that long (don't laugh; you know who you are), each chapter can stand on its own as reference material. Either way, you have a comprehensive guide to Microsoft CRM.

You'll get the most benefit from this book by sitting in front of your computer with CRM on the screen. It's easy to convince yourself that you've got it by just reading, but there's no substitute for trying the steps yourself. Experimenting with sample data is sometimes just the ticket to an epiphany.

Foolish Assumptions

We assume you have some basic computer and Windows skills. If you aren't comfortable with Windows, you need to get yourself up to speed in this area. Find a local class or seminar, or get one of the *For Dummies* books on Windows. Regarding CRM, however, we assume you just returned from a long mission to Mars and need to start using CRM tomorrow.

We also assume you have a basic understanding of database concepts. If you're comfortable with fields, records, files, folders, and how they relate to each other, you'll be fine. If you're familiar with attributes, entities, instances, and objects, even better. If this is already sounding bad, you can seek help at most community colleges or local computer training facilities.

If you're going to be your own CRM administrator (backing up files and assigning usernames, passwords, and access rights), you need to understand records, files, folders, security, operating systems, and networks. If you just want to be a good day-to-day user of CRM, make sure that you understand what a file is and how to locate one using Explorer.

How This Book Is Organized

Some people just have a knack for organization. Our office manager is highly organized, although her desk looks like a tornado swept through it. However, she assures us that she knows exactly where everything *should* be. (And we take no responsibility for her actions if you touch anything.) Anyway, we digress. Organization — without it, this book would be a jumbled mess. To cure that, we've organized the book into six parts, each with at least three chapters. Again, you can read the book from cover to cover (who has that kind of time?), or you can refer to it section by section. Each part (and chapter) can definitely stand on its own, but we recommend that you at least skim through the basics and the table of contents before getting started.

Part I: Microsoft CRM Basics

Just the facts! Part I gives you an overview of what Microsoft CRM is all about and provides a tour of the main windows. We also show you how to use Microsoft CRM offline.

Part II: Setting Things Up

In Part II, we begin with a discussion of how to personalize your workplace and the software. The workplace is command central in Microsoft CRM. From the workplace, you can access the day-to-day stuff, such as your calendar, assigned activities, and service scheduling. You can also set up business units, security, sales processes, and business rules. Setting up workflow and reports are the topics of Chapters 9 and 10 respectively.

Part III: Managing Sales

In Part III, we explain how to create accounts and contacts in your database and how to locate existing records. We also show you how to create and manage activities as well as leads, opportunities, and territories. You find how-to information on notes and attachments. Then we get into the nitty-gritty and discuss some of the more complex functions of Microsoft CRM, such as quotes, orders, and invoices (some of which benefit from integration with an accounting system). In addition, we talk about sales literature and how to track competitors.

Part IV: Making the Most of Marketing

Microsoft CRM 4 explodes with all kinds of capability in the marketing arena. Combining the new Advanced Find function with quick campaigns and a sophisticated campaign management system, Microsoft CRM enables you to do more than just send out e-mails and letters. You'll be able to follow the progress of the campaign, create and delegate tasks, keep track of actual costs compared to the campaign budget, and easily catalog and maintain the responses.

Part V: Taking Care of Your Customers

Customer service is a big issue, no matter how big your company. In this part, we show you how to track and manage customer service issues using cases and the special Service Calendar. We talk about workflow and your business processes and how Microsoft CRM can easily handle incoming service calls and e-mail and their responses using queues. We discuss contracts and tiered levels of customer service and how to organize this division to handle service issues efficiently and quickly.

Part VI: The Part of Tens

As new as Microsoft CRM is, third-party developers have brought many complementary products to the market. We discuss the best and most useful we've found. And, just in case you still need assistance, we also discuss ten ways to get help.

Additionally, two appendixes at the end of the book assist you with converting to Microsoft CXRM 4 and with managing your data.

Icons Used in This Book

You don't want to skip the helpful reminders noted by this icon.

This icon lets you know that some particularly geeky, technical information is coming up. You can look past this if you want.

This icon points you to a trick that will save you time and effort.

Look to this icon to find out what to avoid if you don't want your database to blow up or cause you other types of anguish.

Where to Go from Here

If you're a first-time user, we suggest you begin with Chapters 1–3 to get a solid introduction to the basics of living with Microsoft CRM. Then check out Part III, IV, or V, depending on whether you're in sales, marketing, or customer service, respectively. If you're charged with setting up CRM for your company, you would do well to read Part I and then Part II. If you have questions or comments and want to contact us directly, please send us an e-mail at dummy@ccc24k.com.

Part I
Microsoft CRM
Basics

The 5th Wave   By Rich Tennant

"It's Web-based, on-demand, and customizable. Still, I think I'm going to miss our old sales incentive methods."

In this part . . .

Microsoft Dynamics CRM 4 is technically an update to version 3, but it's really a quantum leap beyond what first came out almost three years ago. In addition to smoothing out a few rough edges, Microsoft has added a *Live* — which, to most of us, means *hosted* — version of CRM. There are also three levels of server software, appropriate for small, mid-level, and enterprise-type organizations.

Microsoft CRM integrates with Outlook and the Web and is now much easier to use. If you're one of the 92 million Outlook users, Microsoft CRM is the comfortable, organizational upgrade you're looking for.

In this first part, you find a general discussion of the features and benefits of Microsoft CRM and how best to navigate through the screens, even if you're navigationally challenged. You can even set up internal announcements; this is discussed in Chapter 3.

Chapter 1

Taking a First Look at Microsoft CRM 4

*P*ersonal information managers (PIM) and contact management systems (CMS) were introduced in the mid-1980s. Both PIM and CMS enabled you to organize the names, addresses, and phone numbers for all of your business contacts. PIMs were superseded by sales force automation (SFA) systems in the late 1980s. Products such as ACT and GoldMine initially combined scheduling functions with contact management. By the mid-1990s, these systems evolved into simple customer relationship management (CRM) systems, attempting to involve not just salespeople but also customer service and management.

Microsoft Dynamics CRM 4 (that's the official name) is the next generation of CRM systems. Microsoft CRM is based on .NET (pronounced *dot-net)* technology, pioneered by Microsoft. Not only does Microsoft CRM have functionality for sales, customer service, and now marketing, it takes great advantage of the Internet, or more specifically, Web services. This Web service focus is what defines the .NET strategy. In a nutshell, Web services enable applications to be easily integrated, rapidly configured to meet your business needs, and extended to both internal and external users.

Tracking Your Contacts

Microsoft CRM has a record type or entity called a *contact*. A contact, in this sense, is a person. It's a concept taken from Microsoft Outlook. In fact, contact records from Outlook are directly transferable into contact records in Microsoft CRM.

Microsoft CRM calls company records *accounts*. Companies (accounts) and the people who work at each of them (contacts) can be related to one another within the system.

A *contact* is a person and an *account* is a company. A *customer* is either a person or a company.

We often hear company executives say that their most important corporate asset is their database of prospects and clients. We couldn't agree more. Neglecting, for the moment, all the powerful tools within CRM, the most basic thing is what pays off the quickest. And *that* quick payoff results from having one central, organized, accessible, repository for all the information relating to your customers and prospects. Even if you never create any workflow rules, never connect the system to a Web site, or never automate your quotation system, you'll be miles ahead just by organizing your data into one coherent database.

You want to store other kinds of information in Microsoft CRM, too. The system is going to be your universal reference tool — your Rolodex, your personnel directory, and your Yellow Pages all in one place. You also want to have records for vendors, employees, and competitors.

In addition, Microsoft CRM holds important information that will help you manage and make better-informed decisions about your business. That information includes opportunities to track your sales cycles, cases to track customer service issues, and campaigns to track the results of your marketing campaigns.

Communicating with the Outside World

Far and away, the primary reason that companies lose accounts is that the customer thinks no one is paying attention. Microsoft CRM gives you the tools to counteract this perception, which, with regard to your firm, is certainly a wrong one. Right?

A handful of ways exist to communicate with customers, and CRM handles most of them:

- ✓ **Scheduling calls and appointments:** Of course, you'll schedule all of your calls and appointments using CRM through Outlook.

- ✓ **Faxing:** This is built into Microsoft CRM Small Business Edition.

- ✓ **E-mailing:** Outlook is the champion of all e-mail systems. It's practically the de facto standard. Whether you're operating in online or offline mode, you have the ability to integrate your e-mail with the CRM system. This includes the ability to create e-mail templates and e-mail merge documents to rapidly communicate with your customers.

- ✓ **Printing:** You can merge and print letters as long as you have Microsoft Word (which, as part of the Microsoft family of products, is well-integrated with CRM).

Integrating with Accounting

In the early years of CRM systems, many companies were reluctant to allow their salespeople access to accounting information. Fortunately, the pendulum has swung back, with the best thinkers realizing that it's helpful for salespeople to have more knowledge, not less. Microsoft has developed links to a line of applications it owns called Dynamics (of which Microsoft Dynamics CRM is a part). These links include the ability to share customer, product, invoice, and billing information.

Links to other accounting packages, such as those from Intuit and Sage SAP, are provided by third-party developers.

Why integrate?

Surely no sales manager wants his or her people spending their time trying to close another deal with an existing customer when that customer hasn't paid for the previous six orders stretching over the last eight months. Nor would a discerning sales manager want a salesperson quoting a deal that would put customers over their existing credit limit without taking the credit situation into account. By integrating Microsoft CRM with your accounting system, your users and sales managers have the information they need to avoid these situations.

Conversely, before a credit manager calls an existing client in an effort to collect a past-due payment, it may be important for the manager to understand that the sales department is on the verge of closing a megadeal with that very same client. Although the credit department would certainly want to collect that money, understanding the current sales situation may affect how the credit manager's conversation is conducted.

Other accounting systems

Most competitors claim to have integration with one or more accounting packages. Most of the time, a third party does this integration, and that situation has some major disadvantages. If you're relying on three separate companies — your CRM vendor, your accounting vendor, and a third-party developer — to coordinate your front-office and back-office operations, you could be in trouble.

One of the ongoing problems occurs when your CRM vendor or your accounting vendor upgrades. That upgrade immediately requires an upgrade to at least one of the other packages. Microsoft has gone a long way toward solving this dilemma because it controls both ends and the middle. Look for integration that is much better coordinated than what has been available in the past.

Setting Up Business Processes

One of the most powerful features in Microsoft CRM is workflow rules. These rules provide a way to automate many routine functions in your organization, such as following up with standard letters after an appointment or alerting members of your team to account-related deadlines.

If you prefer to have Microsoft CRM work for you, rather than you work for it, you should consider implementing workflow rules after you get past the initial effort of organizing all your data.

Every business has processes. Sometimes they aren't well documented, so they aren't obvious. An example of a process is how your company handles leads from prospective customers.

While designing and customizing your soon-to-be CRM system, you should also analyze (and improve) all of your processes.

Good process development has several basic principles:

- ✓ **Assigning tasks:** The first principle is properly assigning responsibility. Each task that needs to be accomplished should have one primary person assigned to it, not a team of people.

✔ **Feedback:** Every step of every task should be confirmed. Amazon.com has this procedure down pat. If you aren't sure about proper feedback, order a book from Amazon. Almost any *For Dummies* book will do. When you place the order, you get an order confirmation. When the book is shipped, you get a shipping confirmation. And you may very well get some after-the-fact follow-up. (All in an effort, of course, to sell you more books). Their process is well done, and you may want to pattern your processes after theirs.

✔ **Escalation:** Just because a phone call is assigned, don't assume that it will be completed. Plan your processes under the assumption that, even with the best of intentions, things fall through the cracks. Give each team member a reasonable amount of time to accomplish a task. If the task isn't completed, make sure that the next person on your organization chart is notified. Continue escalating and notifying until something is done about the situation.

✔ **Reporting and measuring:** It isn't a real process unless you can measure it and then improve it. Design into each process an appropriate report that allows the necessary analysis that leads to continual improvement. A good way to begin designing a process is to mock up the reports first. These reports help determine what data is necessary for proper tracking.

With workflow rules, you can program the business process you design. Workflow rules can access any of the data files in Microsoft CRM and create activities for your users or send out correspondence through fax or e-mail. These rules can notify you of overdue activities and can escalate important issues.

Implementing business processes within the scope of workflow rules is the heart and mind of a good CRM system and is also probably the most under-utilized area of CRM. Too often, companies relax after their data is properly imported and their users have received a little training. Properly implemented workflow rules will pay you back for your investment many times over. Do not neglect this powerful feature!

Coordinating Microsoft CRM with Your Success Plan

A disappointing number of CRM projects don't live up to their expectations. The first issue to consider is the one of expectations. The second issue involves planning.

If all your expectations are built on what you heard from your salesperson or what you read in the promotional materials, you may be in for an unpleasant surprise. And, of course, the old axiom applies: If you fail to plan, you plan to fail. Microsoft has released a comprehensive CRM planning guide. It's available on their Web site at `www.microsoft.com/downloads/thankyou.aspx?familyId=1ceb5e01-de9f-48c0-8ce2-51633ebf4714&displayLang=en`, or at `www.consultcore.com/dummies.htm`

Defining your goals

You may be tempted to wing it. Maybe someone promised the sales staff that a system would be in place before the next annual sales meeting, and that was 11 months ago. If you're thinking you have a month to buy the software and get it implemented, forget about it. You should do your project in bite-sized chunks, with measurable goals at each step.

The first step in a project with the complexity of a Microsoft CRM implementation is to do a needs analysis. Most of the more sophisticated dealers do this for you, although you should expect to pay for it. Some dealers offer a free needs analysis. Remember, you always get what you pay for.

A true needs analysis involves interviewing representatives from each department that will be using the system. It involves collecting a considerable amount of information on what is being done at your company today and how you want that to change. It involves determining what software may meet your requirements and doesn't presume that it's necessarily Microsoft CRM or any other system. A needs analysis includes detailed pricing, schedules, and the assignment of responsibilities.

We think a good needs analysis (or at least a detailed, written plan) is an essential ingredient to a successful implementation.

Making Microsoft CRM part of your client-retention program

Out of the box, Microsoft CRM comes prepared to assist you with closing business with new customers. It has records for leads that are expected to grow into opportunities. It has fields in the account and contact records that are meant to assist you in organizing your efforts to make a deal.

With a little forethought and customizing, you can use Microsoft CRM to ensure that you keep the customers you already have. CRM vendors have put little emphasis on customer retention, but it is relatively simple and will provide that return on your investment that everyone looks forward to generating.

Microsoft provides some documents that you can refer to if you decide to go it alone. Look in the *Planning Guide* for basic planning documents to make sure you get the most out of your system. The Planning Guide can be downloaded for free from www.consultcore.com/dummies.htm

Implementing a pilot program

Everyone is conservative by nature when thinking about spending money. So a pilot program is often a useful way to make sure the project will be successful. Typically, a pilot program involves a select group of users, not the entire company. If you're going to go this route, make it a representative sample, not just the brightest or most enthusiastic people and not just people in one small department.

Many projects never get beyond the pilot stage because a hundred or a thousand steps are needed to implement any project like this successfully. Invariably, as the pilot project struggles to the finish line, you find two or three nagging items that have not been conquered. And these unresolved items are what everyone is suddenly focused on. In some people's minds, these unfinished items remain a good reason to declare failure or to refuse to move on to the full rollout.

Before beginning the pilot, you must define what determines success. Write these conditions down and make them known to all. If they're met, trigger full rollout automatically.

Live versus On-Premise

Probably the most significant development in version 4 is the appearance of the Live version of Microsoft CRM. *Live* actually just means *hosted* or is sometimes also referred to as *software as a service (or SaaS)*. All of this terminology comes down to one thing: with Live, you don't buy it, you rent it. The On-Premise version is the more traditional, "you buy it, you install it, you own it" variety.

With Microsoft CRM Live, you don't own the software. Instead, you temporarily (as long as you keep paying) own the right to use the software on someone else's server, either a third-party hosting company's server or Microsoft's itself.

Everything seems to come full circle. In the beginning of the computer era, software ran on big, mainframe servers, and we all shared time on them. Then, in the early '80s, the IBM PC revolutionized how we all computed. Suddenly, we were all one-on-one with our own computers. And that gave most of us a feeling of control over what we were doing. There was no longer any pleading with a computer operator to please, please load the tape that has the data we need.

Operating systems and software became so complicated by the late '90s that there was a movement toward leaving the management of servers and software to hosting companies. In the CRM field, this movement was lead by Salesforce.com, the pioneer in hosted CRM. Microsoft's response to the growing enthusiasm for hosted systems is CRM Live. The landscape is a bit more crowded now, however, with entries from Entellium and from Kyliptix.

There are several concerns among people considering whether to adopt a hosted version or an On-Premise version, including:

- ✔ Security
- ✔ Access
- ✔ Total cost of ownership

These are discussed in greater detail in the next few sections.

Security

Many people had an initial unease about having some unknown person or entity managing their most critical data — namely, their customer lists. This author was among those with that skepticism. But we need to look at the reality.

Most organizations, especially smaller ones, don't have the sophisticated kind of data centers that hosting companies possess. Good hosting companies do daily backups, have server redundancy, have multiple hosting sites in case of natural disaster, and have disaster recovery plans. The good ones always keep their operating systems current and update the application software you're using with the most current patches.

If your organization doesn't have the resources to do all of this, your skepticism should be tempered by the realization that your data is probably more secure with a professional hosting company than it is being managed by the boss's brother-in-law who comes in one evening a week.

Access

Another issue with hosted systems is actually getting to the data. If you don't have Internet access you can't log into the system. Yes, there is an offline version of CRM, which is discussed below. However, many people believe it's critical for them to work with their data even when no Internet is available. Let's be honest with ourselves here. There are very few places most of us go without access to the Internet. Okay, airplanes, at least so far, although several major airlines have recently announced plans to provide in-flight Internet access.

Typically, whether you're at home, in a hotel room, at a customer site, or at the local coffee shop or burger joint, some kind of Internet access is almost always available. This argument about needing consistent access is becoming less and less tenable.

Total cost of ownership

How do the costs between owning and renting compare? Typically, CRM systems, and software in general, has a life expectancy of three to seven years. How long you use a particular piece of software has a profound effect on its cost of ownership and how well renting compares to buying.

In general, if you're going to use the software for only a short time (24-36 months or less) renting is almost always the more cost-effective approach. However, there are many factors. We have designed a spreadsheet you can use to analyze your situation. The spreadsheet allows you to enter your own numbers and then displays a graphic illustrating the five-year comparative costs of hosted vs On-Premise software. You can download the spreadsheet for your own use at www.consultcore.com/dummies.htm. Figure 1-1 illustrates a typical scenario. In the figure, we used $59 per month per user as the hosted cost and a little over $1,000 per license for the purchase option.

Figure 1-1: The total cost for a 25-user hosted system versus that same system On-Premise.

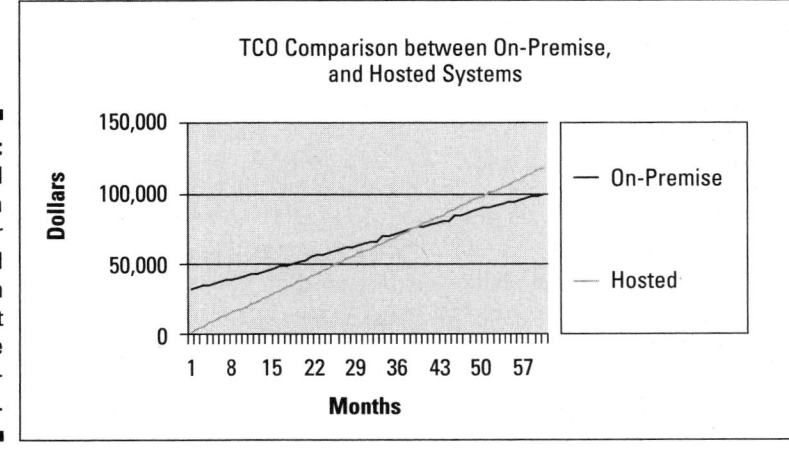

TCO Comparison between On-Premise, and Hosted Systems

— On-Premise

— Hosted

Being Mobile

So, what do you do when you're on an airplane from New York to Johannesburg for 16 hours without Internet access? Well, we suggest you read a book or watch a movie, but if you really need to be productive, you can be. Microsoft CRM provides offline access to your CRM data.

You can select the data you need to take with you on the road and download it to your laptop via Outlook. While disconnected, you can review and update data related to your accounts. When your feet are back on the ground and you have Internet access, you can synchronize your data with the Microsoft CRM server.

Microsoft CRM Mobile — as of this writing (spring 2008) the CRM Mobile functionality that allowed you access via various handheld devices, such as BlackBerries and Treos, hasn't yet been released for version 4. If you want to operate remotely with a handheld device, keep your eye out for Microsoft's release, which is imminent, or you can search out a third-party product.

Server Editions

Every server running Microsoft CRM 4 requires a server license. Three levels of licenses are available:

- ✔ Workgroup
- ✔ Professional
- ✔ Enterprise

These are discussed more fully in the next few sections. There ought to be a convenient and cost-effective path to upgrade from one level to the next. There doesn't seem to be, so your initial purchase decision needs to be well considered.

Workgroup

The Workgroup Server license is intended for the smallest organizations. You get five user licenses, and that's it. You can't expanded it beyond five. This is a competitive and cost-effective approach if you're certain you won't ever grow beyond this number. If you do outgrow the Workgroup Server license, you'll need to buy either a Professional or an Enterprise license.

Workgroup Server runs on Windows Server 2003 and Windows Small Business Server 2003.

Professional

If you "go Professional," you're limited only by the number of user licenses you purchase — and you can always buy more as you grow. The Professional license supports *single tenancy,* which means you can install only one copy of the software on one server. Although that may sound like the right ticket, the Enterprise license provides a lot more flexibility and power.

Professional runs on Windows Server 2003 and Windows Small Business Server 2003.

Enterprise

The whole "multi" family comes into play when you own the Enterprise Server license. This applies to multi-tenancy, multi-currency, and multi-language. Even if you have no intention of being a hosting center for other companies, you can have a complete test bed with the Enterprise license. That means you could have a development version, a test version, and a production of CRM. That's a good thing!

If you operate in several countries, you can take advantage of multiple currencies and multiple languages. John in New York can work in English and enter forecasts in dollars while Miguel in Buenos Aires can work in Spanish and enter his forecasts in pesos.

Migrating from one version to another

As of this writing, Microsoft just doesn't have a good plan for migrating from one version to another. For example, if you outgrow the Professional Server and now want the Enterprise Server, you need to buy and install Enterprise Server *without any credit for the fact that you already own most of it.* So, you and your CRM analyst need to do the best possible job of planning for future growth.

We haven't seen a good migration plan from the Live version to On-Premise either. All in due time, probably. We almost always recommend the Enterprise Server. You won't be likely to outgrow that one!

Using Microsoft CRM Successfully

The difference between a successful implementation and a flop is often the investment of a little more time, thought, money, and commitment. Microsoft CRM won't let you down as long as you do the following:

- ✔ **Have a needs analysis completed by a competent dealer.** Spend the money. It's well worth it.

- ✔ **Make sure that every user finds an advantage to using the system.** Otherwise, you won't get good acceptance or consistent use, which will inevitably lead to the collapse of the system. You have to sell your team on it. Solicit ideas from team members. Have each of them invest in the effort.

- ✔ **Plan your technology infrastructure.** Microsoft CRM demands a series of servers (or at least a Small Business server) and good network connectivity. You may need to update your operating systems and install SQL and Exchange servers.

- ✔ **Organize your existing data.** You probably have your data in more places and formats than you realize. Take a survey of all your users so you know the location of all the data. Plan to eliminate unnecessary records and collect as much missing information as possible.

- ✔ **Install your Microsoft CRM software and customize it with regard to any additional fields and reports you need.**

- ✔ **Set up your organizational structure with business units, roles, and teams.**

- ✔ **Import all the data and train your users almost simultaneously.** As soon as training is complete, you want your users to have immediate access to their own data so they can start using it before they forget what they learned in class.

- ✔ **Don't take your eyes off of your data.** As soon as you turn your back on the data, it will turn into garbage. Put someone in charge of data integrity.

- ✔ **Plan to continually improve the system.** The system will never be finished and will never be perfect. It's a process that evolves and changes as your organization changes. Don't lose sight of where you came from.

Chapter 2

Using the Outlook Client — Or Not

*M*icrosoft CRM is all about choices. It is very empowering, but it can also get confusing. It can be used in two ways: through the Web or through Outlook (offline or online).

In this chapter, we look at the various ways to access Microsoft CRM. Microsoft calls these *clients*. The three clients in which you can access Microsoft CRM are:

✔ **The online Outlook client:** Access MS CRM within Outlook. The CRM data is read over the internet on the corporate server.

✔ **The offline Outlook client:** Access MS CRM within Outlook without an Internet connection. When you are back online, you will automatically synchronize with the corporate server.

✔ **The Web client:** Access MS CRM with Internet Explorer 6.0 and higher.

We use the Microsoft CRM Web client in the figures throughout this book. Except as described in this chapter, the other clients look and feel about the same. Most people use either the Outlook clients or the Web client, but you don't really have to make a permanent choice: You can log into one in this session and into another in your next session.

In Microsoft CRM 3, the functionality of the Outlook client was significantly less than that of the Web client. In version 4, that gap has narrowed considerably.

The Microsoft CRM Online Outlook Client

The Outlook client requires that you have software on your computer. This is the first difference between the Outlook client and the Web client, which requires no Microsoft Outlook 2003 / 2007, and Internet Explorer 6.0 sp1 or higher software on your computer. The significance is that when you have any client software on your computer, you need to do a small amount of maintenance. You'll need to be sure that you're on the same version of the software as that of your server. Microsoft Outlook 2003 / 2007 is part of the Microsoft Office suite and is purchased independently from CRM. MS CRM comes with integration software that enables MS Outlook to communicate with it. Before installing MS CRM Outlook software, the client must have Outlook and Internet Explorer 6.0 sp1 or higher installed.

The "online" part means that you're using Outlook online. (That is, you must have Internet access.) When you interact with Microsoft CRM using the online Outlook client, you're updating the main database directly.

One of the differences between the Outlook client and the Web client is that the Outlook client offers you the option of simultaneously updating your Outlook data when you update your CRM data.

When you open Outlook with CRM installed, you see some new items on the Outlook toolbar (Figure 2-1), in the Shortcuts pane (Figure 2-2), and in the CRM folder (Figure 2-3). As you click on these new tools, you'll see that the associated Microsoft CRM objects appear in the main Outlook screen. These Microsoft CRM objects look and work like their counterparts in the Web client and in the offline Outlook client.

The CRM Outlook software is a single application that works in two different modes: Online and Offline. *Offline* simply means you are caching your data locally because you have no internet connection. When you do have a connection, you will be automatically synchronized with the server. An option to go Online/Offline is an option in the toolbar.

Figure 2-1:
The
Microsoft
CRM
toolbar.

The Microsoft CRM toolbar is a set of six horizontal icon/text combinations that appear below Outlook's normal menu and e-mail options toolbar. This custom toolbar lets you create record types and activities that coexist in Microsoft CRM and in Outlook. It includes the following tools:

- ✔ **CRM:** This screen shows you which version of CRM you are on.

- ✔ **New Activity:** Lets you schedule an appointment that appears in both Microsoft CRM and in Outlook. You can link the appointment to an account, contact, or opportunity in Microsoft CRM.

- ✔ **New Record:** Lets you add a new contact record, which appears in both Microsoft CRM and in Outlook.

- ✔ **Track in CRM:** Lets you convert selected e-mail messages into Microsoft CRM activities. In this way, you can store and view the e-mail messages on the Activities tab associated with a specific account, contact, or opportunity.

- ✔ **Set Regarding:** Let's you set a parent record, in CRM, for the new activity created.

- ✔ **Advanced Find:** Let's you search on multiple fields to find records.

The CRM Outlook Shortcuts contains six folders: Marketing, Resource Center, Sales, Service, Settings, and Workplace. (See Figure 2-2.)

- ✔ **Marketing:** This folder allows you to create and manage leads, campaigns, and sales literature.

- ✔ **Resource Center:** This folder contains information for the new user, including best practices and training material.

- ✔ **Sales:** This folder allows you to create and manage accounts, contacts, leads, and opportunities.

- ✔ **Service:** This folder allows you to create and manage cases and contracts. This is also where the knowledge base is configured.

- ✔ **Settings:** This folder contains administrative tasks. Here you can manage announcements, set up users and security, configure e-mail options and rules, and configure your system settings.

- ✔ **Workplace:** This folder allows you to create and manage your calendar, personal work items, and knowledge base, and it reports all in one area. You can also work with your accounts and contacts in this area.

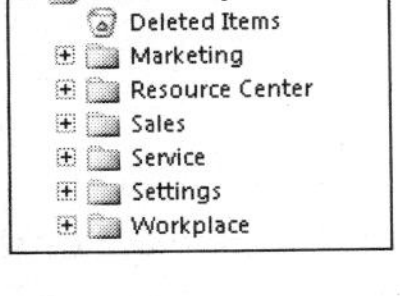

Figure 2-2:
The Outlook
Shortcuts
pane.

```
⊟ 📋 Microsoft Dynamics CRM
    📄 Deleted Items
  ⊞ 📁 Marketing
  ⊞ 📁 Resource Center
  ⊞ 📁 Sales
  ⊞ 📁 Service
  ⊞ 📁 Settings
  ⊞ 📁 Workplace
```

The CRM menu offers the following options (see Figure 2-3):

- ✔ **New Activity:** Lets you schedule an appointment that appears in both Microsoft CRM and in Outlook. You can link the appointment to an account, contact, or opportunity in Microsoft CRM.

- ✔ **New Record:** Lets you add a new contact record that appears in both Microsoft CRM and in Outlook.

- ✔ **Go To:** An option that allows you to select one of the six shortcuts: Marketing, Resource Center, Sales, Service, Settings, and Workplace.

- ✔ **Advanced Find:** Lets you search in multiple fields to find records.

- ✔ **Synchronize with CRM:** This option synchronizes your local data with Microsoft Outlook.

- ✔ **Go Online / Offline:** Allows you to take your CRM data locally (Go Offline) so that you have full access to CRM functionality when disconnected from the internet. Go Online synchronizes your local data with the server database and then continues to use the server database until you go offline. This option is extremely handy if you are on the road often.

- ✔ **Import Data**: Allows you to import records into CRM from an external file.

- ✔ **Duplicate Detection**: Allows you to define rules that constitute duplicate records and define how to merge them together.

- ✔ **Options:** Allows you to set your personal settings, such as default records per page, which items to synchronize (contacts, appointments, and so on), configure your Workplace, set formats (currency, time display, date display, and so on), and your base language.

- ✔ **Modify Local Data Groups:** Allows you to create groups of records, based on field values, to synchronize with Outlook.

- ✔ **Change Organization:** This option allows you to uninstall Outlook CRM software or re-configure it to point to a different server database. (For example, if you have the software installed but move to a different company.)

- ✔ **Disable Toolbar:** Because most of the options listed here are accessible via the shortcuts or CRM Toolbar, you may wish to simply disable this toolbar.

- ✔ **Check For Updates:** This option checks the Microsoft Web site for any updates to the software.

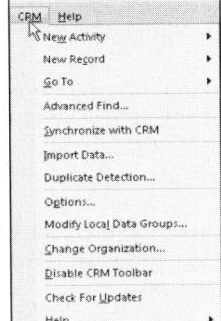

Figure 2-3:
The CRM
Menu.

The Microsoft CRM Offline Outlook Client

The Microsoft CRM offline Outlook client looks and works like the online Outlook client. The difference is that you're offline, so the offline client must store its data right on your laptop computer. The advantage of the offline Outlook client is that you can use your computer on airplanes, at client sites, or anywhere else where you don't have Internet access.

The disadvantage of the offline Outlook client is that the data isn't written directly to your server database. Instead, it's written to a local database that you later synchronize with the server database when you're back online. You don't see changes to the server database — and online users don't see changes to your database — until you synchronize your data.

In addition, synchronization can cause data conflicts. This isn't a Microsoft CRM problem: All synchronizing databases have data conflicts, and they all need conflict resolution rules. This all sounds very academic, so let's look at a simple example:

Suppose you're offline and you edit David Lee's telephone number to 703-367-9571. Before you synchronize, someone at the main office edits that same number to 703-367-9572. There is now a potential data conflict. Only one of you will "win."

Microsoft CRM uses the following conflict resolution rule: The person who is synchronizing the data "wins." That means that changes in the laptop database overwrite changes on the server when you log back on. That also means that if you use the offline Outlook client, you should synchronize your data as soon as possible after you make changes.

When you sync from the server to your laptop, there should be no data conflicts because you presumably haven't made any changes in your offline client since the last time you went online.

Note that Microsoft CRM 4 has a new diagnostic tool that identifies records that cause problems with synchronization. See the section, "What's New in Microsoft CRM 4.0 Outlook Client," later in this chapter, for details.

As noted in the Online Outlook Client section, you launch the synchronization from the Microsoft CRM toolbar. Select the Go Offline option (assuming that you're online at the time). This lets you synchronize your current CRM data with your local computer or, if you're offline and are going online, send all changed data from your local computer to the CRM server (Go Online).

The Microsoft CRM Web Client

The Web client is the access method used in the examples throughout this book, so we don't go into much detail here.

With Web access, you don't need any software on your computer. You can actually access your system from the lobby or business center computer in a hotel.

You must do all setup and configuration tasks through the Web client. However, as we mentioned earlier, you can use any of the clients during any session. You don't need to make a permanent selection of which client to use.

What's New in Microsoft CRM 4 Outlook Client

Microsoft CRM 4 improves on version 3 by adding a number of new enhancements and features. These improvements, guided by customer evaluation, are focused on end-user benefits, support for global organizations (in the form of multi-language packs and currencies), and increased application scalability (running multiple instances of CRM 4 on the same physical machine).

Because you will not likely be working with CRM 4 in the back-end, the following enhancements are focused on regular usage of CRM.

✔ **The Diagnostic Tool:** This is a standard part of the Outlook client. In Windows, navigate to Start➪All Programs➪Microsoft Dynamics CRM 4.0➪Diagnostics, to invoke the tool.

The Diagnostic Tool can identify records that cause problems with synchronization, and it can identify and resolve CRM add-ins that have been disabled. It can analyze your log files and report to your support desk so that your support people can provide you with better support. It can check for updates and disable your system if you don't have a mandatory update installed.

✔ **User interface enhancements:** These enhancements include the following:

- Promote up to 20 contact or appointment records at a time from Outlook to Microsoft CRM. This saves time by allowing the end-user to highlight 20 contacts in Outlook and click on a single button to send them to MS CRM.

- Synchronize tasks (available in version 3) as well as telephone calls, letters, and faxes (all new in version 4).

- Set the Regarding feature for e-mail messages. (This links the e-mail from Outlook to the parent account in MS CRM.)

  You do this by clicking Track in CRM on the toolbar. After saving the record, click View in CRM. If you're using Outlook 2003, click Regarding. If you're using Outlook 2007, click Set Parent or Set Regarding. Then click Save and Close.

- In Microsoft CRM 4, you can enter data into Outlook *or* into the CRM windows, which means that you can now enter data into a custom CRM data field.

- *Auto Resolution for lookup fields:* When you're searching for a value, you can get a list of all records meeting your search criteria.

- *Converting activities:* Convert an activity to an opportunity (available in 3.0) *or* to a lead, an opportunity, or a case. On the Actions toolbar, click Convert Activity and then select from the options.

- *Mail merge:* In version 3, mail merge worked only from the Outlook client. In 4, it works from the Web client as well.

✔ **Reporting services enhancements:** These enhancements include the following:

- *Report Wizard:* This allows you to create reports using an easy to follow graphical display on demand. (In version 3, it was not possible to create reports within CRM.) This Report wizard allows you to group data; summarize data (totals and subtotals); present data in tables, graphs, and charts; and print without exporting to Excel.

- *Export to Excel:* This was available in version 3. The new features include exporting data from related entities and editing queries after you create your spreadsheet.

✔ **Offline synchronization improvements:** These improvements include the following:

- *Background synchronization:* Instead of clicking Go Offline and waiting while synchronization runs, you can synchronize continuously in the background. (Note that this puts an extra load on your server.)

  You can set this by doing the following: From the Outlook client on the CRM menu, click Options, then click the Synchronization tab, and select Synchronize Local Data Every X Minutes. It defaults to every 15 minutes. The smaller you make the time interval, the greater the extra load on your server.

- *Changes to default synchronization settings:* These are intended to reduce the load on the server. You can still change the settings if you like.

- *Contacts aren't synchronized:* These include only your Outlook clients, not all of the contacts in Microsoft CRM.

- *Only records owned by the user are synchronized.*

- *Address book synchronizes every 24 hours:* You can change this by clicking Set Personal Options and then Synchronization. From the resulting screen you can change all of your sync settings.

Chapter 3

Navigating the Microsoft CRM System

*I*n this chapter, we explain the main features of the most commonly used screens — like the workplace — and provide you with the skills to get from one screen to another without getting lost. The workplace, by the way, is the central repository for everything that you have going on in your life as far as CRM knows.

Whirlwind Tour of the Screen

The workplace is the first thing you see when you start Microsoft CRM, so that's where we begin our discussion of what's what on the screen. Figure 3-1 shows a typical workplace screen.

Many elements in CRM are context sensitive, which means that what they contain differs depending on what part of the program you're viewing, what access rights you have, or both. In addition, you can change your personal settings (as we describe in Chapter 4). Those personal settings may further influence what you see on each screen. And, one more caveat: Microsoft CRM is highly customizable. If someone in your organization or your CRM dealer has already customized your system, your screens may not be exactly the same as those that came out of the box. (For this book, we used all out-of-the-box screens.)

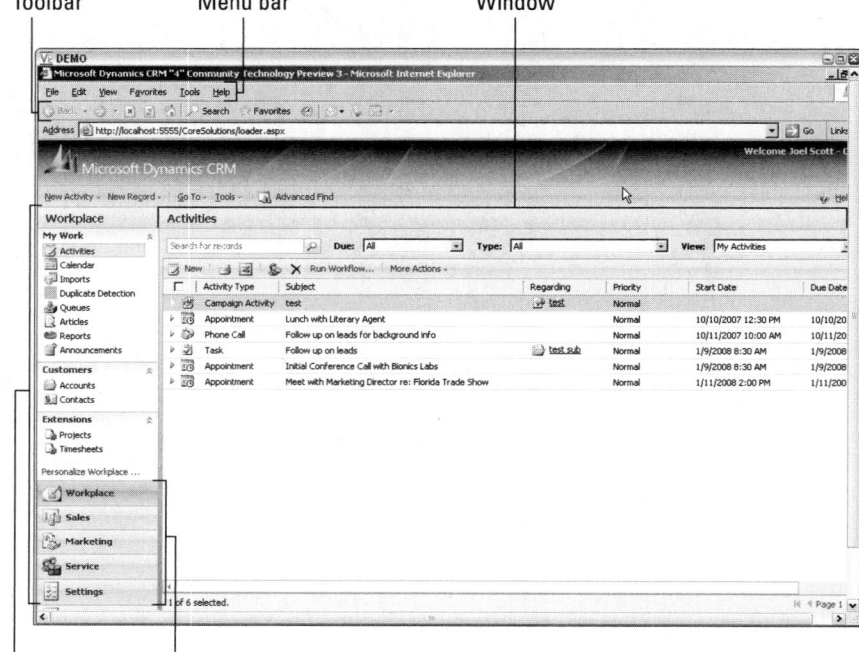

Figure 3-1:
A typical
workplace
with the
navigation
pane on the
left and the
Activities
window on
the right.

If you've used Microsoft products before, you'll find that some of these elements are familiar.

Navigation pane

The navigation pane is the column on the left side of the screen. As mentioned, many screen elements are context sensitive, but no area is more so than the navigation pane. The navigation pane is split into two major areas. Which button you click at the bottom — Workplace, Sales, Marketing, Service, Settings, and Resource Center — determines what you see at the top. Click Sales, for example, and you might see a screen like the one in Figure 3-2.

No matter which module you're working in, the navigation pane is always available, and you can use it to get back to the workplace at any time. For those people just getting started with a CRM application or those coming from a simpler system, it's easy to get lost in what may seem to be a myriad of similar screens. The Workplace button in the navigation pane is always there for you, like a trail of bread crumbs leading you home.

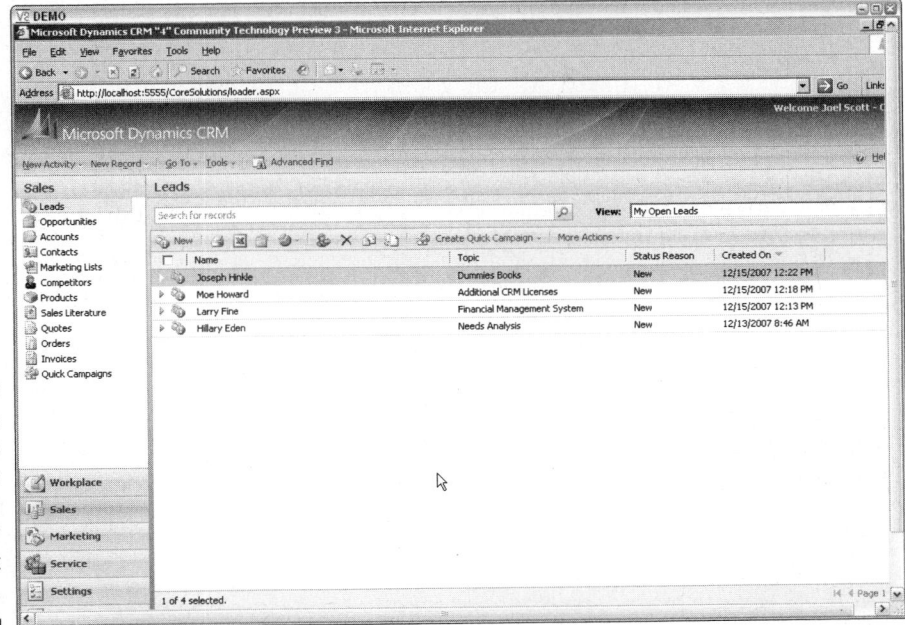

Figure 3-2:
Clicking the
Sales button
displays a
list of your
current
leads.

If you're suddenly lost while entering information, remember that Microsoft CRM doesn't automatically save data for you. So click the Save button (the disk icon) on the toolbar before returning to the workplace.

Status bar

At the very bottom of the screen is the status bar with several indicators. The *Done* indicator tells you that CRM has finished retrieving the information you requested. If CRM hasn't finished, you see an indication of what's currently loading. If you see a pop-up icon in the status bar, hover your mouse over it, and it will tell you whether pop-ups are blocked. The final indicator shows your current Internet security properties. The possibilities are Internet, Local Intranet, Trusted Sites, and Restricted Sites.

Window

The largest part of the screen is what we simply call the *window* (labeled in Figure 3-1). What you see here depends first on which navigation button you've clicked (Workplace, Sales, Marketing, Service, Settings, or Resource

Center) and second on what you've clicked in the upper part of the navigation pane. For example, in Figure 3-3, we've clicked Workplace and then Accounts (under Customers).

At the top of the window is the name of the area you're currently working in. Directly below the title of the window, you see the Look For field and its Find button, as well as the View menu. You use these elements to filter records. We talk more about filtering records later in this chapter in the "Filtering and Searching for Records" section.

Next up is a row of toolbar buttons, such as the New button and a printer icon. The toolbar in Figure 3-3 also shows two buttons with drop-down menus, Create Quick Campaign and More Actions. Click the down-pointing arrow, and a list of options appears. Quick Campaigns are part of marketing and are discussed in Chapters 19 and 20.

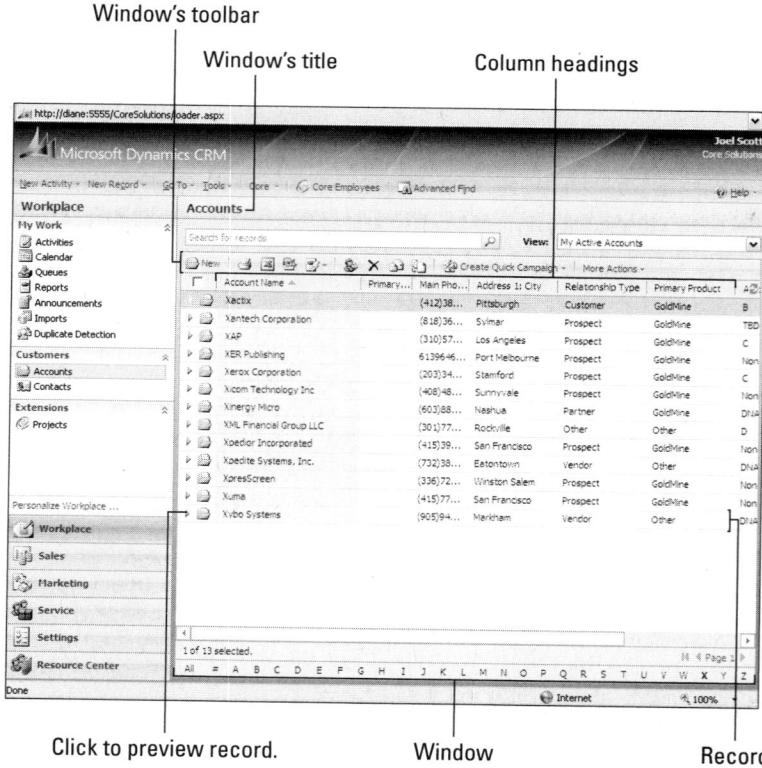

Window's toolbar

Window's title   Column headings

Figure 3-3:
The
Accounts
window.

Click to preview record.   Window   Record

Records are displayed in the main display area of the window. You can view any record that appears here by simply double-clicking it. To preview additional details about a record displayed in the window, click the arrow to the left of the record name. A small window, called the *preview,* appears in the lower part of the screen with more fields than CRM shows in the listing in the main window. However, you can't edit a record in the preview window.

At the top of the record list, you see the column headers. Click a column header to sort the records into ascending or descending order. To change the sort order for a particular column, click the column header again.

To select one record for some type of action, such as sending an e-mail, highlight the record. You can select all the records on a page by clicking the top check box (the one that is a column header).

Selecting all the records in the manner just described selects only those records displayed in that particular window, one screen at a time.

Many windows, particularly those with a list view such as the Accounts window, have a refresh button just to the right of the column headers. If you've modified a record but there's no evidence of that change in the window, click the refresh button.

Several elements appear at the bottom of the window. The first is the scroll bar. Next, you see a row indicating how may records appear in the window and how many of those records are selected. The current page number is on the far right. When a list has more than one page, the arrows surrounding the page number are no longer dimmed, and you can use them to move from one page to another.

The final element (in the list view) is the CRM alphabet bar. Click a letter in the alphabet bar, and you see only records beginning with that letter. This is a quick way to sort and find records.

First Things First — Signing On

Now that we've described some of the basic screen terminology, it's time to talk about navigating through the CRM system. But before you can navigate to and through Microsoft CRM, you have to sign on. Although that sounds like a simple thing, you might encounter a gotcha or two.

Microsoft CRM doesn't require a separate login for the program, like other CRM systems you may have used. It's integrated with Microsoft Active Directory, which means that it gets your login information from your computer. However, before you can access CRM, your administrator must set you up in the system with at least one security role. Your role in the organization and your access rights determine, to a large part, what sections of the system you can get to and what you can do when you're there. For more on roles and access rights, see Chapter 8.

If your browser has a pop-up blocker enabled, this may prevent you from even getting into Microsoft CRM. From the Internet Explorer main toolbar, go to Tools⇨Pop-up Blocker⇨Turn Off Pop-up Blocker. However, this may not be enough if you have other pop-up blockers enabled. For example, if you use Yahoo!, it has its own pop-up blocker (on its main toolbar) that you must also disable. You may also need to add the MSCRM URL as a trusted site in your browser.

The Workplace Is Your Starting Point

The mysteries of Internet connectivity and pop-up blockersare one thing to conquer. The next is actually getting CRM to appear on your screen. There are two common ways to access CRM – either directly via Outlook or via your web browser. I have the URL for my CRM system as one of my favorites in my browser. After you enter your username and password and click OK, CRM automatically brings you to your workplace. Ta da!

If you're working directly on your LAN, you might not get prompted for a username or password because your IT dept may have automated this step for you.

The workplace isn't only the first place you see after signing on, it's the place you should always go back to if you find yourself adrift in a sea of screens. Just click the Workplace button in the bottom portion of the navigation pane to go back to the workplace.

The CRM program contains six modules: Workplace, Sales, Marketing, Service, Settings, and Resource Center. The three application modules — Sales, Marketing, and Service — can contain many individual records, such as an account (a company your business works with), a contact (an individual your business works with), or a case (a record relating to a service issue). In this section, we discuss how to get to the application modules and, from there, how to get to individual records.

Navigating at the application level

You can navigate to the three application modules from the workplace in two ways: the navigation pane or the Go To menu (on the menu bar). Our choice is to use the navigation pane, which contains buttons for all six modules (including the workplace). If you instead choose the Go To menu, you are presented with a drop-down list of the same six choices available in the navigation pane.

The Settings module is one you'll visit infrequently, when you want to change a personal setting on your system. That leaves the three application modules: Sales, Marketing, and Service, plus the Resource Center. Depending on your role in your organization, you'll probably spend most of your day in just one of these modules.

At the application level, the windows you see are similar to those of the workplace, but they do have a few differences. Figure 3-4 shows a sample Sales/Opportunities list view.

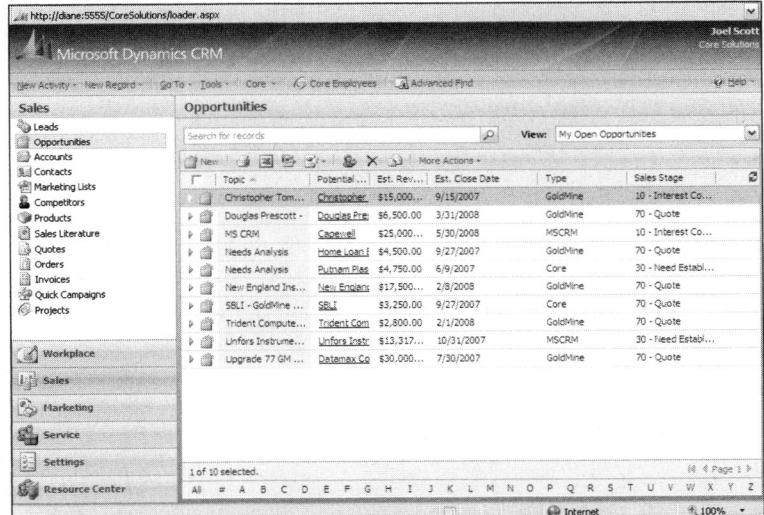

Figure 3-4: Everyone I should be in touch with all the time.

Navigating at the record level

From the application level, you can drill down to the record level, where the meat of your data actually lives. To access the record level, you simply double-click a record in the particular window's listing. Figure 3-5 shows a typical contact record. The record level shows detailed information about each subarea (Contacts, Leads, Opportunities, Accounts, and the like).

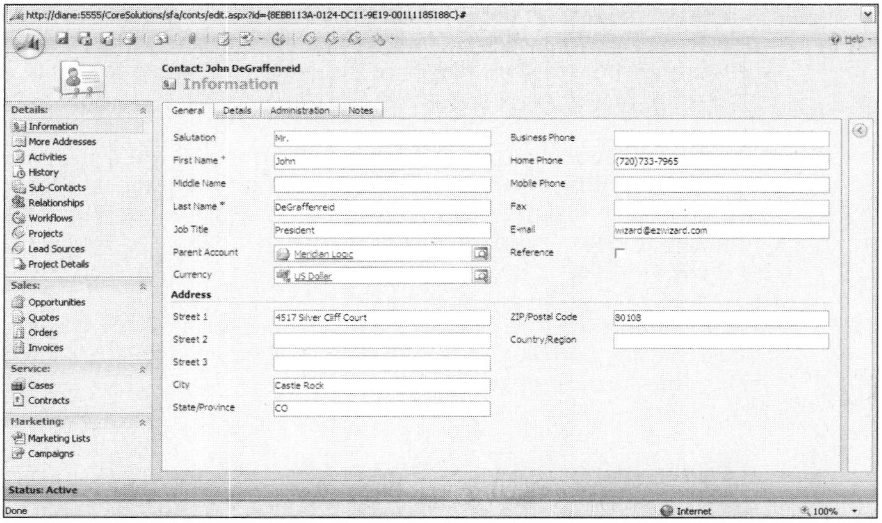

Figure 3-5:
A typical
contact
record.

Your first navigation lessons

Navigating through the Activities window is typical of more general navigation through CRM. You almost always need to create and edit appointments (which are a type of activity), so we use appointments as an example here. You can create (also called *schedule*) an activity in many ways, but the fastest and easiest way is to use the workplace:

1. **At the bottom of the navigation pane, click the Workplace button.**

2. **At the top of the navigation pane, click Activities.**

   The Activities window appears.

3. **On the Activities window's toolbar, click the New button.**

   The New Activity dialog box appears.

4. **Double-click the icon for the activity you want to create.**

   You're creating an appointment, so you double-click Appointment. A window appears for entering the relevant information, as shown in Figure 3-6.

5. **Enter text in all the necessary fields.**

   For an appointment, enter the subject (why you're making the appointment), the account or contact with whom you're scheduling the appointment, and all scheduling information. For more detailed information on how to fill out these fields, skip ahead to Chapter 14.

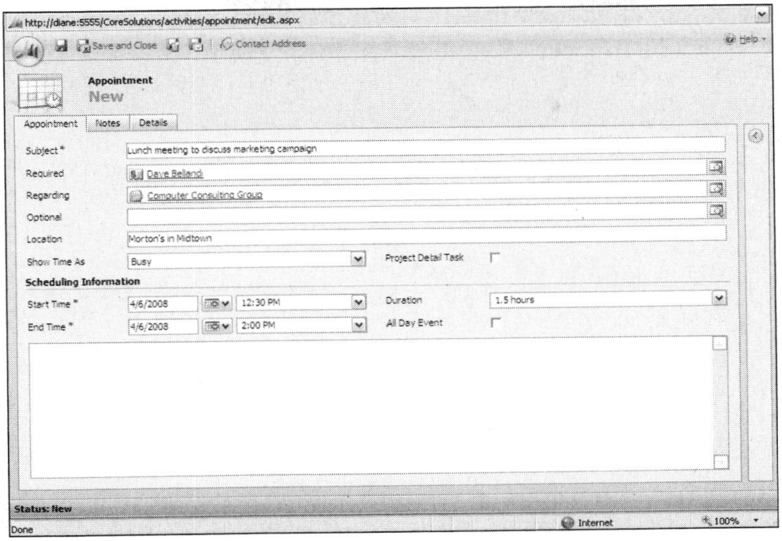

Figure 3-6:
Scheduling
an appoint-
ment.

6. **CRM doesn't save anything until you tell it to, so click the Save and Close button (below the menu bar).**

   You return to the workplace.

Now that you've created an appointment, you can practice changing one. This should be even easier. We'll start from the Activities window:

1. **In the Activities window, find and then click the activity you want to edit.**

   The activity opens, enabling you to review and change it. If you were changing an appointment, you'd see a screen similar to Figure 3-6.

2. **To change a field, highlight it and make your edits.**

   For example, you might want to change the scheduled time for an appointment.

3. **Before leaving the window, make sure you click the Save and Close button.**

   You return to the workplace.

Now that you've worked on creating, viewing, and editing an appointment, take a moment to check out another area of CRM: announcements. From the workplace, click Announcements (under My Work) in the upper part of the navigation pane. In the Announcements window, members of your team can post messages to everyone about company-wide events or issues. For example, you might use an announcement to send reminders about an upcoming price change or a revised holiday schedule.

Figure 3-7 shows some typical announcement postings. Clicking the link in the Announcements window brings you directly to that posting. The posting can include a link to a Web site containing additional information, if the person posting the announcement decides to include it.

If an announcement is too long, or if several active announcements are displayed, a scroll bar appears at the right side of the window so you can review all the posted material.

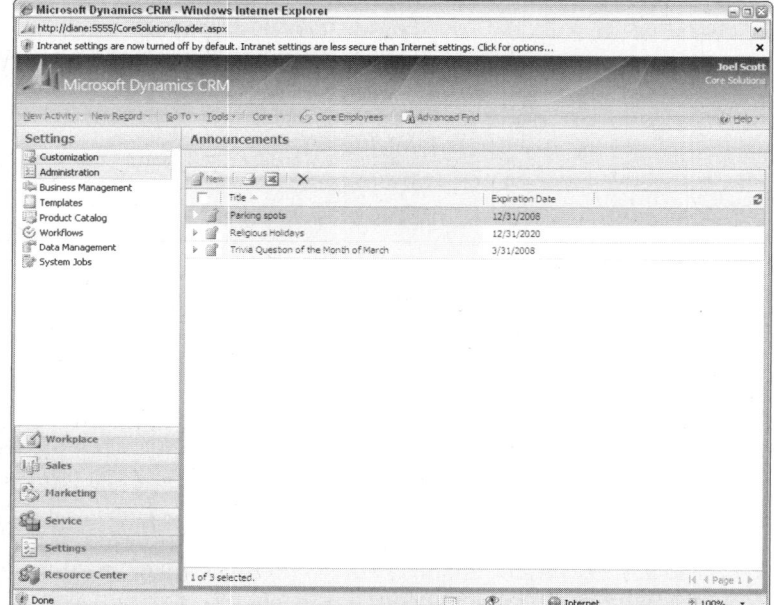

Figure 3-7:
A typical
company
announce-
ment
window.

Filtering and Searching for Records

Since the dawn of mankind, humans have organized things. Of course, if you organize things, you have to filter and search through them at some point. It could be argued that you have to filter and search before you can organize, but that's sort of like trying to determine which came first, the chicken or the egg. Well, Microsoft CRM doesn't answer that question, but the program does offer you an advanced, user-intuitive filter and search capability.

Filtering records

Now how is filtering different from searching? Basically, a *filter* is a type of search, in that you give the program search criteria and the filter function hunts down all the records that meet your search definition. You can apply this filtering to a list of contacts or leads (people you'd like to sell your product to), to documents in the knowledge base (a database of documents), to service activities (customer issues), and more. You can use the function to find one record or a thousand records.

In almost every workspace in Microsoft CRM, you'll see a Search for Records field below the window's title and a View field to the right, as shown in Figure 3-8.

You use the Search for Records field to enter information free form. If you're looking for an article on brakes, for example, you can type **brakes** in the Search for Records field. If you're looking for the guy who just called you at the help desk (and got cut off) but all you remember is his first name, Rico, you can type that first name in the Search for Records field. You might also notice a magnifying glass icon at the right side of the Search for Records field. Keep reading because we tell you how to use that icon in the next section.

Right next to the Search for Records field is the View field. Basically, this tells the program where to search for and what to search while hunting for the text you entered in the Search for Records field.

Here's where the filter function shows its teeth. The options you find in the View field drop-down box depend on what section of Microsoft CRM you're working in. For example, if you're in Workplace, under Contacts, the options are geared towards contacts, such as Active Contacts, My Active Contacts, and Inactive Contacts. If you're in Marketing, in the Campaigns workspace, you get options such as My Campaigns and Launched Campaigns.

Searching with the magnifying glass icon

Throughout Microsoft CRM, you'll find a magnifying-glass icon to the right of many fields. Whenever you see the magnifying glass, there's a Look Up Records dialog box waiting for you. Using this look-up feature, you can search almost anything.

Just click the magnifying glass. Like the filter function, the options you see in the Look Up dialog box depend on the field the icon is next to. Figure 3-9 is the one you'll see most often because it lends itself to most searches performed in Microsoft CRM. The drop-down list offered in the Type field can have as few as two options to search in (say, Accounts and Contacts) or as many as eleven, depending on the type of record you're looking for.

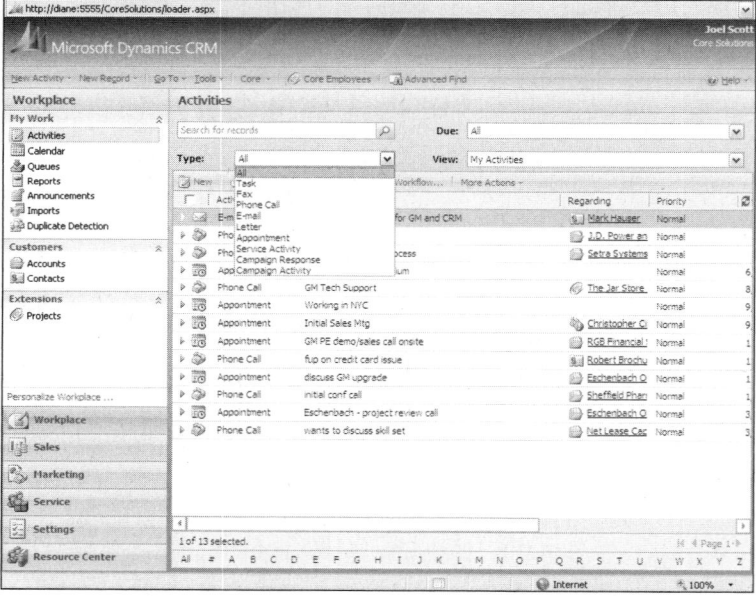

Figure 3-9:
The most common Type dialog window. This one comes from the Activity scheduling window.

Searching with the Form Assistant

The Form Assistant is basically a wizard guiding you through the entry of fields on forms. You can access and complete every field with a magnifying glass using the Form Assistant, which is a window that appears on the right side of virtually every form There is a skinny panel on the right side of the form which you expand to access the Form Assistant, or you use CTRL-SHIFT-F. See Figure 3-10.

Keep in mind that what the Form Assistant shows depends on the field you want to complete.

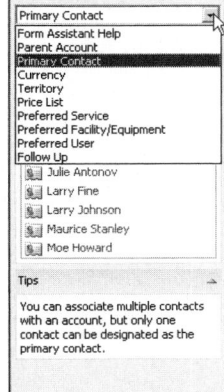

Figure 3-10:
Your friendly neighborhood Form Assistant.

Searching with the Advanced Find feature

Almost all CRM software programs have some sort of advanced search feature, but they rarely measure up to the workhorse built into Microsoft CRM. You can search for almost *anything,* from addresses to queues to roles to views. The other cool thing is that you can access Advanced Find throughout the program (in the main menu bar).

In this section, we look at using the Advanced Find feature locate selected accounts. In this example, we search for accounts in NY or in NJ. (You can find even more ways to use Advanced Find in Chapter 16.) Follow these steps:

1. **Click the Advanced Find button on the main menu bar, or choose Tools⇨Advanced Find on the menu bar.**

   Your location in the program doesn't matter. You can access Advanced Find from Marketing, Sales, Service, the Resource Center — even Settings. The Advanced Find dialog box appears, as shown in Figure 3-11, so you can define the values of your search.

2. **Click the drop-down arrow to the right of the Look For field to select the area or item you want to search.**

   The list has 49 items (or more if you have customized field views). Browse through them to see the available options. The options in the Use Saved View field depend on the category you select in the Look For field. Experiment by selecting various options in the Look For field and then seeing your options in the Use Saved View field.

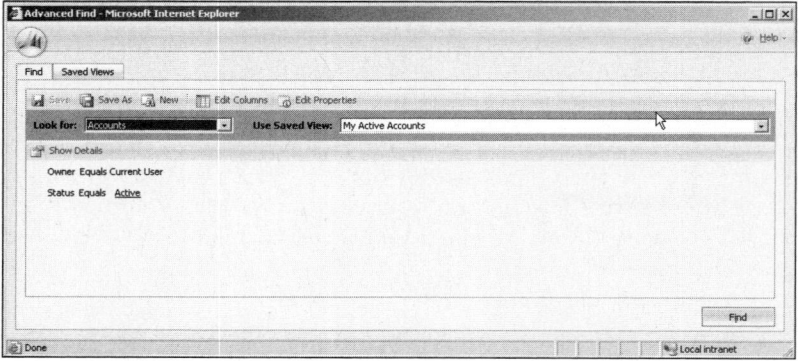

Figure 3-11:
With
Advanced
Find, your
search
options are
almost
limitless.

3. (Optional) Click the drop-down arrow to the right of the Use Saved View field to select the area or item you want to search.

If you don't see any saved searches that suit your needs, skip that field and continue on with the next step.

4. Choose your search criteria.

  a. Move your cursor to the word Select below the window's toolbar in the Advanced Find window.

  A field appears with a drop-down menu.

  b. Click the field to open the drop-down box.

  c. Select a field from the drop-down menu.

  For example, if you select the State/Province field, this tells Microsoft CRM the search you're about to conduct looks first in the State/Province field.

Note that after you make the State/Province selection, the word *Equals* appears next to it. To the right of *Equals* is the phrase *Enter Value*. The options in this third lookup file depend on the choices made earlier.

5. Choose the modifier.

  a. Hover your cursor over the word Equals to display the field.

  This should default to Equals, but always check before continuing. We want Equals in this case, but you can also choose from Does Not Equal, Contains, Does Not Contain, and so on.

  b. Click in the field to open the drop-down box and select the option you need.

6. Enter the value for your search.

  a. Move your cursor over the words Enter Value and click in the field that appears.

Again, these options depend on choices made in the previous steps.

b. To follow along with the example, enter NY in the field.

By using the Group function you can select multiple values. In the example shown in Figure 3-12, we search for Accounts in either NY or in NJ. These *must* be grouped with the "Or" function because no Account can possibly be in *both* States. Whether you are connecting values with ANDs or ORs, you have to specifically add a step each time.

7. Click Save.

A window pops up, asking for a title of your search.

8. Enter a name for your search and click OK.

This convenient feature saves your search for future use.

Click the arrow by the Use Saved View field to see all saved searches. Searches in System Views are available to everyone. Those in My Views (including the one you just saved) are available to you.

9. In the Advanced Find window, click Find (in the lower-right corner) to activate the search.

A new window appears showing you a list of all accounts meeting your search criteria, as shown in Figure 3-12.

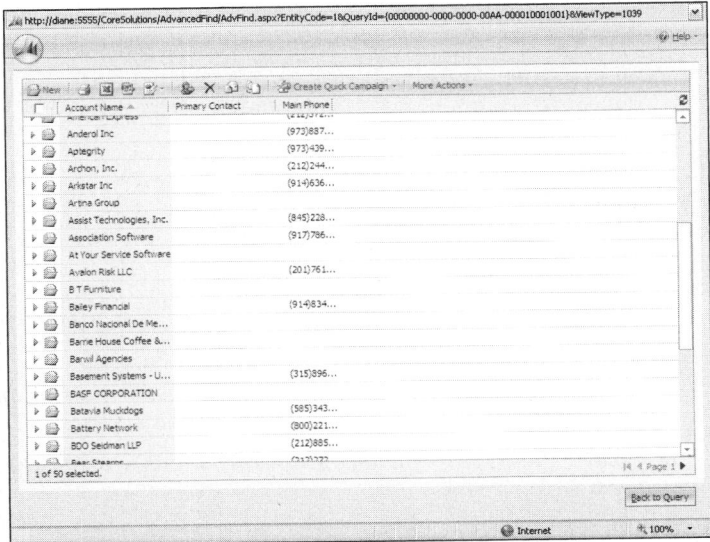

Figure 3-12:
Another
successful
search
using
Advanced
Find!

Don't see what you want? Or worse, your search results returned a gazillion more hits than you thought it would? You can always click Back to Query to return to your search criteria for further definition.

Using the Resource Center

The Resource Center is a new goodie in version 4. The link to it is prominently displayed at the bottom of the navigation pane. A typical Resource Center window is shown in Figure 3-13.

Within the Resource Center, you find links to all sorts of help, white papers, and community forums. You have access to a variety of problem-solving content, including current blog posts, newsgroup answers, and articles. You can find more detailed information on the Resource Center in Chapter 28.

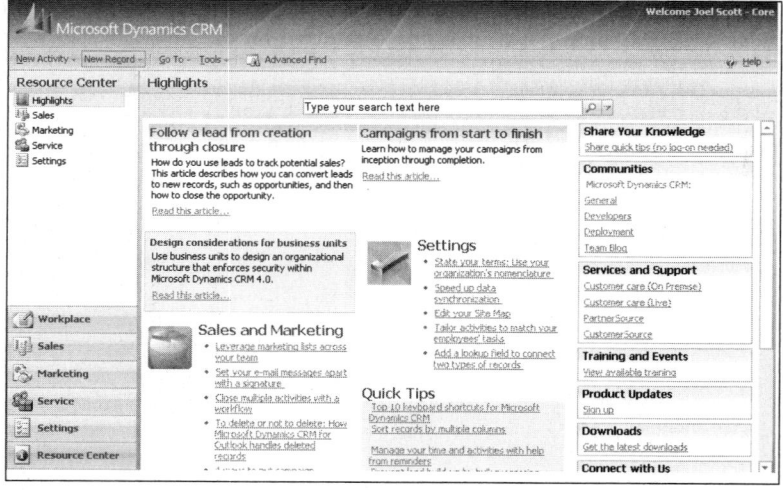

Figure 3-13:
A typical
Resource
Center
display.

Part II
Setting Things Up

The 5th Wave   By Rich Tennant

"The top line represents our revenue, the middle line is our inventory, and the bottom line shows the rate of my hair loss over the same period."

In this part . . .

In Part II, you discover how to make the software fit you and your organization. You read about personalizing the system around your work habits and schedule. You find out about security and access rights, territories, roles, and business units.

If your organization is divided into departments (that is, business units), you find out how to emulate that structure in CRM. We discuss territories, which are usually the province of the sales manager, in this part as well.

If you're going to do quotes in CRM, setting up a product catalog is almost a necessity; you find that information in this part also.

Because workflow is a key component to automating the system around your company's business processes, Chapter 9 discusses designing and then implementing workflow.

With Microsoft CRM, you can use built-in reports or create your own. In Chapter 10, you find out how to run those reports and how to develop template documents.

Chapter 4

Personalizing Your System

. . . .

In This Chapter

▶ Accessing your personal settings

▶ Choosing your default start page, currency, and time zone

▶ Setting up your workplace screen and choosing e-mail and language preferences

▶ Understanding your user profile options

▶ Establishing roles, teams, and office hours

. . . .

*O*ne of the first things you should do is set your personal options to control the way Microsoft CRM displays information. You can use these personal settings to streamline the system so it best suits your function in the organization and your style. For example, you can determine which window appears when you start Microsoft CRM each day. If your role is strictly in customer service, you might want the system to go directly to the list of your cases.

In this chapter, we discuss the choices you have and how to set them. It's unlikely that you'll need to change every option, but it's good to know what's available.

Customization is important, and the process shouldn't take long. A little attention to customization now will enable you to work more efficiently as you become familiar with the system.

Tailoring the System to Suit Your Needs

You can streamline your use of CRM by setting your regular workday hours, how you want your scheduled activities to appear, the starting point for the system each morning, and many other options. Options like these are called your *personal settings.* Basically, you're telling Microsoft CRM how you like to operate.

To access your personal settings from the Web Client, follow these two steps:

1. **At the bottom of the navigation pane, click the Workplace button.**

   An option to Personalize Workplace appears in blue just above the Workplace button.

2. **Click the Personalize Workplace option.**

   The Set Personal Options window appears, with the Workplace tab displayed by default, as shown in Figure 4-1.

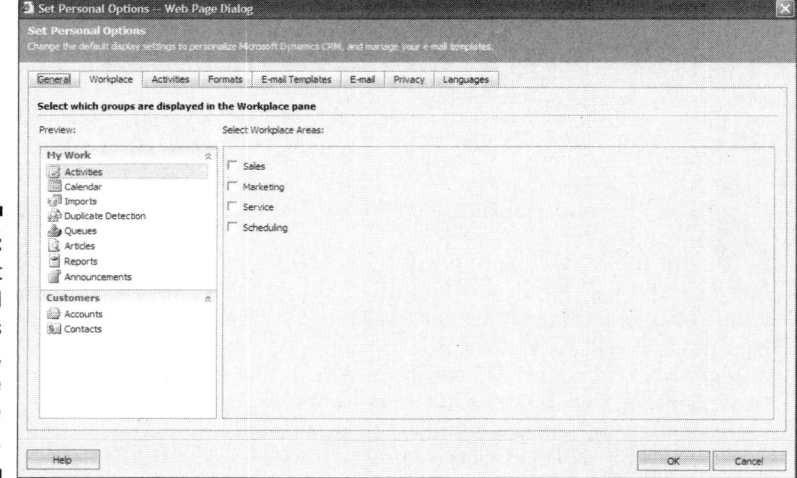

Figure 4-1:
The Set Personal Options window, showing the Workplace tab.

CRM provides you with eight tabs, each of which affects various default settings and how information is displayed. Most of these settings do not affect anyone other than *you,* so you should set them to please yourself. All dates in MSCRM are converted to Universal Time when entered into the database; make sure your time zone is set correctly if you share data with other users in different time zones.

In the sections that follow, we cover adjusting the options on these tabs. After you make changes on any of them, make sure to click OK to save your changes. To see the results of any changes you make, log out and then back in.

General tab: Customizing a variety of user preferences

Click the General tab (called Miscellaneous in prior versions of Microsoft CRM) contains settings for what you want the system to display upon startup, how many records you want to see at one time, how you want the Find function to work, which time zone you work in, which currency you use, and whether you'd like to display CRM in high contrast. The General tab is shown in Figure 4-2.

The first group of options on the General tab pertains to your default start page. The Default Pane drop-down list offers you these six choices:

- ✓ **Workplace:** This folder allows you to create and manage your calendar, personal work items, knowledge base, and reports all in one area. You can also work with your accounts and contacts in this area.

- ✓ **Sales:** This folder allows you to create and manage accounts, contacts, leads, and opportunities.

- ✓ **Marketing:** This folder allows you to create and manage leads, campaigns, and sales literature.

- ✓ **Service:** This folder allows you to create and manage cases and contracts. This is also where the knowledge base is configured.

- ✓ **Settings:** This folder contains administrative tasks. Here you can manage announcements, setup users and security, configure e-mail options and rules, and configure your system settings. You can probably eliminate this option as a reasonable choice. Selecting Settings means that every morning when you sign on, CRM automatically starts up by allowing you to change your Settings. This isn't something you're likely to do regularly. In fact, you'll probably set it and forget it.

- ✓ **Resource Center:** This folder contains information to the new user including best practices and training material.

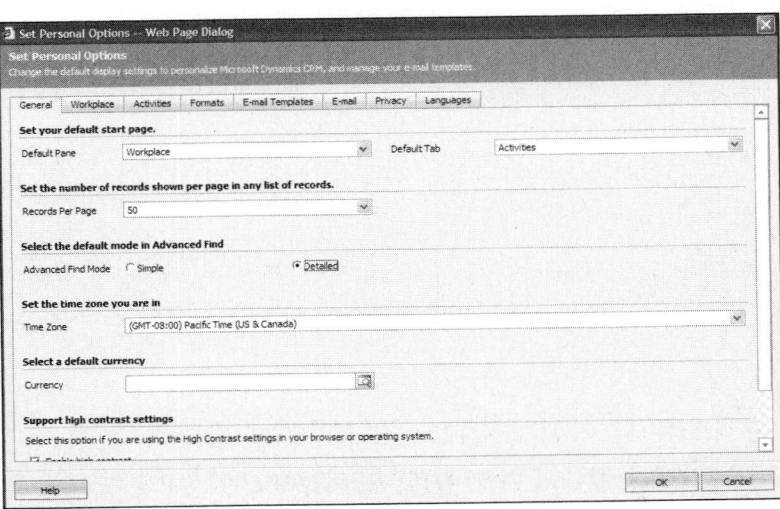

Figure 4-2:
You can tell the system how you want to operate, rather than have it be in charge of you.

Note that the selections you see in the Default Tab option change depending on your selection in the Default Pane option. For example, if you select Settings as your default pane, you will see options for administrative tasks such as user security, announcements and email rules. If you select Service as your default pane, options for cases, contracts, and knowledge base appear as selections in the default tab.

If your job function is primarily in sales, marketing, or customer service, it might seem logical to select one of those choices as a starting point for your day. This *might* work for you. However, we prefer to come in each morning and see what's on our agenda. This is best accomplished by setting the Default Pane option to Workplace and the Default Tab option to Activities or to Calendar.

To set your default start screen, follow these steps:

1. **Set the Default Pane option as desired.**

   To do so, click the down arrow to the right of the field and then make a selection. The options in the Default Tab option will change, but you won't be able to see that until you position your mouse in that field.

2. **Set the Default Tab option as desired.**

3. **Click the OK button (at the bottom of the window).**

   Your new options are saved, but you won't see the effect of this until the next time you log into CRM.

Now on to the next option on the General tab — Records Per Page. Depending on the size and resolution of the screen you're using, you may want to change the number of records that appear in each list. The smaller your screen or the lower your resolution, the fewer lines you may want displayed at any one time. On the other hand, if you have a large number of records and prefer just scrolling up and down, set the number of records shown to a large number, perhaps 100 or more. The default is 50 records per page; we usually set ours a little higher.

Advanced Find Mode allows you to create more complex searches and save search criteria for future use. You can take best advantage of this feature by selecting the Detailed option. If you select the Simple mode instead, you can use predefined searches but cannot create new ones yourself. Even if you have no intention of creating Advanced Find searches right now, don't limit yourself by selecting Simple.

The Time Zone drop-down list contains time zones from all over the world. Choose yours. The goal of setting your time zone is to coordinate your activities with other members of your team who may be dispersed throughout the world. This assists in coordinating conference calls among team members.

For example, suppose you are in New York and set up a conference call with a team member in Sydney, Australia. If you schedule your call for 4 p.m. Monday, the call shows up on your Australian counterpart's activity list for 8 a.m. Tuesday (her time) — if she's selected her correct time zone as well, that is.

The Currency box allows you to select the currency you'll use when working with Quotes, Invoices, Orders, and Opportunities.

The Enable High Contrast option improves the display of buttons and icons in your system. Select this option if you have it selected in your operating system or Web browser (such as Internet Explorer). (Selecting this option will automatically reload your page.)

Workplace tab: Simplifying your navigation pane

You use the Workplace tab in the Set Personal Options window (refer to Figure 4-1) to define your role in your organization and to tailor the workplace. (As you may recall, a workplace is a page that allows you to create and manage your calendar, personal work items, knowledge base, reports, accounts, and contacts all in one area to show any combination of sales, marketing, service, and scheduling information.) When you select the Marketing option, for example, marketing lists, campaigns, and quick campaigns become available to you in the navigation pane. This list of options may look different depending on how your system administrator or implementation partner defined the options when setting CRM up.

Simply click to add the check mark from each of the four options in turn. As you do so, more areas are displayed in the Preview panel on the left of the check boxes you are clicking on. When all four workplace areas are turned on, the maximum areas are available.

We recommend that you select just the one or two roles you usually play in your organization. Selecting more won't damage anything but will clutter the screen with functions you don't need. Our advice? If you're in sales, select Sales or Sales plus Marketing. If you're in customer service, select Service or Service plus Scheduling. If you're in Marketing, don't clutter up your workplace with Service schedules but do select the other three. Remember that the workplace simply consolidates information from different areas as mentioned earlier. If, for example, you selected only Sales to be displayed in your workplace but later needed access to Service information, you can simply click on the Service short-cut in the left navigation pane. (For more on this, please refer to Chapter 3.)

Activities tab: Displaying appointments and setting your work hours

Activities is the third tab in the Set Personal Options window. This is where you to specify your default calendar view and the hours that you're typically in the office, as shown in Figure 4-3.

A good choice for the Default Calendar view is Weekly, which is shown in Figure 4-4. The calendar view, whether daily, weekly, or monthly, displays only appointments and none of the other activities, such as scheduled phone calls or tasks. If you want to use any of the calendar views and you want a realistic picture of what's on your schedule, make everything an appointment. Please note that these options affect what you see in the graphical calendar (calendar view). We think a better option is to use the Activities view, which shows all types of scheduled activities including appointments and phone calls. (Please refer to Chapter 2 for more on using Outlook Client and synchronizing MS Outlook with CRM.)

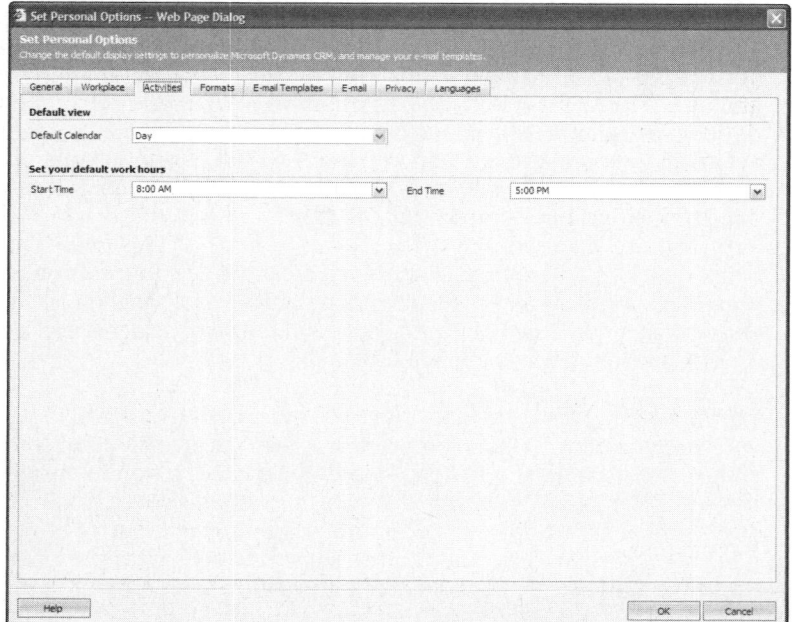

Figure 4-3:
The
Activities
options.

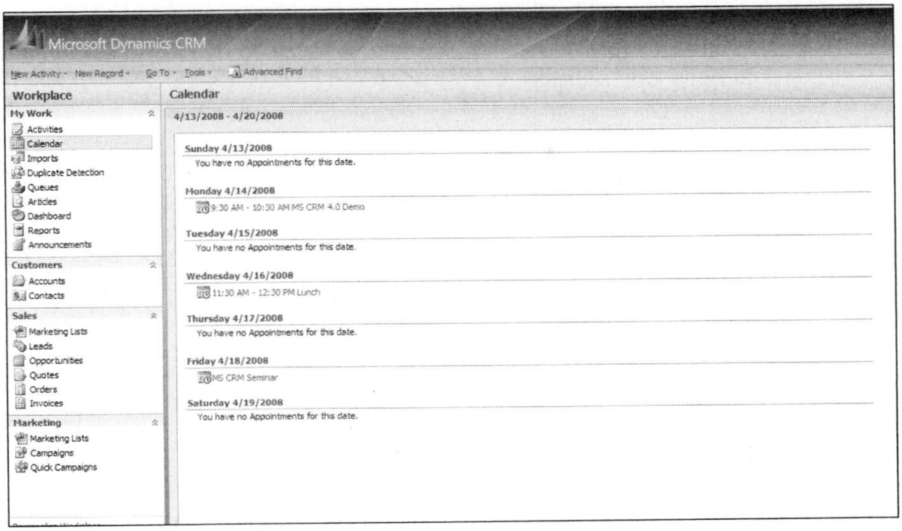

Figure 4-4:
The weekly
calendar
view.

The second set of options (Set Your Default Work Hours) enables you to specify your typical workday hours. Although a Start Time of 2 p.m. and an End Time of 3 p.m. sounds appealing, you should set this more realistically as it affects your calendar as well as scheduling. By default, your workplace calendar displays the hours you've selected as your regular work schedule. This is also what everyone using the system sees as your official work hours. Enter them wisely; other users of the system will schedule your calls, appointments, and so on, within that range of hours. If you (or others) happen to schedule an appointment outside those normal hours, it will still appear on your calendar.

Formats tab: Adapting CRM to your part of the world

The Formats tab (see Figure 4-5) enables you to select from a pre-defined list the manner in which CRM displays numbers, currency, time, and dates. For example, if you choose the English (United States) option from the Current Format drop-down list, when you log into CRM you see numbers 123,456,789.00, currency with a dollar sign preceding it, time 8:30 AM, the short date in the mm/dd/yyyy format, and the long date with the day of the week preceding the day, month, and year.

You can additionally extend the pre-defined list by clicking the Customize button and adjusting the options in the window that appears.

Figure 4-5:
The Formats
options.

E-mail Templates tab: Speed the process of handling e-mails

The E-mail Templates tab enables you to create and customize templates (pre-defined e-mails, e-mail body, subject, and so on) for almost every type of record (account, contact, opportunities, and so on) in the database, assuming your security level allows this. (We describe security and access rights in Chapter 8.) The ones you create in this section are available only to you. To create templates for the entire organization, use the Settings tab of Microsoft CRM.

This important feature enables you to create a powerful array of standard documents that you can use, for example, as automatic responses (see Chapter 9 for more on working with workflows) to inquiries about your products or services. This is a great way to expedite your response to sales inquiries. Unlike fine wine, leads never improve with age. From a list of templates you create, you can choose any template and create a *bulk e-mail,* also known as a *direct e-mail* or an *e-mail blast.* Bulk e-mail is a way to send multiple e-mails at one time easily and automatically. Some people associate this with spam. As long as you're legitimately responding to someone's inquiry or have received permission to send electronic communications (also called *opt-in mail*), it is *not* spam and may be an effective way to handle many routine business activities, including newsletters and special announcements.

It is probably to your professional advantage to include a way for your e-mail recipients to opt out of receiving e-mail from you. For more information, read the CAN-SPAM Act of 2003 at www.ftc.gov/bcp/conline/pubs/buspubs/canspam.shtm.

See Figure 4-6 for an example of e-mail template titles. From the E-mail Templates tab, you can apply any of the templates to an email, or you can create new templates by clicking the New button and following the instructions in Chapter 12.

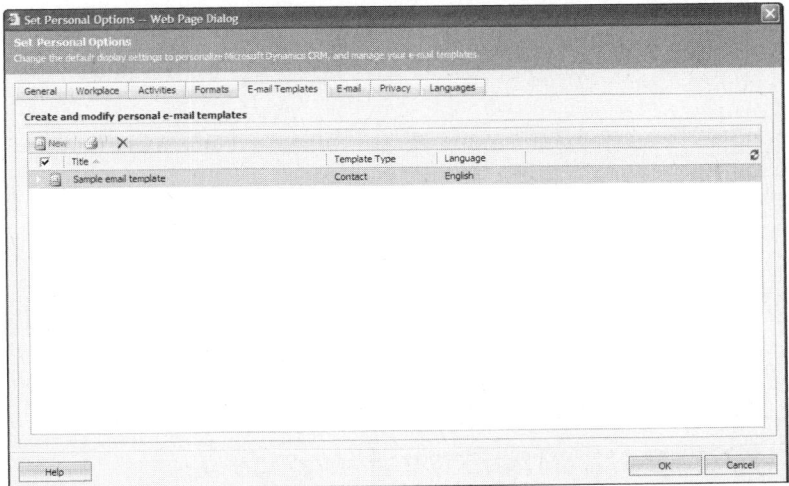

Figure 4-6:
Seasoning
your e-mail
templates
to taste.

E-mail tab: Routing your CRM messages

The E-mail tab (see Figure 4-7) allows you to better control the onslaught of incoming e-mail by letting you choose which type of e-mails are automatically tracked in CRM. Your options are All Emails, Emails in Response to Those You Sent Out or All Emails from Your Accounts, Contacts, and Leads in Your CRM System. Microsoft has incorporated a token-based system into the system which allows it to know if the e-mail should be copied to CRM or not.

From the Track drop-down list, if you select All E-mail Messages, all e-mail that would normally go to your Outlook inbox goes also to Microsoft CRM 4.0. If you select E-mail Messages in Response to CRM E-Mail, only those messages sent in response to e-mails sent from Microsoft CRM are brought into Microsoft CRM automatically. If you select E-mail Messages from CRM Leads, Contacts, and Accounts, only e-mails from leads of customers are will be saved in CRM.

Each method has its strengths and weaknesses. As a general rule, if you use the Outlook Client for Microsoft CRM, you should have Microsoft CRM automatically capture e-mails with the tokens. If you typically use Internet Explorer to access Microsoft CRM, select All E-mail.

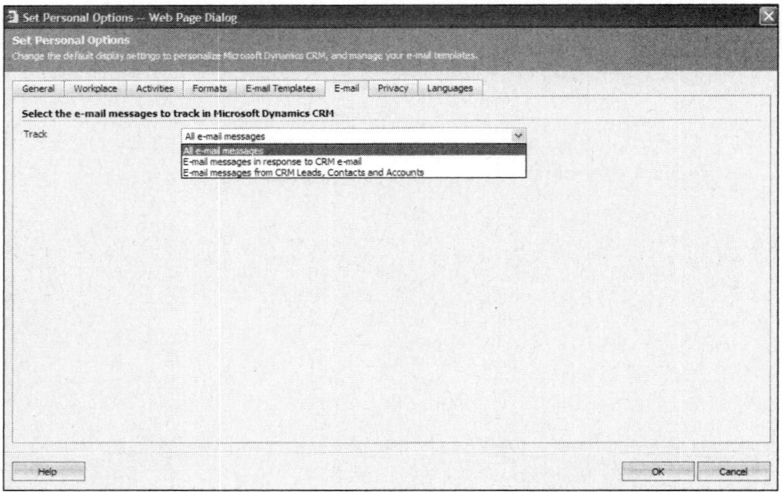

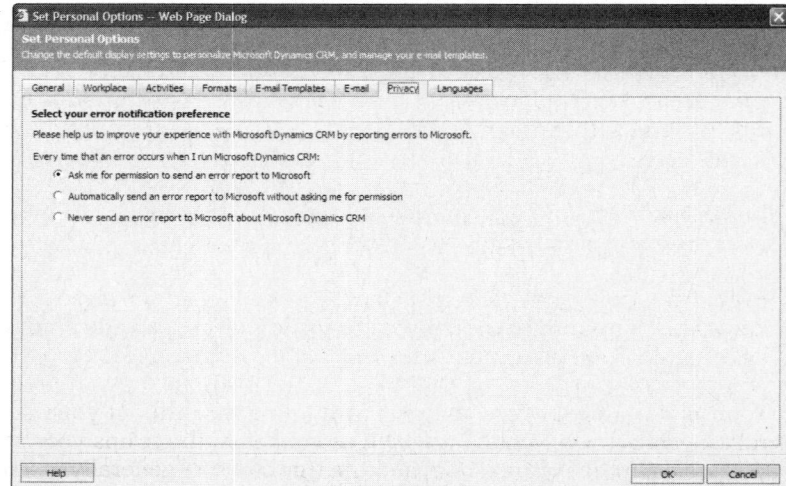

Figure 4-7:
Select
which
e-mails to
track.

Privacy tab: Indicating when to report errors to Microsoft

Users of Windows XP will immediately recognize the options presented here (see Figure 4-8). As with Windows, when MS CRM encounters an error, it can send a detailed report to Microsoft. You can tell MS CRM to do so in three ways: automatically, only with your permission, or never send a report. A good practice would be to have an administrator set this option up as most end-users aren't sure what to do when they see this prompt.

Figure 4-8:
Handle
those error
messages.

Language tab: Choosing the language you see onscreen

The last tab, Languages, allows you to select the language in which the main interface and help files are presented. (See Figure 4-9.)

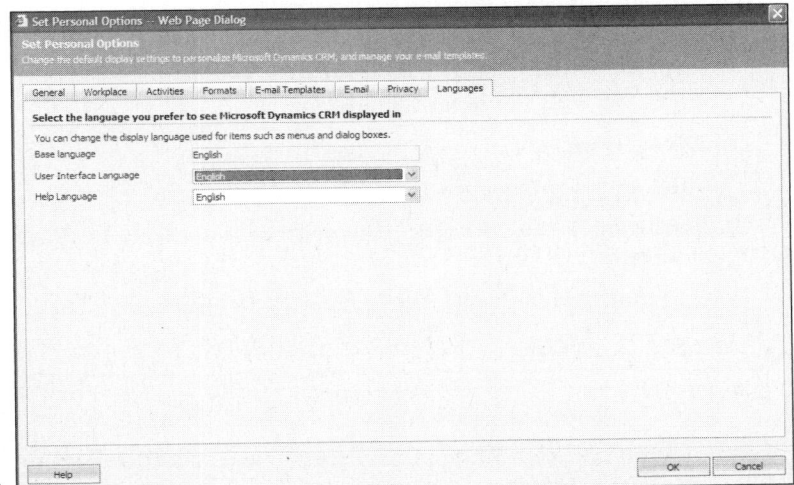

Figure 4-9:
Select your
language.

Establishing Your User Profile

Setting your user profile means telling the system (see the tip below) who you are and your role in the organization.

Your user profile coordinates you with your organization, so it's critical that your profile is set up before you and the other users really start using the system. The settings can always be changed as you go along and as your roles change.

Depending on the rights you have to the system, you may need to approach your system administrator to change your user profile.

Even if you don't have the rights to tinker with these settings, you should know what options are available so you can at least provide input to the system administrator.

Your user profile enables you to record information about yourself and your relationship to your company, such as your title, the teams you work on, your roles in the organization, and the times you're generally available. Your user profile settings enable you to participate in one or more team activities (a team is a group of users which work together on specific records) and to have a specific role in those activities. (Please review Chapter 6, "Managing Business Units and Teams," for more information on teams and roles.)

Anyone can view anyone else's user profile in both the web and outlook clients, but administrative rights may be required to make changes.

To navigate to the user profile area, follow these steps:

1. **At the bottom of the navigation pane, click the Settings button.**

   A window with 10 choices appears.

2. **Select Users.**

   The Users window appears.

3. **Double-click the user (you) whose profile needs to be reviewed or changed.**

   A window similar to the one in Figure 4-10 appears.

Figure 4-10:
Your user profile information.

Your user profile may be displayed as read-only if your security settings don't allow you to edit it. If this is the case, your system administrator has to make any necessary changes for you.

Your user profile contains seven categories, each of which is displayed in the upper part of the navigation pane. These seven categories are divided into two groups: Details and Service. The Details group applies to everyone; the Service group applies specifically to customer service personnel. We discuss Service groups in detail in Chapter 22.

Under the Details group are the Information, Teams, Roles, Quotas, and WorkFlows categories. You should go through each category sequentially to view how your record is set up and determine whether any changes are required. Each of these categories defines a different aspect of your role in the organization, as we discuss in the sections that follow.

Providing general information about yourself

When you click Information in the navigation pane, you see the User window, with two tabs: General and Addresses. (Refer to Figure 4-10.) The fields labeled in red are required; everything else is optional but recommended. Most of
the fields on the General tab are self-explanatory, but these deserve further explanation:

- ✔ **Domain Logon Name:** The server or entire set of resources running your CRM system.

- ✔ **Business Unit:** The organization to which you directly report.

- ✔ **Manager:** Your manager's name. (This field may be important if your system is designed to automatically escalate issues from one level of management to another.)

- ✔ **Territory:** Particularly in sales, efforts are usually divided into regions or territories. Each salesperson is usually associated with one territory.

The Addresses tab allows for two separate addresses. Everyone in your company should use these the same way. We recommend that you use the office address as the Mailing Address and your home address as the Other Address. It could just as well be the other way around, but everyone in your company needs to conform to the same method. This is because of the way they are stored in the database. Inconsistent entry makes it difficult for automating certain tasks such as mailings to employees.

Joining teams to share records

You use Teams, the next selection in the navigation pane, to group users who have the same basic role or who might need to share records.

Each user can be assigned to one or more teams. For example, you may be involved in your company's consulting efforts and also have some sales responsibilities. By assigning yourself to both the consulting team and the sales team, you assure yourself of being included in correspondence and meetings for those two groups. All the teams in a particular organization are displayed on the left. On the right are the teams to which the user is assigned.

Viewing security roles

Roles is the third selection in the navigation pane. Click the Roles option in the navigation pane to display the Roles window. Highlight the specific role you want to see and then click Manage Roles from the window's toolbar.

Microsoft CRM comes with a number of well-defined access rights, each associated with different roles that people perform in a company. For example, there's a well-defined set of access rights for an individual salesperson and a different set for the manager of customer service. You should have at least one role and could have several. These assignments are normally part of the initial configuration of the system and are usually the responsibility of your administrator.

Announcing which hours you'll be working

This is where each user's standard schedule is housed. You establish the typical work week and then add specific time off. If your organization runs more than one shift, the Work Hours area is where you indicate which shift each person is working. You can use this area also to indicate you're working or on vacation.

To view or edit your work hours, follow these steps:

1. **At the bottom of the navigation pane, click the Settings button.**

2. **Select Users.**

   The Users window appears.

3. **Select the user whose work hours you want to view by highlighting that user and clicking Work Hours from the navigation pane.**

   The window shown in Figure 4-11 appears.

4. **In the top-left area, click the Set Up button.**

   This button is the key to managing each user's work hours. Three options appear, enabling you to set a new weekly schedule, set a unique schedule for one day at a time, or schedule time off. Each option displays a simple entry screen.

5. **Choose an option, fill in the entry screen, and then click OK.**

Monitoring workflows

The final category under Details is Workflows. The Workflows screen allows you to monitor processes defined in your system. (These processes are simply workflow jobs, such as automated follow-up calls for every new leads, which are scheduled, running, or completed in the system.) We discuss workflows in detail in Chapter 9.

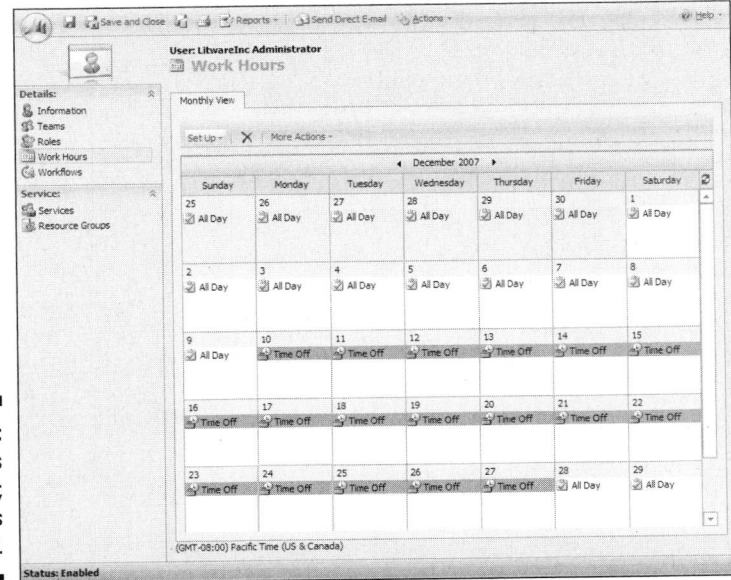

Figure 4-11: Sometimes at work; sometimes not.

Chapter 5

Managing Territories

*T*erritories, teams, and business units are three organizational concepts that are so closely linked that you need to understand all three before deciding how to handle any one of them.

Territories are customer records managed and maintained by one or more people in an organization. A *team* is a group of users who work together on specific records. As one can imagine, some records might contain sensitive information and some may contain information that may be viewed by others but not edited. For example, Person A reports to a Manager A who reports to Region Manager A. Region Manager A has full access to all his own records as well as those accounts managed by his subordinates. The subordinates in turn cannot edit accounts that are outside their territories or managed directly by a supervisor. A *business unit,* then, is where an administrator creates and manages security settings that dictate who can access what information.

Typically, you establish territories to manage sales in bite-sized chunks. You probably want to develop a sales quota for your company in each territory and then check forecasted sales and closed sales against the quotas you've set. (We talk more about assigning quotas and forecasting sales in Chapter 11.) You may also want to use territories as a way to ensure that customers are equitably distributed among salespeople. By using Microsoft CRM, you can measure equitable distribution by geography, the number of customers, account revenue, or some combination of all three factors.

Territories come into play when assigning accounts and when reporting on them. In this chapter, we explain how to set up territories, business units, and teams.

Setting Up Sales Territories

Every account record has one field called Territory. After you define your territories, you assign the proper territory to each account record. You can do this by manually selecting a territory for each account record from a drop-down list that your database administrator sets up, or you can use workflow rules to automatically assign an account to a territory based on state, province, zip or postal code, or some combination of these.

Don't use telephone area codes for territory definitions. Area codes change too often and, in the U.S., aren't geographically consistent. On top of that, with many people using cell phones or Internet phones, it's hard to relate phone numbers to geography.

Implementing workflow rules is a powerful way to have Microsoft CRM do a tremendous amount of work for you. For example, an administrator can create a workflow rule that automatically attaches to every new record; the rule checks the physical location of that account or contact and assigns it to a territory. Setting up such rules is appropriate for this or any kind of procedure that's well defined and frequently repeated. See Chapter 9 for a discussion of workflow rules.

An administrator can assign each user to a single territory and designate the user as either a territory user (a member of a team) or as the territory manager.

The task of setting up and managing territories is usually reserved for people with administrative rights. If you don't already have territories defined, this is a good time to do so. Follow these steps:

1. **At the bottom of the navigation pane, click the Settings button. (If you are using Outlook Client, click on Settings under the Microsoft Dynamics CRM folder in Outlooks navigation pane.)**

2. **Click Business Management in the navigation pane.**

   The Settings window with its 11 options appears. The options are as follows:

   - **Fiscal Year Settings:** This is where you configure your company's settings for its fiscal year and options on how they are displayed.

   - **Facilities/Equipment:** This is where you manage people and the services you provide for your clients. In example, you can schedule a technician to go onsite and fix a printer. The technician may need certain equipment for this job.

   - **Resource Groups:** A *resource group* is simply a team of people who provide services for clients. This is where you would create and manage them.

- **Services:** Services are jobs scheduled for a customer. These appear as calendar activities for the users who are scheduled to perform the tasks.

- **Subjects:** This is where you create and manage various areas on knowledge in a hierarchy. An example would be a company knowledge base.

- **Relationship Roles:** This is where you create and manage a correlation between the records in your system. For example, you may wish to create relationships between distributor and seller accounts.

- **Business Closures:** This is where you define the days in the year that the company will remain closed.

- **Queues:** These are scheduled activities that need attention or need to be closed.

- **Sales Territories:** This is where you create and manage territories. (Sales territories are discussed later in this chapter.)

- **Sites:** A *site* is a physical location of a business. This is where you would manage, per site, services you provide.

- **Currencies:** Currencies help determine the price of products you track in your system. (Products are discussed in Chapter 7.) They are also used to determine the price for various transactions, such as purchase orders.

3. **Select Sales Territories.**

   The Sales Territories window shown in Figure 5-1 appears. This is a typical view displaying the territories already in your system, presumably put there by your system administrator or by a sales manager.

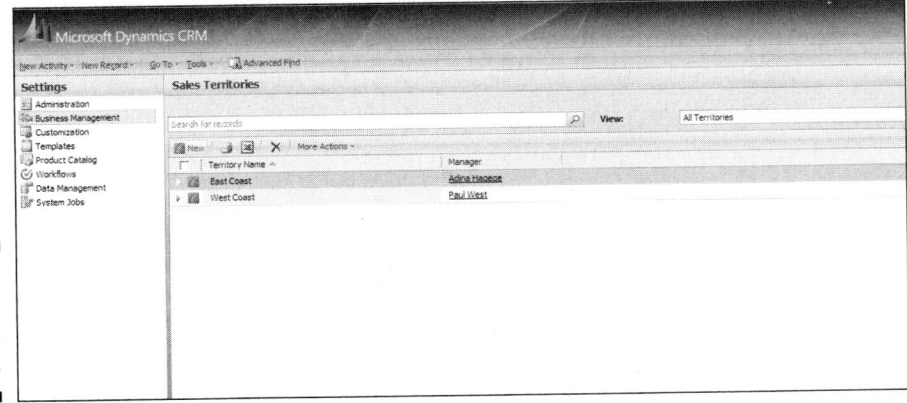

Figure 5-1: The territories in your system.

4. On the Sales Territories window's toolbar, click the New button to add a new territory.

The Territory: New window opens.

5. Fill in the General tab as follows:

a. In the Territory Name field, enter a unique territory name.

b. To the right of the Manager field, select a territory manager for that territory from the drop-down list.

c. If your territory name isn't self-explanatory, be sure to enter a description.

For example, if the Territory Name is New England, you should list the individual states in the Description field. See Figure 5-2.

6. At the top of the screen, click Save (the disk icon).

Note that the Members option in the navigation pane is available. The users assigned to a territory are called *members* of that territory. After you set up a territory, you can add users to that territory.

7. Add a user (member) to the territory as follows:

a. In the navigation pane of the territory, click the Members button.

b. On the window's toolbar, click the Add Members button.

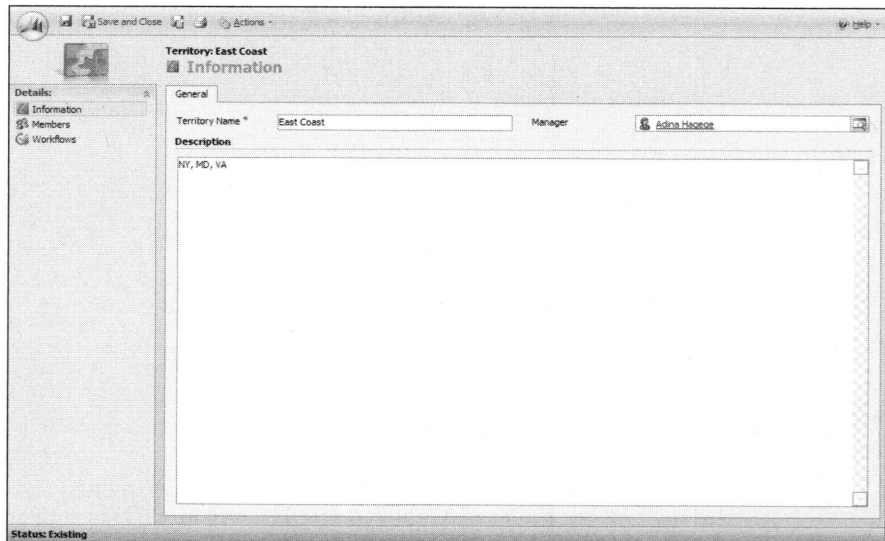

Figure 5-2:
Enter and
define the
territory.

You see a list of available users in the Look Up Records window. Because an administrator can assign an individual user to only one territory, the available users display in Figure 5-3 shows only unassigned users.

c. *From the available users, select one or more users (that is, members) for a territory.*

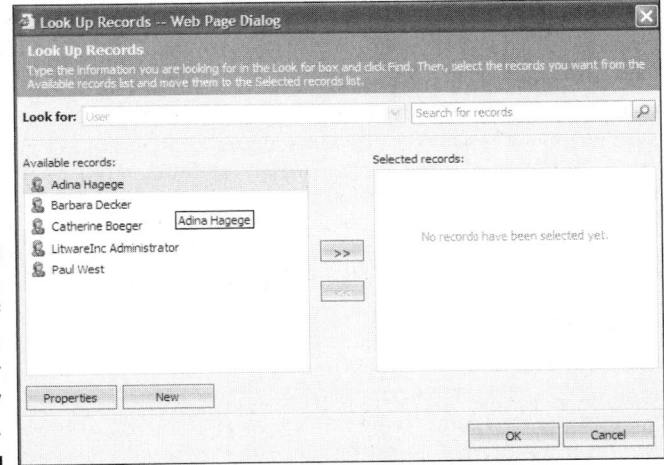

Figure 5-3: Display of available users for territory assignment.

8. **After you finish adding users to a territory, click the Save and Close button.**

    You return to the Sales Territories window.

Sometimes you may *think* that you need to assign someone to more than one territory. For example, if the Mid-Atlantic manager leaves, you may need to have the New England manager temporarily take over both territories. You do this by defining a new territory that encompasses both the New England and the Mid-Atlantic regions.

Managing Territories

If you plan to assign accounts to territories, you need to ensure that the Territory field for every account is filled in. You can do this by establishing workflow rules that automatically assign territories based on the City or State fields.

You can ensure that every account is assigned to a territory in these ways:

- ✔ **Make the Territory field a Business-Recommended field.** (Creating Business Recommended fields is a system administrator function.) This designation turns the field label blue, indicating to the user that entering data in this field is important. The business recommended designation does not force the entry of data.

- ✔ **Make the Territory field a Business-Required field.** (This is also a system administrator function.) With this designation, which turns the field label red, no one can save the record unless the field is filled in.

- ✔ **Send missing data alerts by using a third-party alert system,** such as KnowledgeSync (which we discuss in Chapter 27). An alert system sends a pop-up alarm or report to a user or manager when a new record is saved without critical data. Since KnowledgeSync is not part of MS CRM but an add-on tool, we will not cover how to set it up.

After you do everything possible to make sure every account is assigned to a territory, you'd think you'd be done with it. But, things change. Salespeople leave or are reassigned. New salespeople appear. Territories are merged. It isn't enough to just assign a salesperson to a territory. You must be vigilant to ensure that the assignments still make sense.

When customers are assigned to a territory or reassigned, someone should notify the account manager. In a perfect world, you would also notify the customers that they have a new account manager.

Although notifying account managers when you assign accounts to them seems obvious, the software has no built-in function to make this happen automatically. If a salesperson already has several hundred accounts, he or she may not notice for a long time when a half dozen new accounts are added to the list.

Workflow rules (discussed in Chapter 9) are an effective way to provide this notification. Failing that, you can resort to the old-fashioned method of either telling the salesperson or printing a report of existing customers and highlighting the new ones with a yellow marker.

The second notification needs to go to the client. Whenever an account manager changes, it's critical to inform all affected customers. With the appropriate workflow rules, you can accomplish this by an e-mail, a fax, a template letter, a scheduled phone call, or a visit.

Chapter 6

Managing Business Units and Teams

*T*he combination of business units and teams allows extreme flexibility in organizing your CRM implementation. At first it can be confusing: "Is marketing a business unit or a team?" However, this chapter provides you with a better understanding of how to use each organizational structure.

The essential difference between the two is that business units are hierarchal, potentially consisting of parent and children business units, while teams can cut across this hierarchy. As an example, let's assume that you have some standard business units: Sales, Marketing, Product Development, and Service. Let's also assume that you are starting development of a new product: X. You might create a team, Product X, that includes members from each of the business units. In this manner, teams offer you greater flexibility than you could get by simply having business units.

In this chapter, you see how to create and configure both business units and teams.

Managing Business Units

A *business unit* is analogous to a division or a profit center in a company. But the concept of business units in Microsoft CRM allows more flexibility than the simple concept of divisions in a company. Rather, business units are more like organizational charts. They also play a large role in the security model of Microsoft CRM.

For example, suppose a software dealership has three main business units: software, hardware/networking, and professional services. One or more of these units might have subunits. Maybe the software business unit is further divided into three brands of software. Each of those three is also a business unit. The security division might be divided into the firewall, the spyware, and the antispam units.

To set up business units, follow these steps in either the Outlook or Web client:

1. **At the bottom left of the navigation pane, click the Settings button.**

2. **Click Administration in the upper right of the navigation pane.**

3. **Click Business Units on the right.**

   The screen shown in Figure 6-1 appears.

4. **On the Business Units window's toolbar, click the New button.**

   The Business Unit: New window appears, as shown in Figure 6-2.

5. **Give your new business unit a name and change the Parent Business field if necessary.**

   Notice that the default Organization business unit is automatically selected as the Parent Business. This top business unit is created when you install CRM and every new business unit must be a child of that Business Unit or of some other Business Unit. You can select a different Parent Business Unit by clicking the lookup (magnifying glass icon).

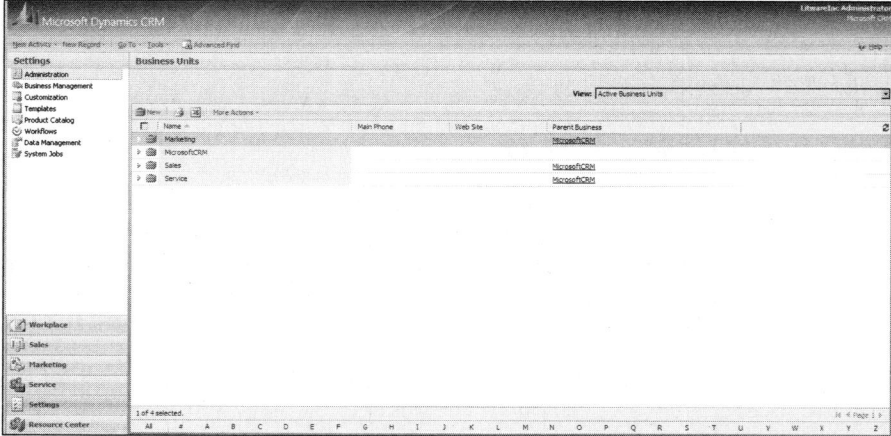

Figure 6-1:
Business units for a typical company.

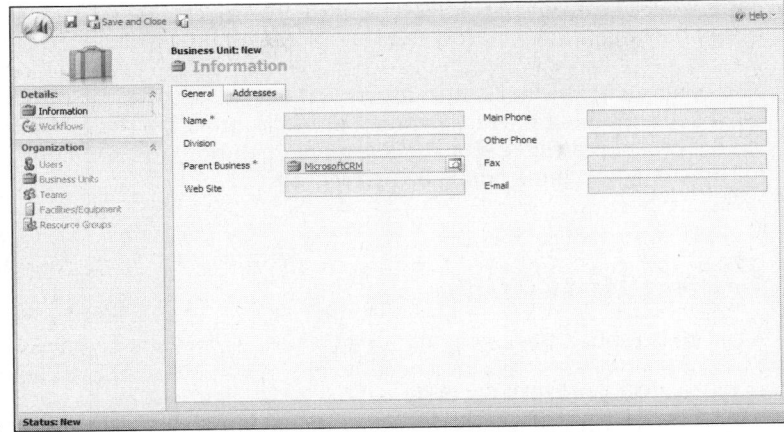

6. **After filling in the relevant fields (by default Name is the only required field), click Save and Close.**

   Notice that The system returns to the Business Units window, where you see your new business unit.

After you create a business unit and link it to its parent unit (and maybe even give it some children), you can reorganize your business units at any time by changing the parent business unit of your business units.

After you create your business units, you can assign teams of users to them. That's the topic of the next section.

Managing Teams

You might have a team of people who work together to service customers in a particular territory. Perhaps you have a separate team for each territory. Or you may have teams that are made up of users with similar skill sets. For example, you might have a sales team, a marketing team, and a technical support team. In this case, you'd want to assign your teams to business units.

Unlike territory assignments, in which each user can be in only one territory, each user can be a member of many teams. In all likelihood, this will be the case, with a typical user being a member of, say, the sales team, the process brainstorming team, and the summer-picnic planning team.

The concept of sharing is also important to teams. Although you can't assign an account to a team, you *can* share an account with a team. In this section, we describe creating teams and assigning members to teams. See Chapter 8 for more on Assigning and Sharing records.

Creating teams

After you create a business unit, you can create and assign teams to that unit. To create a team and assign it to a business unit, follow these steps using either the Web or Outlook client:

1. **At the bottom of the navigation pane, click the Settings button.**
2. **Click Administration in the navigation pane.**
3. **Select Business Units.**
4. **Double-click the business unit to which you want to assign one or more teams.**

   The Business Units window appears.
5. **In the upper part of the navigation pane, select Teams.**
6. **On the window's toolbar, click the New Team button.**

   The screen shown in Figure 6-3 appears.

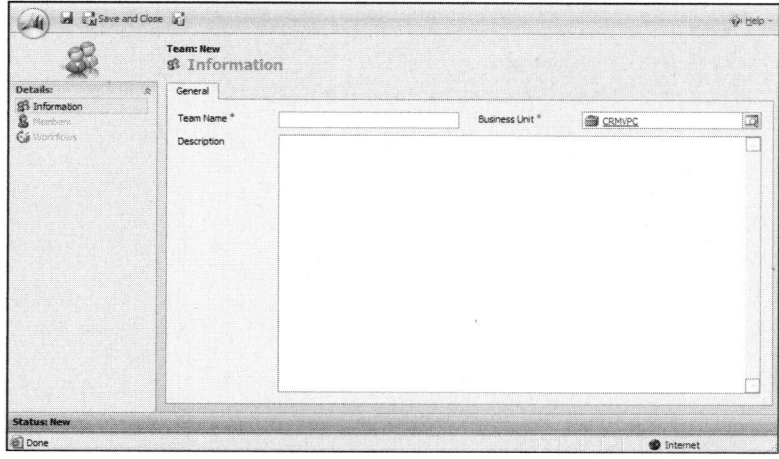

Figure 6-3:
Creating a
new team
for an
existing
business
unit.

7. **Fill in the Team Name field.**

   The business unit you selected in Step 4 is automatically filled in for you, although you can change this association by clicking the magnifying glass to the right of the Business Unit field.

8. **Click Save and Close.**

   The system returns to the listing for that particular business unit.

If you create a team without assigning it to a specific business unit, by default it's assigned to the overall parent unit. After a team is assigned to any business unit, you can't reassign it to another business unit. However, you can disable the team and start fresh with a new team.

Assigning users to teams

When you initially create a team, it has no members. But after the team is created, it's easy to add or later remove members.

To add one or more members to a team, follow these steps:

1. **Double-click the team you created.**

2. **At the top of the navigation pane, select Members.**

3. **On the window's toolbar, click the Add Members button and then click the Find button.**

   The Look Up Records dialog box appears, as shown in Figure 6-4.

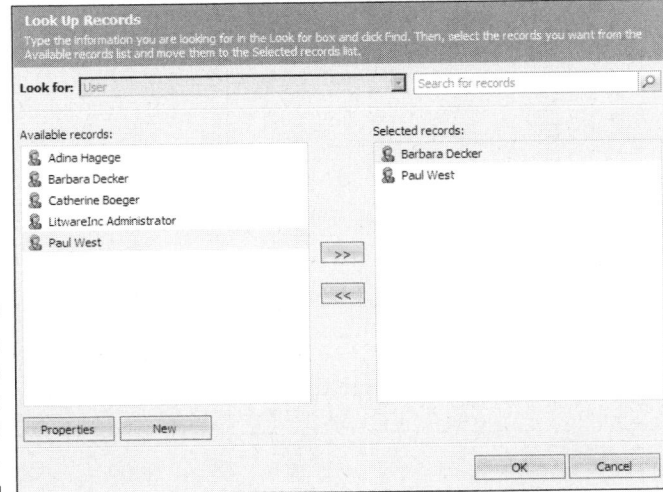

Figure 6-4:
Add some members to your new team.

4. **In the left panel, double-click each member that you want to add to your team.**

5. **When you've finished assembling the team, click OK at the bottom of the window.**

   The system returns to that team's listing.

In this chapter, you've seen how to define and create territories, business units, and teams. You can assign each user to only one territory, but each user may be a member of several teams and business units. By assigning users to teams, you can easily share and shift responsibilities between teams.

Chapter 7

Using the Product Catalog

*P*roduct catalogs, whether they're paper or virtual, are a great invention. And product catalogs aren't just for consumers! They also make excellent reference tools for your sales and customer service staff.

With Microsoft CRM, your company can create a brawny, capable, all-inclusive computer-based product catalog. That way, you can quickly and easily find all the items and services you sell (nix thumbing through pages). This chapter shows you how to set up this valuable resource.

Overview of the Product Catalog

Within a product catalog, you can create pricing schedules and assign them to your customers as default schedules. This way, Bob's Big Discount Warehouse gets the wholesale pricing schedule, and the National Organization for Toasters gets nonprofit pricing. Using these assigned pricing schedules and the quote generation feature of Microsoft CRM (refer to Chapter 16), your salespeople can generate accurate quotes quickly. Quotes beget orders and orders beget invoices and invoices beget bucks (most of the time).

You can create a number of pricing schedules, for any reason. These schedules can be as simple as retail, wholesale, and nonprofit pricing or as complex as seasonal pricing or tiered membership pricing. Chapter 16 details how to create and use the pricing schedule to your company's advantage.

The product catalog can link to opportunities, competitors, and product literature. In fact, the product catalog has its tentacles into virtually every aspect of the system.

If you're integrating with one of Microsoft Dynamics' back-office accounting systems, you can set up the product catalog in the accounting system and link to it rather than set up the catalog in Microsoft CRM. If you're integrating with an accounting system other than Dynamics, you can upload that system's product list directly into the CRM product catalog. When integrating with these systems, any data from the accounting side normally overrides what you entered previously in the CRM product catalog.

If you use an accounting application other than one from the Microsoft Dynamics family, there are solutions for you, too. See Chapter 27 for some add-ons that simplify this work.

It's a good idea to read this entire chapter before you build your product catalog. This will give you an overview and allow you to do some planning.

When you're ready to start building your product catalog, we recommend that you use the order suggested by Microsoft, which we follow too:

- ✔ Discount lists
- ✔ Unit groups
- ✔ Price lists
- ✔ Products

To start your planning, categorize your products and services and organize and simplify your pricing schedules. This is also a good time to check and update your inventory lists. Take out products you haven't sold since President Nixon was in office. And while you're at it, update your pricing. Remember, the cost of living has increased considerably since you founded the company (36 cents for a gallon for gas, anyone?).

Getting to the Product Catalog Window

You create a product catalog in the Product Catalog window of Microsoft CRM. You don't have to venture out of this section while creating your catalog — although we recommend venturing out of your cubicle for a leg stretch once in a while.

Now that you've stretched your legs and shared the latest rumor, it's time to get to work. Start by going to the Product Catalog window, as follows:

1. **At the bottom of the navigation pane, click Settings.**

   The Settings section expands in the top left with the Administration section highlighted.

2. **Click the Product Catalog section in the upper left.**

   The four components of the product catalog appear in the Product Catalog window.

As mentioned, we recommend that you create your product catalog in the order that Microsoft indicates. So that's what you do next.

Creating a Discount List

Discount lists control how prices change based on the quantity of the product or service being purchased. You can set your discounts in two ways:

✔ By percentage

✔ By reduction according to a set dollar amount

For example, a seasonal sale in which you offer a 10 percent discount on all purchases calls for a percent discount list. Offering $5 off for every touchdown the high school team makes during the weekend game is a set dollar amount discount.

To set up a discount list, you first need to get to the Product Catalog window, as explained in the preceding section. Then follow these steps:

1. **In the Product Catalog window, click Discount Lists.**

   All existing discount lists are displayed, as shown in Figure 7-1.

2. **On the Discount Lists window's toolbar, click the New button.**

   The Create Discount List window appears.

3. **In the Name field, enter a title for your new discount list.**

   We recommend a unique and self-explanatory title so that others will be able to identify the list. In our example, we entered **Summer Special Discount**.

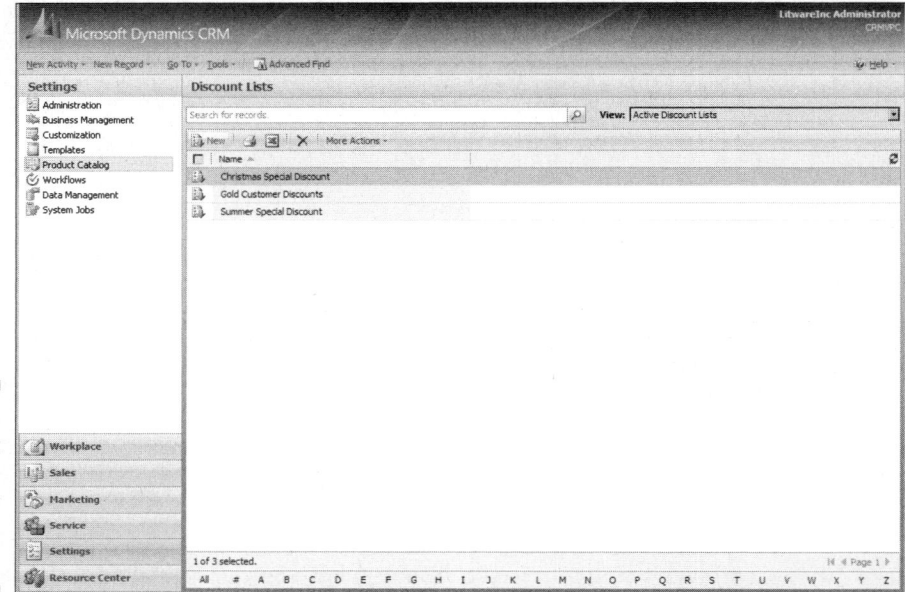

4. Choose the type of discount that you want to offer your customers.

The Percentage option is based on a percentage of the regular price. The Amount option is based on a set dollar amount deducted from the regular price. To follow along with our example, select Percentage.

5. Click OK.

The Information window for your new discount list appears. (The navigation pane has three options: Information, Discounts, and Workflows. The Information display is the default display.) Note the top of the window; whatever you named your discount list appears here.

At this point, you can continue with creating the discount list, or you can exit the discount list by clicking Save and Close.

6. Enter some descriptive information for the discount list in the description box.

For example, you can add a note about the limitations of the discount (such as **limit 4**).

7. In the navigation pane, select Discounts.

The Discount section of your discount list appears, as shown in Figure 7-2. This is where you begin entering the details for this discount.

8. Now to make your discounts, click the New Discount button on the toolbar.

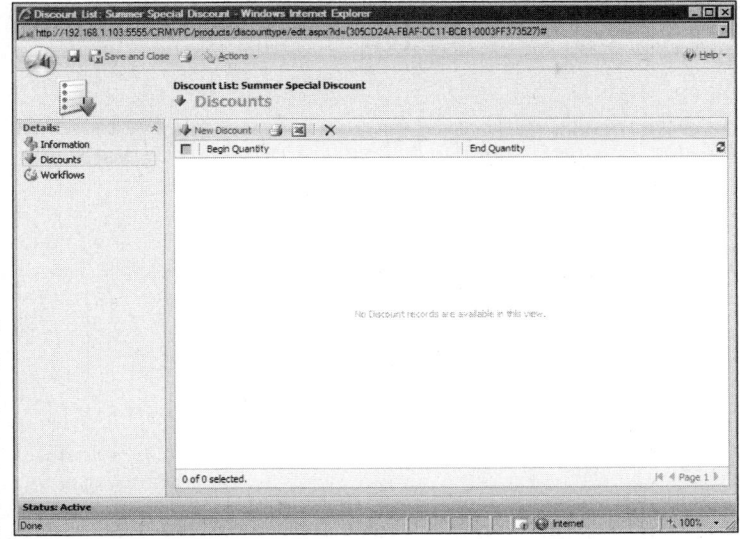

Figure 7-2:
The
discount
workspace
of your
discount list.

9. **In the Discount: New window that appears, enter the following information for your discount:**

   a. *The beginning and ending quantity:* The program calls these Begin Quantity and End Quantity.

   b. *Your discount amount:* If you chose Percentage in Step 4, this line says Percentage. If you chose Amount in Step 5, this line says Amount ($). When entering the amount, don't enter the symbol (% or $).

10. **Click the Save and Close button to return to your discount list.**

11. **To enter another line item, go back to Step 8.**

    You can enter as many line items as you want to establish the necessary price breaks for this discount list. For example, if you want to offer price breaks for quantity purchases, you might create a line item for a discount for 1–10 items purchased and another one to assign a price for 11–20 items.

12. **To save this list, click Save and Close in the Discount List window.**

Make sure that you don't overlap quantity ranges. For example, suppose your first discount covers the first nine items sold, and you have a larger discount for ten items and above. You enter 1–9 for the first discount and 10–99 for the second discount. But what if you sell time and break it down in 15-minute increments? The undefined quantity between 9 and 10 could be an issue. We suggest that you break down time increments into decimals when entering quantities for time.

Creating a Unit Group

A *base unit* is the smallest or most common means of tracking an item sold. Typical base units are pounds, gallons, hours, days, and tons.

A *unit group* defines how individual items are grouped into larger quantities. For example, suppose that you sell books individually, by the case, and by the pallet. A unit group of books shows how a book relates to a case and a case to a pallet. Using this example, if you sell 2 cases of books, with 20 books to a case, the system knows that you sold 40 books.

To create a unit group, follow these steps:

1. **In the Product Catalog window, click Unit Groups.**

   If you need help finding the window, see the earlier section titled "Getting to the Product Catalog Window." The screen shown in Figure 7-3 appears.

2. **On the window's toolbar, click the New button.**

   The Create Unit Group dialog box appears.

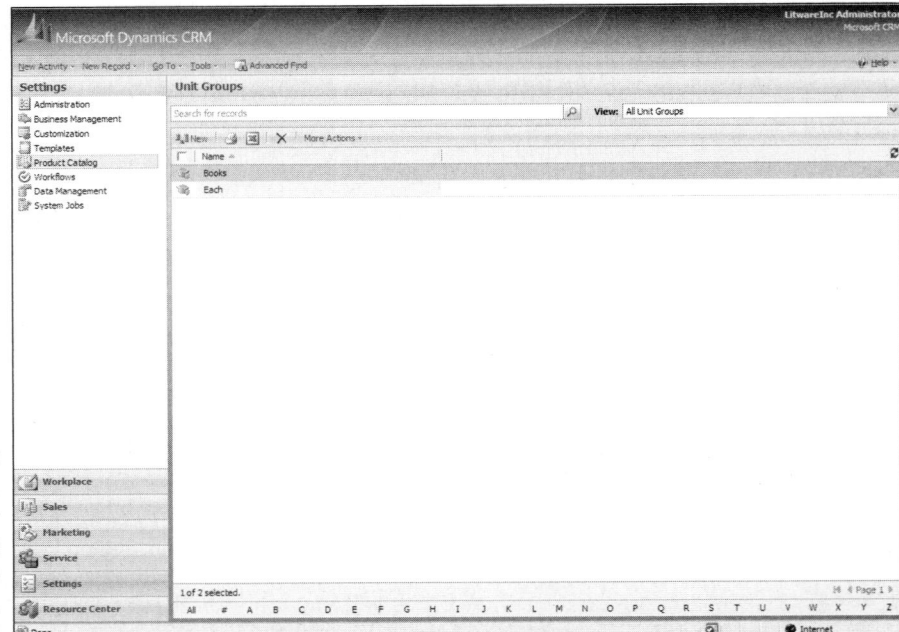

Figure 7-3:
This is your
main Unit
Groups
display.

3. **Enter the following information for your unit group:**

   a. *Name:* This is the name of your unit group. For our example, we're calling this unit group **Books**.

   b. *Primary Unit:* This is the smallest unit by which the product can be sold. The primary unit is also known as the *base unit.* Enter **Each** as the Primary Unit.

4. **Click OK.**

   The Information window, which is the default display, appears.

5. **At the top of the navigation pane on the left, click Units.**

   The Unit Group: Books window appears. (If you named your unit something else, that name would appear instead of *Books.*) This is where you'll add your units to your unit group.

6. **Click Units on the left and then on the toolbar of your new Unit Group, click New Unit.**

   The Unit: New window appears.

7. **For each of the three units (book, case, and pallet in our example), do the following:**

   a. *Enter the name.*

   This is where you enter the name of each unit. To follow along with the example, enter **Book** (the first time through), then **Case**, and then **Pallet**.

   b. *Enter the quantity.*

   Again, to follow along with the example, enter a quantity of **1** for Each because this is our base unit. The Case quantity is **20**, meaning that each case contains 20 base units. The Pallet quantity is **10**, meaning that each pallet contains 10 cases.

   c. *Enter the base unit.*

   The base unit is the smallest increment of this new unit you're creating. Continuing with the example, you can see that Each has no base unit (because it *is* the base unit and was determined in Step 3 to be the Primary Unit). Case has a base unit of Each, and Pallet has a base unit of Case. Use the magnifying glass to browse for the unit you want to set as the base unit. All units, with the exception of the primary unit, must have a base unit.

   d. *Click the Save and Close button.*

A quick note for those keeping score: The columns in the Unit Group workspace are listed in a different order than those in the Unit: New window.

8. **Click the Save and Close button.**

   You're returned to the unit group that you're working on, as shown in Figure 7-4.

9. **To save the unit group, click the Save and Close button again.**

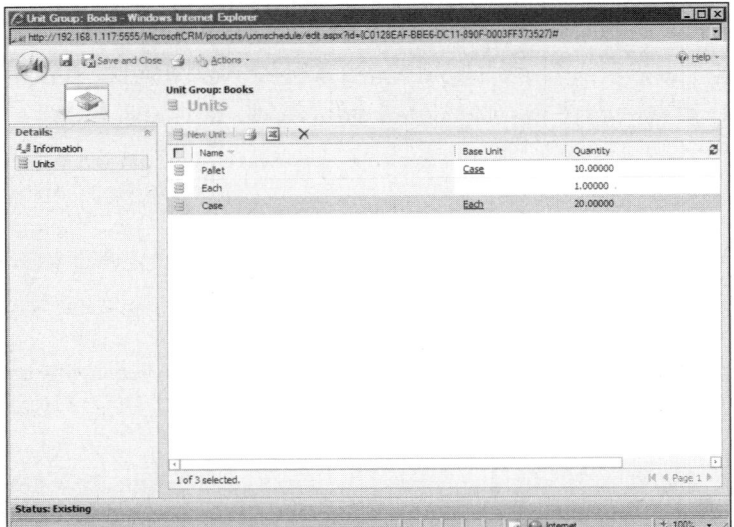

Figure 7-4:
We've added units to the group.

Creating a Price List

Price lists are the backbone of all your opportunities and quotes. Your company may have more than one price list, such as a retail price list and a wholesale one. You could also have separate price lists for government and nonprofit customers. You can add a default price list to each contact or account, but you can override this when you create quotes and invoices. (See Chapter 16.)

If your company uses an accounting system and wants to integrate it with Microsoft CRM, keep in mind that the interface normally provides all of this information and overwrites your price lists with the information from the accounting system. With the integration provided to Microsoft CRM, much of this functionality is disabled because it is controlled by the accounting application.

Here's how you create that price list:

1. **In the Product Catalog window, click Price Lists.**

   The Price Lists window, similar to the one shown in Figure 7-5, appears.

2. **On the window's toolbar, click the New button.**

   The Price List: New window appears. The navigation pane displays three choices: Information, Price List Items, and Workflows. Price List Items and Workflows aren't available until you've saved the price list.

3. **Enter a name for your price list.**

   Required fields are in red. The Name field is required, but the start and end date fields aren't. In our example, we created the "It's Too Cold!!" price list to offer special prices to match the dropping temperatures. However, winter lasts only so long, so we've set the price specials to end in February.

4. **Click Save (the disk icon next to the Save and Close button).**

   Clicking Save allows you to continue with the next part of the process, adding price list items. However, if you aren't ready to enter your price list items or need to get out of this window for some reason, just click the Save and Close button.

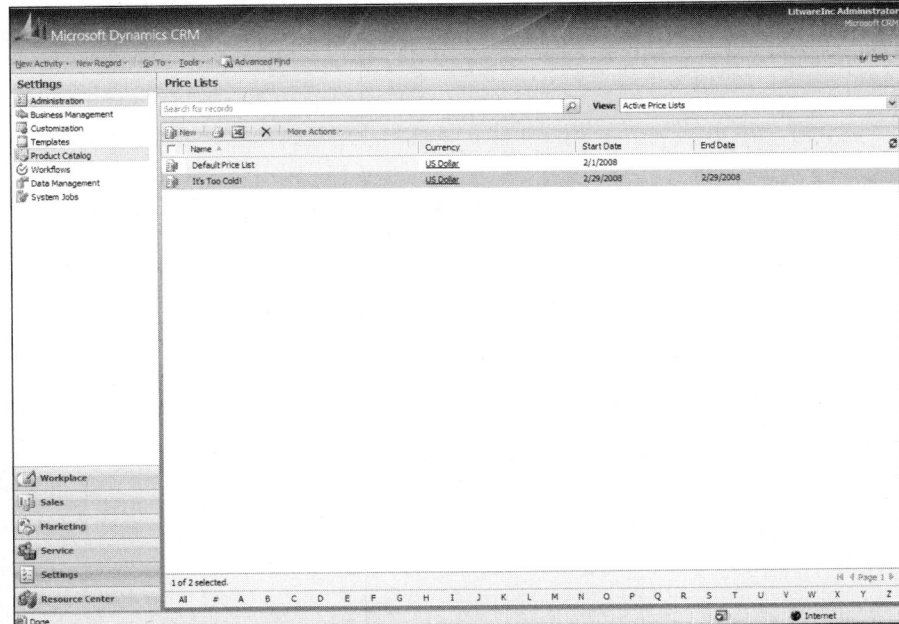

Figure 7-5:
Manage and create your price lists from this screen.

5. **In the navigation pane on the left, click Price List Items.**

6. **On the Price List Items toolbar, click the Add Price List Item button.**

   The Price List Item: New window appears, as shown in Figure 7-6.

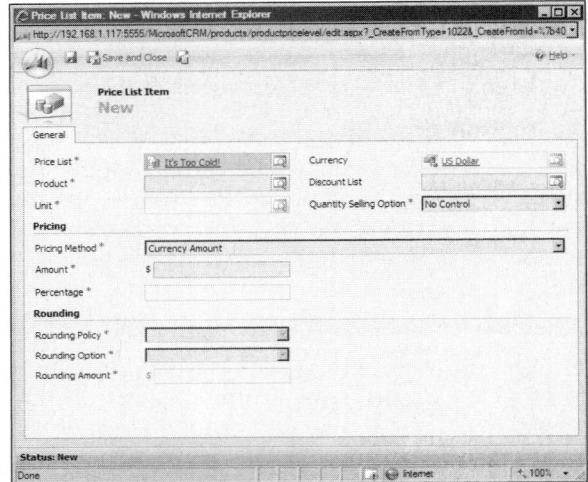

Figure 7-6:
Enter the
information
about your
item here.

7. **Enter your price list information in the available fields.**

   Some fields must be filled in by using the magnifying glass to the right of the field. The magnifying glass opens a Look Up window. You can fill in other fields freehand or by using the drop-down boxes. As with other screens in Microsoft CRM, the fields in red are required.

   a. *Price List:* This is filled in automatically by the program. However, you can change the price list by using the magnifying glass.

   b. *Product:* Use the magnifying glass to find the product you want in this price list. Microsoft thwarts the Minions of Chaos by allowing your staff to enter only predefined choices from the product list.

   c. *Unit:* Use the magnifying glass to make your selection. This field isn't enabled until you select a product.

   d. *Discount List (optional):* Use the magnifying glass to find the discount list you created earlier in the chapter and link it to your price list. By adding a discount list to work in tandem with the price list item, your staff can create thorough pricing to quote your customers. (See Chapter 16 for details on generating quotes.)

   e. *Quantity Selling Option:* This is where you define the quantities in which you'll sell your product. Choose No Control, Whole, or Whole and Fractional. This feature really comes in handy if you sell fractional services such as help desk or prorated time products.

  f. Pricing Method: Six options are available: Currency Amount; Percent of List; Percent Markup — Current Cost; Percent Margin — Current Cost; Percent Markup — Standard Cost; Percent Margin — Standard Cost.

  g. Amount ($): Enter the dollar amount for the price list. The Amount option is available only if you chose Currency Amount under Pricing Method. Don't include a dollar sign.

  h. Percentage: Enter the percentage for the price list. Don't include the symbol (%).

  i. Rounding Policy: Your rounding policy tells the system how to round percentage calculations to arrive at a specific price. Your options are None, Up, Down, and To Nearest. Rounding applies only when the pricing method is based on percentage. If you selected Currency Amount for the Pricing Method, this field isn't available.

  j. Rounding Option: This option works with the Rounding Amount field. For example, select Ends In here and .00 in the Rounding Amount field if you want to round to the nearest dollar. Select Multiple Of here and enter .05 in the Rounding Amount field to round to the nearest nickel. If you selected None for the Rounding Policy or Currency Amount for the Pricing Method, this field isn't available.

  k. Rounding Amount: Fill in the amount on which you want to base your rounding, as described in the preceding entry. If you selected None for the Rounding Policy or Currency Amount for the Pricing Method, this field isn't available.

8. Click Save and Close to save your price list items to your price list.

As mentioned, the fields in red are required. If you've missed one (due to excessive caffeine intake or hunting down who burned the popcorn), the program will remind you.

By creating price lists, you build an easy-to-use system to generate price quotes for your customers. Microsoft CRM uses the price lists, discount lists, and price list items to automatically calculate client costs, so your salespeople can focus on selling and not math.

Adding Products

Your products — without them, you wouldn't have a business, right? From the first entrepreneurial caveman, businesses are made because someone has a product to sell. We use the term *product* as a general term to encompass products, services, the help desk — basically whatever you build your business around.

Now, because the Minions of Chaos love mischief, Microsoft has taken a smart step in preventing them from running amok in your system: Only system administrators are allowed to add new products. That means that if Sam the Salesman can't find the entry for the Hop-n-Pop toaster, he won't be able to add entries that could create confusion when you want a report or when other salespeople are looking for the Hop-n-Pop. Can you imagine if he added the product as hopnpop, Mary in the next cube added it as HnP, and then Carey added it by the model number X900? How could you run a report on how many of those have sold?

Another function of Microsoft CRM allows you to group products sold as a *kit*. Take your Hop-n-Pop toaster, sell it with bagels and organic preserves, and you have the Bagel Buff Gift Basket. You can also create special kits to simplify your sales and ordering processes or to get rid of some stuff that you don't want anymore — clearance, anyone?

You can also *relate* individual products to substitute products. This is a handy function for your salespeople when Mrs. Reynolds wants a Hop-n-Pop toaster but you sold the last one two days ago. By relating this product to a substitute, your salesperson can easily recommend the equivalent HotHopPop toaster.

If you're a system administrator, follow these steps to add a new product to your product list:

1. In the Product Catalog window, click Products.

A list of your active products appears, as shown in Figure 7-7.

2. On the Products window's toolbar, click the New button.

The Product: New window appears with three tabs, as shown in Figure 7-8.

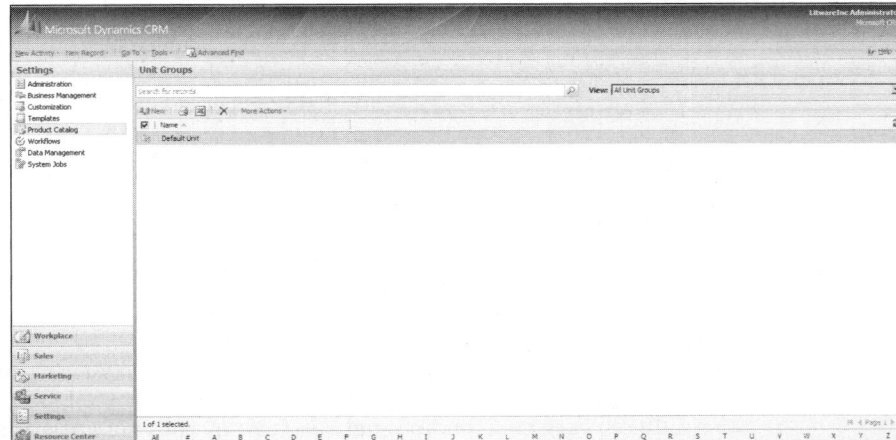

Figure 7-7:
The active products screen.

3. **Fill in the General tab.**

The General tab, which is the default tab, is where you enter most of the information for your product. You can fill in some fields freeform, others using the magnifying glass (thwarting those Minions of Chaos), and still others with the Form Assistant. For details on using the magnifying glass and the Form Assistant, see Chapter 2.

The following fields are mandatory:

a. *ID:* If your system is integrated with your accounting system, the ID is the item number used by the accounting system. Through this field, the accounting system updates (and overwrites) information in each product record.

b. *Name:* This is descriptive text entered freehand. But it can also be populated by your accounting system if it's integrated.

c. *Unit Group:* If your system isn't integrated with accounting, select the unit group that includes the units by which this product will be sold.

d. *Default Unit:* This is the unit you would typically sell the product as. For example, if you sold the book, *Toasting the Night Away,* as a single product, the default unit would be Each. If you were selling nails, the default unit might be Box.

e. *Default Price List:* Earlier in the chapter, we discuss price lists. This field relates an individual product to a default price list (wholesale, retail, dealer, government, and the like) you've set up. When salespeople go to make that quote, they'll actually get the price list attached to the customer record. However, if no price list is attached to the customer record, the system defaults to the price list indicated for the product itself. You can't assign a default price list to the product until you save the product (use the Save button rather than the Save and Close button) and associate the product with a price list item. Until you do this, you see a warning message that the default price list isn't set.

f. *Decimals Supported:* If you can't divide your product (books, for example) into fractional quantities, enter **0**. If fractional quantities are possible, you can use up to five decimal places.

g. *Currency:* This field is used to compute prices for you products. It is also used compute the costs of business transactions such as sales orders.

The following fields are optional, but we find them helpful in building a product catalog and entering products:

a. *Subject:* This field allows you to group your products for reporting.

b. *Product Type:* The four default product types are Sales Inventory (usually physical goods); Miscellaneous Charges (fees, such as for restocking); Services (such as consulting or annual maintenance fees); and Flat Fee (for example, handling or shipping charges).

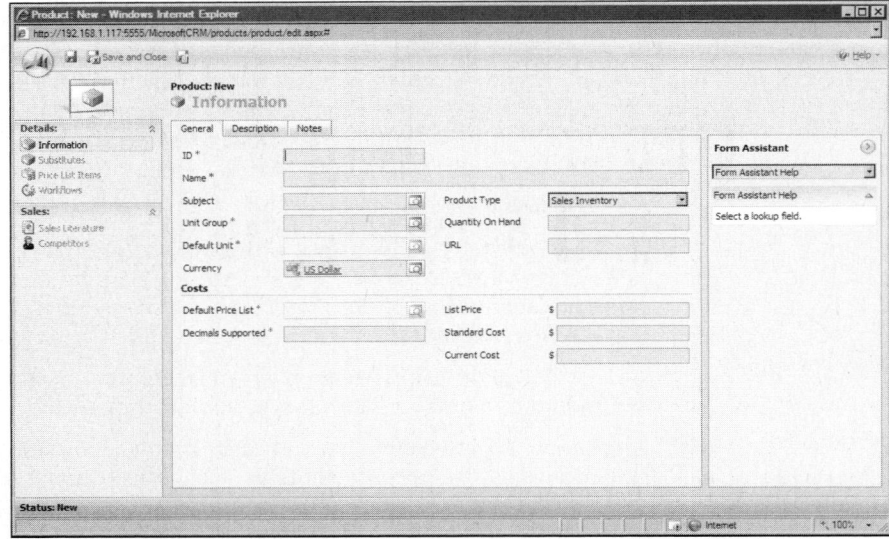

Figure 7-8:
Enter your
new
product
information
here.

c. *Quantity on Hand:* The number of items in stock. This field is controlled by the back-office system if you have integrated it.

d. *URL:* The Web address related to this product. This is a handy place to get up-to-date product information.

e. *List Price, Standard Cost,* and *Current Cost:* The price on a generated quote is based on these fields.

4. **On the Description tab, you can enter vendor and part number information.**

   Having the vendor and part information can be helpful, especially if you sell similar products with similar names. Entering information on this tab isn't mandatory, but it does offer you another opportunity to identify your product.

5. **The Notes tab is for freeform notes and information about your product.**

   Suppose that your product comes in other colors. Instead of making the salesperson back up a few screens to see what colors you offer, you can list the colors here, too.

6. **After you enter all of your product information, click Save and Close to return to your product catalog. (Refer to Figure 7-7.)**

   Remember the motto of computer users everywhere: save, Save, SAVE!

Ta-dah! Now you've entered your product into your product catalog! Give yourself a pat on the back.

Chapter 8

Understanding Security and Access Rights

*I*n this day and age, security is important. As technology advances, so do the hackers, virus writers, and other malevolently minded folks. With Microsoft CRM, you should be concerned with two types of security: physical security and internal security.

Physical security is a defense against everyone you don't know and don't want to meet. These are the people who have nothing better to do than develop and propagate viruses or, worse yet, spend their time hacking into your system to either paralyze it or steal your stuff. This type of security is generally handled by firewalls, routers, and other types of hardware and software. Because the vast majority of CRM installations run only on your intranet, this type of security is beyond the scope of this book. For more information, see the Microsoft *Implementation Guide.*You can download the Implementation Guide by going to www.microsoft.com/downloads and searching for "Microsoft Dynamics CRM 4.0 Implementation Guide." In fact, searching for just "Microsoft Dynamics CRM 4.0" will result in dozens of downloads regarding CRM including the latest security patches.

You can keep up on the latest at the Microsoft CRM Community site at

    http://community.dynamics.com/

Be sure to check this Web site regularly to ensure that you are fully up-to-date on any security issues specifically affecting Microsoft CRM.

The second type of security, *internal security,* is aimed at your own usually well-meaning team members. Some organizations, such as brokerage houses, deal with internal security by requiring the restriction of certain records, even from members of their own staff. In other organizations, salespeople's opportunities need to be hidden from the other salespeople. In our company, we find it occasionally important to keep e-mails away from prying eyes.

CRM has quite a bit of built-in security. And your system administrator, perhaps with several people from your management team, will probably be charged with setting up security and access rights within Microsoft CRM. In this chapter, you find out about the types of security you should consider and how to regulate your internal security.

No form of security is ever foolproof. Although Microsoft CRM provides a sophisticated security system, this issue should remain a high priority. Security threats can come from anywhere: from your staff (innocent mistakes or not-so-innocent sabotage) and from outside hackers.

Remember, no system is foolproof (remember the *Titanic*?), but you can develop an efficient compromise and make your system user-friendly and hacker-unfriendly.

And, don't forget about the Minions of Chaos — always back up your data.

Security Overview

Microsoft CRM's security focuses on meeting the needs of most organizations in two ways:

- ✔ Role-based security
- ✔ Object-based security

Role-based security in Microsoft CRM allows you to assign a role to a user, such as Sales Manager, that controls what the user can do and has access to. Your installation can also define its own roles to meet your requirements. See the upcoming section, "Looking at Predefined Roles" to have a look at the security roles that exist out of the box Many of these will work as-is or require only slight tweaking.

Object-based security in Microsoft CRM focuses on what access the roles have to primary and extended entities (such as leads, opportunities, contacts, accounts, and cases). So, in this way, you could possess the role of Sales Manager and have access to change opportunities (an object) but only read cases (another object).

Essentially a user's rights depend on what Role they are a member of and what Object they are working with. Although a Sales Manger (Role) might have full access to Leads (Object) they may only have limited access to Cases (Object). On the other hand, the opposite might be true for a CSR (Role). CSRs might have full access to the Cases (Objects) but limited access, if any, to Leads (Object).

Setting Restrictions with User Privileges

Privileges are the most basic security options in Microsoft CRM and are generally set up by your administrator. User privileges determine what a user can and can't do, such as creating records or deleting records. (We recommend that only a system administrator be allowed to delete records.) Altogether, a user can have eight basic privileges, as follows:

- ✔ **Create:** The ability to create new records.

- ✔ **Read:** The ability to read or view the record.

- ✔ **Write:** the ability to change the record.

- ✔ **Delete:** The ability to delete the record.

- ✔ **Append:** The ability to link the record to another record.

- ✔ **Append To:** The ability to link other records to this record.

- ✔ **Assign:** The ability to change the record owner or "Assign" to another owner.

- ✔ **Share:** Similar to assign but without changing the owner. If you share a records with another user then they will have nearly the same rights as you on that record depending on their roles.

Further Defining Permissions with Access Levels

The next step above privileges, *access levels* help determine which records the user privileges should apply to. In other words, your privileges may include the ability to delete account records, but your access level determines exactly which records you are able to delete. Microsoft CRM defines four access levels from user (least authority) to organization (most authority), as follows:

- ✔ **User:** You only have access to your records.

- ✔ **Business Unit:** You have access to all the records in your business unit.

✔ **Parent:** You have access to all the records in your business unit and all subordinate business units.

✔ **Organization:** You have access to all records in the entire organization.

Many organizations deal only with the User and Organization Access Levels. This depends mostly on corporate policy and culture. Some organizations allow everyone access to everything and others have a more "your contacts and my contacts" mentality. The Business Unit and Parent access levels allow for very complex access rights more suitable for very large organizations with complex organizational structures.

You can learn more about setting up CRM to mimic your organizational structure in Chapter 6.

Looking at Predefined Roles

The concept of *roles* marries privileges and access rights. Microsoft CRM comes with 13 predefined roles that are typical of a midsized organization, as shown in Figure 8-1. Making use of these predefined roles saves a lot of time that would otherwise be spent setting up specific access rights for each user.

If you're going to make *any* changes to the default roles, we recommend that you use the functionality Microsoft provides, called Role Copy. Refer to the online help on how to use this.

Online help is available in the upper-right corner of virtually every screen in CRM.

Security Roles	
New ✕ More Actions ▾	
☐ Name ▲	Business Unit
CEO-Business Manager	MicrosoftCRM
CSR Manager	MicrosoftCRM
Customer Service Representative	MicrosoftCRM
Marketing Manager	MicrosoftCRM
Marketing Professional	MicrosoftCRM
Sales Manager	MicrosoftCRM
Salesperson	MicrosoftCRM
Schedule Manager	MicrosoftCRM
Scheduler	MicrosoftCRM
System Administrator	MicrosoftCRM
System Customizer	MicrosoftCRM
Vice President of Marketing	MicrosoftCRM
Vice President of Sales	MicrosoftCRM

Figure 8-1: You get these standard roles out of the box, but you can add more.

In this section, we show you how to look at the roles that Microsoft CRM ships with. Each of these roles has a complete set of predefined privileges and access rights. The prototypical sales manager, for example, is given a default set of privileges and access rights. To see the settings for any of the default roles, follow these steps:

1. **In the lower left part of the navigation pane, click the Settings button and then click Administration sub-section in the upper left.**

   The Administration window appears on the right. (Remember that non-administrative users will not have access to the Settings area.)

2. **Select Security Roles on the right.**

   The Security Roles window appears, listing all existing roles. (Refer to Figure 8-1.)

3. **View a role by double clicking it in the list.**

   For instance, if you double click the Salesperson Role, the Role: Salesperson window appears.

4. **Click the Core Records tab.**

   A screen similar to the one shown in Figure 8-2 appears. The Core Records tab contains all the toggle switches to turn access rights on or off and is the central storehouse for role information.

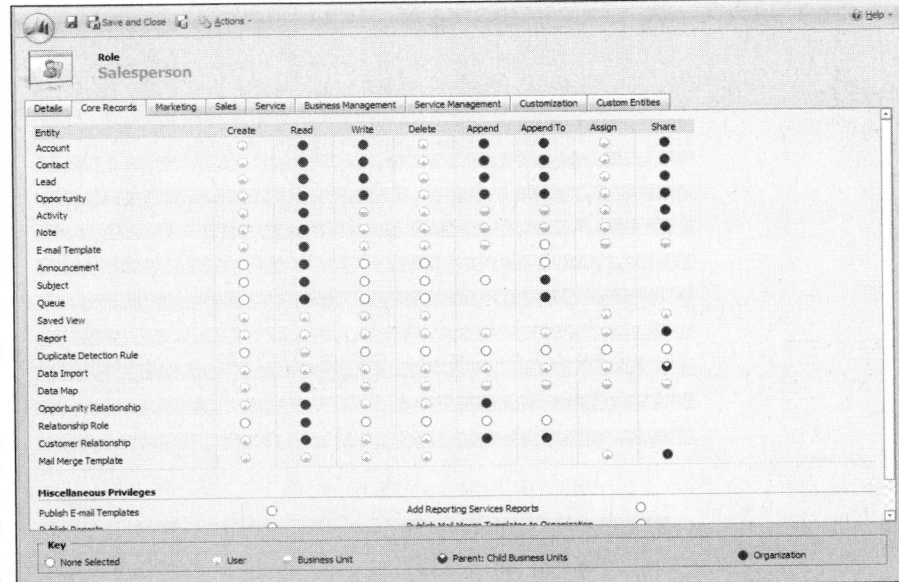

Figure 8-2: The Salesperson's rights regarding Core Records.

5. **Click each tab in turn to see all the objects that the role can access at various levels.**

6. **Click the Save and Close button to return to the Security Roles window.**

If your business has specific business rules you need to enforce, you should seek help from your system administrator or implementation partner.

Assigning Roles

After you have defined a role by either copying or editing and existing role, you need to assign it to the user. Every user in the system must have at least one role to access the system.

A user can have more than one assigned role. For example, someone could have a role as a systems administrator and as a mailroom clerk. Not a very likely combination but still possible. When a single user has multiple roles with different privileges and access rights, the role with the less restrictive privileges takes precedence. So, even when your systems administrator is functioning as a mailroom clerk, he or she will have the maximum levels of access rights.

If your organization is complex or you don't understand Microsoft CRM's concepts of roles, we suggest that you consult with an expert to help you in setting up your roles and assigning them to users. See Chapter 28 for more information on when and where to go for help.

To add a role to a user of the system, just follow these simple steps:

1. **At the bottom left of the navigation pane, click the Settings button and then click Administration in the upper left.**

   The Settings window appears.

2. **Select Users.**

   The Users window appears, listing all current users.

3. **Double-click a username.**

   The User window appears.

4. **In the navigation pane, click Roles.**

5. **At the top of the Roles window, click Manage Roles.**

6. **Select the roles you want this user to have and then click OK.**

7. **Click Save and Close.**

Sharing Information with Others on Your Team

Microsoft CRM has powerful security and record-sharing tools. If keeping certain records or data confidential is necessary for your company, that's no problem. Usually more critical than keeping data confidential, however, is your ability to share information with other members of your team.

Defining a team

Before you set up your CRM system, we suggest that you do a bit of homework and planning. So get your management staff together and order pizza, because you have some brainstorming to do. You'll want to figure out your *business units* (think divisions or remote offices) and then assign users to those units.

Typically, the users assigned to a particular business unit are also members of a *team*. Each user in CRM can be a member of one or more teams. The concept of a team allows for a convenient sharing of records. (For more on teams, see Chapter 6.)

Sharing and assigning

You can easily *share* records and activities with members of your team, and you should. Sharing a record is like asking your buddies to help you when you need it. Rest assured: If you ask them, they'll return the favor. By sharing and distributing the workload, you, your team members, and your customers all benefit. While you're on vacation, team members who have access to your data while you're away can still help *your* clients.

You can also *assign* records and tasks. Assigning is a little more like telling another user on the system to handle the assignment. (It's more like delegating than sharing.)

Unsharing

Whatever you share you can *unshare*. If you turned over access to your clients while you were on vacation, you can retake control upon your return. In most work environments, this is a far better solution than sending your clients e-mails telling them you'll be away for two weeks and they should just relax until you get back. And it's certainly a better approach than not letting your clients know that you'll be away at all.

Sharing and Not Sharing Data

The concept of sharing is also pertinent to security. Assuming you have sharing privileges, you can regulate who else in your organization has access to your records. By sharing your records with another user or a team, you're granting access to people who wouldn't otherwise be able to view or modify those records.

Sharing records

Granting sharing privileges to someone who already has organizational rights (the highest level of access rights) really doesn't accomplish anything. Similarly, if you try to deny sharing rights to someone with organizational rights, nothing's going to change. That's like telling the boss he or she can't look over your shoulder.

Sharing is a good tool if, for example, you're working on a deal in New York and need to bring in a co-worker from Detroit. Under normal security, your co-worker wouldn't be able to view your records. By sharing, you can give him or her access to the record to help work the deal.

You can share almost any kind of record, but here we use an account record as an example. Follow these steps to share an account with one user or a whole team:

1. **Navigate to the object you want to share using the navigation pane on the left of the main CRM screen.**

   For this example click on Sales and then Accounts.

   The Accounts list appears on the right.

2. **Open a record by double-clicking it.**

   The General tab for the account appears.

3. **On the menu bar (at the top of the screen), choose Actions⇨Sharing.**

   The window shown in Figure 8-3 appears.

4. **In the Common Tasks pane on the left, select Add User/Team.**

   The Look Up Records dialog box appears, as shown in Figure 8-4.

5. **In the Look For field, select User or Team and then click the Find button which looks like a magnifying glass.**

   All available users or teams are displayed. Alternately, you could enter some text in the text box to the left of the Find button to narrow the results.

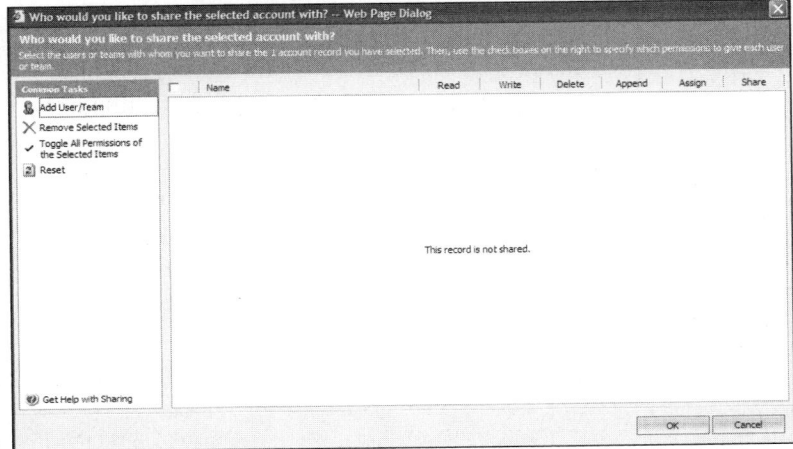

Figure 8-3:
Setting up
one or more
records for
sharing.

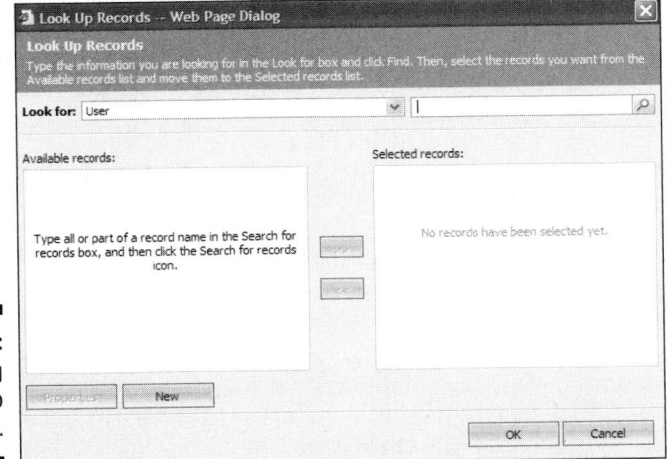

Figure 8-4:
Selecting
someone to
share with.

6. **Double-click any user (or team) from the list in the left panel.**

   Another method is to highlight the user (or team) and click the right-facing arrow button. The user (or team) is transferred to the right pane in anticipation of sharing the record with that user or team.

7. **Click OK.**

   The window shown in Figure 8-5 appears.

Figure 8-5:
Granting
sharing
permissions.

8. **Specify which permissions you're allowing for this record.**

   To do so, select or deselect each of the check boxes that relate to the rights you're granting.

9. **Click OK when you're satisfied that you've shared enough rights.**

   The window for the record reappears, but now these other users have as much access to the record as you've granted them.

Sharing multiple records

You can share multiple records by Shift-clicking them or Ctrl-clicking them from the list and then clicking More Actions from the tool bar and selecting Sharing. This brings you to the same screen as in Figure 8-3, and from there the process is the same as sharing a single record.

Unsharing records

If you can share it, you can unshare it. For example, before going on vacation, you may want to share all your records with one of your peers. When you return, you probably want to unshare them and resume your usual tasks. To unshare a record, follow these steps:

1. **Navigate to the record you want to unshare.**

2. **On the menu bar (at the top of the screen), choose Actions⇨Sharing.**

3. **Click the Share check box to remove the check mark.**

   If you granted sharing rights to more than one user, you can eliminate multiple users' rights by clicking each of their Share check boxes on this one screen.

4. **Click OK.**

   The system returns to the General tab of the account record.

Assigning records

If you can share it, you can unshare it. For example, before going on vacation, you may want to share all your records with one of your peers. When you return, you probably want to unshare them and resume your usual tasks. To unshare a record, follow these steps:

1. **Navigate to the record you want to assign.**

2. **On the menu bar (at the top of the screen), choose Actions➪Assign.**

   You will see the Assign Account box pictured in Figure 8-6. (Assuming it's an account that you are assigning.)

3. **Select either Assign to me or Assign to other user.**

   If you are assigning to another user then use the provided lookup to select the user.

4. **Click OK.**

   The system returns to the General tab of the record and it is now assigned to the new user.

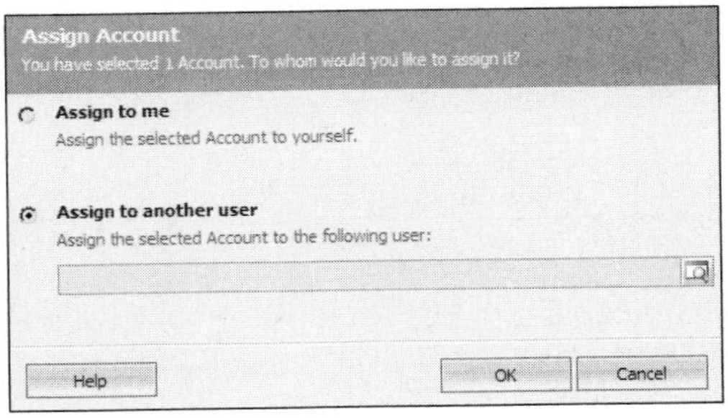

Figure 8-6:
Assigning an account.

Assign Account
You have selected 1 Account. To whom would you like to assign it?

○ **Assign to me**
   Assign the selected Account to yourself.

◉ **Assign to another user**
   Assign the selected Account to the following user:

Help   OK   Cancel

Streamlining the assignment of permissions

If you share with multiple people or multiple teams, you can end up having to deal with quite a few check boxes to manage in the Common Tasks panel, which you see at the left side of the screen after you choose Actions➪ Sharing. Microsoft CRM provides three additional options in the Common Tasks panel to streamline your efforts:

- ✓ **Toggle All Permissions of the Selected Items:** After you've selected one or more users using the check boxes to the left of their name, this option acts like a *toggle switch* (it turns all permissions on and off) for for the selected users. This is an easy way to grant permissions across the board for multiple users.

- ✓ **Reset:** This is like a do-over button. Selecting Reset brings you back to the settings you had before the last time you clicked the OK button.

Chapter 9

Implementing Business Rules and Workflow

*W*orkflow. I know what you're thinking. Workflow? What is that? Well, as one of the most powerful functions of Microsoft CRM, workflow is the nearest thing you'll find to a money machine.

The Workflow Management System takes your manual business rules (or procedures) and turns them into an automated system. Without workflow, you'd have a database with names, addresses, and a schedule, but the database by itself wouldn't do anything. With workflow, Microsoft CRM becomes a system that farms your existing accounts for additional business, helps you hunt for new accounts, and ensures that important tasks don't slip through the cracks. Whooaa. That's a pretty hefty statement, isn't it? However, by providing you with electronic business alerts — such as automatic calls for accounts or automatic follow-up e-mails — Microsoft CRM can step beyond being your contact/account database and become an important part of your business and corporate culture.

You probably have many business rules already in place, even if they aren't set in writing and mentioned all the time. For example, do you return a phone call to a client who asks you to call him back? That's a business rule, and work-flow might automate that business rule by sending you an electronic reminder message — again and again — until you actually make the call. Your business rule has now become a workflow rule. I like to call this one "auto-nag."

Now, before you start plugging in workflow rules, we recommend that you review all your current business processes. This may take some time. You should consult with the CEO, his or her assistant, the sales department, the marketing department, you get the idea. This is also the best time to do spring cleaning. Get rid of business rules that worked before the advent of the Internet, and update others or make new ones. Automating an ineffective procedure is like building a faster Edsel. The speed is there, but it's still an Edsel.

In this chapter, we touch on the general principles of implementing workflow rules and then provide you with an example of a typical rule. You also find the background and basis to design and implement at least some simple workflow rules of your own. However, keep in mind that the creation of complex workflow rules is probably best left to professional Microsoft CRM consultants or dealers.

Workflow Components

Let's start from the beginning. Workflow may sound complicated, but when you get the knack of it, it's fairly simple. Workflow has two main modules: Manager and Monitor.

- ✔ **Manager:** Enables you to develop and use the workflow rules feature, which is nothing more than a system to automate the business processes you already have and use.
- ✔ **Monitor:** Provides a display of the current status of each rule. You can see exactly which processes are running and which ones may be waiting for a triggering event.

Limitations of Workflow

Although Workflow is a powerful utility, it isn't Super Program and does have some limitations. For example:

- ✔ Workflow can monitor data and events within the Microsoft CRM database but not outside it, unless you write a custom .NET assembly. (More on .NET assembly in a moment.)
- ✔ A workflow rule can check for data in more than one object (accounts or contact records) at one time, but it's limited to a few entities. For example, a workflow rule can look through all of your accounts to notify you of any that are missing telephone numbers, but a single workflow rule can't check for accounts that are missing phone numbers *and* have open cases more than two weeks old.
- ✔ Workflow rules have difficulty checking for the absence of an event, meaning they can alert you to an open or uncompleted appointment but don't tell you about stuff that wasn't scheduled but should have been. (It's a software program, not a mind-meld machine.)

An important step in creating your workflows is to think through the flow itself carefully. What are the exceptions? What conditions should terminate the process? For example, if someone buys something, workflow should start treating the person as a new customer and not as a prospect.

Creating Workflow Rules

For creating your workflow rules, we recommend that you use members of your staff who work with the product on a daily basis, both on the administrative side and the operations side. This way, you cover your business processes from all angles.

Now, we do suggest letting your company's system administrator be the only person to implement workflow rules. The process of creating rules can scary, humorous, or just outright sad. (Just spend an hour or two watching C-SPAN!) We think the best way to approach the process is with a small team of individuals from both the business side and the tech side. The business guys will say "We need to make sure that the managers get notified of every account that's not touched in 90 days." Then the data or tech person will say "What's a touch?" "What's an account?" and "Who's the manager?" This exchange can be frustrating, but it is necessary. If you don't go through it, then on Monday morning the CEO might receive a flood of e-mails indicating that hundreds of records in the database, including vendors and competitors, have not had a completed sale in the last 90 days.

One of the most common tasks your company may want to automate is the assignment of an account manager to a newly created account. We use that as our example for creating a workflow rule:

1. **Choose Settings and then Workflows in the navigation pane of CRM Web client.**

   The Microsoft CRM Workflow Manager window appears, as shown in Figure 9-1.

2. **Click New.**

3. **Enter a name for the workflow and select an entity type.**

   The Entity Type option is the type of record (account, contact, lead, and so on. See chapters 12 & 13) that your workflow rule focuses on. Click the down arrow to the right of the field to open the drop-down box and choose the entity you want to work with. For this exercise, we chose Account for Entity Type.

4. **Select the New Blank workflow radio button and then click OK.**

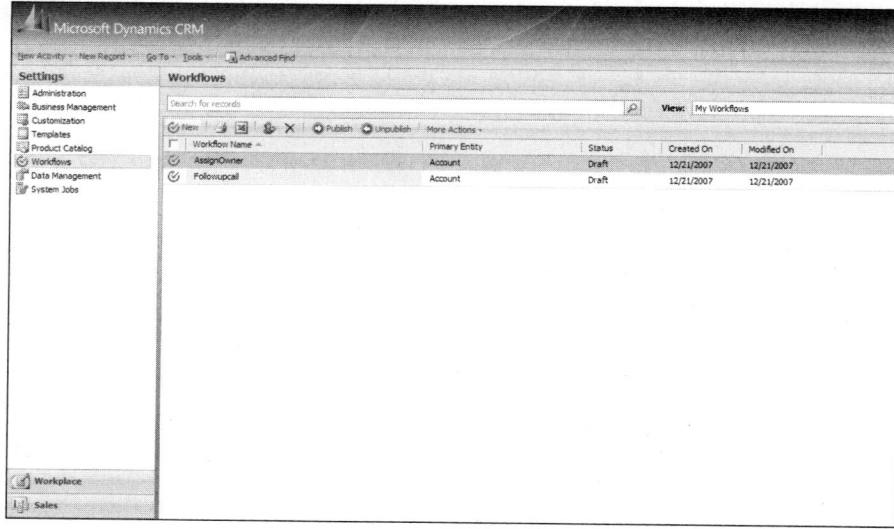

Figure 9-1:
The
Workflow
Manager.

5. Select the Record Is Created check box.

The Workflow form should appear as shown in Figure 9-2. Note that the Entity field is already filled in with your choice from the preceding step. For our example, we chose Start when: Record is created because we want the creation of a new record to trigger this workflow rule.

The other options to automatically trigger a workflow are:

- *Record status changes* (run Workflow when the status field changes)

- *Record is assigned* (run Workflow when the Owner field changes)

- *Record attributes change* (run Workflow when the button to select attributes has been clicked)

- *Record is deleted* (this one's pretty obvious and a good one to use to audit deletions)

6. Click the Add Step drop-down list and then a list appears with the following choices, as shown in Figure 9-3:

- *Check Condition:* This is basically an IF...THEN construct.

- *Conditional Branch:* This is an ELSE...THEN to be attached to the above Check Condition.

- *Default Action:* This is an ELSE to be attached to a Check Condition.

- *Wait Condition:* This pauses workflow until the condition is met.

- *Parallel Wait Branch:* This indicates a separate pause to wait for a condition. This one is useful for creating timeouts or escalations in your workflow logic. For instance you might have a wait condition waiting for a call to be made and Parallel Wait condition set to alert someone after certain amount of time that the call has not been made.

- *Create Record:* Creates a new CRM record of any entity type.

- *Update Record:* Updates a CRM Record.

- *Assign Record:* Reassigns a record to a different user.

- *Send E-Mail:* This one does your laundry — no, wait! It sends an e-mail!

- *Start Child Workflow:* Branches to a child workflow. A *child workflow* is a workflow that cannot be run on its own but only when called from a *parent workflow*. If you have a given group of steps that many workflows will use then you may want to create a child work-flow of the steps and then just reference the child workflow from the other workflows.

- *Change Status:* Changes the status field of the record.

- *Stop Workflow:* Immediately stops the process of the workflow.

7. **Select Check Condition.**

Three lines of information are added to the Workflow details area at the bottom of the screen. The first line is a text box containing the words Type a Step Description Here.

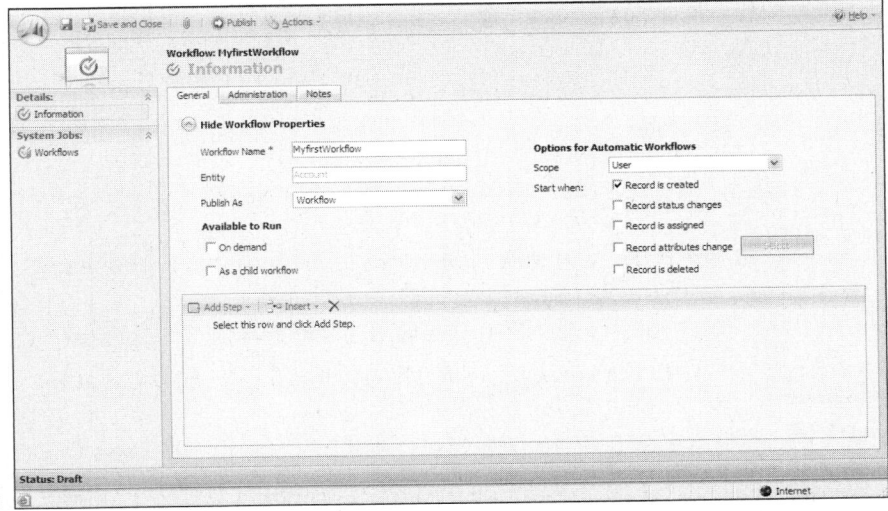

Figure 9-2:
Create your
workflow
rule and
don't go
wild now!

8. In that text box, enter the description of this step.

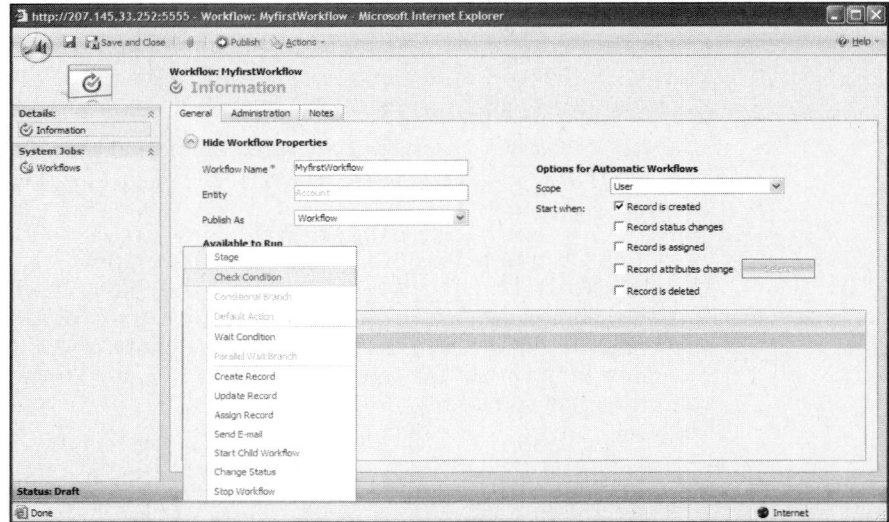

Figure 9-3: Everyone needs a Check Condition option.

9. Highlight *<condition>* **(click to configure) in the workspace.**

The Specify Condition form appears as shown in Figure 9-4.

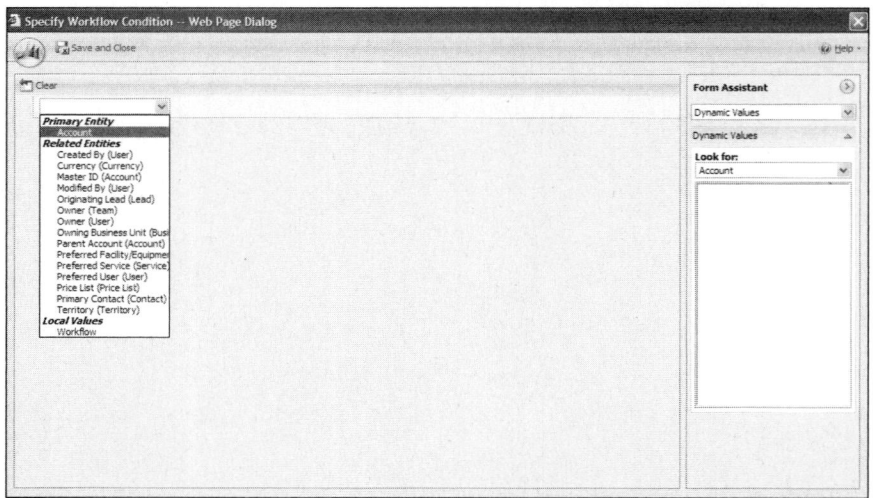

Figure 9-4: Check it out!

10. **Hover your cursor over the word Select and a drop-down box appears. Click the down arrow and select a table.**

    In this example, we're working with the Account table, so select Account.

11. **Hover your cursor over the word Select, which appeared to the right of where you selected Account, and another drop-down appears. Click the down arrow and select a field.**

    Just about every field in the table selected in step 10 is available here. Select the field to which you'd like to apply the workflow rule. For example, if you want to assign only records in Massachusetts to your account manager, Ted, you'd choose the Address1: State/Province field.

12. **Hover your cursor over the word Select next to the State field you selected, click the down arrow, and then select Equals.**

    The Contains, Begins With, and Ends With operators can produce surprising results if you don't carefully consider what data these expressions might find. For example, if you search for records containing *East*, you also get records containing *beast*.

    In our example, we're testing for Accounts in Massachusetts, so we select Equals.

13. **Hover over the words Enter Value next to the Equals condition and enter MA in the text box that appears.**

    For example, if you selected State in Step 11, you could put the state here in the Static Value field. If you wanted to compare two fields, you could select another field by selecting a Dynamic Value from the forms assistant on the right.

    Now your new Workflow condition should look similar to Figure 9-5.

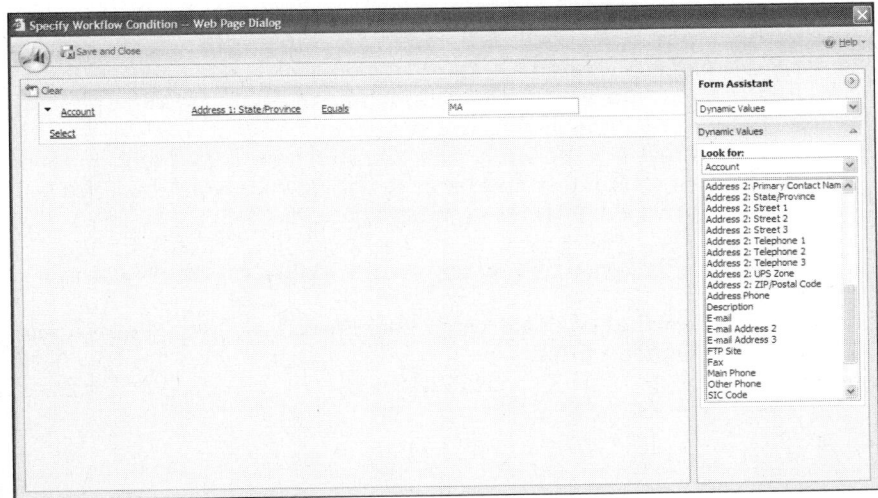

Figure 9-5:
Complete
Workflow
Condition.

14. **Click Save and Close.**

    You return to the main Workflow screen.

15. **Back on the main Workflow creation screen Highlight *Select this row and click Add Step* under the condition you just created.**

    The action you select tells the program what you want done when the condition you set in Steps 8 through 11 is met. A list of actions and their descriptions is available in the "Workflow Glossary" at the end of this chapter.

16. **Select Assign Record from the Add Step drop-down menu.**

17. **Enter the account manager name or click the find button next to the field to search for a list of system users.**

18. **Click Save and Close.**

19. **To make the rule available, click Publish.**

    If you forget to do this, your perfectly good new rule will sit there forever, forlorn and lost.

20. **Click Save and Close to return to the main workflow manager window.**

Testing a new rule

Throughout this book, you can find reference to our office manager's arch nemeses, the Minions of Chaos (MoC). They love to sneak inside your database and wreak havoc. Remember this because they can make an appearance at any moment, now that you've created your workflow rules.

Back to the workflow rules. They're complete and ready to go, so you load them up and away you go, right? Negative, databoy.

Loading an untested workflow rule on your active database is an invitation to the MoC, who want nothing more than to get in and show you any errors or glitches that are on your live system by bringing your system to a grinding halt as that workflow rule runs amok on your data. Okay, this is dramatic, but we must stress the importance of testing your workflow rules *before* you make them live features of your Microsoft CRM.

The good news is that testing your workflow rule is easy. Here's how:

1. **Now that you've created your workflow rule, go ahead and start Microsoft CRM.**

2. **Create a condition in your database that triggers the workflow rule.**

   For example, if you set your workflow rule to trigger on every new account created in the system, go ahead and create an account and remember to save, Save, SAVE and Close the record.

3. **Reopen the record you just created so you can check for the intended result.**

   If the rule said to assign every new account to Bob, you'd check to see whether Bob is listed as the owner.

If you don't see the desired result, you either failed to activate your rule, or you need to review the rule criteria and specifics to determine the cause of the problem. Always go back and check out how you built the workflow rule first before assuming there's a bug in the program — because most computer errors are the result of operator error.

In large, mission critical environments there would most likely be a development or test system that mimics the live system in every way possible. These systems allow you to test possible solutions without the danger of damaging your production data.

Creating On-Demand (manual) rules

An On-Demand rule is a rule that can only be invoked manually — not automatically (at least not directly). Essentially it is a Workflow that doesn't have any of the Start When: boxes checked and instead has the Available to Run: On Deman box checked. For those of you designing complex workflow rules, you can call manual rules by another rule. By *calling,* we mean that each rule should do one or two simple things and should then trigger, or call, another rule if more functionality is needed.

Speaking of calling, try to avoid creating a giant workflow-rule Godzilla. Instead of one massive process, it may be easier to put together a series of simple manual rules that call each other. You can also do what computer programmers do (no, not change people's passwords for fun): Create small modules of code, or in this case, workflow rules that you can reuse for many different applications.

Remember that you have to activate a workflow rule after you create it, as the last step. On-Demand rules, just like all the other rules, must be active before you can invoke or call them.

On-Demand Workflow rules are great if everyone remembers to invoke or trigger them. The key word here is *remembers.* In today's offices, most people are so busy answering the phone, dealing with customer service issues, and making sales calls that things are bound to slip through the cracks. We suggest that you create a system with a master workflow rule that automatically attaches to every new record and begins a sequence of calling additional rules as conditions in that record warrant.

Creating follow-up rules

Almost every business does some sort of follow-up with its customers, and yours is probably no exception. You may want to send a thank-you e-mail for a recent purchase, or you may want to schedule calls to accounts that have had no activity for 60 days. This is called a *follow-up rule,* and it's usually a manual one. The steps are similar to creating a rule in the first place, so we'll just touch on them here and make sure we point out the variations.

One of the most common tasks your company may want to automate is the scheduling of a call to a newly created account. We use that as our example for creating a follow-up rule. As mentioned earlier, the steps mostly mirror the ones you use to create a workflow rule.

To create a manual rule that schedules a follow-up activity for the owner of an account, follow these steps:

1. **Choose Settings and then Workflows in the navigation pane of CRM Web client.**

   The Microsoft CRM Workflow Manager window appears, as shown in Figure 9-1.

2. **Click New.**

3. **Enter a name for the workflow and select an entity type. For this example we will use the Account entity once again.**

4. **Select the New Blank workflow radio button and then click OK.**

5. **Click On Demand and uncheck Start when: Record is created.**

   This is a slight variation. In the list used to create a workflow rule, you selected the Record Is Created option instead.

6. **Click the Add Step drop-down list and then select Check Condition.**

7. **Click in the box where it says *Type a step description here* and type a description to describe this step of the workflow. Something such as "Where State = MA" should suffice.**

8. **Click *<condition> (click to configure),* which opens the Specify Workflow Condition screen.**

9. Hover your cursor over the word "Select" and a drop-down box appears. Select Account from the box.

10. Hover your cursor over the word "Select" to the right of where you just selected Account. Another drop-down box appears. Select Address1: State/Province.

11. Hover over the word Select that appeared to the right of the the last selection you made and select Equals from the drop down box that appears.

12. Hover over the word Select that appears to the right of the last selection and enter MA in the text box that appears.

13. Click Save and Close.

14. Back at the main Workflow screen click on "Select this row and click Add Step" under the condition you just created.

15. Select Create Record from the Add Step drop-down menu.

16. Select Phone Call from the drop-down menu of the Record you're creating and then click the Set Properties button to the right of the drop down.

    The Create Phone Call window appears, as shown in Figure 9-6. Here, you can specify what tasks the follow-up rule should perform when it is called, or triggered.

17. Enter a subject and a description for this new activity.

    For example, in the Subject field, you might enter New Account or Assigning an Account Manager to a new Account.

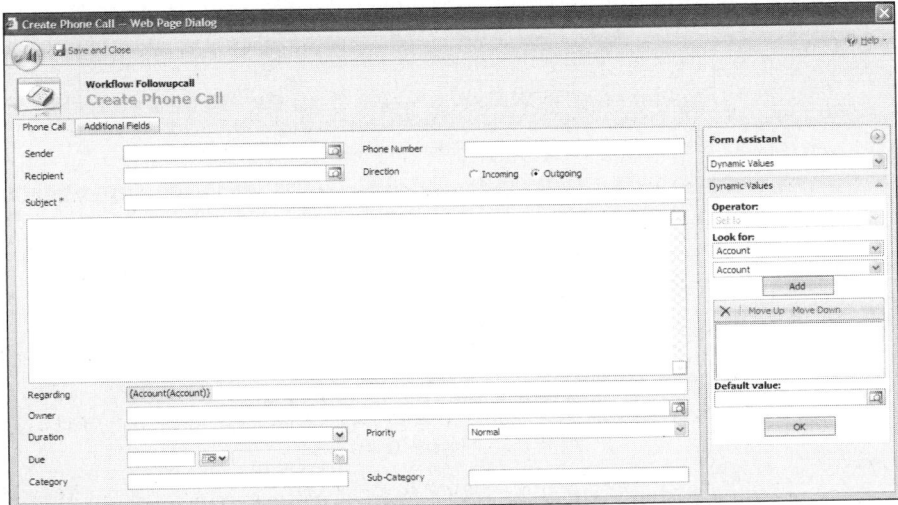

Figure 9-6:
This activity can create a task, phone call, fax, or letter.

18. **Enter a due date and a priority.**

    The due date isn't so much an actual date but a length of time you want the system to wait before it sends the letter or fax or prompts you to perform the task or make the phone call. The priorities are low, normal, and high.

19. **Click Save and Close.**

    You're taken to the main window of the workflow you just created. Remember, rules do nothing unless you publish them.

20. **To make the rule available, click Publish.**

21. **After it's published, click Save and Close to return to the main workflow manager window.**

Testing a manual rule

Remember the Minions of Chaos mentioned earlier? They don't discriminate between automatic rules and manual ones, so you'll want to test these as well.

The steps for testing follow-up rules are different than those for testing automatic ones. Here's how you do it:

1. **Create a condition in Microsoft CRM that triggers the original rule.**

   A good example is the New Account workflow rule we just created.

2. **In Microsoft CRM, use the navigation pane to find and highlight the account.**

3. **In the window's toolbar, click Run Workflow.**

   The Workflow dialog box appears.

4. **Select your workflow process from the list and then click OK.**

   The process begins to run invisibly.

5. **Go to the workplace and click Activities in the upper part of the navigation pane.**

   You should see the follow-up activity listed there (if the activity was assigned to you, anyway).

Monitoring Your Workflow

Now that you have all of those workflow rules processing merrily away, you want to see them all on one screen, without having to go to every account or contact to see whether a rule has been applied. You can do this through the Workflow Monitor. Like Workflow Manager, Workflow Monitor is visible from within the CRM Web client. It also keeps a log of processes that are currently active and records which ones have already run.

There are two ways to view the Monitor:

✔ **Click a record that the workflow applies to, then click Workflows in the navigation pane to see the status of workflows on that record.**

The Workflow Monitor window appears, as shown in Figure 9-7. In this display, you can see Workflow process attached to the selected record and along with some brief information regarding each Workflow.

✔ **In the navigation pane, click Settings and then click System jobs. The Settings area is generally only accessible by end users so they will need to use the first method.**

You can sort the items by clicking the header for each column. You can also export the log to an Excel spreadsheet by clicking the Excel icon.

The Workflow Monitor only shows workflow rules that have been triggered. Even though you may have additional rules activated, they remain invisible to the Monitor when an event triggers them.

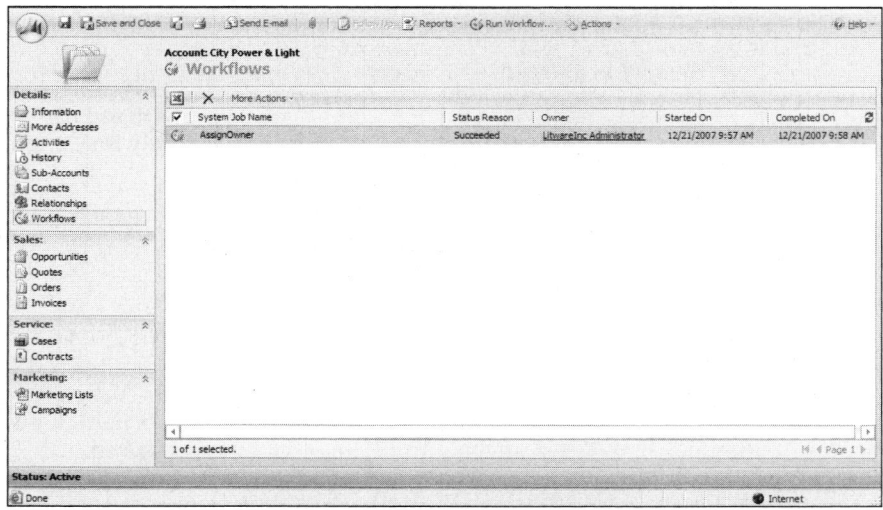

Figure 9-7: Success at last!

Workflow Glossary

Throughout this chapter, we tell you to select an event, or choose an action, or set a condition. Maybe you're wondering what, exactly, constitutes an event, action, or condition. Well, we list them all here, in a one-stop, look-see that's easy to find.

Events

In Microsoft CRM, an *event* is the trigger condition that initiates a workflow rule. For example, you can set a workflow rule for Assign, and anything that is assigned has that workflow rule applied to it. Microsoft CRM has four events:

- **Record is created:** This trigger fires whenever a new record is created for the selected entity.

- **Record status changes:** CRM monitors whether records have changed state from active to inactive or vice versa and this event is fired when this happens.

- **Record is assigned:** This event fires when a record is assigned (or reassigned).

- **Record attributes change:** This event fires when one of the selected attributes (or fields) changes for the selected entity.

- **Record is deleted:** This trigger fires when an entity is deleted.

- **On Demand:** Only workflow rules marked On Demand can be invoked manually. To perform this invocation, select Apply Rule from the Actions tab of the Workflow Manager window.

Conditions

Every business process is triggered by some change in a *condition*. That condition might be a change in a data field, a due date being passed, or a record being created. The various conditions of the Workflow Manager (visible in Figure 9-3) enables you to initiate an action based on a field or an activity that has changed or an amount of time that has transpired.

The options for possible conditions are as follows:

- **Check Object Conditions:** This enables you to drill down to a specific field in a record. For example, if the State field is New York, you can take an action to assign the New York sales rep to the account. Based on the type of field (whether it's a numeric, text, or a date field, for example), various operators are available.

✔ **Check Activities:** By checking activities, you can initiate actions based on scheduled or completed activities.

✔ **Else If:** This enables you to nest additional condition statements saying that if the first condition is false, evaluate the second condition.

✔ **Wait for Conditions:** Workflow can wait for a specified amount of time until the specified criteria becomes true before the rest of the rule is completed. This can be the cornerstone of an activity escalation plan. For example, if a lead is assigned to a sales rep, the system can be instructed to wait for three days before checking to see whether a user has created an appointment. If the system finds no evidence of an appointment, a message can be automatically sent to the sales rep or the sales rep's manager.

✔ **Wait for Timer:** This is similar to Wait for Conditions, but this condition can make sure that an assignment is handled within a specified time limit. For example, you can monitor a high-priority tech support call that must be returned within an hour by using Wait for Timer.

Actions

Actions are a series of operations performed after conditions have been evaluated as true. You can enact nine activities:

✔ **Create Activity:** This schedules a task, phone call, fax, or appointment.

✔ **Send E-Mail:** This powerful utility enables CRM to send a confirming e-mail, on your behalf, to a customer who has just placed an order or notify a sales rep when a lead is assigned to him or her.

✔ **Create Note:** CRM can automatically attach a note to a record. For example, CRM could create a note that places an account on hold when payment becomes overdue.

✔ **Update Record:** You can use the Update Record action to modify individual fields in records. Many fields in each record are not, by default, displayed on the screen. You can use Update Record to modify visible as well as invisible fields.

✔ **Change Status:** Different types of records are assigned different types of status. The Change Status action enables the workflow system to change a record's status automatically based on conditions being met.

✔ **Assign Entity:** Workflow can automatically assign cases to customer service reps based on a topic, or it can assign an account to a sales rep based on a territory. For example, if a customer calls about a malfunctioning transporter, the case can be assigned to Molly, your most experienced customer service rep.

- ✔ **Post URL:** This action sends a Web site address of another business to a data field. For example, when a new account is created, you can post the Web site address in the Web Site field.

- ✔ **Run child workflow:** Basically, this is one process or rule calling another one. By using this technique, you can program a large number of simple workflow rules, with each rule potentially calling another rule.

- ✔ **Stop:** This brings your process to a halt.

- ✔ **Call Assembly:** This option contains any custom .NET assemblies that your administrator or implementation partner has registered with Microsoft CRM. Refer to the SDK documentation to add your own assemblies here. You can download the SDK from `www.microsoft.com/downloads`. Search for "CRM SDK".

To workflow infinity and beyond . . .

Microsoft CRM also allows you call a small piece of code called a *.NET assembly* that does some custom functions. For example, if you want Microsoft CRM to check the credit on one of your customers and update the customer record with the customer's FICO score, you can write a small .NET assembly that calls another application to get that information and then updates Microsoft CRM. Based on the returned score, Microsoft CRM can then finish processing the rest of the rule you set up.

A third-party business alert system, KnowledgeSync, enables you to look at multiple databases and multiple types of records. We describe KnowledgeSync in Chapter 27. If you anticipate the need to build sophisticated rules and alerts, and you don't want to write custom code, you may want this add-on program.

Chapter 10

Creating and Running Reports

In This Chapter

▶ Adding report categories

▶ Creating reports

▶ Editing reports

▶ Removing reports

▶ Running reports

▶ Using Excel as a report writer

*N*ow that you've started to put data into Microsoft CRM, you're ready to get that data out. An easy way to analyze data in Microsoft CRM is to run a report. But what if one of the pre-installed reports isn't what you're looking for? In fact, experience tells us that it's very unlikely that the prebuilt reports are going to be exactly what you want. So what now?

Prior to Microsoft CRM 4, custom report creation was left to people who could author reports in SQL Reporting. Not an easy task for the average user. But don't worry, because version 4 has a built-in Report Wizard. The Report Wizard is simple to use, especially if you're familiar with using Advanced Find. (See Chapter 3 for more on Advanced Find.)

The Report Wizard provides limited design features. Designing reports with the Report Wizard allows for grouping and sub-grouping of data, column selection, some data summary, and graphing. Reports with graphs can also have the additional capability of drilling down to the details that represent the graph.

Adding Report Categories

In Microsoft CRM, you can aggregate reports by category. Out of the box, there are four categories: Sales, Service, Administrative, and Marketing. You can add your own categories to the list as well. Although you can find reports in more than one category, Microsoft has segregated the reports based on the following:

- ✔ **Sales reports:** Collect all the activities associated with a sale, from the lead through the actual sale. These reports can also provide statistical information about accounts, lead sources, competitors, and products.

- ✔ **Service reports:** Provide statistical information related to contracts, cases, and summaries of knowledge base articles. These reports provide quick analyses of which products require the most support and where your service representatives are spending the most time.

- ✔ **Administrative reports:** Provide summary information about your Microsoft CRM users.

- ✔ **Marketing reports:** Describe accounts, campaigns, lead source effectiveness, and other areas of interest to the marketing department. The reports provide summary and detail information across accounts, campaigns, and lead sources.

You can add your own report categories. To do so, follow these steps:

1. **In the navigation pane, click Settings.**

   The Settings navigation options appear at the top of the navigation pane.

2. In **the navigation pane, click the Administration icon.**

   The Administration options are now available on the right.

3. **In the Administration pane on the right, click System Settings.**

   Settings are divided by tabs. Click the Reporting tab on the right.

4. **Click Add on the right.**

5. **Create the new category.**

   For our scenario, we added a category called Stephanie's Reports.

6. **Click OK.**

7. **Click OK on the bottom.**

   Your new category appears in the report area.

Navigating the Report Area

Prior to designing our first report, let's take a look at the report area of Microsoft Dynamics CRM. To access the report area, follow these steps:

1. **In the navigation pane, click the Workplace button.**

   The Workplace navigation options appear at the top of the navigation pane.

2. **In the navigation pane, click the Reports icon.**

   The reports listing now appears on the right.

The top right of the report screen has the View drop-down list, like all other areas in Microsoft CRM. In this case the values in the drop-down list include the report categories.

The report toolbar has several icons. From the right, the first icon is More Actions. Clicking the More Actions icon reveals a menu with the following options:

- ✔ **Run Report:** Run report is obvious and works in the same manner as double-clicking the report.

- ✔ **Edit Default Filter:** When you add reports to the system, they're filtered to display the data desired. Microsoft CRM allows the user to edit the filter at runtime; that way, the user can customize the data displayed without actually editing the report. In the More Actions menu, Edit Default Filter allows the system administrator a way to edit the default filter used by the report at runtime, should the user not edit the filter.

  To understand report filtering, first run a report without filtering:

  1. **Double-click the Account Overview report.**

     The Report filtering criteria appears. (See Figure 10-1.) You could change the default filtering now, but don't do so just yet.

  2. **Click Clear at the top left.**

     This removes all filtering for the report.

  3. **Click Run Report on the bottom right.**

     The report's listing now appears on the right. (See Figure 10-2.)

  4. **From the report screen, click Edit Filter on the top left.**

     The report filtering window appears. Defining the filter criteria is much like working with Advanced Find. (See Chapter 3 for more on Advanced Find.) In this example, we filter the company name.

  5. **Click Select and choose Account Name.**

     For this example, we filter the report based on Account Name. However, you can choose a different field based on your filtering requirements.

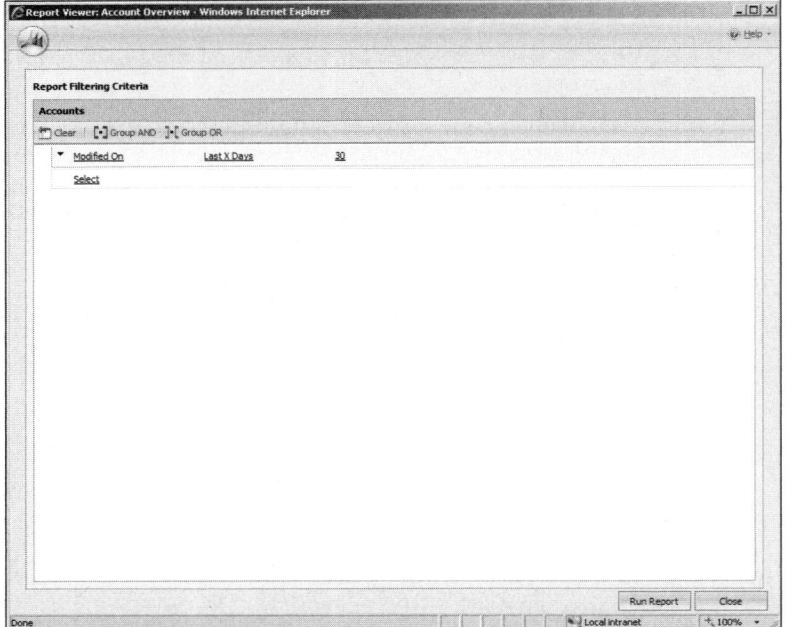

Figure 10-1:
The report filtering screen.

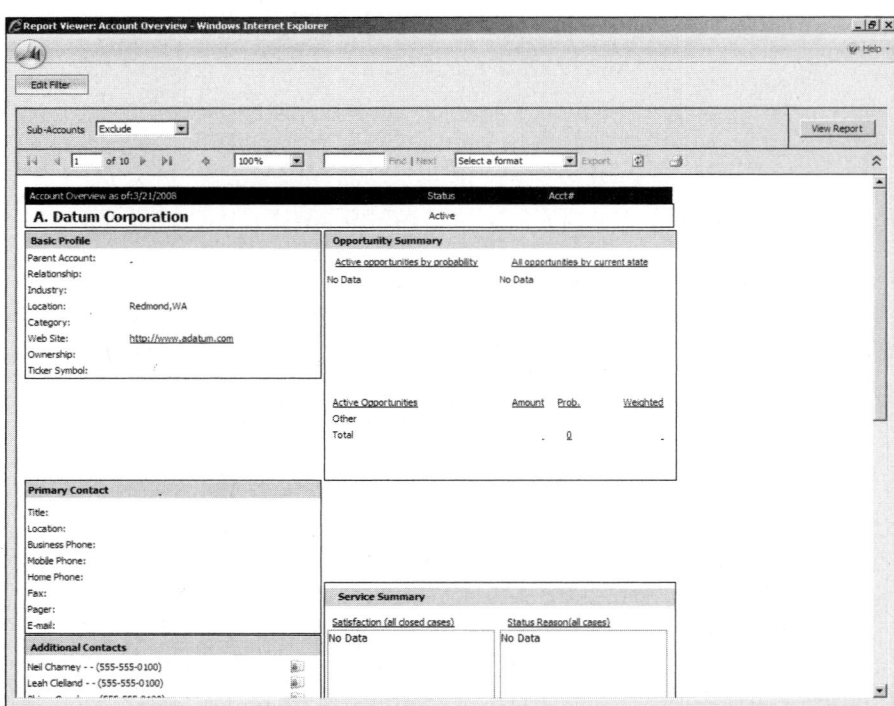

Figure 10-2:
The report without filtering.

6. Make sure the operator shown is Equals.

If you need to change the operator from equals, simply click the word Equals.

Because you chose Equals, this value must match *exactly* the company name in the account area. Choose your operator carefully. If you want to return all records in which the company name begins with the letter A, you would choose Begins With and not Equals. To learn more about selecting the proper operator, see Chapter 3.

7. Place mouse over Enter Value and type a company name.

If necessary, you can add more sophisticated filtering prior to running the report. To do so, click Select below your first criteria and repeat steps 5–7.

8. Click Run Report on the bottom right.

Figure 10-3 shows a filtered report based on the Account Name.

Reports are also filtered based on user security. This happens regardless of the filter criteria chosen. Therefore, users running reports will only have access to records via the reports that they can access via the CRM interface.

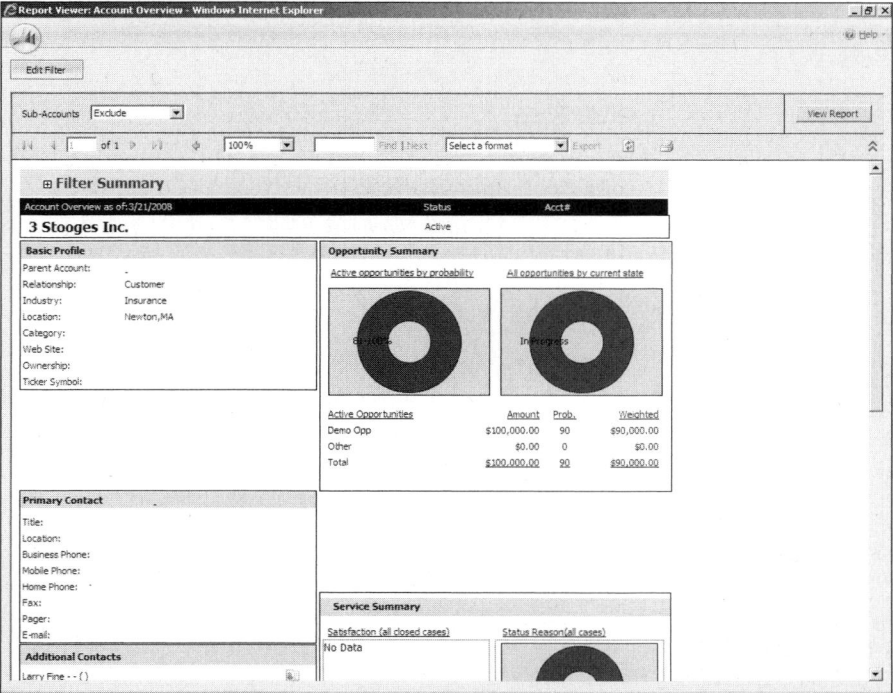

Figure 10-3:
The filtered
report.

From the More Actions menu, the Edit Default filter allows the system administrator a way to edit the default filter used by the report at run-time, should the user not edit the filter. Follow the preceding steps for filtering a report to edit the default filter (after you've chosen Edit Default Filter from the More Actions menu).

✔ **Schedule Report:** This is a wonderful way to create a report snapshot. *Report snapshots* are analogous to pictures in that they are frozen in time. When a snapshot is created, it preserves the report and data at the time the snapshot was created. Rerunning a report snapshot, then, shows the same data every time. This is in contrast to running the actual report, which will dynamically update the report with the most current data.

Reports snapshots cannot be created unless the Microsoft CRM Connector for SQL Reporting Services is installed. If you try to create a snapshot and receive such an error message, speak with your Microsoft CRM partner.

Microsoft CRM allows for eight snapshots per report. You can create snapshots manually or via a schedule. To create a report snapshot, follow these steps:

1. **On the Report area toolbar, select More Actions⇨Schedule Report.**

   The Schedule Report Wizard runs.

2. **Select either On Demand or On a Schedule.**

   Both are similar; however, On Demand has fewer options. In this list, I choose On a Schedule.

3. **Click Next.**

   The Select Frequency form opens. The schedule varies based on the selection on the left.

4. **Create a schedule for your report and click Next.**

5. **Depending on your selection in Step 4, pick start and/or end dates.**

6. **Click Next.**

   The Define Report Parameters form is displayed.

7. **Fill in the appropriate parameters. If you don't need to edit the default filter, click Next; otherwise, edit the default filter.**

8. **Review the snapshot criteria and click Create.**

9. **Click Finish.**

✔ **Sharing:** Sharing is the last option in More Actions. Remember that snapshots contain data. They have the data that was available to the user who created the snapshot. Sharing the report with a user who otherwise wouldn't have access to sensitive data when running the report means that user now has access to that data when viewing a snapshot.

The other report toolbar icons work like their brethren on other forms, and we don't cover them in this chapter.

Using Viewing Options

After you've run the report, you may have noticed the viewing options just above the report. Let's take a look at all those options. (Depending on the report you're running, not all of the options that follow are displayed.)

- ✔ **Group By:** Group By options vary by report. Choose this to group report data.

- ✔ **Page navigation:** If your report has more than one page, you can move through them using these VCR-type controls. From left to right, the first button (First Page) takes you to page one of the report. The next button (Previous Page) takes you back one page from the page currently displayed. The third button (Next Page) takes you to the next page. The last button (Last Page) takes you to the last page of the report. The display between the second and third button tells you the page you're on and the total page count.

- ✔ **Display size:** Next to the navigation options is a box showing the size of the display. Click the arrow for the drop-down list to modify the size of the report.

- ✔ **Find | Next:** This field enables you to search for specific text in the report. You can use * as a wildcard to search partial text. (For example, typing **Mart*** will find Martin.) Just fill in the Find field and click Find. You're taken to the first result. To move to the second result, click Next.

If the text you enter in the Find field appears in the report on a page previous to the one you're viewing on the screen, the search will come up empty. So, when conducting a search using the Find field, always jump to the first page of the report before clicking Find.

You can drill down on summary reports (or graphs) to see the underlying detail. For example, if you open the Sales Pipeline report, you see a single bar in the graph. Change the Group By to Sales User and click View Report. You now have multiple bars representing your sales team. Click a bar and you're presented with a table of data representing the selected bar. Move your mouse over any of the items in the left column (Opportunity). Your mouse turns into a hand. Click and drill all the way down to the actual opportunity record.

Exporting and Printing Your Report

Exporting report data is just what it sounds like — the movement of data from inside Microsoft CRM to outside Microsoft CRM. Let's look at exporting your spiffy report.

Printing is a form of exporting. To print your report, just click the little printer icon in the line above the report. You'll get the basic Print dialog window, where you can make the usual selections.

For the most part, when we use the term *export* in this business, it describes sending the data to another application. In Microsoft CRM's case, the data doesn't export to just Microsoft products. You can create your report in HTML (good for display on your company Web site) or export it to an Adobe Acrobat file.

Follow these steps to export a report:

1. **With the report on the screen in the Report Viewer window, click the Export drop-down list and select the application.**

   Your choices are HTML, Excel, Web Archive, Acrobat, TIFF, CSV (comma delimited), and XML.

2. **Click the word Export.**

   You see a familiar screen, asking whether you want to open the file or save it to disk. Your computer thinks you're downloading a file from a Web site, so you're asked whether you want to open it or save it. If you choose to open it, you have the option to save it from the report window.

3. **Decide whether to open or save the file and then click OK.**

   After a moment, your report opens in the format you selected.

When you select one of the export formats, the associated application opens and displays the report. Interestingly, no matter which selection you make, the report opens in a browser window. (Remember that Microsoft CRM is browser based.) So, for example, if you select Microsoft Excel as the export format, the report opens in essentially a browser version of Excel, and all of Excel's menus will be available.

Microsoft CRM 4 uses SQL Server 2005 Reporting Services as its primary reporting tool. Should you desire to learn the Reporting Services design tool, you will need Microsoft Visual Studio. You can find a free version at www.asp.net. We suggest you try the Report Wizard first, as it is much easier to learn. So read on.

Accessing the Report Wizard

Before designing a report with the Report Wizard, we suggest you sketch your design. After doing so, you're ready to create a report with the Report Wizard.

If you read the "Navigating the Report Area" section earlier in the chapter, you now know your way around the report area in Microsoft CRM, and you're ready to create a new report.

What is our scenario for this report? The sales manager of Mega Corp, Stephanie, would like to create an opportunity pipeline report, grouping data by sales person or owner and sub-grouping by state and ordering by revenue. She has three sales people; Zach, Ethan, and Rachel. Let's take a look at how Stephanie would go about creating the report. Follow these steps:

1. **In the navigation pane, click the Workplace button.**

   The Workplace navigation options appear at the top of the navigation pane.

2. **In the navigation pane, click the Reports icon.**

   The reports listing is now available on the right.

3. **Click New to Create a new Report.**

   The Report: New dialog box opens. (See Figure 10-4.)

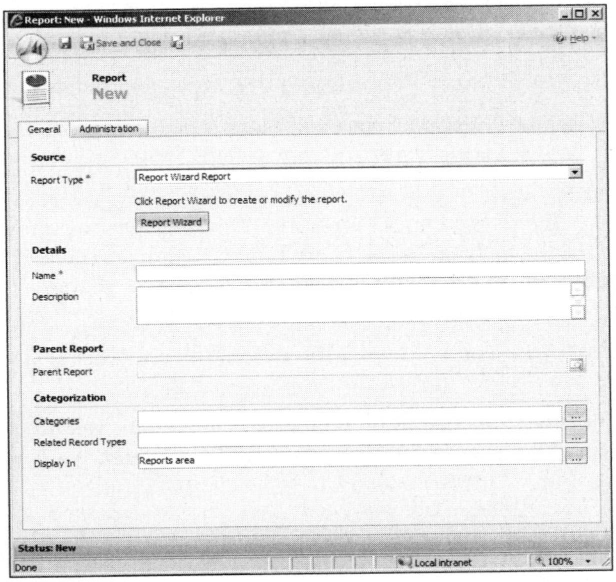

Figure 10-4:
The Report:
New dialog
box.

4. **On the General tab, click the Report Wizard button.**

   The Report Wizard dialog box opens. (See Figure 10-5.)

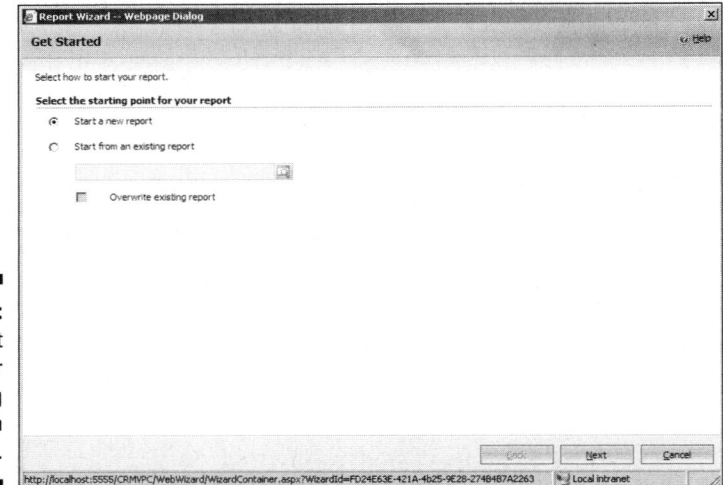

Figure 10-5:
The Report
Wizard for
creating
custom
reports.

5. **Select the Start a New Report radio button and click Next.**

   The Report Properties dialog box opens.

6. **Enter a report name and description.**

7. **Select a primary record type. (See Figure 10-6.)**

   In our case, the Primary Record type that we select is Opportunities.

   Leave the Related Record Type field blank for this report. You could add a related record if your report displays fields from a related entity.

8. **Click Next.**

   The Report Filtering Criteria dialog box opens.

9. **Click Clear icon to reset the report filter.**

   You can now enter your own filtering criteria. Of course, you don't have to click Clear in this step. Leave the default filtering criteria when it matches your desired filter criteria.

   Report filtering criteria can be changed at run-time. See the section, "Navigating the Reports Area," earlier in this chapter.

10. **Click Next.**

    The Lay Out Fields dialog box opens.

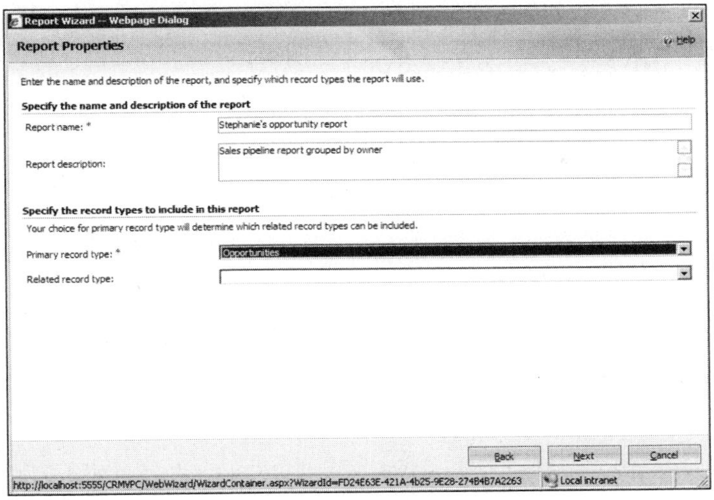

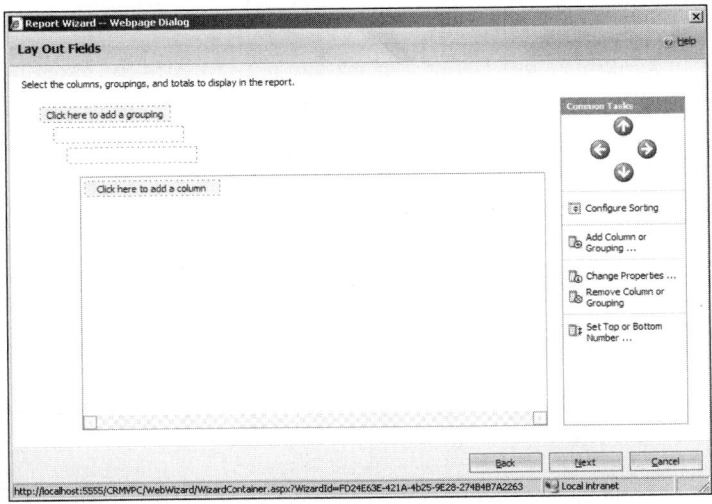

Figure 10-6:
Selecting
the entity
to report
on. In our
example,
the entity
is Opportu-
nities.

11. **Click "Click here to add a grouping" to set the report's highest level grouping (see Figure 10-7) and add a field to group by.**

The Add Grouping dialog box opens. You can group your report in three levels. For example, group first by date, then by sales rep, and lastly by product.

Figure 10-7:
Grouping
the report.

12. In the Add Grouping dialog box, leave Opportunities in the record Type drop-down list. Select Owner in the Column field, and leave remainder of the fields as-is.

13. Click OK.

Back to the Lay Out Fields dialog box.

14. Click the "Click here to add a column" option.

The Add Column dialog box opens.

15. Select a Column for the report.

We're adding only Opportunity fields, so make sure the Record Type field says Opportunities. If you'd like to add fields from related entities, change the drop-down list to the desired entity. Select the field you'd like to have in the left-most column (Stephanie chose Topic), and set the column size. The largest column width is 300 pixels, and 25 pixels is the smallest. Add more columns as desired.

16. Click OK.

17. Repeat Steps 15 and 16 to add additional columns.

18. Click Next.

The Format Report dialog box is displayed.

19. Select Table Only or Chart and Table.

For now, select Table Only. You can't choose Chart and Table without a number field that is summarized; we cover that in the next numbered step list.

Summary choices relate to the type of number field.

20. Select Table only, click Next.

The Report Summary dialog box is displayed.

21. Click Next.

The Report Successfully Created dialog box opens.

22. Click Finish.

The report new/edit dialog box opens.

Before we alter the report settings, let's return to step 19 above, the one in which we chose Table Only. If we'd like to include a chart, we would have instead chosen Chart and Table. However, that option may not have been available to us. To access Chart and Table we need a field in the body of the report summarized. Let's back up to step 15 above and make the necessary changes so we can select Chart and Table.

15a. **Highlight an existing field and click Change Properties on the right.**

The Edit Column Properties dialog box opens. Note, you MUST change the properties of a number field and not a text field. Otherwise you won't be able to perform 16a below.

16a. **Change the summary type to the option that best fits your data.**

We chose Sum.

17a. **Click OK.**

The dialog box closes.

18a. **Click Next.**

The Chart and Table option is now available. Choose:

- **Show table below chart on same page:** This displays the table and the chart on the same page.

- **Show chart. To view data for a chart region, click the chart region:** This option lets you click on the chart and drill into the report table for the details not displayed by the chart.

19a. **Select a chart type. Click Next.**

The Customize Chart Format dialog opens.

20a. **Depending on your selections in step 15, you'll be able to select which fields are displayed as data slices and values. Decide if you want to show data labels and legend and click Next.**

The Report Summary dialog box opens.

21a. **Click Next.**

22a. **Click Finish.**

At this point we've created a new report using the report wizard. However, we're not done yet. We need to set up where we want to display the report, the associated categories, and several other options. Then we need to run the report to see if we're happy with how it looks.

Report Settings

When we click Finish (step 22 above) the New/Edit Report dialog box opens. (See Figure 10-4.) We're now ready to complete the remaining options on the form and run it.

The options on the General Tab are:

- **Report Type:** Report Wizard Report, Existing File, or Link to Web Page. If you've followed the steps above and created a report using the Report Wizard, leave this alone. If you're adding a Microsoft SQL Reporting Service Report (SRS Report), then choose one of these options:

  - *From Existing File:* An "existing file" is a report already uploaded to your report server.

  - *Link to Web Report:* This choice lets you link to other reports that have not been uploaded to your Microsoft CRM report Web server.

- **Name:** The report name. You can rename your report here. If you are naming a SRS report name, you'd be changing the display name in Microsoft CRM and not the actual name.

- **Description:** Add any report description you deem appropriate.

- **Parent Report:** This pertains to sub-reports that are totally or partially displayed in another report — the parent report. For our example, leave this field blank.

- **Categories:** Select the categories under which your report can be found. To learn more about categories, see the section "Adding Report Categories," earlier in this chapter.

- **Related Record Types:** This controls the location (lists and forms) in which the report will be available. For example, to ensure that this report is available in the local opportunities list (the reports available from the opportunity form), select Opportunities.

- **Display In:** Controls where reports are displayed, as follows:

  - *Forms for related record types:* When a form is open, the report is accessed via the report icon on the form toolbar.

  - *Lists for related record types:* The report can be accessed from the local toolbar when viewing a list of data. To find the report list, click on an entity from the navigation bar, such as Accounts. A report icon is available on the toolbar above the list of records returned.

  - *Reports area.* The Reports area is where we began this chapter. Access the reports area by clicking Workplace on the navigation bar, then Reports.

Now you're ready to save the report and run it! Here's all you need to do:

1. **Complete the report as necessary.**

   We want our report to be run from the Reports area and from the list of opportunities, so we completed the form as follows:

   - *Related Record Type:* Opportunities.

   - *Display In:* Lists for related record types and Reports area.

2. **Click Save or Save and Close on the toolbar at the top of the form.**

3. **Click Run Report from the toolbar to view the report.**

    Your new report is displayed.

Editing Reports

You can use the Report Wizard to edit reports created with the Report Wizard, but you can't use the Report Wizard to edit reports created elsewhere. That means that you would have to use Microsoft SQL Reporting Services to edit any report created with Microsoft SQL Reporting Services. Such reports aren't covered in this book.

Only users with the appropriate rights can add, edit, or delete reports.

After you've created a report with the report wizard, you may want to make some changes to the report. To do so, follow these steps:

1. **In the navigation pane, click the Workplace button.**

    The Workplace navigation options appear at the top of the navigation pane.

2. **In the navigation pane, click the Reports icon.**

    The reports listing is now available on the right.

3. **Highlight the report to be edited and click Edit Report on the toolbar above.**

    The Reports dialog box opens.

4. **Click the Report Wizard button.**

    The Report Wizard appears.

5. **Leave the default selections as they are and click Next.**

6. **Change the Report Name, Description, Primary Record, and Secondary Record Types and click Next.**

7. **Edit the report filter and click Next.**

8. **Click the group or column to change and click Change Properties.**

    You can change the Column Width field and Summary field (if it's a numeric field).

9. **To remove a column or group, click it and click Remove Group or Column. Similarly, to add a group or column, click Add Group or Column.**

10. **Click Next.**

11. **Edit the layout and click Next.**

12. **Select the chart type (if your selection in Step 11 included a chart).**

13. **Customize chart type and click Next.**

14. **Click Next.**

15. **Click Finish.**

    The report now reflects your changes.

To remove a report from the report area, follow these steps:

1. **Navigate to the report area.**

2. **Click the report you'd like to remove.**

3. **Click the black X on the report toolbar.**

4. **Confirm deletion.**

Creating Excel Reports

Throughout the CRM system, you find the ever present Excel icon. Often in this book, we refer to the fact that you can export data from Microsoft CRM to Excel and further manipulate that data. When you've created an Excel spreadsheet that you'd like to run often with refreshed CRM data, you can do so by saving your Excel file as a report.

Let's say that Stephanie would like to create an Advance Find (refer to Chapter 3 for more on Advanced Find) to show opportunities closing in the next 30 days with estimated revenue greater than $50,000. She saves the Advance Find, which is now visible in the Opportunity view.

Stephanie exports data to Excel and reformats the spreadsheet, and then she would like to run the spreadsheet and have the data change dynamically. To do this, she would follow these steps:

1. **On the Navigation Bar, click Sales.**

    The sales-related icons appear at the top of the navigation bar.

2. **Click Opportunities.**

    The Main Opportunity form opens to the right.

3. **Click the Excel icon on the toolbar.**

The Export Data to Excel dialog box opens. The dialog box provides three export options, as follows:

- **Static worksheet with records from this page:** With this option you export the data and the columns visible on the grid. Selecting this option makes the Make This Data Available for Re-Import by Including Required Columns option available at the bottom of the form. To learn more about this option, see Appendix A.

- **Dynamic PivotTable:** Select this option when you want to see your data in a pivot table. When selected, you can select your columns (see step 4). Also, this is dynamic so if you save the spreadsheet the data will refresh each time the saved spreadsheet is run.

- **Dynamic worksheet:** Similar to the pivot table, but you create an Excel worksheet instead of a pivot table.

4. **Select an option (we chose Dynamic Worksheet) and click Export.**

   The File Download dialog box opens.

5. **Click Open.**

   The Excel spreadsheet opens.

6. **If prompted, select Yes.**

7. **Edit the spreadsheet as you see fit.**

   Because the worksheet or pivot table is dynamic, it reflects changes in the data whenever you run it. For example, the spreadsheet might have two opportunities with estimated revenue of $100,000; when you rerun it, if a third opportunity exists with estimated revenue of $50,000, the resultant total in the Excel spreadsheet is $150,000.

8. **Save the Excel Spreadsheet.**

   We suggest you select Save As Excel and save the report with a name you prefer such as, `Open Opportunity Report`.

9. **In Microsoft CRM, click Workplace on the Navigation Bar.**

   The workplace options now appear at the top of the navigation bar.

10. **Click Reports at the top of the Navigation Bar.**

11. **In the report, click the New icon on the toolbar.**

    The new report dialog opens. (See Figure 10-4.)

12. **Change the Report Type to Existing File.**

13. **For File Location, browse to the file you just saved.**

14. **Add categories.**

    For more information, see the section, "Report Settings," earlier in this chapter.

15. **Choose the Related Record Type.**

    In our example, we chose Opportunities.

16. **In Display Area, select Lists for Related Records.**

    The spreadsheet now is available in the toolbar above the Opportunity grid.

    The Related Record Types and Display In fields control the location in which your reports will be visible. The Categories field controls the categories in which a report will be displayed in the main reports area (Workplace ⇨Reports).

    To share your report with others in your organization, complete steps 17 and 18. Otherwise, skip to step 19.

17. **Click the Administration Tab.**

18. **Select Organization in Viewable By.**

19. **Click the Save Icon or Save and Close.**

Part III
Managing Sales

The 5th Wave   By Rich Tennant

"Oh, we're doing just great. Philip and I are selling decorative jelly jars on the Web. I run the Web site and Philip sort of controls the inventory."

In this part . . .

This part deals with the sales side of your organization. CRM has four types of customer records: leads, opportunities, accounts, and contacts. This part explains all four and shows you how to enter and manage them.

Organizing the sales team with quotas and forecasts is the starting point and is detailed in Chapter 11.

We discuss leads and opportunities, which are near and dear to every salesperson, in Chapter 12. Chapter 13 focuses on accounts and contacts.

Activities, which are tasks such as appointments and phone calls, are associated with each of the four record types, and we discuss them in Chapter 14. Saving your notes and attachment documents is discussed in Chapter 15.

The quotes and orders and invoices that come from setting up your product list are all discussed in Chapter 16. If you have any sales literature or any competitors, you find out how to handle both of these in Chapter 17. Sales processes, important in the design of your workflow, are discussed in the last chapter of this part.

Chapter 11

Setting Sales Quotas and Dealing with Forecasts

. . . .

. . . .

Toward the end of every year, our sales team sits down and develops a plan for the coming year. That plan includes the products we will sell, who will sell those products, and a guideline for how much of each product our account managers will sell (we hope). That guideline translates into a quota in Microsoft CRM.

The quota not only helps us budget for the coming year but also gives us a series of quarterly milestones. Failure to meet quotas or milestones causes midterm reevaluations or sometimes something worse. Meeting or exceeding our goals is what keeps our company healthy and happy.

In this chapter, you find out how to set quotas for salespeople, how to log forecasted sales against those quotas, and how to adjust these forecasts and quotas as you go along.

How a Manager Sets Up Quotas

Quotas relate to your company's quarterly fiscal periods. Before you can set up a quota for anyone, Microsoft CRM needs to know your company's fiscal periods. Fiscal periods may be set only once, and the task should probably be performed by someone with a title like CFO.

Fiscal year settings

Quotas are usually related to the time period in which accountants measure profits and losses — that is, the fiscal period. Accountants have devised a variety of fiscal years. They can be based on calendar years or can end on other seemingly random dates. A fiscal year can be divided semiannually or quarterly.

You can set the fiscal year options only once. You can't change these settings after you set them.

To set a fiscal year, follow these steps:

1. **Near the bottom of the navigation pane, click the Settings button and then select Business Management.**

   Eleven customization topics appear.

2. **In the Settings window, select Organization Settings.**

   The Business Management Settings window appears.

3. **Select Fiscal Year Settings from the list.**

   The Fiscal Year Settings window appears as shown in Figure 11-1.

Figure 11-1:
Creating your fiscal year information.

Fiscal Year Settings
Select fiscal year settings for Microsoft Dynamics CRM.

Fiscal Settings

Set the fiscal period.

Start Date *	1/1/2007
Template *	Quarterly	☐ Monthly period name based on month name

How do you want to display the fiscal year?

Fiscal Year *	YYYY	Named Based On *	Start Date

How do you want to display the fiscal period?

Fiscal Period *	Quarter 1

How do you want to connect the fiscal year and fiscal period?

Display As *	P1 FY2 (Space)

Help   Cancel

http://192.168.29.200:5555/CoreSolutions/tools/fiscalsettings/dialogs/fiscalsettings.aspx   Internet

4. **Enter the starting date for your fiscal year in the Start Date field and select your intended interval for measuring revenue from the appropriate drop-down menu.**

   The required Template field allows you to specify your fiscal periods. The rest of the fields in this window allow you to specify the naming conventions your company uses and to formatt the periods.

You need to enter the fiscal year information carefully and correctly because you get only one shot at it. The system displays a warning message to this effect. *You can't enter sales quotas until you've entered the fiscal year settings.* If you set up your fiscal year beginning at some future date — let's say it's December, and you are setting up your system for the following year — you won't be able to enter sales quotas until you reach that future date.

   5. **Click OK to save your entries.**

Setting up a salesperson's quota

After the fiscal year information is set, you need to establish quotas. Of course, before you can enter quotas into the system, your management team must develop a business plan and sales plan and coordinate the quotas with that plan.

To set up the quota for a user (salesperson), follow these steps:

   1. **Near the bottom of the navigation pane, click the Settings button.**

   2. **In the navigation pane, select Administration.**

      This selection brings you to a window with five topics as shown in Figure 11-2.

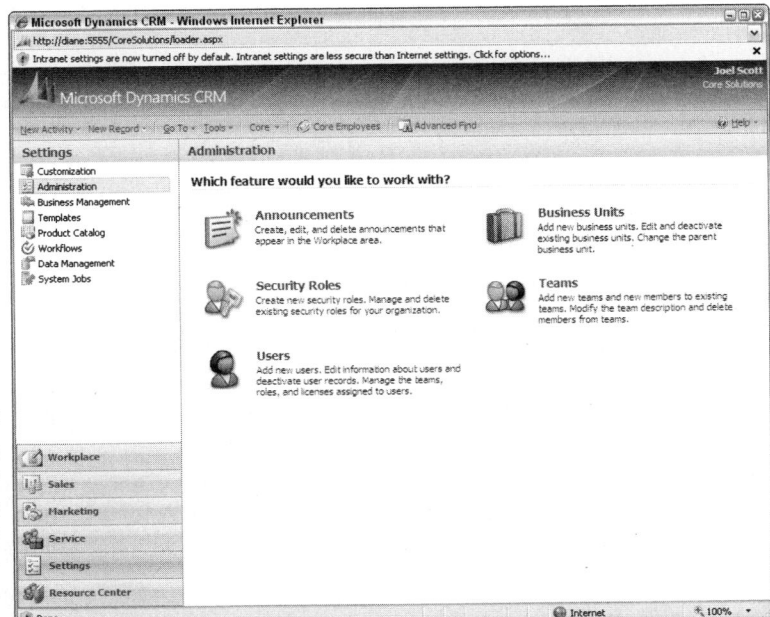

Figure 11-2:
The major functions within Administration.

3. **Select Users.**

   A list of all available users of the system appears.

4. **Select one or more salespeople.**

   Although *users* is a more general term than *salespeople,* usually only salespeople have quotas. To select more than one salesperson, hold down the Ctrl key while clicking with the mouse. If a group of salespeople has the same quota, you can set quotas for the group all at once.

5. **From the menu bar (at the top of the screen), choose Actions⇨Manage Quotas.**

   The Manage Quotas dialog box appears, as shown in Figure 11-3.

   If you've selected more than one user, you may get a warning message. If this is the case, the new quota you're about to enter will override any existing quota. If that isn't your intention, you can cancel the operation; you return to the list of users (Step 3), where you can make another selection.

Figure 11-3:
Entering a sales-person's quota. In this example, three salespeople were selected, each of whom will be getting the same quota.

Add New Quotas -- Web Page Dialog		
Manage Quotas		

You have selected 3 Salespeople. Set the quotas of the Salespeople by entering values in the boxes. Any existing values will be overwritten when you click OK.

Fiscal year: 2007

Currency: US Dollar

Period|Start Date	End Date	Quota
Quarter 1 2007	1/1/2007	3/31/2007	$ 0.00
Quarter 2 2007	4/1/2007	6/30/2007	$ 0.00
Quarter 3 2007	7/1/2007	9/30/2007	$ 0.00
Quarter 4 2007	10/1/2007	12/31/2007	$ 0.00

OK   Cancel   Apply

http://192.168.29.200:5555/CoreSolutions/_grid/cmds/dlg_addquota.aspx?K   Internet

6. **On the right side of the window, fill in each period's quota.**

   These quotas will apply to every salesperson you selected in Step 4. However, nothing happens until you click the Apply button.

7. **Click the Apply button at the bottom of the dialog box.**

   The quotas are saved. This is an important step. If you click OK without applying your changes, nothing is saved.

8. **Click the OK button at the bottom of the dialog box.**

   You return to the Quota window.

9. **If you want to enter a quota for another salesperson, repeat Steps 4 through 8.**

Entering Sales Forecasts

Anyone who's been in sales for more than a day has wrestled with sales forecasting in some fashion. This wrestling match may have been with some formal system or may have been a manager demanding to know when that big deal is going to finally go down. Without reasonably accurate sales forecasts, it's difficult for management to steer the boat.

Forecasts in Microsoft CRM are part of the Opportunities section of the program (in the Sales module). The words *forecast* and *opportunity* are nearly synonymous in this system.

To enter a new opportunity, follow these steps:

1. **Near the bottom of the navigation pane, click the Sales button.**

2. **At the top of the navigation pane, select Opportunities.**

   The Opportunities window appears on the right, as shown in Figure 11-4.

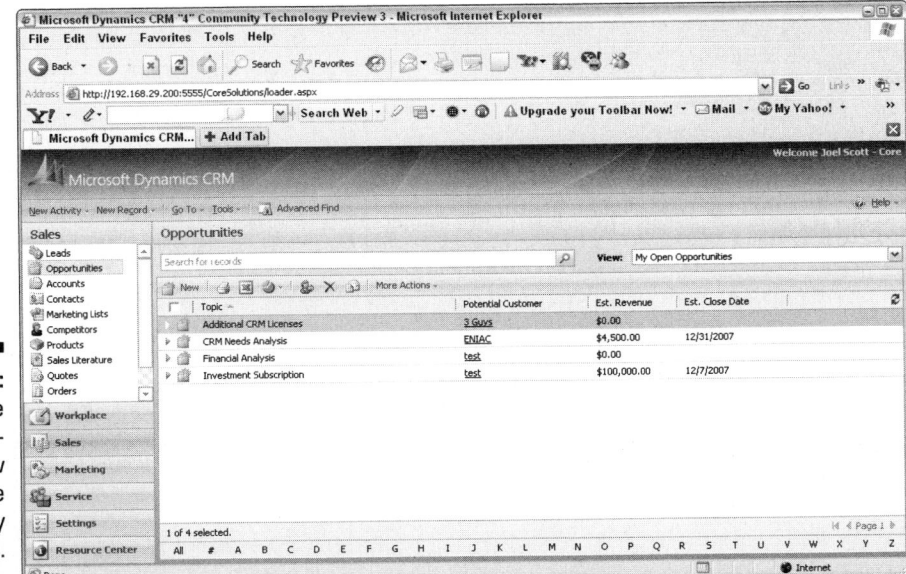

Figure 11-4:
The opportunities window with some data already entered.

3. **On the Opportunities window's toolbar, click the New button.**

   The Opportunity: New window appears, as shown in Figure 11-5. On the General tab, the Topic, Potential Customer, and Currency fields are all required fields.

4. **In the Topic field, enter a general description of the product or service you're selling.**

   For example, you might type **Residential Swimming Pool Installation** or **Client Retention Consulting Engagement**.

5. **Fill in the Potential Customer field as follows:**

   a. *Click the magnifying glass to the right of the Potential Customer field so you can link the opportunity.*

   Every opportunity should be linked to an account or to a contact.

   b. *In the Look For field, select Account or Contact.*

   To follow along with the example, select Account.

   A customer can be either an account (a business) or a contact (a person) and a forecast can relate to either entity.

   c. *Enter a portion of the potential customer's name and then click Find to locate the specific account or contact to which you're linking this opportunity.*

   (We discuss the Find function in detail in Chapter 3.) The Look Up Records dialog box appears, as shown in Figure 11-6.

   d. *In the Account Name field, select an account.*

   The General tab of the Opportunity: New window reappears.

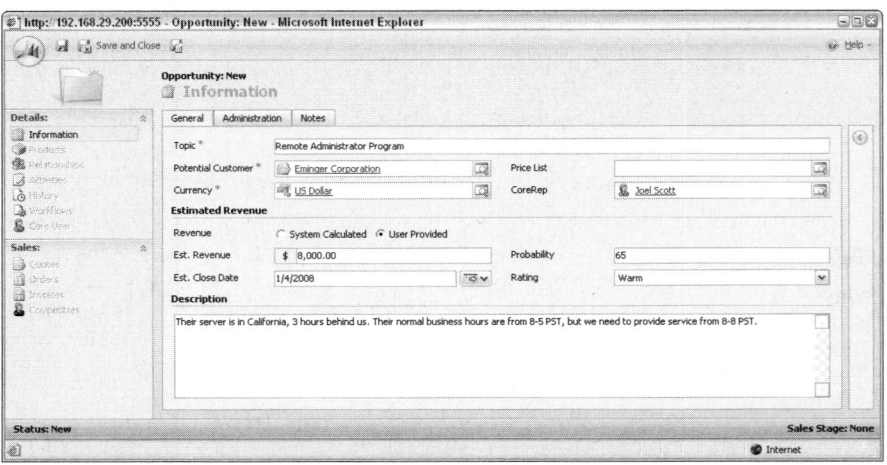

Figure 11-5: Entering a new opportunity.

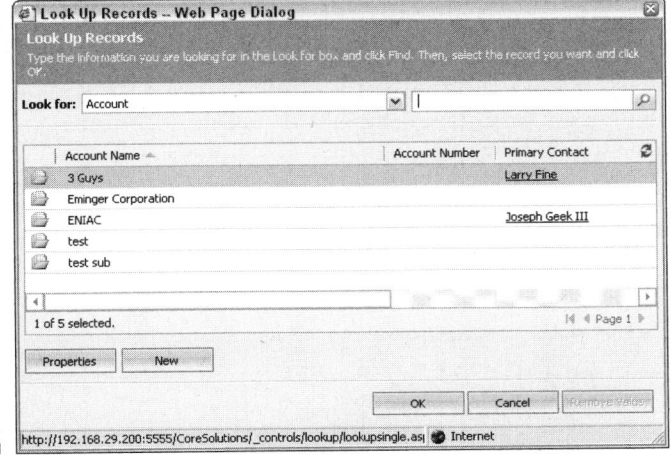

Figure 11-6:
The accounts that correspond to your search criteria.

6. **For the Revenue option, select User Provided.**

   If you've set up price lists, you may be able to have the system calculate the price of your list of products and services. In this example, we assume that you don't have price lists that apply, so you need to do a manual entry of the price.

7. **In the Est. Revenue field, enter the estimated revenue from this opportunity.**

8. **Fill in the Est. Close date field using the calendar at the end of the field.**

9. **In the Probability field, enter the probability of closing the deal.**

   If your company uses a sales process automated by workflow rules, this field may be auto-populated.

10. **If you want, make a selection in the Rating drop-down list.**

    You can rate the deal Hot, Warm, or Cold, but the Probability field covers this.

11. **In the Description field, add any comments.**

    You might notice that a Notes tab is associated with this new opportunity. There's no rule for using the Description field versus the Notes tab. However, for complex sales that take a long time to close or involve a team of people, we use the Notes tab so each note is time stamped and date stamped. For simpler and shorter deals, we use the Description field.

12. **Click the Save and Close button.**

    You return to the Opportunities window.

Updating Your Forecasts

Forecasts have a tendency to get stale quickly. We recommend that you review and revise your forecasts at least once a week. These revisions need to focus not only on the estimated close date but also on every field that may have changed.

To update a forecast, follow these steps:

1. **Near the bottom of the navigation pane, click the Sales button.**

2. **At the top of the navigation pane, select Opportunities.**

   The Opportunities window appears. If the opportunity you need to update doesn't appear, check the View menu in the upper-right corner to make sure you're looking at My Open Opportunities or Open Opportunities.

3. **Select the opportunity in question.**

   The detailed information for the opportunity appears, as shown in Figure 11-7.

4. **Make your modifications.**

   Although much of the forecast is for your own benefit and is meant to keep you on track, the forecast is also probably being reviewed by the sales management team. Reasonable and realistic estimates are always better than pie-in-the-sky guesses.

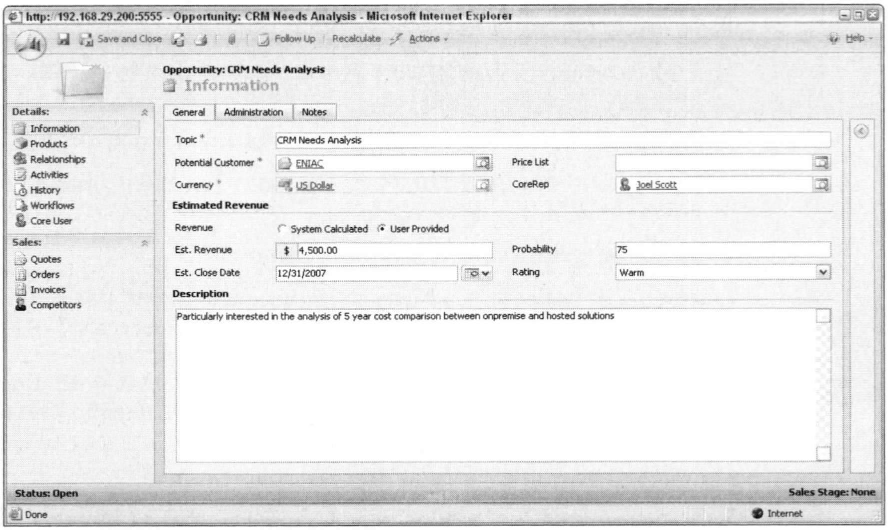

Figure 11-7: It's all in the details.

5. **Click the Save and Close button.**

   The Opportunities window reappears. From here, you can review or edit another opportunity that needs attention.

Examining the Forecasts

Microsoft CRM has built-in reports that focus on opportunity management: opportunity reports and pipeline reports.

Opportunity reports are typically simple line reports with subtotals or totals. You can filter and sort them by territory, potential revenue, closing probability, salesperson, and many other fields.

Pipeline reports and charts generally involve a little math. If you are a sales manager, you may want to see how much each salesperson is likely to close this quarter. A pipeline report can show this to you, either in tabular or graphic form, by multiplying the potential revenue by the probability.

Your dealer or a knowledgeable systems administrator can customize these reports, as well as set up additional custom reports. However, that customization is outside the scope of this book.

Printing a report

To select a report for printing or saving, follow these steps:

1. **Near the bottom of the navigation pane, click the Sales button.**

2. **At the top of the navigation pane, select Opportunities.**

   The Opportunities window appears.

3. **In the View drop-down list, select the opportunities you want to report on.**

   For example, choose My Open Opportunities if you want to see only your own deals, or choose Open Opportunities if you want a more company-wide report (assuming you have the rights to see these).

4. **On the window's toolbar, click the Reports button.**

   The system displays a list of all available reports. Our copy of the software lists three reports: Competitor Win Loss and Lead Source Effectiveness and Sales Pipeline.

5. **Select a report from the drop-down list as shown in Figure 11-8.**

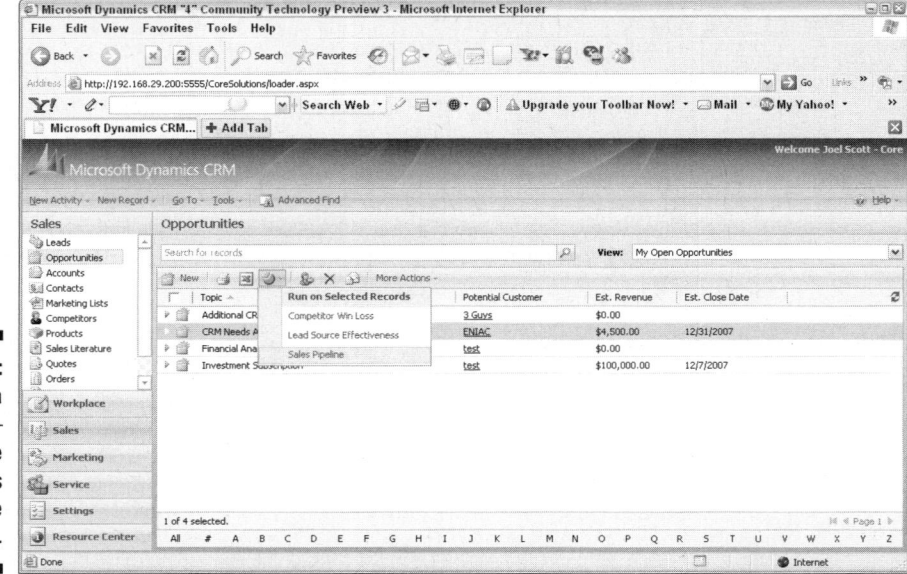

Figure 11-8:
Selecting a
report —
like the
Sales
Pipeline
Report.

After the system processes all the data, the report appears on your
screen.

6. **Print or save the report.**

Using Excel to examine forecast data

Sales forecasting is one of the most critical aspects of the sales process at
our company. It allows each salesperson to track his or her progress, and the
information in the combined sales forecasts gives management a view of
coming attractions. Most importantly, this same information allows workflow
rules to ensure that no sale falls through the cracks.

You can export your forecast data directly to a local copy of Excel on your
computer. Then, if you have even a little facility with Excel, you can manipulate the data and look at it in a tabular or in a graphical presentation. (If you
need help with Excel, get a copy of *Excel 2007 For Dummies,* by Greg Harvey
[Wiley Publishing].)

To export your forecast data to Excel, follow these steps:

1. **Near the bottom of the navigation pane, click the Sales button.**

2. **At the top of the navigation pane, select Opportunities.**

   The Opportunities window appears.

3. **In the View drop-down list, select the types of opportunities you want in your Excel export.**

4. **On the window's toolbar, click the Excel icon.**

   A screen appears with several worksheet choices.

5. **For the simplest kind of export, select the first option and then click Export.**

   CRM loads your data into a local copy of Excel. You can then calculate totals, add columns with calculated values, or even create graphs.

6. **For more sophisticated dynamic Excel tables, select the second or third choices.**

   Dynamic worksheets automatically update their data as you change the data in another application.

Chapter 12

Handling Leads and Opportunities

- -

- -

*I*n CRM-speak, a *suspect* is a person or a company with whom you may do business someday. In all likelihood, your suspect hasn't yet heard of you. A *prospect* is the next level up. Your prospect has heard of you and may have even expressed some interest in doing business with you. Microsoft CRM refers to both suspects and prospects as *leads*.

An *opportunity* is a lead that has matured enough to deserve serious attention. But before you can begin to turn leads into opportunities, you need to enter your lead data (such as contact information, the source of the lead, and what the prospect is interested in) into CRM.

Actually, you can promote a lead to an account record, a contact record, or an opportunity record, or to any combination of these three. The subtle benefit of promoting a lead to an opportunity is that you can forecast a sale associated with an opportunity. You can also link each opportunity to a price list, which helps determine the pricing in a quote.

You need to create an opportunity record before you close your opportunity (whether by winning or losing the deal). You create opportunity records manually by just typing them in, by importing them from outside files (such as Excel), or by converting them from leads. Importing data from Excel is discussed in Appendix A.

Workflow rules enable almost complete automation of your selling process, moving opportunities from one sales stage to the next. Workflow is part of the process of handling opportunities and is discussed in some detail in Chapter 9.

In Chapter 16, we discuss what happens when you close an opportunity and turn it into the real deal. In this chapter, we talk about entering leads and moving them through your sales process with the intention of turning them into full-fledged opportunities.

Processing Leads from Suspects

Leads may come to you from many sources. Some of the most common sources are referrals from existing customers, mailing lists you've rented or purchased, inquiries from your Web site, and responses to marketing campaigns.

Leads get into CRM in essentially two ways. You can enter them manually or you can import them, typically from an Excel file. If your CRM system is integrated with your Web site, you can automate the entry of leads from the Web. It's likely, though, that you'll want some expert help for that. Chapter 21 deals with Web integration and Chapter 28 discusses when and how to access some expert help. You're probably going to enter leads manually if you have only a few sporadic leads or if you don't have them available in a convenient electronic format. In this section, we discuss getting leads manually into your CRM system and what to do with them after they're there.

Getting to the Leads window

You can access everything about leads and opportunities from the Sales module. And everything about leads starts at the Leads window, which is shown in Figure 12-1. To get to that window, click the Sales button near the bottom of the navigation pane. Then, at the top of the pane, select Leads. That's it.

As you go through the standard Lead windows, you can see about 20 data fields. As with most data entry windows throughout CRM, many more fields than that are available. Those fields have been hard-coded into the database structure but remain invisible unless your system design people make them available. In the case of lead records, for example, 95 fields are available, should you need to track more information about your leads. Your administrator or dealer can add fields, if needed.

Creating a lead manually

Your marketing department's efforts are supposed to create leads. Microsoft CRM thinks of a lead as a potential customer that may or may not have expressed interest in your company's products. For example, the marketing department might purchase a list of potential users. Or various types of advertising might generate inquiries. In any case, the resulting contact information has to get into the CRM database.

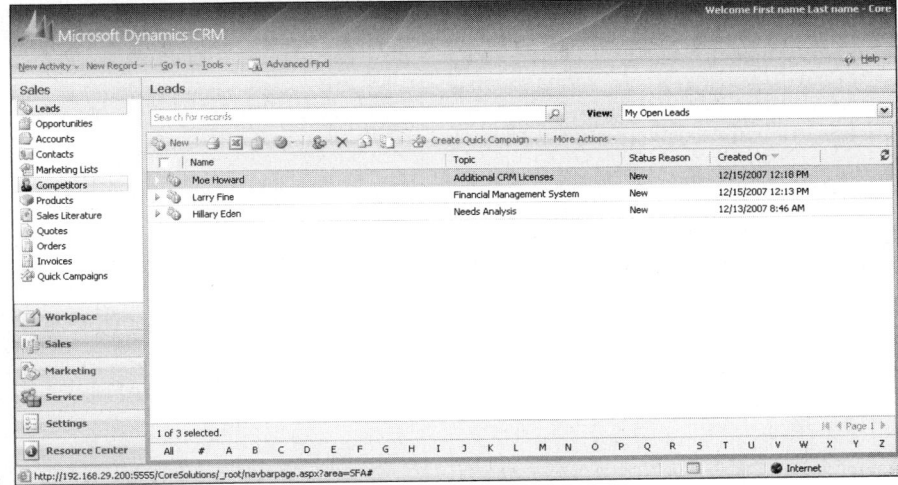

Figure 12-1:
Your work
with leads
starts here.

Unless you have an electronic list or your CRM system is hooked to your Web site, you're probably going to be entering leads the old-fashioned way — by typing. In this section, we discuss the easiest way to manually enter those hard-won leads. Just follow these steps:

1. **On the Leads window toolbar, click the New button.**

   The Lead: New window appears, as shown in Figure 12-2, with four tabs: General, Details, Administration, and Notes.

2. **Fill in at least the required fields, which are highlighted with red asterisks.**

   If the General tab isn't already selected, click it. For the Topic field, enter the product or service that the prospect is interested in.

   The Company Name field is a required field, so you must enter a company name even if your lead is an individual. When we encounter that situation, we simply enter X as the default company name. If you have the name of an individual or any other relevant contact information, enter that as well.

   Although the E-Mail and Lead source fields aren't system-required, they should be at least business-recommended fields (in blue). The e-mail address field is on the General tab, and the Lead source field is on the Details tab. Make sure you enter as much information as you can in the General, Details, and Administration tabs.

3. **When you're finished, click the Save and Close button at the top of the screen.**

    The system returns to the Leads window, where you can create another lead, access a lead, or move on to another function.

Aside from the obvious contact information, such as company name, contact person, and phone number, you should focus on collecting data that will enable you to follow up both immediately and over the long term. E-mail addresses and specific product interests are key ingredients to properly following up on leads, and they're critical for campaign management and electronic marketing.

Modifying a lead

You can modify a lead by navigating to the Leads window, clicking the lead, and then making the necessary changes in the various tabs of the lead's record. Remember to click Save and Close before leaving the record.

If the lead you're interested in isn't displayed in the list, check the View menu in the upper-right corner. This menu contains several options in its drop-down list that expand or contract the number of listings displayed, as shown in Figure 12-3. For example, if you're looking for a lead that hasn't been assigned to you, try selecting Open Leads from the View drop-down list. Depending on your access rights, you may be able to see additional leads this way.

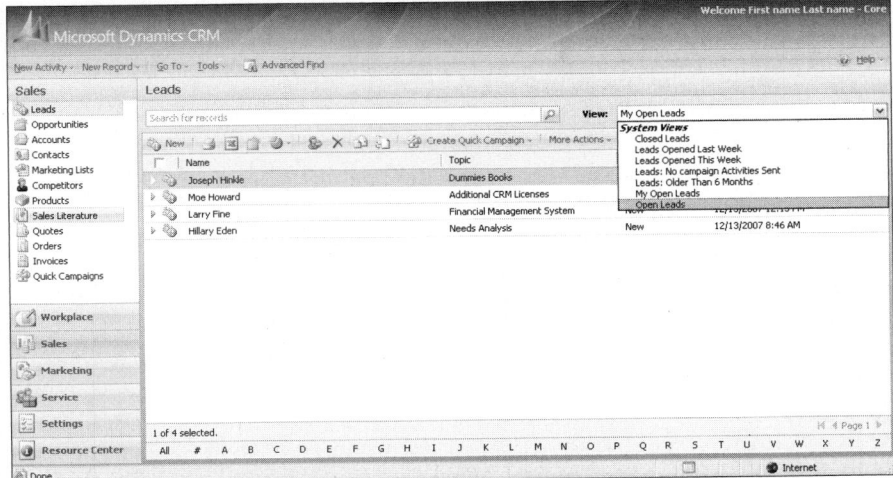

Figure 12-3:
Expanding
the list of
leads.

If you don't find your lead in any view, it may have been converted to an account, a contact, or an opportunity. That's good news, but it means you may have to look under those other record types for your data. We discuss accounts and contacts in Chapter 13 and opportunities later in this chapter. If your lead has been *disqualified*, which is just another way of saying, "forget about it," refer to the upcoming "Resurrecting a lead" section.

Giving up on a lead

When you've decided that you have no hope of generating anything worthwhile from a lead, you can *disqualify* it. You do this as follows:

1. **In the Leads window (refer to Figure 12-1), double-click the specific lead you intend to give up on.**

   The General tab for that lead appears.

2. **Click the Convert Lead button near the top of the window.**

   The Convert Lead dialog box appears as shown in Figure 12-4.

3. **To disqualify the lead, select the Disqualify option.**

   All the choices above the option become dimmed.

4. **Select a reason for the disqualification from the Status drop-down menu and then click OK.**

   The lead now shows up only in the Closed Leads view in the Leads window.

Convert Lead
Specify whether to convert this lead into one or more of the following options or to disqualify it.

- ○ **Qualify and convert into the following records**
  - ☐ Account
  - ☐ Contact
  - ☐ Opportunity

  Potential Customer [_____] 🔍

  Currency [💲 US Dollar] 🔍

  ☐ Open newly created records

- ◉ **Disqualify**

  Status [Lost ▾]

  [OK] [Cancel]

http://192.168.29.200:5555/CoreSolutior 🌐 Internet

Figure 12-4:
Converting a
lead.

Deleting a lead is possible but not recommended. Deletions are permanent, and deleting a lead also deletes any attachments or notes associated with the lead. A far better approach is to disqualify the lead. That way, an audit trail (using that term loosely) remains if needed. And disqualifying allows you to resurrect the lead later if the situation changes.

Resurrecting a lead

Occasionally you get lucky and a lead that you thought had died comes back to life. If you disqualified the lead, you can bring it back without re-entering all the old information. If you didn't heed our advice — see the preceding Warning — and instead deleted the lead, you're out of luck.

To resurrect a lead, perform the following steps:

1. **In the upper-right corner of the Leads window, change the View selection to Closed Leads.**

   The lead you previously disqualified appears somewhere in the list.

2. **In the list, select the lead in question by double-clicking it.**

   The record for that lead appears.

3. **On the menu bar at the top of the screen, choose Actions➪Reactivate Lead.**

   The Confirm Lead Activation dialog box appears.

4. **Click OK.**

   The original record appears. The data that had appeared dimmed while the lead was disqualified is again available for editing and general use.

5. **Click the Save and Close button, and you're back in business.**

   The record is updated and the window closes.

6. **Review the list in the Leads window to make sure that your lead is successfully brought back to life. Make sure to change the Status to "Open Leads" or to "My Open Leads" to actually see your newly resurrected lead.**

Turning a Lead into an Opportunity

Your goal is to turn all leads into opportunities. When you reach that goal, it's time to turn your lead record into an opportunity record. Navigate to the record for that lead and then click the Convert Lead button at the top of the screen. The screen shown in Figure 12-5 appears.

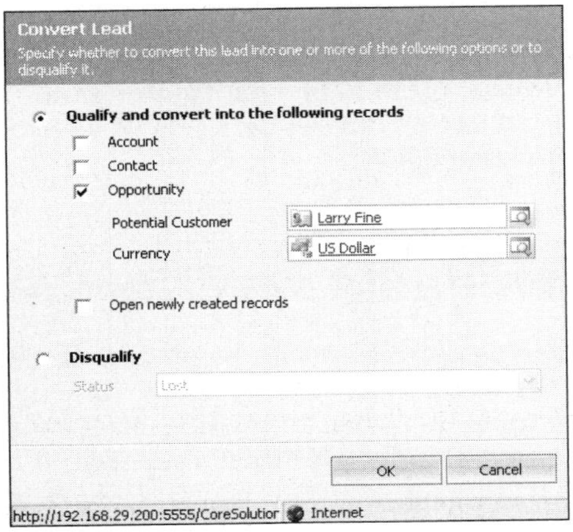

Figure 12-5: Converting a lead to something better.

The first three conversion choices in Figure 12-5 aren't mutually exclusive. If you initially created a lead without establishing any related accounts or contacts, you can do all three conversions in one smooth step now. We discuss accounts and contacts in Chapter 13.

If this potential sale is directly related to a consumer (a person), select the Contact option. If you're trying to sell something to a company, choose the Account option. If you're dealing with a company, you can select the Contact in addition to selecting Account, in which case the system creates an account and a related contact record.

An *account* is a company. A *contact* is a person. A *customer* might be either one.

The third option, Opportunity, converts your lead to an opportunity. If you also elect to create an account record, that opportunity will be related to it. If you don't create an account but do create a contact, the opportunity will be related to the contact. If you have the system create both an account and a contact, the opportunity (and the contact) relates to the account.

An opportunity is always associated with a customer! That's why the Customer field is a required field.

Handling Opportunities

A fine line exists between a lead and an opportunity. Generally, you've crossed the line when you're able to forecast a sale with associated revenue, a potential close date, and a probability for the sale happening. When those conditions are met, you graduate a lead to an opportunity, although your organization may define the transition differently. If you've already written a quotation, you're definitely over the line.

Creating and modifying opportunities

We cover converting a lead to an opportunity in the preceding section. You can also skip entering the lead record entirely and go directly to an opportunity record. We like to do this when an existing client calls and asks for something — even if we aren't ready to forecast a sale yet.

To create a new opportunity, follow these steps:

1. **Near the bottom of the navigation pane, click the Sales button. Then, near the top of the pane, select Opportunities.**

   The Opportunities window appears, as shown in Figure 12-6.

2. **On the Opportunities window's toolbar, click the New button.**

   The Opportunity: New window appears, as shown in Figure 12-7.

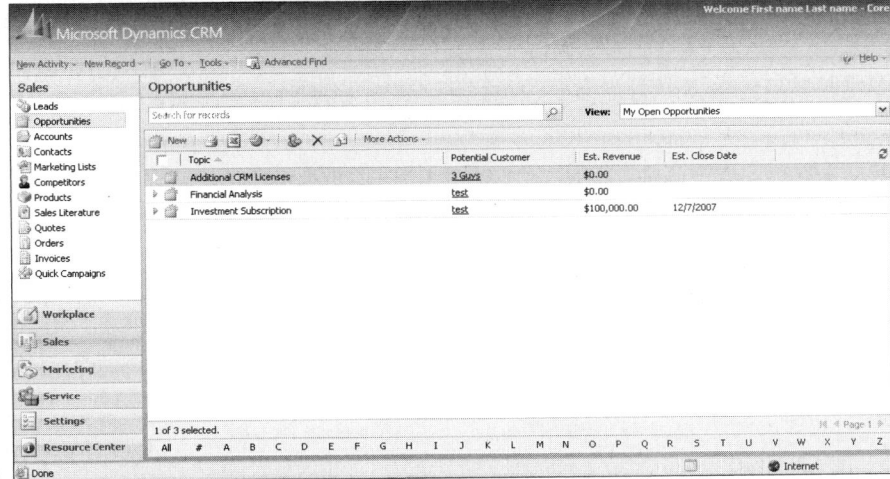

Figure 12-6:
All open
opportuni-
ties are
displayed.

Figure 12-6:
All open
opportuni-
ties are
displayed.

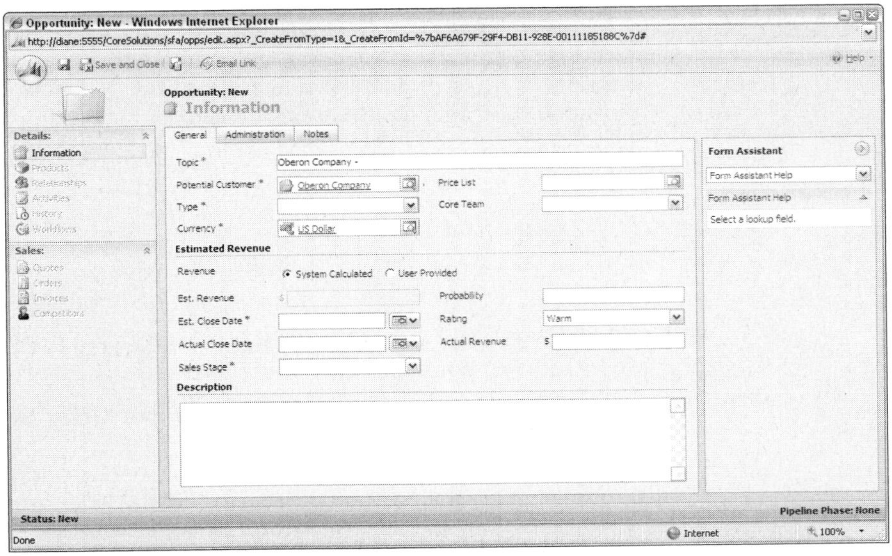

Figure 12-7:
Entering
a new
opportunity.

3. Enter a topic.

Topic, which is a system-required field, is just a description of what you expect to sell — for example, Consulting, Term Insurance, or Transporter System.

4. **Select a Potential Customer (the second required field) to which this opportunity relates.**

   Remember, a customer is either an account (a company) or a contact (a person). If you click the magnifying glass to the right of the Potential Customer field, another screen appears that allows you to browse to and select either an account record or a contact record.

5. **If you have a price list set up, select the appropriate one.**

   We discuss price lists in Chapter 7.

6. **For the Revenue field, if your price lists have been set up, select System Calculated; otherwise, select User Provided.**

   By the way, *you* are the user, so be prepared to enter a forecasted amount if you select the User Provided option.

7. **Enter information in the following fields:**

   a. *In the Est. Revenue field, enter your best guess for the actual revenue you'll receive when you close the deal.*

   b. *In the Probability field, enter a whole number between 1 and 99.*

      Although 0 and 100 are allowed, a 0 probability sale doesn't deserve to be an opportunity, and at 100 the deal must already be closed and turned into an order.

   c. *In the Est. Close Date field, enter the date when you expect to close the deal.*

   d. *In the Rating field, enter a rating.*

      You can select Cold, Warm, or Hot to describe the rating, although the Probability field already does a good job of rating.

   Although none of these are system-required fields, you don't have much of an opportunity if you don't have these estimates.

8. **Click the Save and Close button to save the opportunity record.**

From the Opportunities window, you can update an existing opportunity record by double-clicking the particular record, editing the information in any of the three tabbed areas (General, Administration, and Notes), and then saving the record.

As your opportunity progresses through the sales cycle, you'll want to update it often to maintain the current status of your real pipeline.

Assigning and sharing opportunities

You can assign an opportunity to yourself or to another user. You can share opportunities with other users or teams. For large or more complex opportunities, this is often a necessity.

When you *assign* an opportunity to someone else, you change the record ownership to that user. *Sharing* enables other users to see the opportunity in their My Opportunities view just as if it were their own, but it doesn't change the record's ownership.

To assign an opportunity to another user, follow these steps:

1. **On the menu bar (at the top of the screen), choose Actions⇨Assign.**

    The Assign Opportunity dialog box (available from the Opportunity record itself, not from the Opportunity grid) appears, as shown in Figure 12-8. Although you can assign one or more opportunities to yourself or to another user, you can't assign an opportunity to multiple users or to a team.

Figure 12-8:
You can assign an opportunity to yourself or to another user.

2. **Select the second option, Assign to Another User. You can also assign records to yourself, but your organization may have some rules regarding this.**

3. **Click the magnifying glass to the right of the Assign to Another User text field.**

    A Look Up Records dialog box appears.

4. **Select the user to whom you want to assign this opportunity.**

    The Assign to User text field shown in Figure 12-8 is automatically filled in with that user's name.

5. Click OK.

The system returns to the General tab of that record, even though the opportunity is no longer yours.

You share opportunities as follows:

1. In the Opportunities window, click the More Actions button.

A short list of options appears.

2. Choose Sharing.

The window shown in Figure 12-9 appears.

Figure 12-9:
The
Opportunity
sharing
window.

3. Select which users or teams you want to share this opportunity with and which rights you want to give them.

Unlike assigning, sharing allows you to choose multiple users and even teams of users. For each user or team, you can decide how much authority to give. For example, you might decide to allow everyone to see the opportunity but not make changes to it. Or, if you're going away on vacation, you might share the opportunity with another user and give him or her complete rights to make changes (Write) and to share the opportunity with yet another user. Those choices and selections are shown in Figure 12-9. Chapter 8 has further details on security and rights.

4. Click OK after you've chosen the people or teams and their rights.

The system returns to the Opportunities window.

If you decide to share an opportunity, examine the permissions you grant to other team members. For example, you may want to be judicious about allowing other members the ability to delete or close an opportunity.

Relating opportunities to activities or other records

Opportunity records are often associated with many other types of records. Opportunities can be, and should be, related to accounts, or contacts, or both. (We discuss how to associate an account or contact to an opportunity in the preceding section, "Creating and sharing opportunities.") This makes sense because you're planning to sell something to either a company or a person. You may also want to relate *activities* (such as phone calls and appointments), quotes, orders, invoices, notes, or attachments to an opportunity.

While working on an opportunity, chances are you're generating one or more quotes, making notes, and saving documents or data files that are associated with the opportunity. For example, in our business, CRM consulting, we often need to save sample data files so we can analyze how best to convert a legacy system's data into Microsoft CRM files. All these various files can be linked to the opportunity record.

Here are the steps to link activities or files to an opportunity:

1. **In the Opportunities window, click an opportunity record to see its details.**

2. **On the menu bar (at the top of the screen), choose Actions.**

3. **Select one of the choices shown in Figure 12-10.**

4. **Click the Save and Close button.**

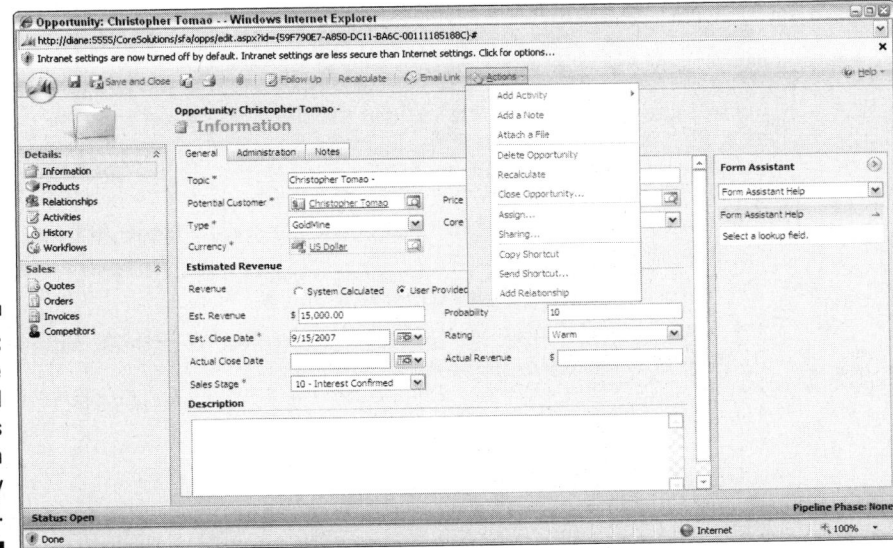

Figure 12-10:
All the potential Actions from an Opportunity record.

Managing stages and relationships

Workflow rules automate your sales process — assuming your organization has a process and the workflow rules are set up to emulate that process. Typically, a sales process has 3 to 12 stages ranging from initial contact to generating a quote, negotiating with the customer, and closing the deal. Every company has a different process with different stages. In fact, a single company may have a different process for every type of product or service it sells.

Setting up your processes is usually the domain of your sales management team, an outside consultant, or a combination of the two.

From the Actions menu, you can advance an opportunity through your predefined sequence of sales steps. We highly recommend this approach, but an intelligently designed workflow is key. Workflow rules are discussed in Chapters 9 and 18.

The Relationships function enables you to link various accounts and contacts. This is often important, particularly in more complex deals. For example, you may have a pending deal with a prospect, and both an outside consultant and a leasing company are involved. Because the consultant and the leasing company are each separate records in your database, you use the Relationship function to link them. From the Opportunities window, you select the appropriate opportunity, select Relationships from the navigation pane on the left, and add new customers to the opportunity.

Closing, reopening, and deleting opportunities

Eventually, whether you win or lose the deal, you need to close the opportunity. This is easy enough to do. To close an opportunity properly, follow these steps directly from the Opportunity form (not the grid view):

1. **On the menu bar (at the top of the screen), choose Actions⇨Close Opportunity.**

   The Close Opportunity window appears.

2. **Under Status, click the appropriate option to indicate whether you won or lost the opportunity.**

3. **In the Status Reason field, select one of the drop-down choices.**

   Microsoft CRM provides two reasons for losing a deal: The order was canceled or you were outsold. We've never seen a salesperson select that second choice. Many other reasons exist for losing a deal, and your system administrator or dealer should help expand this list.

4. **Do one of the following:**

   - *If you won, modify the Actual Revenue field to reflect the agreed-upon price and then enter the Close Date.*

   - *If you lost the opportunity, enter the competitor to whom you lost, if you know that information.*

5. **In the Description field, enter a sentence or two with your final comments.**

   An example is shown in Figure 12-11.

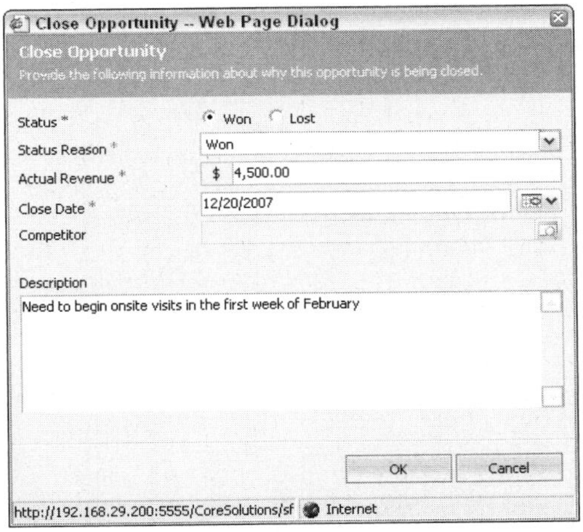

Figure 12-11:
Closing an
opportunity.

6. **Click OK to close the opportunity.**

   The system returns to the General tab of the opportunity.

A previously closed opportunity may resurface and need to be reopened. If so, follow these steps:

1. **In the Opportunities window, make sure the View menu displays Closed Opportunities.**

2. **In the window's list, select the appropriate opportunity.**

   The opportunity's record appears.

3. **On the menu bar (at the top of the screen), choose Actions⇨Reopen Opportunity.**

   The Opportunity's status changes immediately, and you can edit it just as you would any other active or open opportunity record.

You can also delete an opportunity. This may seem like a good idea, particularly if you're upset that you lost a deal. In the long run, however, it's a bad idea because you never know when a deal may come back to life or you may need to refer to your notes on it. Don't do it. Instead, close it and attach a note if need be.

Chapter 13

Working with Accounts and Contacts

*A*ccount and contact records, as well as related lead and opportunity records, hold much of the primary information that your team has or will collect. Depending on the nature of your business, you may use one or both types of records. Microsoft CRM continually refers to accounts, contacts, and customers, so it's important to keep the terms straight. *Accounts* are companies, *contacts* are people, and *customers* can be either companies or people.

Assuming for the moment that you sell to other businesses and that you use account records, you'll also need to use contact records. Each account record can have multiple people (contact records) associated with it. The larger the account, the more people you likely need to track.

If you sell only to individuals, you may never actually use account records to track your customers. In all likelihood, however, you'll want to track more than just your customers in Microsoft CRM. For example, keeping track of your company's vendors in the same database is useful. Your competitors may also be candidates for their own account records if you don't create actual competitor records for them. If you're strictly a B2C company, you will probably still encounter situations like these where you need the account record.

In this chapter, we describe how you add new accounts and contacts and how best to use and access those records after you create them.

Adding and Editing Contacts

You can add a contact record that stands alone, or you can add one that is associated with an account record. Adding or editing contact records is almost identical to the process you follow for account records.

Contacts have a list view just as accounts do. You can access this view from the Sales, Marketing, or Service areas. The Contact database is the same for all three areas of CRM, so all your users access the same contact records.

You can add or manually edit individual contacts in the same way that you handle account. Contact records have a Parent Account field just as account records do. If you do business only with individuals, you may never need the Parent Account field. You should use it, however, if you need to associate a person with a company. Note that you can associate many different people with the same company (account record).

In addition to the manual entry of contact records, Microsoft CRM also comes with an automated wizard-based system for importing contact records. Although the wizard was designed with Outlook files in mind, the import facility can handle other types of data, such as text (`.txt`) files. See Appendix B for more information on importing data.

If you need to perform a significant amount of importing or something more complex than just basic contact information, investigate the third-party import products discussed in Chapter 27.

Adding and Editing Accounts and Subaccounts

The first step in getting started with CRM is to stock it with all the organizations and people you deal with. If you already have the information organized in data files (in Excel, other CRM systems, or accounting data files, for example), you'll be doing some importing. We discuss importing data and converting it to Microsoft CRM's format in Appendixes A and B. If the data is stored in your head (or, worse, someone else's head), you're in for some typing. The basic entities into which this data will go are accounts and contacts.

As mentioned, *accounts* are companies. *Subaccounts* may be divisions of the main company or separate physical locations of the same company. Anything you add in Microsoft CRM, you can edit. And anything you add can be deleted, but a better practice is to deactivate an account rather than delete it. Deactivating an account is like making it go dormant. If you deactivate an account, you can always resurrect the information later if you discover you need it. Deletion is forever.

The ability to add, edit and/or delete records is a function of your security rights.

Old-timers who used version 1 may be looking for the Quick Create function — the lazy person's way to create new records using only required fields. This function bit the dust in version 4.

Every account you add will almost always be associated with one or more contacts (people), so you'll find it easier to create the contact records before you create the account record. You can then easily link the two.

Exploring account records and their four sections

You can get to your account records from each of the three application modules — Sales, Marketing, and Service — and even from the Workplace. In each of those modules, Accounts appears up at the top of the navigation pane.

Each account record has four related tabs: General, Details, Administration, and Notes. You can access these tabs to create a new account, as follows:

1. **At the top of the navigation pane, select Accounts.**

   The Accounts window appears on the right.

2. **On the window's toolbar, click the New button.**

   The Account: New window appears, as shown in Figure 13-1.

The General tab

The General tab has most of the critical contact information for your account, including the required field Account Name. Most of the fields on the General tab are self-explanatory, but the other three tabs deserve a little discussion.

The Details tab

The Details tab contains mostly financial information, such as annual revenue and a company's stock symbol if it's publicly traded. It's the kind of stuff you'll get if you receive data from Dun & Bradstreet or other similar services or list providers. This provides useful demographic information about the account, assuming someone in your organization does the research to fill in the information and keeps it current. The Details tab is shown in Figure 13-2.

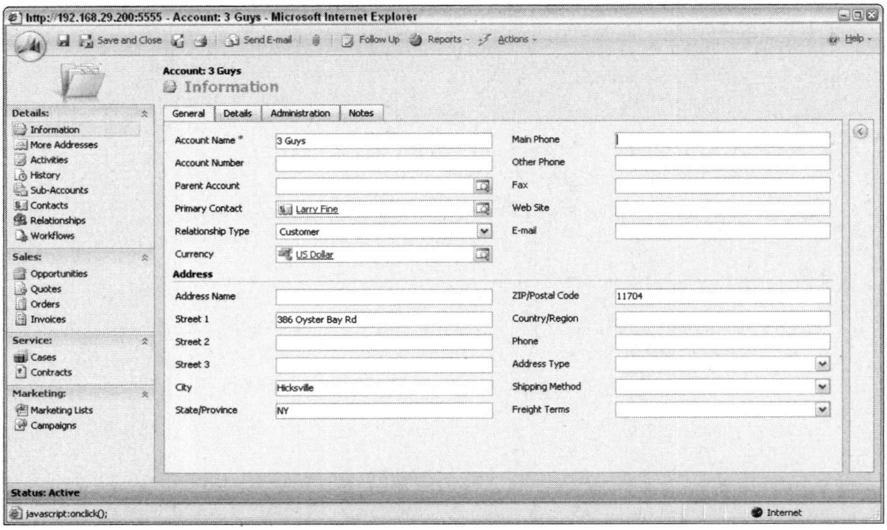

Figure 13-1:
The General
tab is where
you begin
entering
information
about the
account.

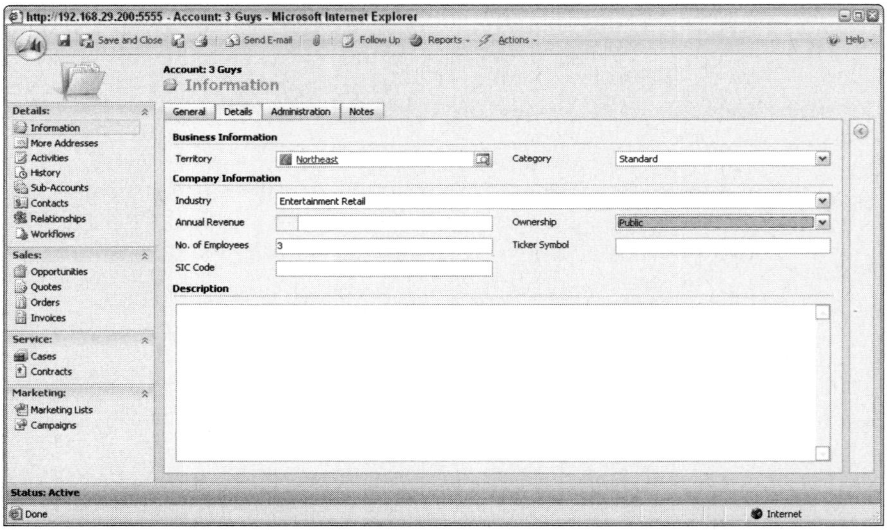

Figure 13-2:
The Details
tab of the
Account
window,
housing
basic
company
demo-
graphics.

The Territory field on the Details tab is one of the most important. Many companies, particularly national or international ones, divide their business into territories usually based on geography. Salespeople, or teams of sales-people, are assigned to each territory and their revenue is tracked.

Territories should be set up in the Settings module. (See Chapter 5 for more information.) Then you can manually select a territory for an account by clicking the magnifying glass to the right of the Territory field and selecting the appropriate territory.

You can also customize the system so that each new account is automatically assigned to a territory or so that accounts are reassigned automatically when it's time to reorganize your territories. See Chapter 9 for instructions on creating workflow rules that can automate these types of processes. Effective design and implementation of workflow may require the services of an experienced dealer or developer.

The Administration tab

The Administration tab, shown in Figure 13-3, is a catchall for accounting, marketing, and service information. The Owner field is the only required field and is filled in automatically with the name of the user creating the record. So, by default, the record owner is the person who enters the information. If that isn't the way it works in your organization, you can reassign the record to another user by clicking the magnifying glass to the right of the Owner field and selecting the proper user.

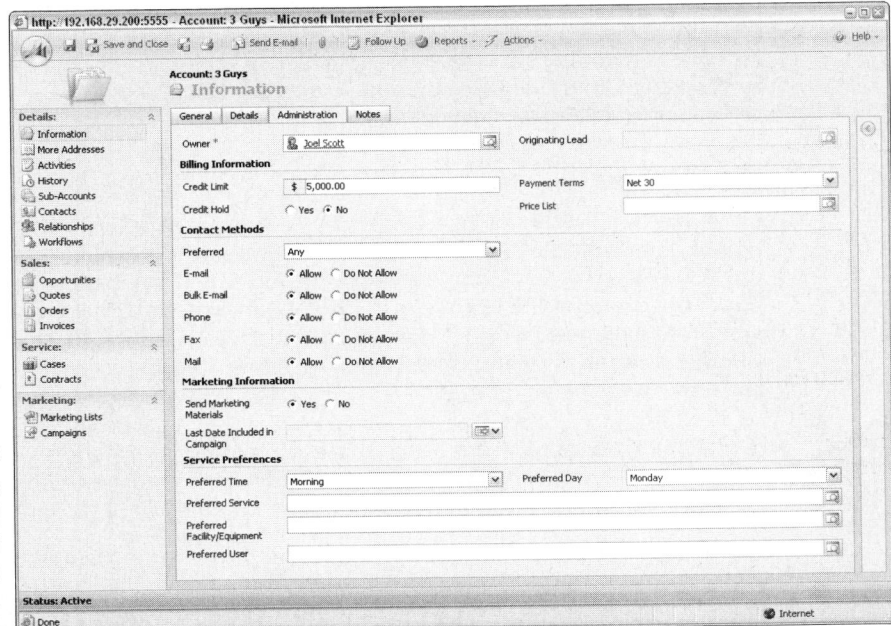

Figure 13-3:
You can add all sorts of information here.

The Originating Lead field automatically keeps track of the source of this account record if it came from a converted lead record. (We tell you how to convert a lead record in Chapter 12.) Your marketing department will definitely want this field filled in accurately so that they can understand which marketing efforts are generating revenue.

The Originating Lead field is a system-generated field, so you can't enter anything into it. To be filled in, the account must be generated from a lead when it is qualified.

It's a great advantage for salespeople to know at least a little bit about their clients' billing and credit situations. The fields in the Billing Information section are prime candidates for integration with whatever accounting system is used at your company. This integration will probably require some custom work and is usually the domain of the business partner who sold you the software.

The fields in the Contact Methods and Marketing Information sections regulate how you market to and correspond with this account. Keeping track of this is increasingly important as more and more laws go into effect regulating how we market to prospects and clients.

Even if you aren't using the Service module, the Service Preferences section contains basic service-related information that can help you tailor manual or automatic responses to service requests. For example, this is a simple place to keep track of the equipment your customer has and who your preferred technician is whenever service is needed.

The Notes tab

The Notes tab starts out as a blank slate: a large area where you can begin typing. You should use the Notes section to record general information about the account. After you finish typing your notes, just navigate to another section. This is one of the few areas in CRM where you don't have to tell the system to save your work. It does so automatically. In fact, CRM also records who created the note and timestamps it. Figure 13-4 shows a Notes tab after a few notes have been entered.

Everything you write in the Notes section is public information — and CRM doesn't have a spell checker or grammar checker. Pay attention to your writing style, and don't enter anything that you wouldn't want a client or a judge to see.

When you've finished filling in data fields in the various tabs, you could click the Save and Close button with each tab. But you can often save some steps by just clicking Save (the disk icon), which activates related actions on the navigation pane.

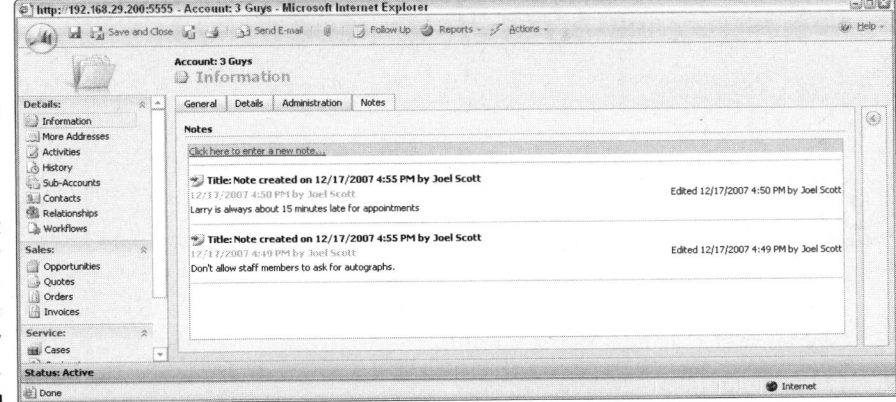

Figure 13-4:
The Notes
tab of the
Account
window
with some
notes
already
entered.

Setting up subaccounts

An account record may be the *parent* of other account records, and those other account records are called *children*. A *child* record is also referred to as a *subaccount*. Typically, you use the subaccount system to subordinate one record to another. An example is when you're dealing with a company that has multiple locations. The headquarters would be the parent account, and each regional location would be a subaccount. By relating the accounts this way, you can use the reporting system to consolidate, subtotal, or total revenue for all the related accounts.

The General tab (refer to Figure 13-1), which is the default window when you are creating a new account record, contains the field that relates one account to another. This field is labeled Parent Account and lists all account records in the system. There is no limit to the number of levels of parenting. In other words, every parent account can have multiple children, grandchildren, great-grandchildren, and so on.

As you create this structure, the best approach is to map out the relationships between the accounts and begin at the top. First enter the parent account and then enter the children. As you enter each child account, click the magnifying glass next to the Parent Account field and select one parent to connect each "generation."

Finding and Viewing Account Information

Almost no matter what your role is, as a user of CRM you'll find yourself looking up accounts, contacts, leads, and opportunities on a regular basis. (Okay, if you're a customer service rep, you may not spend much time checking out sales forecasts or opportunities. In fact, your access rights might even preclude you from doing so.) For the most part though you can locate records in Microsoft CRM in two basic ways: the Find function and the Advanced Find function.

Finding an account by name

You can access the Find function from any of the main windows. Using Find is the simplest and fastest way to locate a record. Figure 13-5 shows a typical list view as a result of a search for accounts beginning with the letter "e."

At the top of the window is an unlabeled, blank search field. The magnifying glass to the right of the field, actually sets this function in motion. You can locate an account in several ways:

✔ Enter the first few letters of the account name in the search field and click the magnifying glass. All the accounts beginning with those letters appear in the list. Click the account in the list to navigate to that account record.

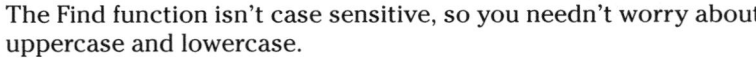

The Find function isn't case sensitive, so you needn't worry about uppercase and lowercase.

✔ Enter part of the account name preceded or followed by an asterisk (*). If you want to locate all the companies that have LLC in their names, you can enter **LLC** in the search field. This locates all the accounts that start with LLC. If you think LLC may occur in the middle or at the end of the name, however, you can generalize your search by using ***LLC***.

✔ Click a letter of the alphabet at the bottom of the grid and scroll through the listing of all companies that begin with that letter. This approach is useful if you have a small database — but if you have hundreds of accounts that span multiple pages, one of the other techniques is easier.

Figure 13-5: The Search function makes it easy to find records. This figure shows the results of a search for accounts starting with "e".

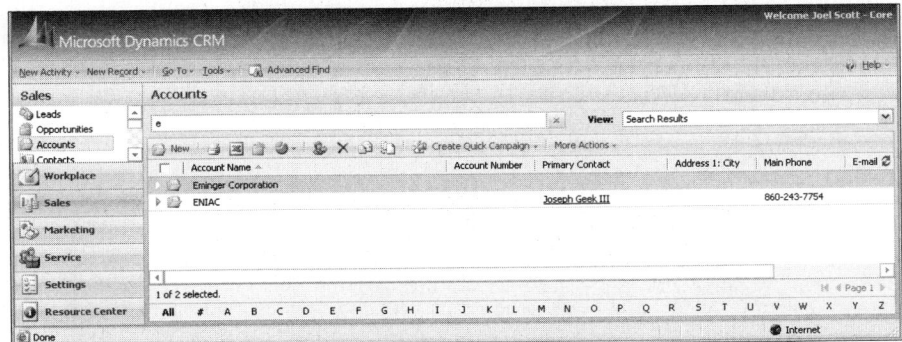

Using Advanced Find to perform a more sophisticated search

The Find function enables you to locate an account record quickly if you know the name of the account, or part of the name as long as that's the only criterion by which you're searching. Advanced Find, however, provides a more powerful search capability, enabling you to locate specific records (and activities) based on multiple fields, even if those fields are in different entities. When you use Advanced Find, you can specify one or more search conditions. For example, you can find items by account name, city, and the name of the salesperson responsible for the account. You may want to find all the A-level accounts in your city and send them an invitation to a seminar.

Your search can contain Boolean operators, such as AND or OR. While using Advanced Find, you can also enter an asterisk when performing a search (for example, when you're searching for an account, a user, or a contact).

The values you enter aren't case sensitive. For example, if you're entering a state code, Microsoft CRM will find the same records whether you enter **CT** or **ct**.

Boolean logic dictates that conditions within parentheses are evaluated before conditions separated by ANDs. ANDs are evaluated before ORs. However, the Advanced Find function doesn't have parentheses and evaluates expressions in the order in which they appear in your search.

To do a search with Advanced Find, follow these steps:

1. On the main toolbar, click the Advanced Find button.

The window shown in Figure 13-6 appears.

Figure 13-6:
A sample
search is
already
entered.
Just as with
diet pills and
exercise
equipment,
your own
results
may vary.

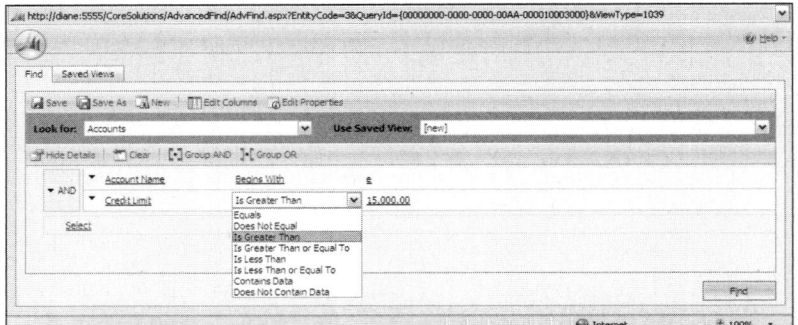

2. In the Look For drop-down list, select the appropriate choice.

In this example, the Look For list allows you to specify which record type Advanced Find will focus on. After you select the record type (in this example, Accounts), all related fields are available to you. You now proceed to the selection of specific fields, conditions, and values.

3. In the first row, select a field (in this example, Account Name) from the drop-down list by clicking the down arrow to the right of the field name.

Based on the field you choose, the system selects your available choices for conditions. You can see all the possible conditions by clicking the down arrow to the right of the Condition field.

4. Choose a condition.

The most commonly used conditions are Equal, Does Not Equal, Contains, Begins With, Contains Data, and Does Not Contain Data. Click the condition you want from the drop-down list. In the example, we chose Greater than.

5. Enter a value in the Value field.

Microsoft CRM allows you to have multiple values in this field *for those fields that have drop-down lists*. Relationship Type is an example of such a field. If you separate individual values with a semicolon (;), the system treats that semicolon as if it were an OR condition.

6. **Continue to the next row to add search criteria.**

   If you run out of rows, click the Select button to begin another row of criteria.

7. **Select two or more rows you want to connect with either AND or OR and then select the Group And or the Group Or button.**

   To the left of the two selection criteria, a box appears with either an AND or an OR inside. You can change your choice by selecting the down arrow within that box.

8. **Click the Save As button if you'd like to name your query and retain it for future use.**

9. **Click the Find button in the lower right corner to actually perform the search.**

Assigning and Sharing Accounts

The Actions button at the top of every account window enables you to assign or share your accounts. You can also delete or deactivate an account.

Deleting accounts is usually a bad idea because any records attached to an account, such as contacts or opportunities, also go away. After you delete an account, you can never retrieve the information, and you can't undo the action. Deletion is forever. However, if you had previously set up a subaccount, that subaccount remains.

Deactivating an account turns it off, rendering it inactive. You can't edit an inactive account or associate other types of records with it. It disappears from your usual lookups and is visible only if you specifically search for inactive accounts. The advantage of deactivating over deleting is that you can restore a deactivated account to active status should that become necessary. Any sub-accounts that were associated with the original account continue to be active, however.

Assigning accounts to users

If you go on an extended vacation, you may want to assign an account to another user. Or perhaps the territories your company covers are being realigned, and many accounts need to be tended to by other managers. If you assign one of your accounts to another user, that new person becomes the account owner, and you are removed from that position.

To assign one or more accounts, follow these steps:

1. **In the upper part of the navigation pane, select Accounts.**

   The Accounts window appears.

2. **Choose the accounts you want to reassign by clicking (highlighting) each account listing.**

   You can select multiple accounts by using the Shift key or the Ctrl key. The Shift key selects all the accounts from the first one you selected to the one you're currently positioned on. Hold down the Ctrl key and click to select noncontiguous accounts.

3. **Click the Assign icon (the little guy with the green megaphone).**

   The Assign Accounts window appears.

4. **Click the radio button next to Assign to Another User.**

5. **Click the magnifying glass at the end of the Assign to Another User field.**

   The Assign Account dialog box opens for choosing the new user.

6. **Select the new user and click OK.**

   The system returns to the Accounts window. You won't see the reassigned account in the list unless you change the View to Active Accounts.

Sharing accounts

Sharing is a little different from assigning. *Sharing* one of your accounts doesn't remove you from ownership; it merely adds additional users to the team servicing that account.

To share one or more accounts, follow these steps:

1. **Go to the Account List View and select all the Accounts you want to share.**

   You can select multiple Accounts at one time by using the Shift key or the Ctrl key. The Shift key selects all the Accounts from the first one you selected to the one you're currently positioned on. The Ctrl key allows you to randomly select individual Accounts.

2. **On the window's toolbar, choose Actions⇨Sharing.**

   The Who Would You Like to Share the Selected Account With window appears.

3. **Choose the users or the team from the Who Would You Like to Share This Account With dialog box.**

   After you select the users or teams, the system returns you to a List View with check boxes for the security privileges assigned to each user or team. By default, none of these privileges are assigned.

4. **Select the security privileges you want to give to each of the users with whom you're sharing by checking all the appropriate boxes.**

   For details on which type of security privileges each option allows, check out Chapter 8.

5. **To save these sharing specifications, click OK.**

Chapter 14

Creating and Managing Activities

*M*icrosoft CRM 4 comes with a basic activity management system that enables you to schedule or log activities associated with the various records in the database, such as opportunities, leads, contacts, accounts, or cases.

Your calendar is a subset of your activities and displays only appointments. Your activities show a wider assortment of things that take up your time, such as phone calls and miscellaneous tasks such as meeting with your boss or coordinating the company golf outing. In addition, only the appointments on your calendar are coordinated with Outlook. Phone calls and tasks never show up in the main area of Outlook.

Aside from the obvious practice of entering all your activities in the system to ensure that they're properly documented and that you don't forget to do them, workflow rules can also have an important role with activities in your business processes. Workflow rules can look for overdue activities and alert you to them. They can look for activities that should be scheduled (such as following up on a quote that you sent out a week ago or an annual mainte- nance contract that's due next month) and send a series of alerts to the right team members. This is a powerful use of scheduling, but it works well only if everyone on the team is consistently logging his or her activities. (We discuss workflow in detail in Chapter 9.)

The ingredients essential to activity management include viewing existing activities, entering new activities, delegating activities, the inevitable rescheduling of activities, and completing activities. In the next few pages, you'll find out how to manage your activities and, to the extent possible, the activities of others as well.

No Outlook Here

Microsoft designed its CRM product assuming that most users also use Outlook. In this chapter, we discuss how to use Microsoft CRM's activity management system assuming that you *aren't* using Outlook. This is a big assumption, but it helps simplify the discussion of calendar usage.

If you aren't using Outlook, you'll want to look at the Service Scheduling calendar as a way to keep you and your team members on the same page. You won't get any alarms about appointments or due dates. (Maybe you view this as a good thing!)

Chapter 2 covers using Outlook with Microsoft CRM. If you're an Outlook user, consider reviewing Chapter 2 next. Doing so will fill in the holes created in this chapter.

If you're coming to Microsoft CRM with experience using another CRM system, you may wonder where some of the more advanced teamwork functionality is hiding. So, before you start looking around, here are some of the program's shortcomings:

- ✔ To look at everyone else's activities, you have to go to the Service Scheduling area from the Navigation pane. Using Outlook via Exchange provides some assistance here, though, in that it allows for shared calendars.

- ✔ You can schedule other users to do something, but no convenient, automatic way exists to notify them that you did the scheduling. And because you can't see their calendar easily, you may end up scheduling them into a conflict. Outlook's Meeting Request is the answer to this situation. (And you can link Outlook Meeting Requests to CRM, so this is a viable workaround.)

- ✔ You can't set an alarm on any kind of activity to alert you to an upcoming event. Therefore, Microsoft also doesn't have a snooze button in CRM.

- ✔ The system doesn't automatically roll over activities from one day to the next if you don't complete something when you're supposed to. However, activities do remain on your calendar as past-due activities and show up on your activity list as long as you fail to complete them.

Some of these oversights are resolved if you're using the Outlook client. More on that in Chapter 2.

Having now finished our complaints, we must say, in all fairness, that Microsoft CRM enables you to schedule and track all the important activities associated with customers. If you use this feature consistently, you'll always be organized. You'll never forget to do the important things. You'll make more money, live longer, and prosper. But we do still need to easily see and share our staff's calendars. And, we've got to say it one more time: Use the Outlook client if you really want the system to work well for you.

Viewing Your Calendar

To display your calendar, click the Workplace button near the bottom of the navigation pane. Then, near the top of the pane, click Calendar, which appears under My Work. (If nothing appears under My Work, click the plus sign next to it to display the list.) The Calendar window appears on the right, as shown in Figure 14-1.

The service calendar displays the weekly view of appointments *and* service activities. Note that *service activities* are activities associated with the Service module that have not only a user but also company resources. The information is available also in the Service Scheduling window, which allows users to see other user's calendars and activities.

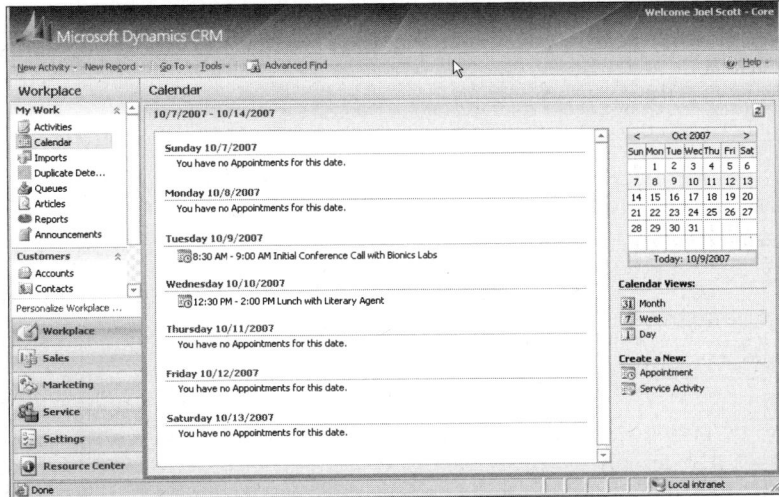

Figure 14-1:
A typical week in the life of a writer.

The area on the far right of the screen contains a calendar you can use to change the date or date range of the calendar display. You also can select from three display modes — month, week, and day.

The calendar is just a subset of your activities (only appointments and service-related activities) with a more graphical view of them.

Viewing Your Activities

If you really want to know what's on your agenda, the Activities window is the place to go to look at your open activities. To get there, select Activities under My Work at the top of the navigation pane. You can also set this as the default screen that shows up every time you start up CRM. This is discussed in Chapter 4. Figure 14-2 shows a typical Activities window. This is probably where your day should begin and where you should spend much of your professional life.

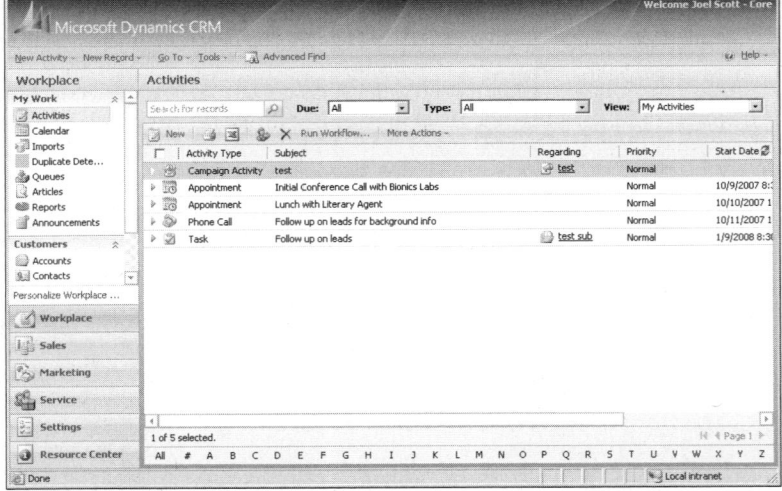

Figure 14-2:
A snapshot of the life of a certain writer.

Figure 14-2 shows the Activities window for appointments, but remember you can manage eight types of activities in Microsoft CRM:

- ✔ Tasks
- ✔ Fax
- ✔ Phone call
- ✔ E-Mail

✔ Letter

✔ Appointment

✔ Service Activity

✔ Campaign Response

Clicking the column title re-sorts your activities by that column, from ascending to descending order. Activities are sorted within each day's display. If you want to adjust the width of a column, drag the border between the column titles. You can change the columns displayed by saving your own Advanced Find searches, or your system administrator or implementation partner can create customized views.

At the top of the window, the Look For field allows you to locate scheduled activities based on the subject. Although you can use the alphabetical listing bar at the bottom of the window to locate Subjects beginning with a particular letter, the Look For field is more flexible. For example, you can enter consecutive characters, such as **flor**, to find activity subjects starting with, say, Florida. You can also use the wildcard character ***** to match any sequence of characters.

If you're trying to find all of your activities, enter ***** in the Look For field and then click the Find button. This displays both open and closed activities. You might think by just choosing My Activities in the View drop-down list, all your activities would be displayed. But you'd be missing the closed activities with that method of searching.

You can use the View menu (in the upper-right corner of the Activities window) to select from one of several views. Your selection of a view works with your Search for Records selection. These views are

✔ **All Activities:** This comprehensive list displays open and completed activities no matter whose they are.

✔ **Closed Activities:** These are all the completed activities the system contains — yours and everyone else's.

✔ **My Activities:** These are the activities on your schedule. This is probably the most important view and the one we use most often.

✔ **My Closed Activities:** These are all your completed activities that the system contains.

✔ **Open Activities:** These are all open activities, whether they belong to someone else or to you. Unfortunately, the default view doesn't show to whom they belong.

✔ **Scheduled Activities:** These are all your scheduled appointments.

Of course, there are no activities to view if you don't enter some in the first place. Creating these activities in CRM is the subject of the next section.

Creating an Appointment for Yourself from the Activities Screen

You can create an appointment for yourself directly from the Workplace, which Microsoft online help suggests. This method is quick, but you can easily cause yourself problems by flippantly agreeing to some appointment without first checking your calendar — or better yet, your activity list.

 An appointment is just a special kind of activity, and that's why we sometimes seem to refer to those two things (appointments and activities) almost interchangeably. The calendar shows only appointments, not tasks or phone calls. If you want to avoid scheduling two conference calls at the same time, for example, use the Activities window instead of the calendar.

You're always better off checking before you schedule appointments. For that reason, we recommend another approach to scheduling your appointments *when working online* in Microsoft CRM:

1. **Near the bottom of the navigation pane, click the Workplace button. At the top of the pane, select Activities (under My Work).**

   Review your schedule here before committing to another appointment or activity.

2. **On the Activities window's toolbar, click the New button.**

3. **Select an activity (such as Appointment) and then click OK.**

   Figure 14-3 shows a typical window for entering appointment details. We describe this screen in detail in a moment.

4. **Fill in the details.**

5. **When you're finished, click the Save and Close button.**

   You return to the Activities window.

The Appointment window is divided into three tabs: Appointment, Notes, and Details. The following fields deserve clarification or further elaboration:

✔ **Appointment tab:** the Appointment tab contains the information that will be transferred to your calendar display.

   • *Subject:* The text you enter in the Subject field appears in the Activities window and the Calendar window. In the weekly view of the calendar, the text wraps so you can see it all. In the daily view, if the text is too long, it's cut off.

   • *Required* and *Optional:* When you click the magnifying glass to the right of each of these fields, CRM presents a window allowing you to specify one or more people involved in the meeting. The first field, Required, is for those people for whom attendance is mandatory. The Optional field is for people not quite so important.

- *Regarding:* This field enables you to attach an activity to one or more records, such as contacts, accounts, or leads. By associating the activity with more than one record, you can then see the activity from any of those records.

- *Start Time* and *End Time:* If you don't enter a start and end time, particularly for appointments, the times aren't displayed on your calendar.

- *All Day Event:* By default, an event is a day-long activity. When you select an All Day Event, you no longer have the option of selecting specific times. However, you can specify the dates; if the end date is different from the beginning date, you create an activity that spans multiple days. Vacations are a good example of an appropriate use of All Day Event.

✔ **Details tab:** The Details tab houses the information on the meeting owner and the organizer — possibly two separate people.

✔ The *organizer* is the person coordinating the activity and isn't necessarily one of the attendees. This is the person you blame when the meeting is messed up.

✔ **Notes tab:** The Notes section is an unlabeled free-form text area that appears on the lines just below the time span and subject on the calendar.

That's what it takes to schedule something for yourself. One of the more powerful features of CRM systems is the ability to schedule activities for other people — that is, to delegate. That's what we discuss next.

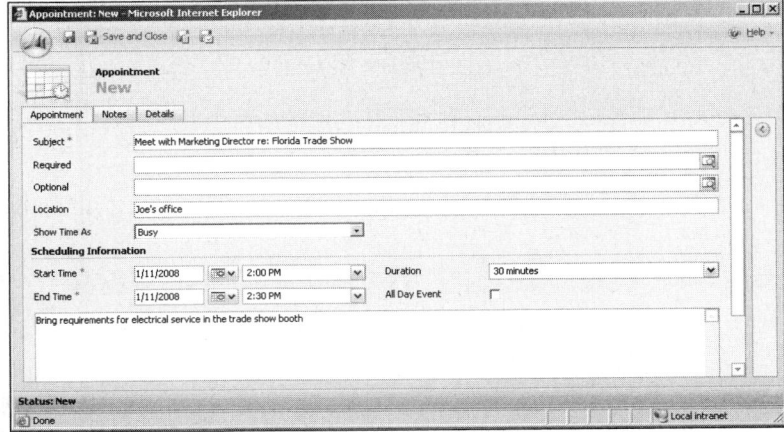

Figure 14-3:
Planning
to meet
with your
marketing
director.

Scheduling for Other People

How you use Outlook determines how you can best schedule activities for others on your team. Specifically, if calendar sharing is enabled in Outlook, scheduling is easy. Even if sharing isn't enabled, you can use Outlook's meeting request functionality to assist in setting up activities for other people. We discuss Outlook in detail in Chapter 2. Assuming you aren't using Outlook, you still have a few options.

Because you can't actually see anyone else's complete schedule using Microsoft CRM, it would be improper to even try to put anything directly on someone else's calendar. So you're left with two options when attempting to schedule the activities of others: e-mail requests and instant messaging.

You can use Microsoft CRM's e-mail system to send an activity "suggestion" to one or more users on your team. You can attach the e-mail to the appropriate record and request that the other users schedule that phone call or appointment. Chapter 2 discusses e-mail in some detail.

The second method for coordinating your activities with other members of your team is to use one of the instant messaging systems. They're free, which makes them even more appealing. The most common ones are Microsoft's Instant Messenger, Yahoo!, AOL, Trillian, and ICQ. In addition, Microsoft CRM version 4 now has an "Integrated Office Communicator" which is really a fancy way of saying that Instant Messaging is built-in. It's your System Administrator's task to set this up if your organization thinks it's appropriate.

Several compelling reasons exist for implementing such a system. You can see who's online and available at any given moment. You can coordinate with users who are widely separated geographically. We like the instant part of the equation also. In addition, some instant messaging systems keep a history of your messages. You could, when the conversation is over, cut and paste the message history into the Notes section of the appropriate record.

In a flash, you can ask another user to call a client and get a confirmation that that task is going to happen. This is an ideal way to respond to a client call requesting service or support.

Assigning an Activity to Someone

When you create an activity, you can assign it directly to yourself (by default) or to another user or to a queue. Similarly, you can reassign an activity to another user or to a queue. When you do reassign an activity, the ownership of that activity doesn't change until the intended user or queue accepts the assignment. You can assign activities from anywhere in CRM, but you can accept them only from the Queues area of the Workplace.

Assigning an activity is our favorite. We love to delegate. To do so, follow these steps:

1. **Near the bottom of the navigation pane, click the Workplace button. At the top of the pane, under My Work, click Activities.**

   The Activities window appears on the right. Based on your selection in the View field, you see some or all of your scheduled activities.

2. **Select one or more activities that you want to assign to someone else.**

   In Figure 14-4, we've selected two activities.

   You can select one or more activities by highlighting those activities and using either the Shift key (for contiguous activities) or the Ctrl key (for noncontiguous activities.)

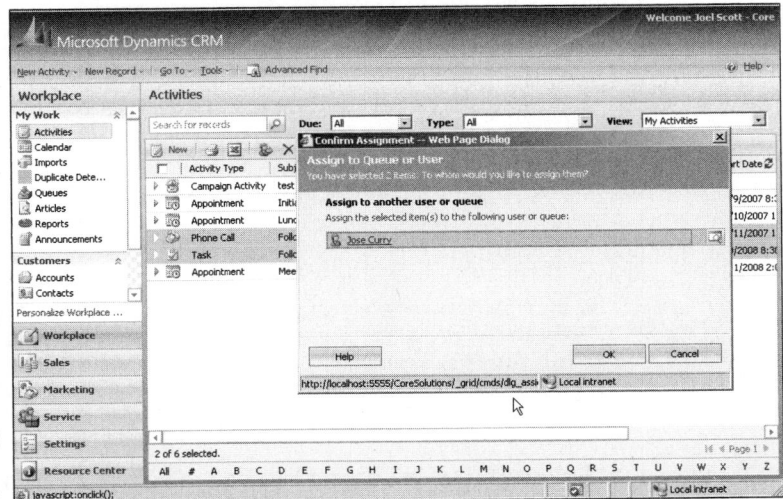

Figure 14-4: Delegating everything you don't want to do.

3. **Click the Assign option from the Activities drop-down list.**

   The Assign to Queue or User dialog box appears, leading you through the sequence of actions to delegate all the activities you highlighted in Step 2.

4. **Click the magnifying glass at the end of the field to see the entire list of users to whom you might assign these activities.**

5. **Select one or more users from the list. Make sure you notify the assignees either by setting an alarm, sending an Instant Message, sending an e-mail, or by yelling down the hall.**

6. **Click OK.**

   CRM returns to the Activities window.

You can also choose to delete activities, but this is generally a poor choice because you can't undo a deletion. If an activity is canceled, you should complete it (see the next section) and include a note that the activity was canceled by the client or by a user.

Completing an Activity

Nothing is as satisfying as getting things off of your activity list. To complete, or close, an activity, follow these steps:

1. **Near the bottom of the navigation pane, click the Workplace button. At the top of the pane, under My Work, click Activities.**

   The Activities window appears on the right.

2. **To follow along with the example, select an appointment that you want to mark as completed.**

   The Appointment window appears, with three tabs: Appointment, Notes, and Details.

3. **Click the Actions button and Add a Note to create a note that will be attached to the record. Save and close the Note.**

   Documenting what you do is important so that the historical trail for this record is complete.

4. **Click the Actions button and complete the activity as shown in Figure 14-5.**

We have a saying in our office: "If it's not in CRM, you didn't do it." A rough translation is that unless you enter your activities and close them when you've completed them, there's no evidence that you did anything. Later, you'll be explaining to a skeptical boss that you really did make those follow-up calls but just didn't bother completing them in CRM. Complete every activity immediately afterwards. Then there's no doubt.

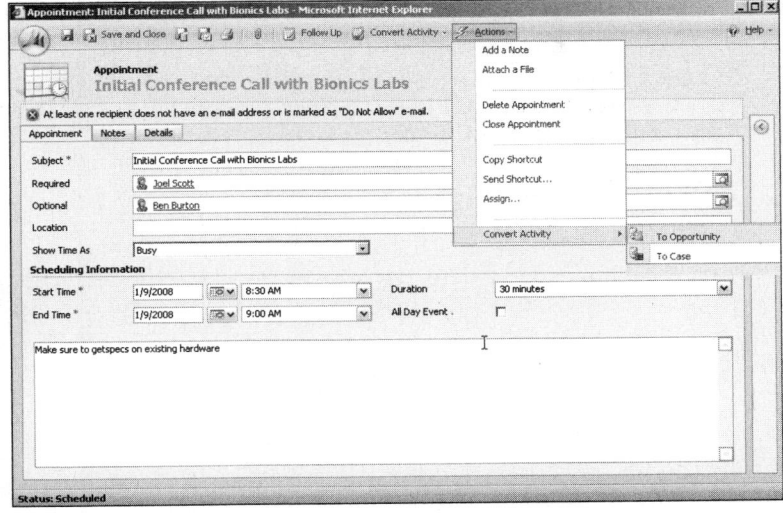

Chapter 15

Using Notes and Attachments

In This Chapter
- ▶ Creating a note
- ▶ Adding an attachment
- ▶ Deleting a note or an attachment

A lmost every type of record in the Microsoft CRM system enables you to post notes and link attachments. Think of a *note* as information that you manually type into the system. For example, if you find out that your main contact at an account is about to leave, you probably want to document that and create an action plan. Meetings and phone calls deserve this kind of follow-up documentation as well. At our company, every meeting and phone call and almost every kind of activity is documented with notes so we have an audit trail of what we've promised or accomplished.

Attachments include a variety of files that are linked to individual records. These files may be the typical Word documents or Excel spreadsheets, or they may be PowerPoint presentations, digital photos, contracts, images of faxes, and so on — almost anything.

In this chapter, you find out how to create and maintain notes and attachments, processes that have been significantly streamlined in version 4.

With regard to relating notes and attachments to other records — you can't do it. Notes and attachments are assigned to the one record they're initially attached to — and that's it. Sorry.

Creating Notes

You can associate notes with any kind of existing record, whether it's an account, a contact, or a case, from the Customer Service area. All of these types of records include a Notes tab. For example, Figure 15-1 shows the Notes tab for a typical account record.

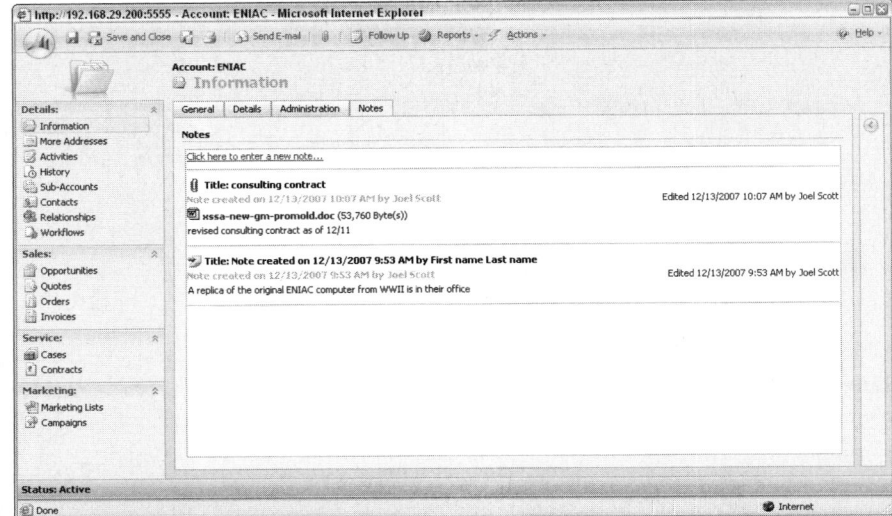

To create a new note relating to a particular account, follow these steps:

1. **At the top of the navigation pane, click Accounts.**

   The system displays the Accounts window. We use accounts here as an example, but remember that what you do here applies equally well to contact, lead, opportunity, and case records. In fact, almost every type of record in CRM has a Notes field.

2. **Select the specific account to which you want to attach a note.**

3. **Click the Notes tab at the top of the account's screen.**

4. **Click the blue hyperlink that reads "Click here to enter a new note."**

5. **Type your text in the rectangular area, as shown in Figure 15-2.**

6. **When you've finished entering text, click Save and Close.**

The next time you return to the Notes tab for this account, you'll see the note you entered, as well as the date and time and your name. This is one of the few areas in Microsoft CRM where you don't have to manually save your work because you simply could have navigated away from your newly entered Note by selecting another option from the navigation pane. You can see the completed note in Figure 15-3.

Notes don't have spell checking or grammar checking. If you're challenged in this department and think that others may end up reviewing your notes (and they probably will), use Word to create your notes and spell check and grammar check them there. Then either cut and paste the Word text into the notes section or attach the Word file, as explained in the next section.

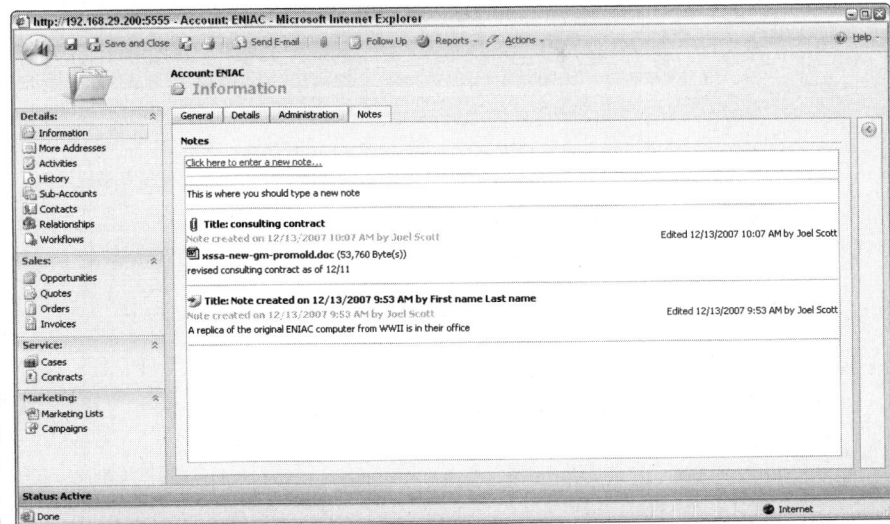

Figure 15-2:
Entering a
new note.

Creating Attachments

Attachments are separate files that you may associate with individual
records such as accounts, contacts, opportunities, and cases. An attachment
can be a Word document, but it can just as well be, say, an electronic set of
blueprints, or a series of digital photos, or a spreadsheet.

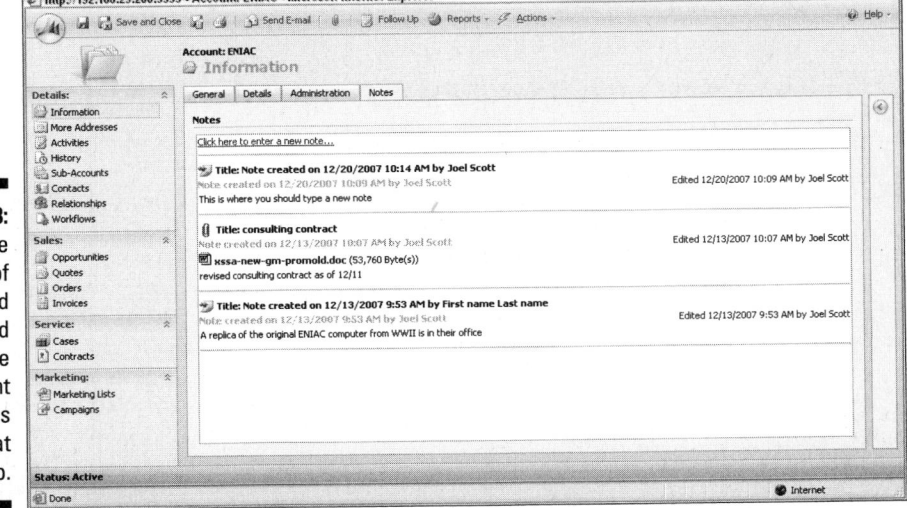

Figure 15-3:
The
evidence of
a completed
and saved
note. The
most recent
note is
always at
the top.

You can add a note but not an associated attachment by using the Notes tab at the top of most records. You can add a single attachment, but you can't make notes, by choosing Actions➪Attach a File. A better and more general approach follows.

To add a note as an attachment, follow these steps:

1. **Navigate to the record to which you want to attach a note or a file.**

2. **On the menu bar (at the top of the screen), choose Actions➪Add a Note.**

   The Note: New window appears, as shown in Figure 15-4. The system automatically fills in the Regarding field.

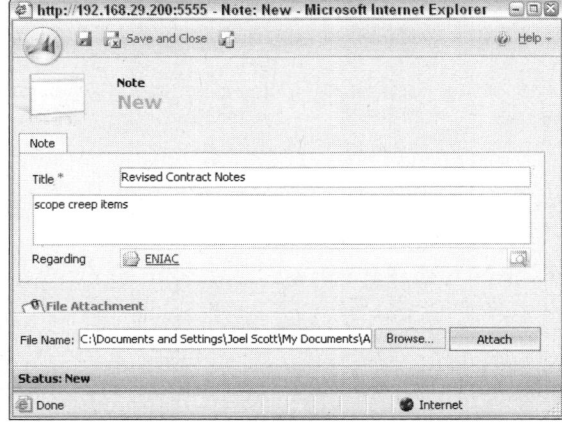

Figure 15-4:
Adding notes and attachments at the same time.

3. **Enter a title in the Title text box.**

4. **Enter a description in the large text box (below the word *Title).***

   The information you type in the larger field is displayed in the listing of all associated notes — *not* what you enter in the Title field.

5. **Use the Browse button to locate and select the file you want to attach.**

6. **Click the Attach button.**

   The system uploads your file to the server for storage. This gives other users (with the proper access rights) the ability to see the file and also gives you access to it from any other computer you may be using later.

You can attach only one file per note. All attachments are stored on the server, so when you're first attaching a file or using it in some way, the system needs to move it using your Internet connection. Virtually any kind of file is a candidate for an attachment. The maximum size of the file that you can attach to a record is defined by your system administrator, but if you expect to upload or download attachments from the server frequently, try not to bog the system down with enormous files. (Video clips, fax images, and the like are often pretty big.)

Deleting a Note or an Attachment

If you need to change the file attached to a record, perhaps because the file itself has changed, you need to delete the original attachment. After an attachment is attached to the note, you can delete the attachment by clicking the Remove button.

To delete a note associated with a record, follow these steps:

1. **Navigate to the record.**

   If you're deleting a note associated with an account, for example, select Accounts from the upper part of the navigation pane and then select the specific record from the Accounts window.

2. **Click the record's Notes tab.**

   All notes associated with this record appear.

3. **Highlight and then right-click the note you want to delete.**

   The text of the note appears.

4. **A context menu appears from which you can select the Delete option. See Figure 15-5.**

   The Confirm Deletion dialog box then appears, telling you that you are about to delete not only this particular note but also any associated attachment.

5. **Click OK to proceed.**

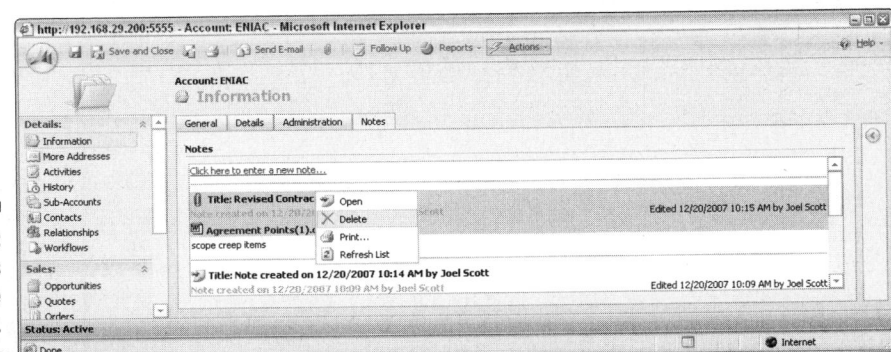

Figure 15-5: Your note is about to bite the dust.

Deleting an attachment without deleting the associated note is now much easier than in prior versions of CRM. Follow these steps:

1. **Navigate to the record.**

2. **Click the record's Notes tab.**

   All notes associated with this record appear.

3. **Double-click the note with an attachment that you want to delete.**

   The text of the note appears.

4. **Click the Remove button in the lower-right corner. See Figure 15-6.**

   A confirmation screen appears with a warning that when you remove the attachment, it's really gone. However, you can always reattach the same file anytime you want to.

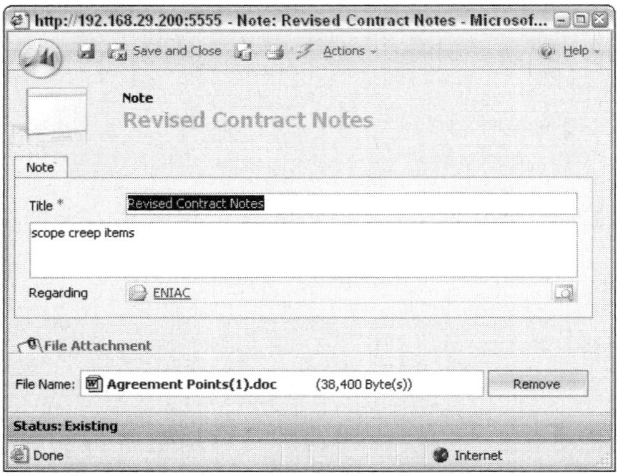

Figure 15-6:
Your attachment is about to bite the dust.

5. **Click OK.**

   Another confirmation screen appears.

6. **Click Save and Close to complete this action.**

Chapter 16

Generating Quotes, Orders, and Invoices

Microsoft CRM manages the entire process of generating quotations, orders, and invoices. An essential ingredient in developing quotes is the product catalog, which we describe in Chapter 7. The product catalog contains your list of products and their prices and discount structures. Microsoft CRM's quotation system draws from these products, prices, and discounts to create pricing specific to each customer.

After you generate a quote and give it to a customer, the best scenario is that the quote comes back as a signed order. The second-best scenario is that the quote comes back for revisions. Even after a quote is converted to an order, however, you can still revise it (until you send it to the accounting system). After an order goes to accounting, it becomes an invoice.

Although the logical flow is from quote to order to invoice, you can also create an order without creating a quote. And, in the same way, you can create an invoice without having created either a quote or an invoice. As you can see, you can start anywhere in the cycle.

In this chapter, we cover how to use Microsoft CRM to create a quotation, turn the quote into an order, and make the order into an invoice.

Creating and Activating Quotes

Several years ago, we met with a very large distributor of paper products. They had been in business for more than a hundred years and had a hundred million dollars of revenue. Their entire quotation procedure was a verbal system. They never even wrote down what price they had quoted. When the customer called back to order something, the salespeople would simply ask what price they'd been given! We never got the go-ahead on installing a quotation system because they didn't think such a thing could possibly work.

If your quotation system involves something more formal than just telling your clients their prices during a phone conversation, you need to generate a formal, written quotation.

Most quotes go through more than one iteration. Initially, you create a draft of your quote. You can continue editing your draft quote until it's ready to send. At that point, you activate the quote (also making it read-only) and send it to the customer.

You can make multiple revisions of an activated quote, and each revision is stored as a separate record. The quote is then either accepted if it's won or closed if it's lost. If it's accepted, it's recorded as part of the order history.

Creating a quote

Most significant sales are preceded by a series of quotes or proposals.

(Many people confuse proposals with quotations. *Proposals* are quotations on steroids; they include a great deal more background, discussion, and analysis in addition to the more typical one- or two-page quotation. CRM doesn't have a built-in proposal system, but you can find third-party proposal systems that integrate with Microsoft CRM in Chapter 27.)

To create a new quote, follow these steps:

1. **At the bottom of the navigation pane, click the Sales button.**

2. **In the upper part of the navigation pane, select Quotes.**

   The Quotes window appears, displaying all your existing quotes.

3. **On the Quotes window's toolbar, click the New button.**

   The quote record appears, as shown in Figure 16-1, with General, Shipping, Addresses, Administration, and Notes tabs.

   On the General tab, the quote ID is a unique, system-generated number that can help you identify the quote later. The revision ID is also created and maintained by the system and enables you (and the system) to

track all the various versions of quotes that you have created and activated. The Quote ID and Revision ID fields are filled in *after* you save the
quote. These fields cannot be filled in and will appear grayed out. For
that reason, clicking the Save button (the disk icon) after you enter the
Name, Potential Customer, and Price List fields is essential. You don't
need to click Save and Close until you have filled in all the relevant fields
in each of the five tab areas.

4. **In the Name field, enter some text that describes what this quote is
all about.**

   For example, you might type **Microsoft CRM Training Class in Maui**.
   After you save all the details of the quote, the text in this Name field will
   appear in the Quotes window.

5. **In the Potential Customer field, select an account or a contact to associate with the quote.**

   To do so, click the magnifying glass to the right of the field to display the
   Look Up Records dialog box for Accounts and Contacts. Alternatively,
   you can select a customer from the Form Assistant on the right.
   Whichever method you choose, select the appropriate record from the
   list and click OK. The system returns you to the General tab.

6. **In the Price List field, use the magnifying glass or the Form Assistant
to select a price list.**

7. **In the Currency field, use the magnifying glass or the Form Assistant
to select a Currency.**

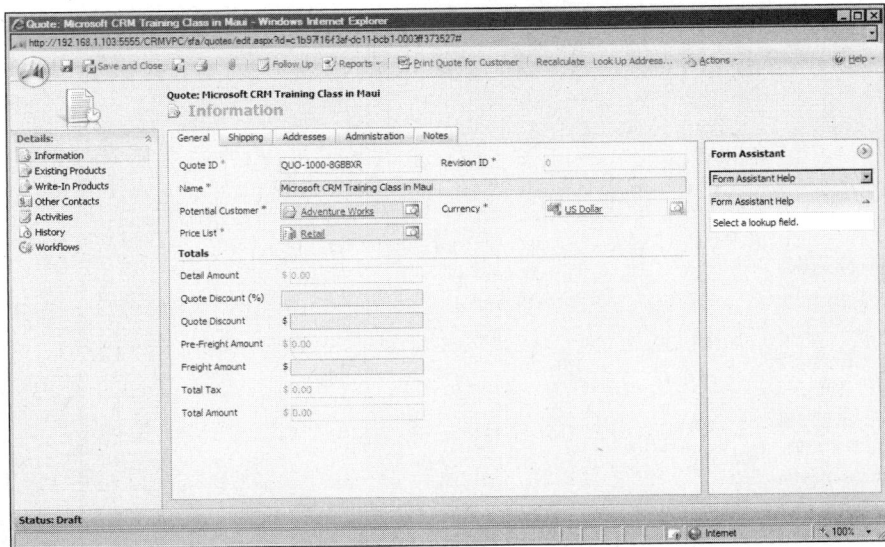

Figure 16-1:
Developing
a new
quote.

8. Now is a good time to click Save (the disk icon).

CRM displays the quote ID number in the Quote ID field. (If you were revising a quote, CRM would also populate the Revision ID field.)

9. In the Totals section of the General tab, enter the Quote Discount and Freight Amount.

Microsoft CRM calculates the total amount and displays it in the last field in the General tab. Several fields on this screen, such as Detail Amount and Pre-Freight Amount, are system generated. You can tell because these fields are outlined in black rather than blue.

10. Click the Shipping tab and fill in the following:

a. Enter information into the Effective From, Effective To, Requested Delivery Date, and Due By fields.

Each of these date fields has an associated calendar display (little grid box icons with a red oval in them) just to the right. (See Figure 16-2.) Clicking the calendar and then choosing a date is usually easier than manually typing a date directly into the field.

b. Enter the Shipping Method, Payment Terms, and Freight Terms.

Each of these fields has an associated drop-down menu. If your system is integrated with an accounting system, these fields can be filled in automatically.

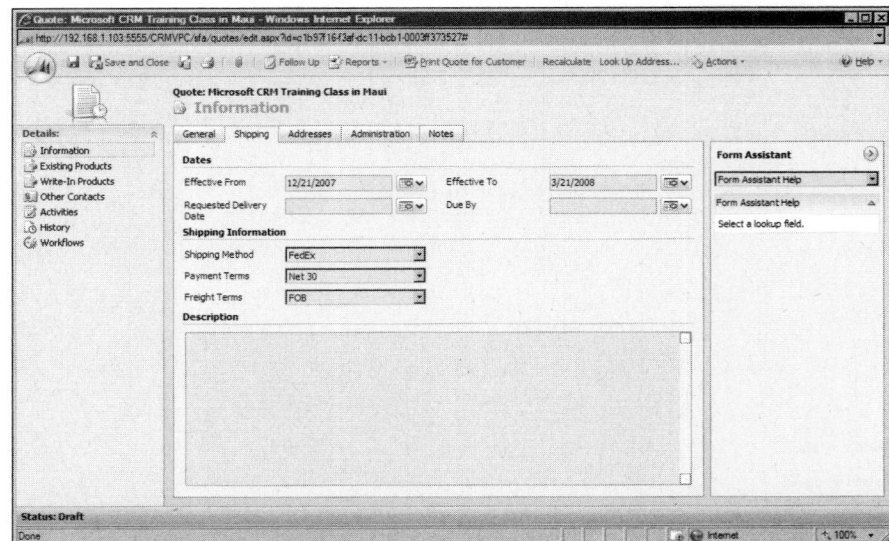

Figure 16-2:
The Shipping tab — delivering the goods.

11. **Click the Addresses tab (see Figure 16-3) and enter the Bill To and Ship To information.**

    To look up this address information, click the Look Up Address button on the toolbar.

    If the customer will be picking up the items, select Will Call for the Ship To option (the first option in the Ship To Address section).

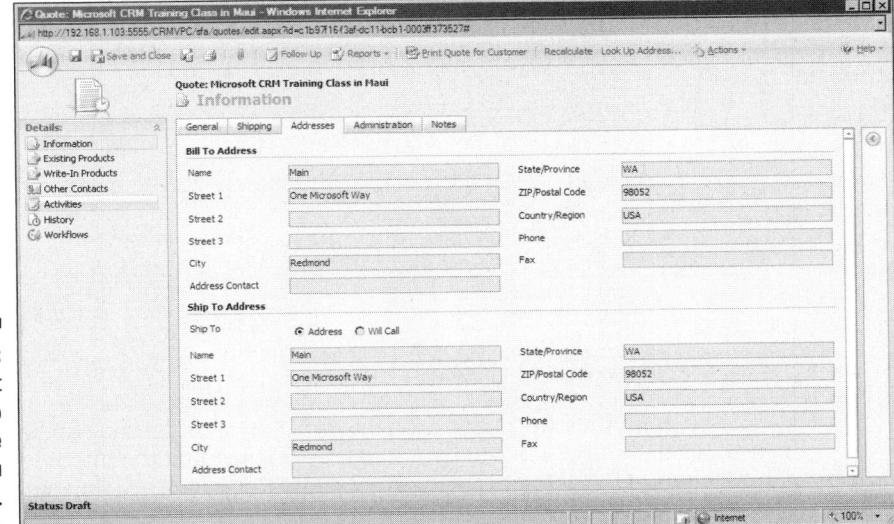

12. **If you want to associate your quote with an opportunity, start the quote from the opportunity screen or do the following:**

    a. *Click the Administration tab. (See Figure 16-4.)*

    b. *Use the magnifying glass in the Opportunity field to find and select that opportunity.*

    c. *Click OK.*

13. **Click the Save and Close button to save your quote.**

    The system returns to the Quotes window.

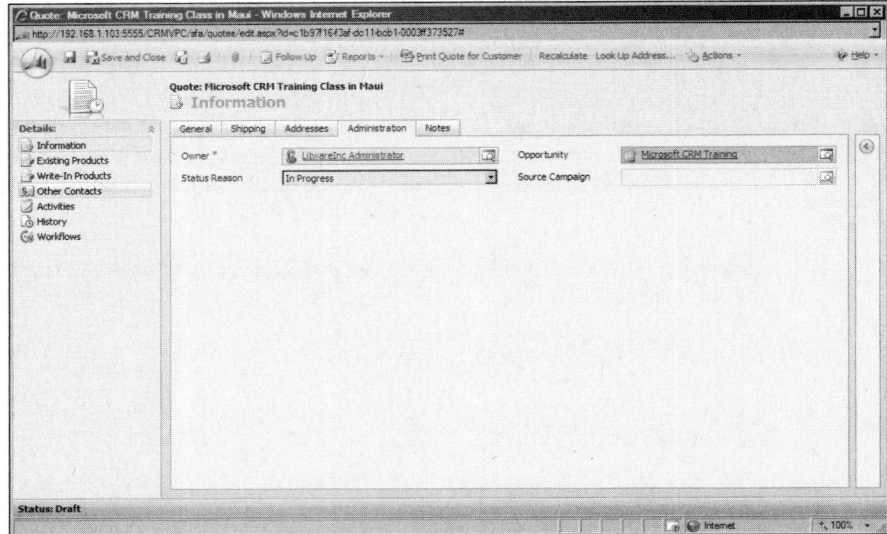

Figure 16-4:
Store admin-istrative details of the quote here.

Activating a quote

When you first create a quotation, it's officially a draft. You can modify the draft as many times as necessary. But before sending the quote to a customer, you must activate the quote. Follow these steps to do so:

1. **In the Quotes window, select the quote you want to activate.**

   The details of the quote appear.

2. **On the menu bar (at the top of the screen), choose Actions⇨ Activate Quote.**

   The quote now becomes read-only, and you can turn it into an order when the time comes.

3. **To save changes and continue working, click Save (the disk icon); to save changes and close the form, click the Close button.**

After you have activated the quote, it's no longer a draft and the system creates an official quotation. If the customer then requests a revision to the quote, you can modify that quote. The system stores an additional record with its own revision ID for each modified quote, so you may have a long series of quotes as you continue to revise activated quotes.

Associating Opportunities and Quotes

Opportunity records house all of your sales forecast information. By associating an opportunity with a quote, you allow the system to calculate the estimated revenue for the opportunity automatically. As you revise an associated quotation by changing products or discounts, those changes to the revenue stream are reflected in your overall forecast.

You can associate a quote with an opportunity or vice versa. If the opportunity doesn't exist yet, you need to create it before you can associate it with a quote.

We go through the steps of associating a quote with an opportunity record:

1. **In the Opportunities window, select the opportunity that needs an associated quote.**

2. **With the opportunity record displayed, click Quotes in the navigation pane (under Sales).**

   A list of all associated quotes appears in the main window.

3. **If no quotes are yet associated with the opportunity, click the New Quote button in the window's toolbar. If quotes already exist, you can edit them if necessary.**

4. **Whether you're entering a new quote or editing an existing quote, proceed with entering the information as detailed in Step 4 of the "Creating a quote" section, earlier in this chapter.**

5. **Assemble the individual items you want listed in your quote by clicking Existing Products from the navigation pane or if you're quoting a custom product or something that isn't in the products list, select Write-In Products from the navigation pane.**

Because we started this exercise from an opportunity record, the quote we just created is automatically associated with this opportunity. No need to do any further association!

Printing a Quote

After you finish developing a quote and activate it, it's a good idea to do a quick Microsoft CRM print. Follow these steps:

1. **From the Quotes window, select the quote you want to print.**

   Your quote record appears on the screen.

2. **Choose File⇨Print or click Print Quote for Customer in the toolbar.**

   A preview of your quote appears so you can review it for accuracy.

3. **When your previewed quote looks okay, you can send it to your printer by clicking the Print button.**

   Your bare-bones quotation prints, displaying the information from each of the tab areas of your quote.

In most cases, this information won't be formatted in your organization's style. The good news is that you aren't locked into a specific quotation format. The bad news is that you need to create a format rather than select from some canned ones.

Your system administrator or dealer can assist with the development of specially formatted printouts and reports.

Converting a Quote to an Order

A successfully presented quote becomes an order. Only a previously activated (status = active) quote can be turned into an order. The steps to change a quote into an order are easy:

1. **In the Quotes window, click the active quote.**

   The details of the quote appear.

2. **On the Quotes window's toolbar, click Create Order.**

   The Create Order dialog box appears, as shown in Figure 16-5. The Status Reason of the quote has automatically changed to Won. You can see the Status in the list of quotes as long as the View is All Quotes. The opportunity is no longer part of your forecasted sales because it's now a done deal. Today's date is automatically filled in, although you can modify this if necessary.

3. **Select the Close Opportunity option and click OK.**

   The opportunity is closed and no longer appears in the list of Active Opportunities (that is, when the View is set to Active Opportunities).

4. **The quote window closes and a new window opens showing the details of the newly created order.**

Generating Invoices from Orders

When you're ready to ship your goods or services to the customer, you use the information in the order to generate an invoice to the customer. Follow these steps:

1. **In the lower part of the navigation pane, click the Sales button. In the upper part of the pane, select Orders.**

   The Orders window appears.

2. **Make sure the View menu (in the upper right) is set to All Orders.**

3. **Select the order you want to make into an invoice.**

4. **Click the Create Invoice button.**

   Microsoft CRM automatically generates and displays the invoice for you. Unless your system is integrated to a Dynamics accounting application, however, that invoice goes nowhere. Your invoice is typically printed (or delivered in some other electronic way) from your accounting system.

5. **Click Save and Close.**

One of the most compelling things about generating quotes, orders, and invoices is CRM's ability to integrate with accounting software. The extent or ease of this integration depends on the accounting software you're using. If you're using Microsoft Dynamics GP, for example, Microsoft has the integration you need. If you're using accounting software not from Microsoft, you'll probably need a third-party module to integrate the two. See Chapter 27 for information on sources for this type of integration.

Chapter 17

Setting Up Sales Literature and Dealing with Competitors

*T*he Sales Literature area is really a document management system. After you set up your subjects (formerly known as the Subject Manager) to provide the structure for your company's document library, you can file individual pieces of sales literature for future reference. (See Chapter 23 for full details about how to set up the subjects.)

Subjects create an organizational structure for your literature, documents, and brochures. Think of it as the Dewey Decimal System for your own library. The Sales Literature area allows you to stock the shelves. And the shelves, by the way, are on the server — not your local computer.

You may also want to keep track of your competitors and their sales literature. This information is particularly important when competing for projects. What you find out (even in a losing battle) may help you win the next one.

Adding Literature

All new literature must be categorized by subject. This means your subjects must be set up with a structure to house your documents. (As mentioned, see Chapter 23 for information on subjects.)

To add a piece of literature — or any document or file — to the Sales Literature area, follow these steps:

1. **In the lower part of the navigation pane, click the Sales button.**

2. **In the upper part of the navigation pane, select Sales Literature.**

   The Sales Literature window appears, as shown in Figure 17-1.

3. **On the Sales Literature window's toolbar, click the New button.**

   The Sales Literature: New window appears, as shown in Figure 17-2. This is the main information screen for entering and cataloging your literature.

4. **In the Title field, enter a title for your article.**

5. **In the Subject field, select a subject as follows:**

   a. Click the magnifying glass to the right of the Subject field.

   The Look Up Records window appears.

   b. Select a subject from the list.

6. **In the Type field, click the arrow and choose an item from the list.**

   This list displays likely topic descriptions for your literature.

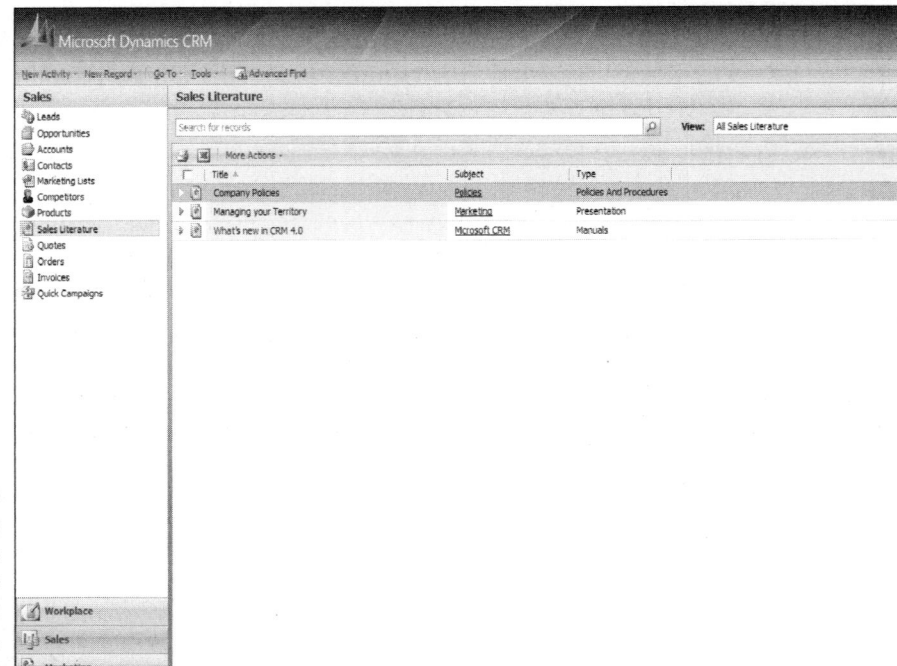

Figure 17-1:
Your sales
literature
appears in a
typical view.

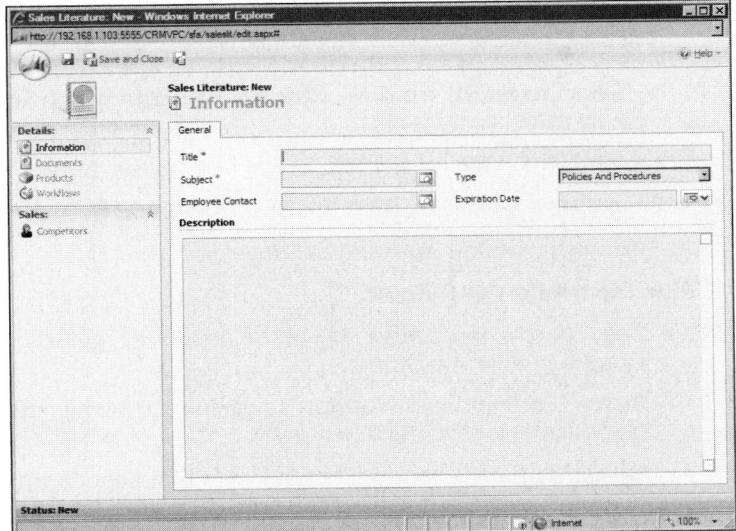

Figure 17-2:
Entering a
new article.

7. **If you want, associate a user with this literature as follows:**

   a. Click the magnifying glass to the right of the Employee Contact field.

   b. Select an employee to associate with the literature.

   This is probably the person on your staff who developed the literature or the one who is responsible for the documentation.

8. **To the right of the Expiration Date field, click the calendar icon and select a date for your document to expire.**

   For example, you may have a sale advertisement or a company policy that expires on a particular date.

9. **If you want, enter an abstract of the document in the Description field.**

10. **Click Save (the disk icon) or the Save and Close button.**

    If you select Save, the system saves what you've entered so far but remains on this same New Literature screen awaiting further edits. If you click Save and Close, the system returns to the Sales Literature window.

So far, you've entered only general information about the document. You still need to attach the document to the listing you just created. Follow these steps:

1. **In the Sales Literature window, click the listing to which you want to add one or more documents.**

2. **In the window's pane on the left, select Documents (under Details).**

3. **On the window's toolbar, click the New Document button.**

   The Document window appears, as shown in Figure 17-3.

4. **Fill in the window as follows:**

   a. *Title:* Enter a descriptive title of the document, possibly including a version number or a date.

   b. *Author:* Enter either the author's name or the name of the person responsible for the document.

   c. *Keywords:* Enter one or more keywords that anyone with access to the database can use later to locate any document with one keyword or a combination of keywords.

   d. *Abstract:* This is a short summary of the document's contents.

   e. *File Name:* This field connects Microsoft CRM to the stored file. You can use the Browse button to the right of the File Name field to locate the document.

5. **Click the Attach button in the lower-right corner of the window.**

   Doing so attaches the document entered in the File Name field and uploads the document to the server.

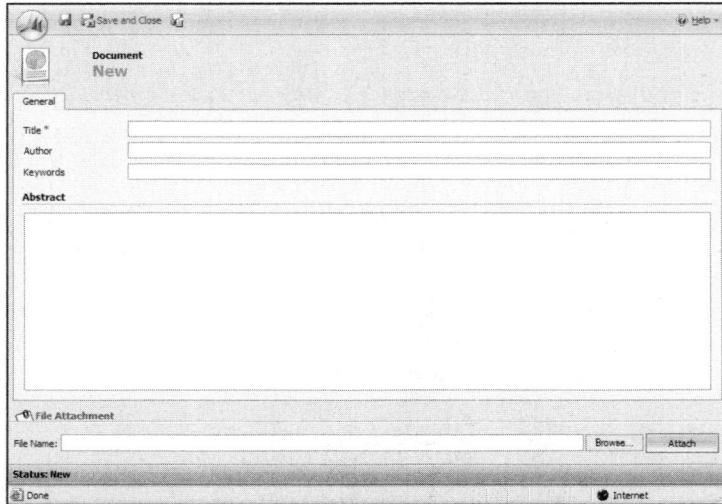

Figure 17-3:
Entering the
specifics for
a piece of
literature.

6. **Click the Save and Close button at the top of the window.**

   The system returns to the listing of documents associated with this particular subject.

   Each title can be associated with multiple documents. When you complete step 6 above, you will be at the Sales Literature main window. To add a new document, simply repeat steps 3–6 above. The structure of the entire title listing is similar to an organization chart, with each parent record capable of having multiple children. For example, you might have a document with pricing and terms and a separate document dealing with confidentiality associated with consulting agreements. This is done by working with subjects. Subjects are a way to organize records and to tie them together. All Sales Literature is categorized by subjects that are created in a hierarchy. We talk more about subjects in Chapter 23.

All documents are stored on the server. If you attach a document that's currently stored locally on your hard drive, Microsoft CRM makes a copy of the document on the server. This way, other users (if they have access rights) will have access to the document. When you need to retrieve the document, you have a choice of downloading it from the server or just opening it directly from the server.

Modifying Literature

Microsoft CRM copies documents to the server so that all authorized team members can use them. Therefore, at least two copies of the same document exist — one on your local computer and one on the server. Users may have their own original copy of the document on their own machine. Keep in mind that you want everyone to work from the same version of the document.

Several document management systems allow multiple users to contribute to the same document, more or less simultaneously. Even Microsoft Word has a facility called Track Changes. Each contributor is automatically assigned a color, and you can easily see who has done what to the document. It's also easy to gracefully remove all signs of editing before printing the final edition.

You need one central repository for the current copies of all literature. That can be the Microsoft CRM server, or it can be another readily accessible server, as long as everyone understands where the active documents are stored. If you use CRM as a document repository, keep in mind any user of the system has access to view and download it.

Assuming that the CRM server is the central library for current documents, follow these steps to edit an existing piece of literature:

1. **In the Sales Literature window, click the row that contains the document you want to edit.**

   The General tab for that subject appears. You will soon have access to the documents so that you can edit one or more of them.

2. **In the pane on the left, select Documents.**

   You see a list of all the documents related to this subject.

3. **Click the document you need to edit.**

   At the bottom of the window is a link to that document. This document, or attachment, is housed on the CRM server.

4. **Click the link to the document and save it on your local drive.**

   You can't edit the document while it's on the CRM server.

5. **Edit the document and save your changes on your local drive.**

6. **Upload the document to the CRM server so other users can access it.**

   If you simply reattach the document, it uploads automatically. Revision numbers aren't automatically associated with revised documents, so you might want to include a revision number in the file name or title of the document. In addition, you can track revisions, at least a little, by checking the Modified On date that appears in the Sales Literature window.

Relating Literature to Competitors

One of the more compelling aspects of the design of Microsoft CRM is the ability to relate one kind of record to another. Suppose you want to associate a piece of sales literature with a competitor. You collect sample brochures from each of your competitors. You then catalog them in the Sales Literature area and relate each brochure to the appropriate competitor. To do this, follow these steps:

1. **In the lower part of the navigation pane, click the Sales button.**

2. **In the upper part of the navigation pane, select Competitors.**

   A list of all competitors appears in the window on the right.

3. **Select the appropriate competitor.**

   The General tab for that competitor's information appears.

4. **In the pane on the left, select Sales Literature (under Sales).**

   The Sales Literature window appears, showing all existing sales literature associated with the competitor you selected.

5. **Select the piece of literature that you want to associate with this competitor by clicking the appropriate row in the list.**

   You can also set up a new piece of sales literature from here, as shown in the "Adding Literature" section, earlier in this chapter.

6. **In the window's toolbar, click the Save button to save your association of sales literature with the competitor.**

Adding and Tracking Competitors

Whenever you're in a competitive situation, knowing as much as possible about the opposition is a good idea. You want to track their strengths so that you can anticipate the ammunition they'll use against you. You want to know their weaknesses so you can exploit them. Yes, it's a tough world out there.

It's a good idea not only to track the products they sell but also to compile as much literature about those products as possible. Your competitor's Web site is a great place to go to compile, download, and cut and paste all the information you can find. To add a new competitor to the database, follow these steps:

1. **At the bottom of the navigation pane, click the Sales button.**

2. **At the top of the navigation pane, select Competitors.**

3. **In the Competitors window's toolbar, click the New button.**

   The data entry window shown in Figure 17-4 appears.

Finding your competitors

You may occasionally find yourself in a competitive situation but not know exactly who your competitor is. Maybe you know the general geographic location of your competitor. The Advanced Find feature may come to your rescue. For example, if you're competing to sell computer clones against another dealer somewhere in Connecticut, you could use the Advanced Find feature to find likely contenders. Choose Tools⇨Advanced Find in the Competitors window to access the Advanced Find feature.

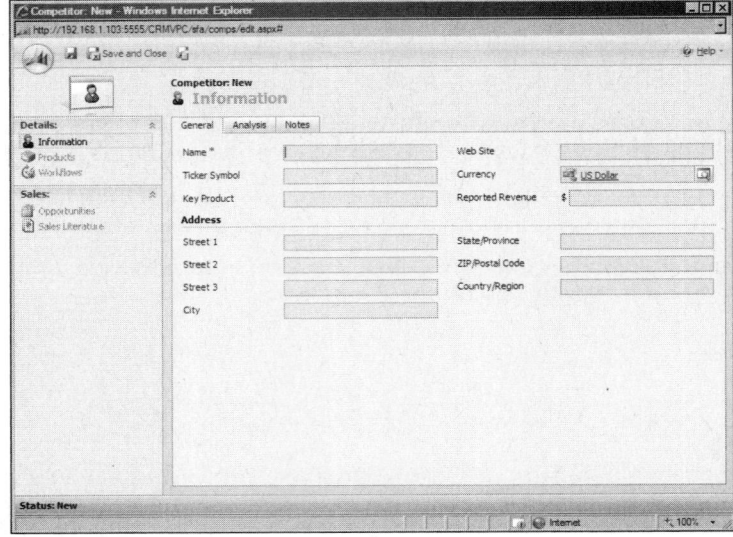

Figure 17-4:
Entering
data on
another
annoying
competitor.

   4. **Enter at least the one required field, Name, and as many of the other fields as you can.**

      Filling in the Key Product and Address fields may come in handy.

   5. **Click the Analysis tab.**

      The Analysis tab has five general, text-based topics for you to fill in. If you've ever taken any Miller Heiman sales training, some of these topics may look familiar.

   6. **In these five fields, enter everything you know or suspect about the competitor.**

   7. **Click the Save and Close button.**

Compiling a library of your organization's literature is one of the more useful things you can do for the group. Whether it's just for internal consumption or, ultimately, for distribution to prospects and customers, having current literature organized in one place and available to everyone speeds up your sales and support efforts. Do it and then make sure you keep it all up-to-date.

Chapter 18

Implementing Sales Processes

*B*usiness processes are intertwined with the workflow rules discussed in detail in Chapter 9. In this chapter, we discuss some of the basic principles involved in designing your processes and how you can implement those design principles in Microsoft CRM.

In the almost 20 years that we've been designing and implementing CRM systems (not always Microsoft CRM, of course), it has been made clear again and again that two basic features allow CRM to earn its keep. The first is its ability to consolidate an entire organization's data into one useful, shareable place. Don't underestimate this.

The second is its ability to automate business processes. The implementation of workflow not only forces you to think about — and then continuously rethink — your business processes but also allows you to replace notoriously inconsistent human activity with automation that always follows the rules.

Sadly, more than 90 percent of CRM implementations never achieve that automation. That initial goal seems to get lost in the effort to get the system up and running and the staff using the software. Too often, we're out of energy and money to invest further in developing the workflow that really makes the investment in CRM pay for itself. If you want to maximize the value of your system, however, don't allow yourself to run out of resources before you finish the entire job.

A good process guides your people through a series of well-documented steps for almost every type of situation. For example, although you can do a quote before properly qualifying an account, any well-thought-out system discourages this. Or you may remember to call a prospect back after sending a quote, but a good workflow-based process won't let you forget.

Earlier in the book, we discuss in detail how to implement one of your well-thought-out processes in the Workflow Manager. (Actually, it may not be one of *your* well-thought-out processes, but it might be similar to one of yours.) Please refer to Chapter 9 for a refresher on workflows.

In this chapter, you find out how to plan your sales stages and how to relate these sales stages and other processes to your CRM system. You also discover the basic principles of process design and how these affect the design of your overall CRM system.

The General Principles

A good business process includes the concepts of alerts, escalation, feedback, and analysis. We describe each of these principles in this section.

Alerts

An *alert,* which is often an e-mail notice or some kind of screen pop-up, is called for when an activity should've been completed but for some reason wasn't. For example, if you've obtained verbal approval and the prospect promises a written purchase order within a week, the system should alert the account manager 10 days later if that purchase order hasn't arrived. (If you're a Type A personality, you may want to adjust your waiting period to 10 minutes.) Please refer to Chapter 9, "Managing Workflows," for an example of setting up a workflow rule.

Alerts are appropriate also as a warning that an upcoming activity is almost due. For example, you might want a polite warning 30 days before a client's annual contract needs renewal.

Depending on the number of alerts you anticipate, you may decide on individual e-mail notices for each alert, or you may want a single e-mail or report that contains all the alerts. For example, you may set up a Workflow which e-mails you a list of overdue purchase orders at the end of the day. A typical sales alert might be to let a manager know on the 18th of the month that a forecasted sale that was slated to close on the 15th hasn't closed yet. If you expect more than two or three of these alerts, you'll be better off planning to put them in a consolidated report that the manager receives. Otherwise, you risk clogging up your manager's in-box with dozens of these warnings, which he or she will soon learn to ignore. KnowledgeSync, discussed in Chapter 27, is a third-party alert messaging application. This is one tool you could use to display on-screen pop-up alerts.

Escalation

When something doesn't get done on time, someone needs to know. Now, you can do this properly, or you can do this in a way that gets everyone upset. Escalations are typically done by e-mail notices, by automatically scheduling activities, or by some combination of the two.

Typical activities that deserve escalation are sales that haven't closed when predicted or customer support issues that haven't been resolved in a timely way.

To be fair, the first step in escalating any issue is to notify the person to whom the issue was originally assigned. There might be a perfectly valid reason why the issue hasn't been resolved, and you should allow the original person to resolve it.

An administrator could set up a Workflow rule which automatically schedules an activity or sends an e-mail when a scheduled activity is overdue. Please refer to Chapter 9 on setting up a Workflow rule.

If the task or issue still hasn't been resolved within a few days, a notice should go to the original person's manager.

 CRM can't send a notice to the manager unless it knows who the manager is. Each user's record has a field for the user's manager's name. Escalating issues is probably the best use of this field. To see users' managers, simply click on Settings on the main navigation pane, click on Administration and then click on users. You will be presented with a list of all configured users. Simply double-click on any user to see his or her Manager.

The typical steps of an escalation plan are as follows:

1. Test to see whether an alert is required. You could do this by setting up a Workflow rule scan for any incomplete assigned tasks. (Refer to chapter 9 on how to set up Workflow rules.)

2. Send an initial alert to the primary user. You could do this by setting up a Workflow rule to send an e-mail to the primary user.

3. Wait a reasonable period (one to seven days, for example) and test again. If the issue still isn't resolved, escalate to the primary user's manager.

4. Test again a reasonable time later. If the issue still isn't resolved, notify the manager's manager. Continue this notification until you run out of management levels. Adjust the waiting period between notifications as appropriate. You could do this by setting up a Workflow rule to send an e-mail to the manager's manager if the incomplete task has not been completed after so many days. In this example, you waited up to seven days to notify the primary manager (step 3), you could wait an additional seven days to notify the manager's manager.

Each time a manager is notified, all users who received prior notifications should be copied.

Feedback and analysis

It isn't a good process unless you can measure it. Losing weight is a process. Before you start that process, you undoubtedly weigh yourself and continue to do so as you work toward your desired weight. Without measuring, you don't know how well you're doing, and you can't make midcourse corrections. Business processes are the same.

If you're implementing a sales process with a focus to move each sale from one stage to the next, you want to measure a number of factors. You probably want to know:

- ✓ **Where and when the lead originated.** The purpose of tracking the source of each new record is to be able to better allocate your marketing dollars by determining which lead sources are best.

- ✓ **Who is working on the lead.** Aside from wanting to give credit where credit is due — that is, commissions, bonuses, or a pat on the back — you also want to identify salespeople who may be having problems with particular types or stages of sales so you can correct these problems.

- ✓ **How long it takes to get from each stage to the next.** If your sales are bogged down at a particular stage, you want to know that and make corrections to your process or workflow.

Planning Your Sales Stages

Microsoft Corporation and Microsoft CRM both follow the sales process called Solution Selling, which was originated by Sales Performance International. If you haven't taken one of the classes, read one of the books that provides an overview of this sales philosophy. We're partial to *Solution Selling: Creating Buyers in Difficult Selling Markets,* by Michael T. Bosworth (McGraw-Hill).

If your company already has a sales process other than Solution Selling in place, that's okay. Microsoft CRM has enough flexibility to allow you to configure almost any kind of process.

Your organization undoubtedly needs more than one process. For example, if you sell software and technical support, the associated sales cycles and techniques are different, and you'll want a process for each type of sale. Also, you may need a different sales strategy just based on the size of the potential deal or even the size of the prospect. For example, you would sell 2 pounds of nails to a homeowner in a different manner than you would sell 200 tons of nails to a home improvement store.

In CRM, sales processes are associated with opportunity records. Although you may consider the sales process to begin when you enter a lead, this isn't the case. The process can't begin until you convert a lead to an opportunity, which we tell you how to do in Chapter 12. We distinguish a lead from an opportunity the same way we distinguish a suspect from a prospect. It isn't an opportunity or a prospect until this potential customer expresses some interest in your products or services. After that happens, you may have an opportunity, and it's time for the sales process to begin.

No immutable laws govern the development of a sales process. The sales process police won't be knocking at your door if you have too few or too many stages, but sales processes do have a few guidelines.

The more complex or the longer your sales cycle is, the more stages you'll need to describe where each deal is in your pipeline. However, the more stages you program into the cycle, the more likely your salespeople will object to being forced to enter unnecessary data or take unnecessary steps. So, the simpler, the better — with an eye toward gathering good information about where sales bog down or at what point a particular salesperson begins to struggle.

In Table 18-1, we present a typical sales cycle. Before you can begin to implement CRM's workflow rules, you must define your process. Start with the table and compare it with your own existing sales steps. Chances are, you don't even have a well-documented set of steps. Now's the time to begin creating that system.

Table 18-1		Typical Sales Cycle	
Stage	*Description*	*Probability*	*Comments*
1	Prequalify	10	Make sure it's the right kind of client.
2	Initial meeting	20	This can be a phone call or a physical appointment; probability increases to 25 if the prospect comes to your office.
3	Qualified	30	Not only are they interested, but their timeframe and financials make a deal possible.
4	Demonstration	40	This is show and tell at their place or, even better, at yours.

(continued)

Table 18-1 *(continued)*

Stage	Description	Probability	Comments
5	Quotation or proposal presented	60	There may be several of these, and you may go back and forth from stage 6 to 5 more than once.
6	Negotiating	75	Always be ready for some give and take.
7	Verbal approval obtained	85	This isn't as good as a written purchase order or a signed check.
8	Purchase order received	99	It isn't a done deal until the money arrives.

Select your simplest product or service and compare the steps you use to the steps in Table 18-1. Then create a table that best follows either the steps you're taking today or, better yet, the steps you think you should be taking.

Before you just jump in and begin programming the workflow rules described in Chapter 9, you need to organize your thoughts. Convene a brainstorming session with the users who are involved on a day-by-day basis with each process you want to automate.

The result of that brainstorming session should be a detailed outline or diagram of the process. Each outline needs to include, for each step:

✓ The action that will be taken

✓ Who will be responsible for that action

✓ What will trigger the action (for example, a change in the data or a missed appointment)

✓ How to escalate if the action isn't completed

After you set this up for each step of the process, it's time to go to Chapter 9 and begin making your new process happen.

Part IV
Making the Most of Marketing

"There's been a lot of interest shown in your home, but no offers. I suggest we either lower the price or start selling advertising space on your virtual tour site."

In this part . . .

Targeting your accounts, which we cover in Chapter 19, is a way to group just those accounts or records that have something in common. For example, you could target every customer or prospect in your state that might be interested in a new line of products you're about to release.

Any marketing person worth his or her salt wants to measure the cost and effectiveness of each marketing campaign, so we cover that in Chapter 20.

And, in a chapter new to this edition, in Chapter 21 we discuss how you can collect information from visitors to your Web site and automatically get that to flow into your CRM system and then, maybe, even use workflow to automatically respond to their requests.

Chapter 19

Targeting Accounts and Contacts

Marketing professionals are often looking for ways to build lists of customers and prospects to help target their marketing message. Your Microsoft CRM system is most likely full of useful marketing data. Fortunately, the developers of Microsoft CRM understand that and provide a multitude of ways to target customers and prospects directly from the CRM system. This chapter addresses the marketing module contained in Microsoft CRM 4.

Target marketing with databases consists of storing critical business data, mining that data, and building lists of people that correspond to a marketing need. This book isn't a primer on database marketing, but that doesn't mean we can't review some basic concepts.

Databases are wonderful tools for storing data and retrieving it. With Microsoft CRM Marketing Lists, we can retrieve individual records, aggregate data, build lists, and perform marketing-related actions against the aggregated lists of data. We can then associate marketing lists with marketing campaigns (as we discuss in Chapter 20). Marketing campaigns store data on the types of channels used to reach your target market: who responded, how much new business was created, and lots more. Analyzing this data helps to improve future campaigns by allowing you to focus on the channels and people that not only respond to your marketing activities but more importantly purchase your goods and services.

Believe it or not, marketing list development starts with database design. A well-designed database allows for maximum output with minimal input. Simply put, a well-designed database puts few data entry requirements on users while allowing the marketing department to query the database at will. We suggest you check with your Microsoft CRM dealer to aid in database design.

Let's take a look at an example to illustrate marketing list development. Mr. Spacely (of *The Jetsons*) wants to make a special offer to customers of his competitive product, Cogswell Cogs. Fortunately, Mr. Spacely had a reader of *Microsoft CRM 4 For Dummies* design his database. His CRM designer added a field to the Account form called Product Owned, which records the product that an account owns, either a Spacely Sprocket or a Cogswell Cog. Mr. Spacely asks his marketing department to create a list of all customers who purchased Cogswell Cogs. His marketing team uses Advanced Find to create the desired list. (For more on Advanced Find, see Chapter 3.) With the list created, the Spacely marketing will create a campaign targeted at Cogswell customers. To learn more about Marketing Campaigns, see Chapter 20.

We recommend that you work with a Microsoft CRM professional organization to help in determining the best approach for designing your database.

Here are some basic rules for designing your Microsoft CRM 4 system, to help you optimally market to customers, prospects, or leads, or any combination of the three:

- ✓ **Track company information on the account form only.** If you need to segment by industry, enter it on the account form and not on the contact form. If you know what industry a company is in, you can safely assume the company's employees also work in that industry. Similarly, when designating companies as prospects or customers, we recommend tracking that information on the account screen.

- ✓ **Enter contact-specific data on the contact screen.** This may seem obvious, but should you want to send out birthday notices, put a birthday field on the contact screen.

- ✓ **Query related entities.** Microsoft CRM is a relational database. The Advanced Find lets you query related entities to help develop a list. If you're unaware of how to relate entities, call your reseller.

Targeting the Right People

Let's not lose sight of an obvious fact: You market to people — not buildings, accounts, opportunities, or anything else. And some people don't want you to market to them. Don't worry if someone opts out of your marketing but somehow ends up on one of your marketing lists anyway; Microsoft CRM has a built-in safety net. (Okay, you may not be trapeze artists, so *safety net* is more of a metaphor.) In any case, the aforementioned *safety net* is found on the Administration tab of the Contact form, as well as the Account and Lead forms under Contact Methods.

Figure 19-1 shows the Contact form's Administration tab. At the top of the tab is the Contact Methods section, where you can adjust the following settings:

✔ **Preferred:** This drop-down list allows you to choose the contact's preferred method of contact.

✔ **E-Mail:** If the contact opts out of e-mail, select the Do Not Allow radio button. Subsequent attempts to e-mail the contact from Microsoft CRM will be blocked.

You can't send an Outlook e-mail to a CRM record that has Do Not Allow set in the E-Mail field. When you click Track in CRM prior to sending the e-mail, you'll receive the message shown in Figure 19-2.

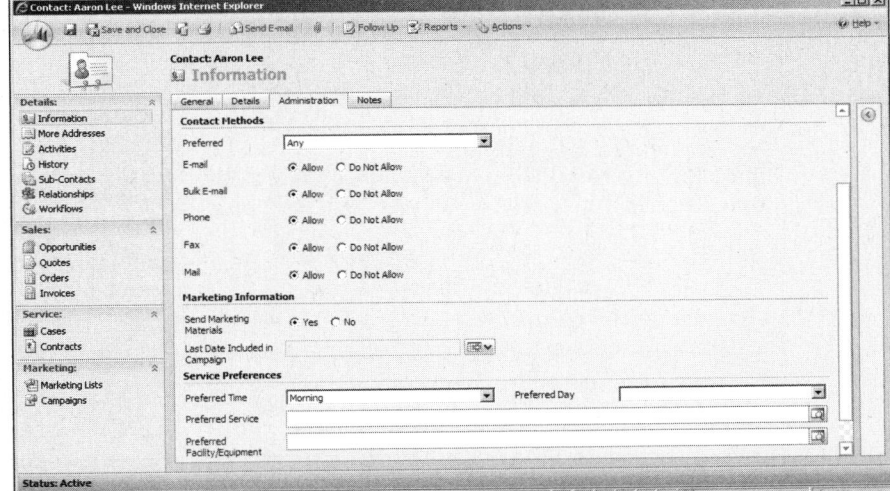

Figure 19-1:
The Administrative tab that's in account, contact, and lead records.

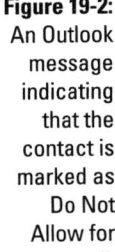

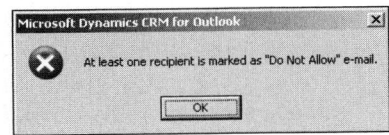

Figure 19-2:
An Outlook message indicating that the contact is marked as Do Not Allow for e-mail.

Chapter 20 covers marketing campaigns; however, it will be helpful now if you understand the distinction between a *campaign* and a *quick campaign* in Microsoft CRM. A quick campaign is a single marketing activity sent to one or more records. A marketing campaign is a full marketing campaign that can have one or more events in a variety of channels, such as e-mail, letter, fax, and more. Marketing campaigns can have associated planning steps, targeted responses, and more.

- ✔ **Bulk E-Mail:** Used for quick campaigns. Records marked "Do Not Allow" with this option will not receive quick campaigns.

- ✔ **Phone:** Indicates a person's desire, or lack thereof, to accept marketing calls from your organization.

- ✔ **Fax:** As with phone, you can indicate whether or not the person will accept fax marketing messages.

- ✔ **Mail:** Indicates whether a person will accept marketing materials that are mailed to them.

The next section, called Marketing Information, contains a radio button for sending marketing materials. Selecting the No radio button for the Send Marketing Materials option prevents all marketing campaigns from going to that contact.

Note that setting Bulk E-Mail to Do Not Allow (in the Contact Methods section, above) prevents all quick campaigns. A Do Not Allow for E-Mail blocks all e-mail to the contact regardless of the selected choices for Bulk E-Mail and for Send Marketing Materials (when the campaign is an e-mail campaign).

Figure 19-3 illustrates the proper settings for a contact with whom you often exchange e-mails, but who has declined to receive your e-mail marketing. In Figure 19-3 we've set: E-mail to Allow; Bulk E-mail to Do Not Allow; and Send Marketing Materials to No.

This contact is now someone with whom we can communicate on a regular basis via e-mail but who won't receive any of our e-mail marketing.

We recommend creating corporate best practices on how to utilize the Contact Methods settings. More and more laws are being passed regulating spam, opt-in/opt-out marketing, and the divulging of contact details to third parties. If you violate any of these rules, your marketing will probably not benefit and may create all sorts of trouble.

We're ready to build that marketing list we mentioned earlier in the chapter. If you've properly designed your database, now you simply need to go ahead and build the list.

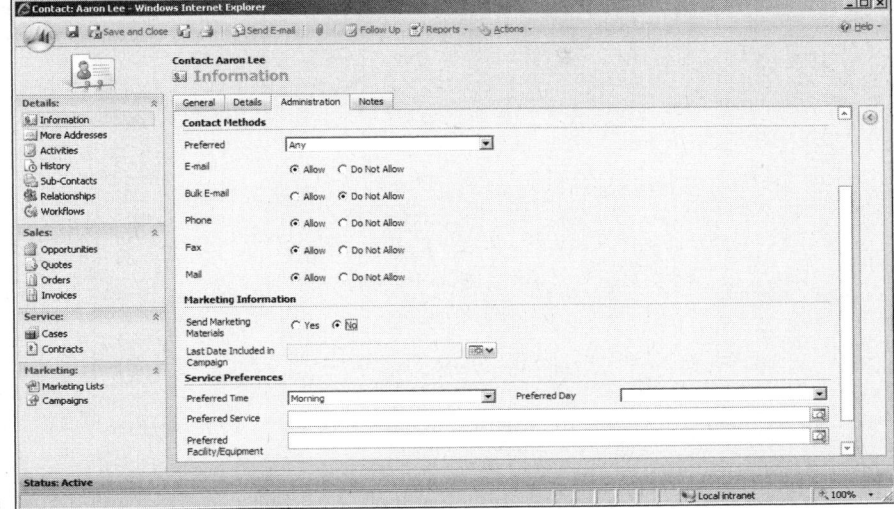

Figure 19-3:
The
Administrative tab
allowing
e-mail
but not
marketing.

Developing and Saving Marketing Lists

Marketing lists differ from Advanced Find in that, after a marketing list is built, it requires human interaction to alter the contents. In contrast, whenever you run an Advanced Find query, the result set that is returned encompasses all the data in the database satisfying the query. If you create a marketing list with 100 records, 100 records will remain in that list forever, unless someone alters the marketing list. In contrast, an Advanced Find query can differ in the number of records returned every time it's executed. For example, an Advanced Find query run for all customers in Massachusetts returns a specific number of records, such as 1,000. If we rerun the Advance Find later in the day we may now return 1,010 records as 10 new customers have been added to the database.

A marketing list isn't dynamic, meaning that marketing list entries don't change automatically with changes to the database as an Advanced Find does. If we create a marketing list based on the Massachusetts Advanced Find, we have 1,000 records in the marketing list. Later, when the Advanced Find returns 1,010 records, the marketing list will continue to return 1,000 records. This allows you to track the original group marketed to regardless of additions made to the database.

Creating marketing lists

Before creating a marketing list, have an idea as to the target audience of your marketing message (such as accounts, contacts, or leads). Then follow these steps:

1. **On the navigation pane, click the Marketing button.**

2. **In the upper part of the navigation pane, select Marketing Lists.**

   The Marketing Lists window appears, as shown in Figure 19-4.

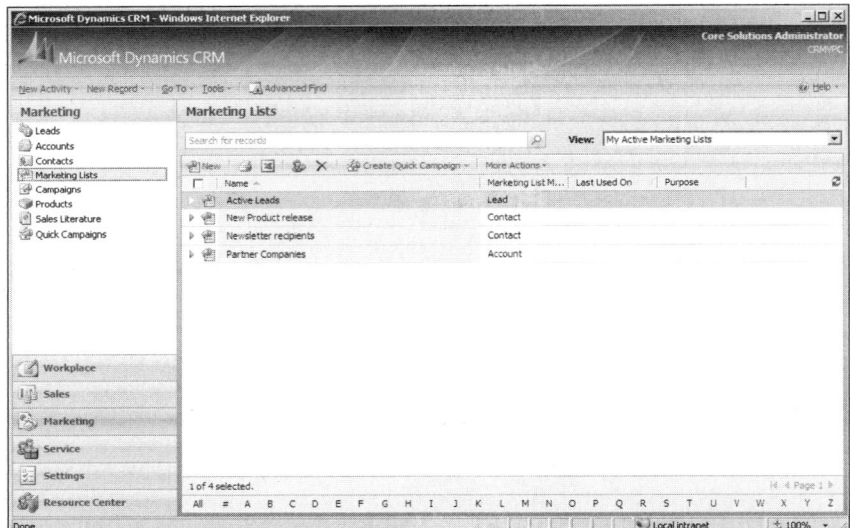

Figure 19-4: Your marketing lists are displayed.

3. **On the window's toolbar, click the New button.**

   The Marketing List: New screen appears, as shown in Figure 19-5. Three fields are required: Name, Member Type, and Owner.

4. **In the Name field, enter a unique name for your new list.**

5. **Select a Member Type from the drop-down list.**

   The Member Type simply indicates whether you're building the list from your accounts, contacts, or leads. You can choose only one of these per list.

6. **By default you will be the Owner; to change ownership of the marketing list to another user, click the magnifying glass icon and select another user.**

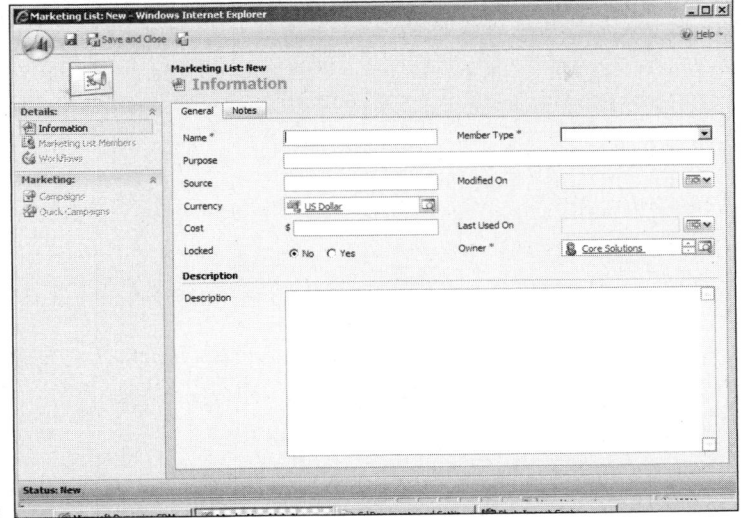

Figure 19-5:
Creating
a new
marketing
list form.

7. **Enter information in the other fields, as desired.**

   If you're building this marketing list based on a purchased list that was imported into the CRM system, indicate so in the Source field. Enter how much you paid for the list in the Cost field. You can enter notes either in the Description field or in the Notes tab. If you use the Notes tab, each note is date and time stamped.

8. **Click the Save button.**

   The navigation menu on the left of the marketing list is now available.

Now you have a list, but it has no records in it. The next section describes how to populate your list.

Adding members to the marketing list

You can populate marketing lists by adding records one at a time or with Advanced Find. The Advanced Find method populates the list with multiple records at a time. Similarly, you can remove marketing list members from the list one at a time or *en masse* via Advanced Find.

In general, if a database relationship exists between the records you'd like to target, Advanced Find is the best tool for the job. On the other hand, should you want to add records without a common thread (no database relationship can be established), the Look Up feature is the way to go. Of course, you could do both. The examples that follow illustrate these points.

To add all contacts where the account type is Customer, use the Advanced Find method. The database relationship between the account records is the account type of Customer. Your list will consist of contacts where the relationship field on the Account form is Customer. This is in contrast to a list created that is not based on a database relationship. For example, a marketing list called Newsletter will contain anyone requesting your corporate newsletter. Other than adding these records to a marketing list called Newsletter, there may not exist any other database relationship between these records.

To add specific members to the marketing list, follow these steps:

1. **On the marketing list navigation pane, click Marketing List Members.**

2. **At the top of the Marketing List Members pane, click Manage Members.**

   Figure 19-6 shows the Manage Members screen.

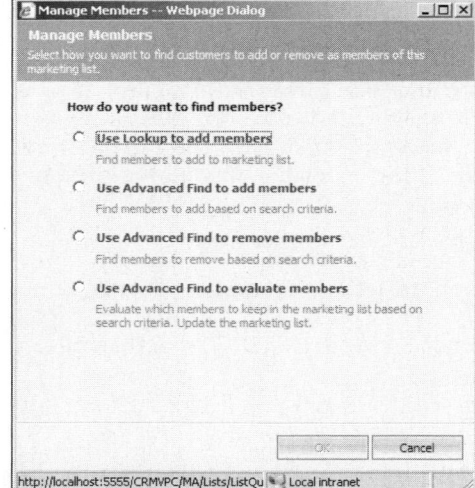

3. **Click the first option, Use Lookup to Add Members, and then click OK.**

   The Look Up Records dialog box opens.

4. **In the Look For field, enter the name of the account(s) you want to add to your list.**

You can enter all or part of the name. We entered ***mo***. The asterisk (*****) is a wildcard that matches any sequence of characters. The **mo** finds any contact record with *mo* in the first or last name. The characters aren't case sensitive and will display *mo* in the first or last names, such as *Moe Howard, Amos Smith* or *Mickey Monaghan*.

5. **Click the Search Icon (magnifying glass).**

   All the contacts with *mo* in their first or last names appear in the Available Records pane, as shown in Figure 19-7. This list may include records you don't want. For example, the figure shows many other people that we don't want to add to our marketing list.

6. **Highlight the records you want to include in your marketing list and then click the >> button.**

   To select a range of records, use the Shift key or the Ctrl key to select multiple records.

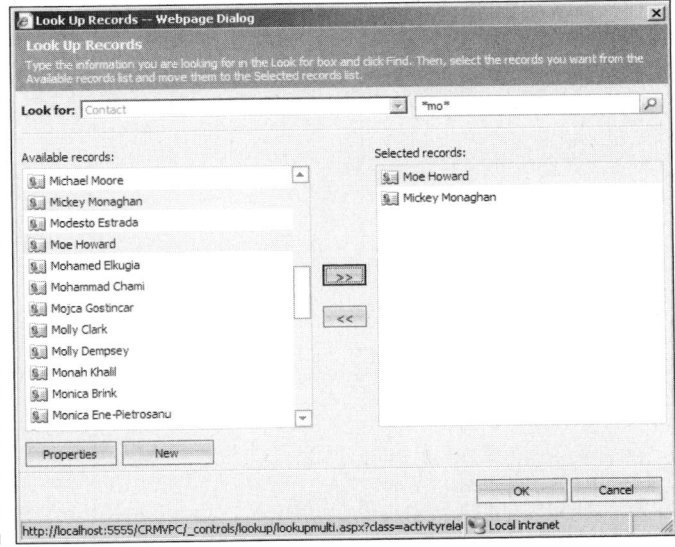

Figure 19-7:
You're adding two of the records displayed.

7. **Click OK when you're finished.**

   The system flashes a message, telling you that it's adding records to your list, and then returns to the Marketing Lists window.

To see the number of records added to a marketing list, follow these steps:

1. **Click Marketing on the Navigation Bar.**

2. **Click Marketing Lists.**

3. **Double-click a marketing list to open it.**

4. **On the Local Marketing List navigation bar, click Marketing List Members.**

5. **The total number of list members is written near the top left of the form. (See Figure 19-8.)**

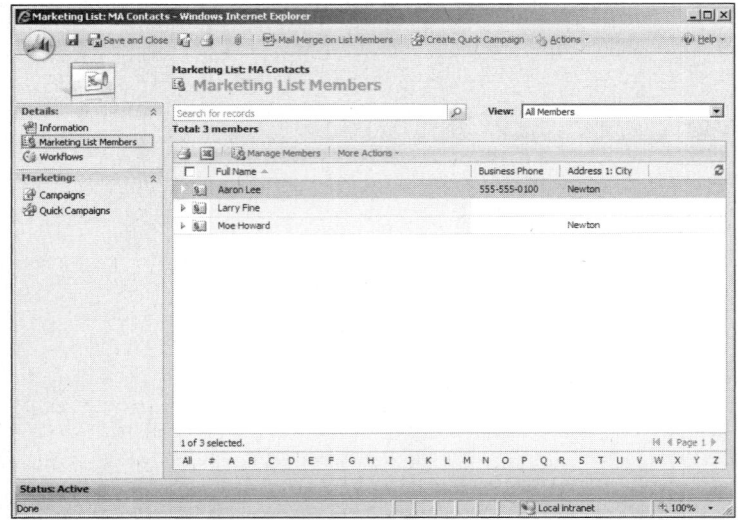

Figure 19-8:
The total number of records added to a Marketing List.

Here's an alternative way to add a record to the marketing list. After you've created your marketing list, you can add members when you're on the Lead, Contact, or Account forms. To do so, just follow these steps:

1. **Open the contact record and Click Marketing Lists on the bottom of the contact navigation pane.**

2. **At the top of the Marketing List Members pane, click Add to Marketing List.**

   The Look Up Records - Marketing List dialog box opens. (See Figure 19-9.)

3. **Select a record.**

4. **Click Save and Close.**

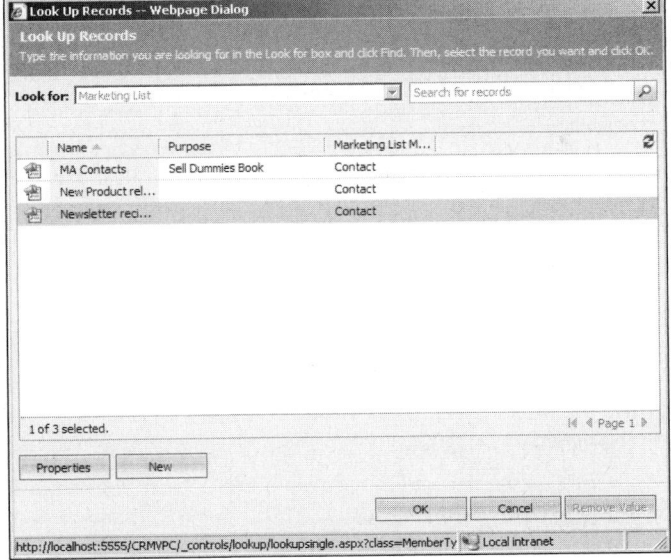

Figure 19-9:
The Look Up
Records -
Marketing
List dialog
box.

Populating a marketing list using Advanced Find

With Advanced Find, you can add many records to the marketing list at one time; you create a query that returns a subset of data. For example, the query you create could be: All contact records in the state of California where the E-Mail field contains data and the contact's title is VP of Operations. This complex query returns all the contact records in the database that satisfy the query. Some benefits of using Advanced Find are:

- ✔ Advanced Find can look at any field within a record, not just the Name field.

- ✔ Advanced Find can look at more than one field in a search. For example, Advanced Find can locate all the accounts in New York that also have fax numbers.

- ✔ Advanced Find can search more than one entity. Your contact list can be filtered by values on the account form or any entity related to contacts.

- ✔ You can save Advanced Find queries for use later.

To create a targeted list using Advanced Find, follow these steps:

1. **On the navigation pane, click the Marketing button.**

2. **At the top of the navigation pane, select Marketing Lists.**

3. **Double-click to select the marketing list you want to populate** (if you have not yet created a marketing list, refer to creating marketing lists above).

   The marketing list form opens.

4. **On the navigation pane, select Marketing List Members.**

5. **On the window's toolbar, click the Manage Members button.**

   The Manage Members dialog box appears.

6. **Click the second option, Use Advanced Find to Add Members, and then click OK.**

7. **The type of record on which you're basing your search is limited to list type; however, you can query related entities, such as the Account entity from Contacts, as shown in Figure 19-10.**

   You're looking for contacts in Massachusetts with an account Relationship Type of Customer. (See Figure 19-10.)

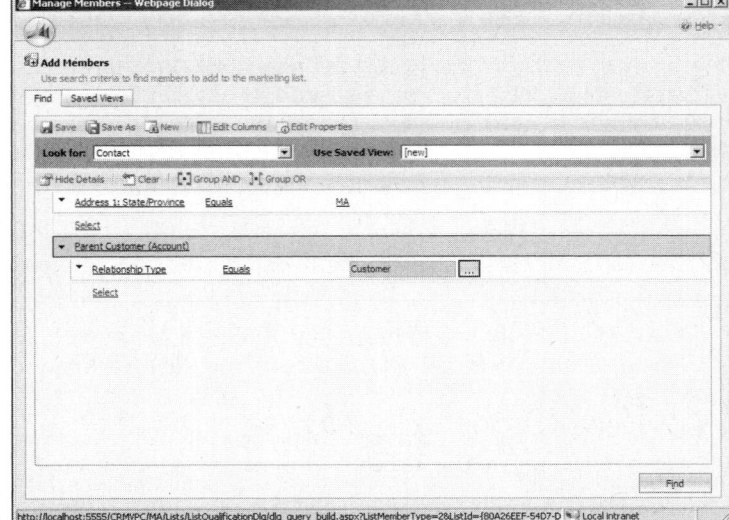

Figure 19-10: Advanced Find for contacts in Massachusetts with an account designation of Customer.

You can also use a saved Advanced Find query by clicking the Saved Views tab and selecting an existing query.

8. **In Figure 19-11, you can add selected members to the marketing list by using Ctrl+click or by clicking the Add All the Members Returned by the Search to the Marketing List radio button. When done, click the Add to Marketing List button.**

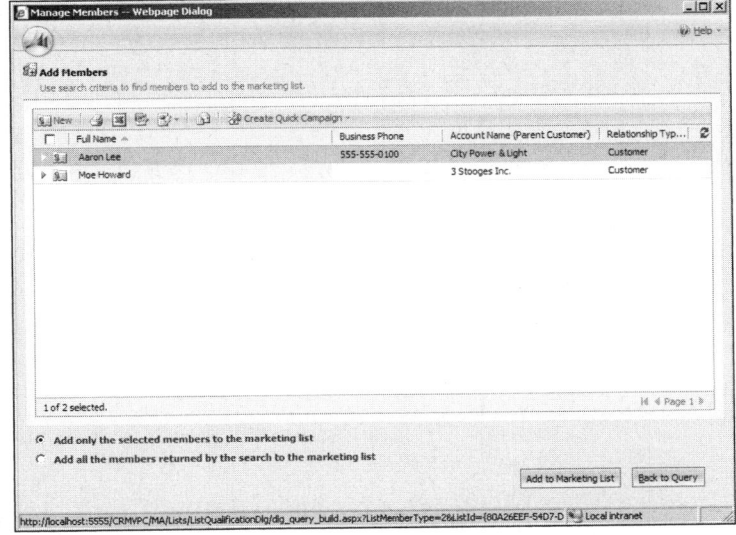

Figure 19-11:
Adding
Advanced
Find records
to a
marketing
list.

9. **If so desired, click the Back to Query button and save your Advanced Find.**

   This adds the Advanced Find to your saved queries.

10. **Click Save and Close to save this new entry as one of your marketing lists.**

After a marketing list is created, it's static. In other words, marketing list members don't change without manual intervention.

Editing a Marketing List

We mention several times that, unlike an Advanced Find, marketing lists are static and can be changed only manually. Why would you want to change a list? One reason is to add people to the list to comply with a request, such as a newsletter opt in. To update a list with many records at one time, you can use Advanced Find in much the same way you use it when creating a marketing list.

To add records, follow the steps in the preceding "Populating a marketing list" section.

You can enter a record into a specific marketing list only once, so don't worry about duplicating the entry.

Removing Records from a Marketing List

There are two ways to remove records from a marketing list. We cover both options in the steps that follow.

To remove records from a marketing list, follow these steps:

1. **Open a contact record.**

2. **On the form's navigation pane, click the marketing list icon second from the bottom.**

   The marketing list view is displayed on the right.

3. **Click the list item (or Ctrl+click several marketing lists) from which you'd like to remove the record.**

4. **On the toolbar, choose More Actions⇨Remove.**

   The contact will be removed from chosen list or lists.

5. **Click OK.**

The second approach is to navigate to a particular marketing list where you have several options to remove records. From the marketing list, you can remove one or multiple records at a time. Let's explore those options:

1. **On the navigation pane, click the Marketing button.**

2. **At the top of the navigation pane, select Marketing Lists.**

3. **Double-click to select the marketing list you want to edit.**

   The marketing list form opens.

4. **On the navigation pane, select Marketing List Members.**

5. **Click the list member or Ctrl+click the members you want to remove.**

6. **On the toolbar, choose More Actions⇨Remove From Marketing List.**

7. **Click OK.**

Alternatively, you can remove records via an Advanced Find query. To do so, follow these steps:

1. **From an open marketing list, Click Marketing List Members on the navigation bar.**

2. **Click Manage Members on the top right.**

   The manage members dialog box opens. (Refer to Figure 19-6).

3. **Select Use Advanced Find to remove members.**

   The Advanced Find query window opens.

4. **Create an Advanced Find or use a saved one.**

5. **Click Find in the lower right corner.**

   The list of members satisfying the search is shown.

6. **Ctrl+click to remove individual members or click the Remove All the Members Returned by the Search from the Marketing List radio button.**

7. **Click the Remove from Marketing List button on the bottom of the form.**

Or, finally, you can remove records with the Use Advanced Find to Evaluate Members option. To do so, follow these steps:

1. **From an open marketing list, click Marketing List Members on the navigation bar.**

2. **Click Manage Members on the top right.**

   The manage members dialog box opens. (Refer to Figure 19-6.)

3. **Select Use Advanced Find to evaluate members.**

4. **Click OK.**

5. **The Advanced Find window opens.**

   In this case, you're going to evaluate the account state and remove any contacts whose parent account isn't located in Massachusetts. Figure 19-12 shows your query.

   Of your three records, Moe and Larry work for a company in Massachusetts, and Mickey Monaghan works for a company located in Washington state.

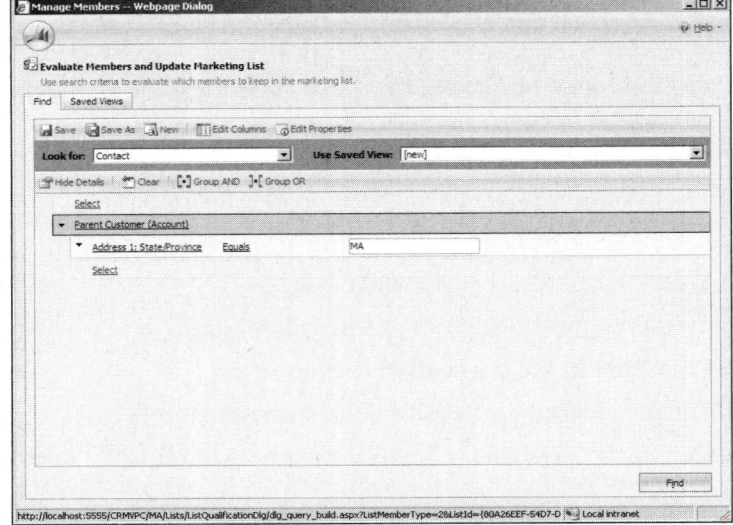

Figure 19-12:
Query to
exclude
records
from the
marketing
list.

6. **Click the Find button.**

Figure 19-13 shows the results. Only two records appear based on the query, which means Mickey will be removed from the list.

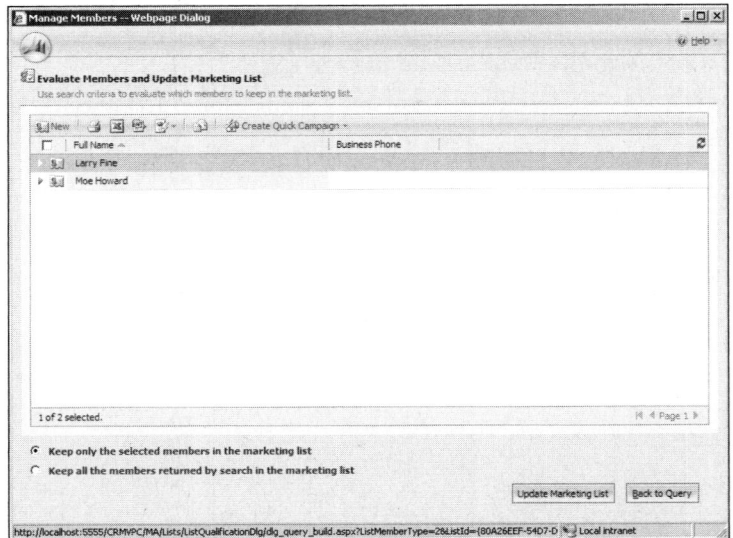

Figure 19-13:
Query
results for
evaluating
members.

7. **Click the Keep All the Members Returned by Search in the Marketing List radio button.**

8. **Click the Update Marketing List button.**

Merging Mail from Marketing Lists

A new feature added to Microsoft CRM 4 is the ability to launch mail merge documents from the Internet Explorer client, a feature only found in the Outlook client in version 3. The mail merge feature enables the user to output data from the marketing list members to Microsoft Word, e-mail, fax, labels, or envelopes.

After you create a marketing list, the Mail Merge on List Members button is available at the top of the screen. Use it to create the mail merge as follows:

1. **At the top of the marketing list form, click the Mail Merge on List Members button.**

   The Mail Merge for Microsoft Office Word dialog box opens, as shown in Figure 19-14.

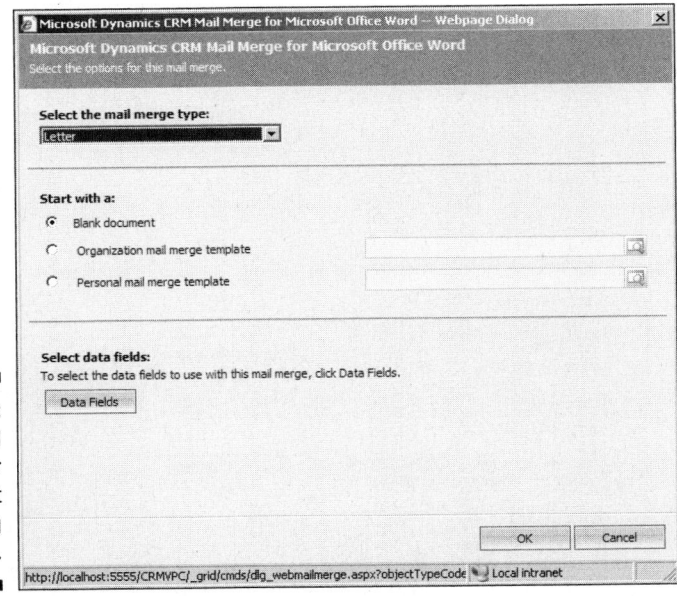

Figure 19-14: The Mail Merge for Microsoft Word Dialog box.

2. **In the Select the Mail Merge Type drop-down box, choose Letter, Email, Fax, Envelope, or Label, according to your needs.**

3. **Choose the type of document to start with: a blank document, or an organization or personal mail merge template.**

   If you choose one of the templates, you'll then have to click the lookup box to the right of your selection. If you have a few templates they will show in the dialog box. Select one and click OK. If you have many templates, you can search for the desired template in the Look For box. When found, click on the template and click OK.

4. **Select a template, if necessary, and click OK.**

5. **Click the Data Fields button.**

   You can select up to 62 fields.

6. **Click OK twice.**

7. **Click Open when prompted with the file download dialog box.**

8. **If macros have been disabled, click Options in Word and enable macros. (See Figure 19-15.)**

   If you're using Word 2007, as we are in Figure 19-15, you'll also have to click the CRM button on the Add-Ins or Mailing tab.

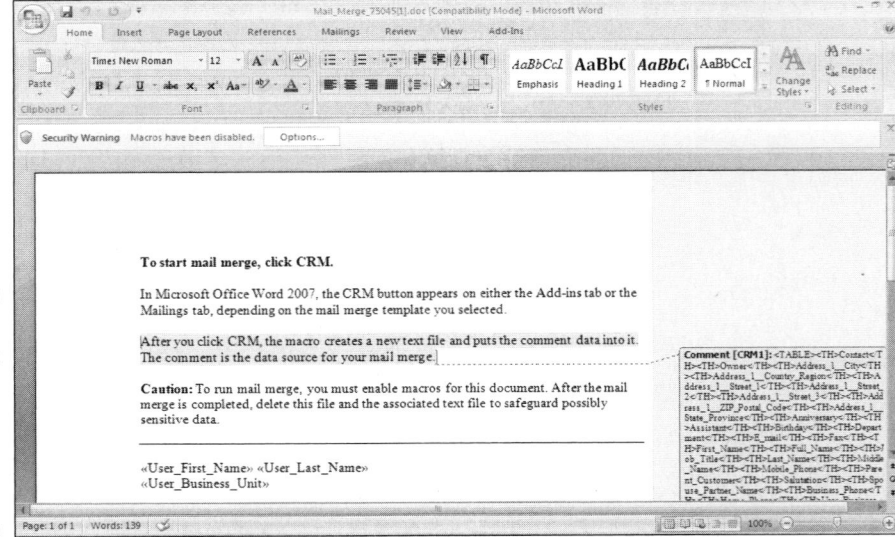

Figure 19-15: A Microsoft Word template with CRM data merged.

9. **Select the data to be merged and click OK.**

   Figure 19-16 shows the data to be merged.

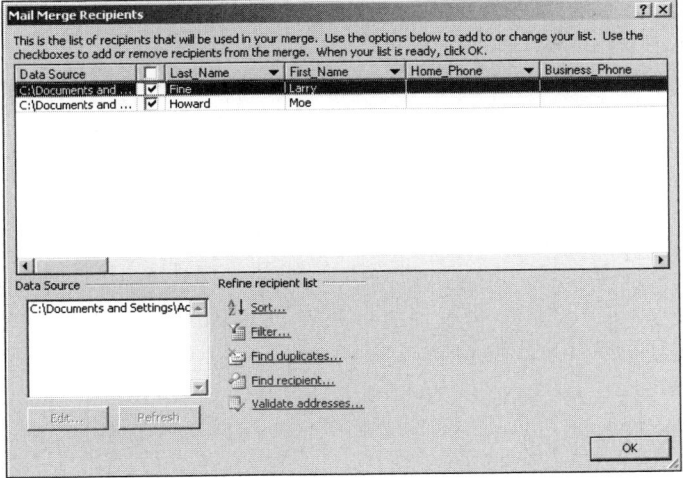

Figure 19-16:
Merging
marketing
list data
with
Microsoft
Word.

10. **In Word, on the bottom right, click Next: Preview your letters.**

    You're merge document shows with actual CRM data merged.

11. **In Word, on the bottom right, click Next: Complete the merge.**

    Your merge documents are now complete. You can print or save or both.

Chapter 20

Managing Campaigns

· ·

· ·

As a Customer Relationship Management tool, Microsoft CRM 4 has an entire module related to marketing. A key component of the marketing module is campaigns. *Campaigns* in Microsoft CRM deals with planning and executing a database marketing campaign. Campaigns are related to database marketing because the campaigns you create deal with data stored in your Microsoft CRM system, and the campaign results will also be stored in your Microsoft CRM system. You need not be a marketing professional to use campaigns. This chapter will introduce you to campaigns, how to execute them and how to record responses.

This chapter logically follows Chapter 19, in which we cull our database to produce lists of customers, prospects, and so on. Now we want to put those lists to good use.

Marketing campaigns can be simple. A campaign can be comprised of a single activity, such as sending a letter, or a campaign can be very sophisticated and comprised of multiple steps. A complex campaign can consist of several phone calls, letters, and trade show attendance involving many people. Whichever campaign is decided upon, marketing managers would like to track campaign response rates. They can then correlate the number of impressions to responses to opportunities and hopefully to new business. This analysis is vital in determining a campaign's effectiveness.

CRM campaigns allow for tracking responses and linking them to sales opportunities. In addition to response rates, campaign managers can track a variety of other campaign-related data and report on results. These tools can help a marketing manager improve planning and execution of future marketing campaigns.

Developing Your Campaign

Microsoft CRM is the tool to carry out and track a marketing campaign, but before you do that, you can use CRM to develop a clearly defined plan for the campaign. Proper planning is an essential component of any marketing campaign (but you already knew that didn't you?). When you're armed with a plan that has clearly stated goals and a well-defined budget, you're ready to execute your first Microsoft CRM 4 marketing campaign.

But before we begin our journey through campaign management with Microsoft CRM 4, let's explore a marketing scenario. Our three funny guys, Moe, Larry, and Curly, are planning to attend the big Comedy Convention in Las Vegas later this year. The Comedy Convention sends a list of attendees to exhibitors prior to the convention. Our three funny guys have decided to use Microsoft CRM to market to the attendee list prior to the meeting in an effort to maximize the number of prospects who visit their booth. Their pre-conference marketing consists of different channels — e-mails, letters, phone calls, and so on.

After the conclusion of the conference, our heroes will post-market to the conference attendees that stopped by the booth. With Microsoft CRM, they will be able to manage campaign responses and the effectiveness of the marketing campaign in terms of related opportunities and hopefully new business.

The following list outlines several important aspects of the benefits of using Microsoft CRM for a marketing campaign:

- **Track budget versus expenses.** Money, money, money. Your budget is extremely important, and you want to make sure you have one established before you start. Then, as the campaign progresses, the cost is automatically calculated in Microsoft CRM. You can enter and adjust information for the total budget of the campaign, the expected revenue, miscellaneous costs, or the total actual cost.

- **Assign promotion codes.** Use promotion codes to help track responses. Track responses by associating different codes with different media outlets.

- **Target products.** Add products to Microsoft CRM and associate those products with a marketing campaign. Now you're experiencing the power of a relational database!

- **Define lists.** All campaigns need at least one marketing list associated with it. *Marketing lists* are collections of accounts, contacts, or leads that have been identified as the target market for a campaign. Marketing list creation can be based on database queries (Advanced Find) or simply by adding users to a particular list or lists. For more on lists, see Chapter 19.

✔ **Collect marketing material.** Now you'll know who received the unique coffee mug you provided as a thank you. Or perhaps the pen that writes underwater to a depth of 60 feet.

You'll also want to set your revenue target and the starting and ending dates of your campaign. We suggest that you put all this together in an outline before building your campaign. That way, you can see any holes in your campaign before they become an issue.

Creating Campaigns

Let's return to our marketing scenario. The Stooges in preparation for the upcoming Las Vegas conference create a campaign in Microsoft CRM. Let's create the campaign together. Just follow these steps:

1. **On the navigation pane, click the Marketing button.**

2. **At the top of the navigation pane, click Campaigns.**

   The Campaigns window appears, Most likely your view will be My Campaigns, but you can switch your view by clicking on the View drop-down list (See Figure 20-1).

3. **On the window's toolbar, click the New button.**

   The New Campaign form is displayed, as shown in Figure 20-2.

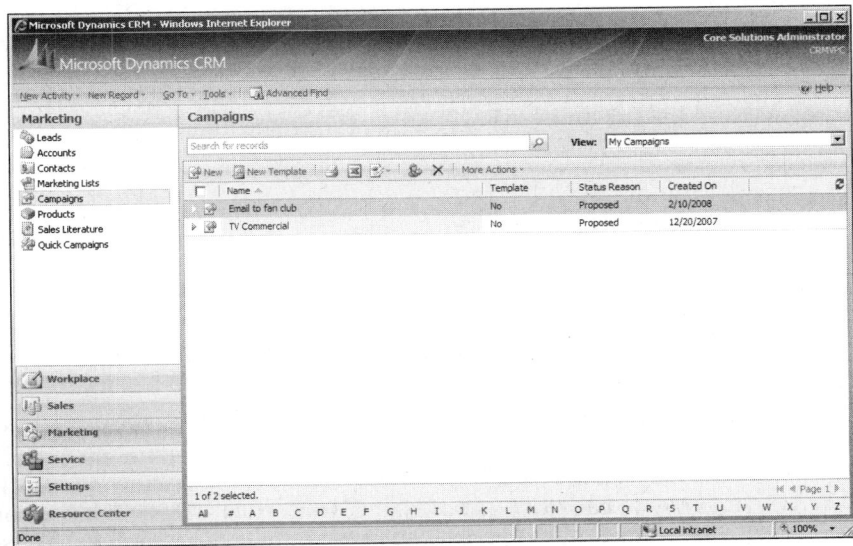

Figure 20-1:
All campaigns start here.

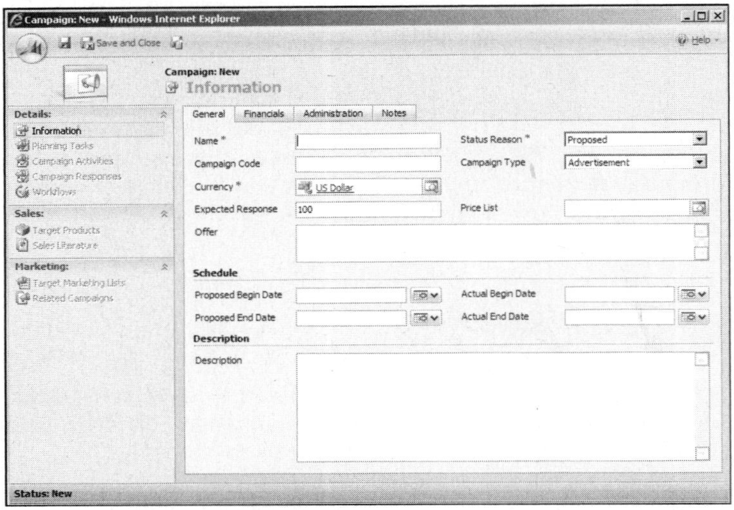

Figure 20-2:
The New
Campaign
form.

4. **Enter a name for your campaign in the Name field.**

   We're entering **2008 Las Vegas Convention**.

5. **Click the arrow to the right of the Status Reason field to select an option from the drop-down list.**

   Because we're creating a campaign here, we choose Proposed. After your campaign is defined and everything is in place, you can change the status to Ready to Launch. The other options are self-explanatory.

6. **Enter your campaign code in the Campaign Code field.**

   You can enter a code (perhaps as part of a marketing gimmick) or let the program assign the code (just leave it blank for now). The campaign code helps you link responses to the campaign for those important reports and demographic data. The assigned code follows the format your system administrator chose in the settings area.

7. **Choose your campaign type from the Campaign Type drop-down list.**

   The options are Advertisement, Direct Marketing, Event, Co-Branding, and Other. Select the option that best fits the type of campaign you are creating.

8. **Next, enter the expected number of responses to the campaign in the Expected Response field.**

   For example, if you're sending 500 mailers and expect a 1 percent response rate, you would put 5 here. This allows you to later measure the actual response rate against what you estimated.

9. **In the Price List field, select a price list to associate with this campaign.**

   If you're using products in Microsoft CRM, we recommend that you choose a price list so that the campaign has something to work from. If you're not using products then leave this field blank. To learn more about using products with Microsoft CRM see Chapter 7.

10. **In the Offer field, describe your offer.**

11. **Fill in the fields in the Schedule section.**

    These fields are optional, but we recommend you complete them. The proposed dates let everyone working with the campaign know when you'd like to execute the campaign. The actual dates allow you to compare actual to proposed.

12. **Enter a campaign description as needed.**

13. **Click Save (the disk icon).**

    Your data is saved, and you can move on to the other tabs.

Now enter information on the Financials tab as follows:

1. **Click the Financials tab. (See Figure 20-3.)**

2. **Complete the Budget Allocated, Miscellaneous Costs, and Estimated Revenue fields.**

   The other two fields (Total Cost of Campaign Activities and Total Cost of Campaign) are calculated automatically as you define and run your campaign.

   We put $35,000 in the budget field and $350,000 in the estimated revenue field. The Stooges want a minimum of a 10x return on any marketing venture.

3. **Remember to click Save (the disk icon).**

   We suggest that you save your data each time you move to a new tab or option within your campaign.

After you've entered your financial information, you can either click the Save and Close button or enter notes in the Notes tab. You can use notes as a running journal of campaign-related interactions. Notes are not required and will not be reported on, so use them as you see fit.

The Administration tab contains basic campaign administration notes (Owner, Created date, date of last modification, and who did the change), which are filled in automatically. The only field you can edit on this tab is Owner. The Owner field defaults to the logged-in username; you can change the owner by clicking the hourglass to the right of the field.

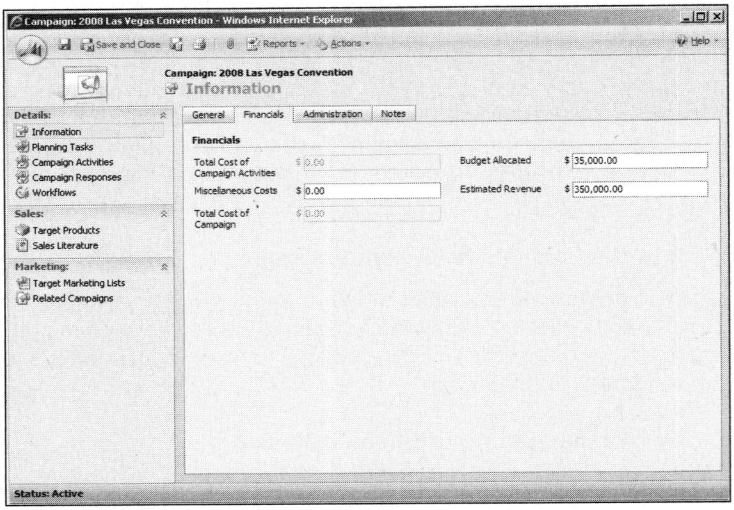

Figure 20-3:
The
campaign
financials.

Planning Tasks

In the case of a trade show, there's often a lot of preparation needed to have a successful conference. The planning tasks could include: reserve booth space, book hotel and flights, ship the booth, order booth related items, and more. All of these tasks are time sensitive and perfect candidates for the planning tasks section. Additionally, each task can be individually assigned to the proper person within your organization. In Microsoft CRM, tasks are simply activities assigned to CRM users. These activities are associated with the campaign and are found in the campaign planning tasks, on a user's calendar, or in Activities (under Workplace). Completed activities remain listed with a Status Reason of "Completed."

In this section, we will explore the creation of Planning Tasks. All you have to do is follow these steps:

1. **On the navigation pane, click the Marketing button.**

2. **At the top of the navigation pane, click Campaigns.**

   The Campaigns window appears. Most likely your view will be My Campaigns, but you can switch your view by clicking on the View drop-down list. (Refer to Figure 20-1.)

3. **Double-click a campaign to open it (or continue to use the campaign you created above).**

4. **On the navigation pane, select Planning Tasks.**

   The Planning Tasks window appears.

5. **On the Planning Tasks window's toolbar, click the New button to create a new task.**

   The Task: New window appears, as shown in Figure 20-4. This window is similar to the one you see when scheduling activities (which we discuss in Chapter 14).

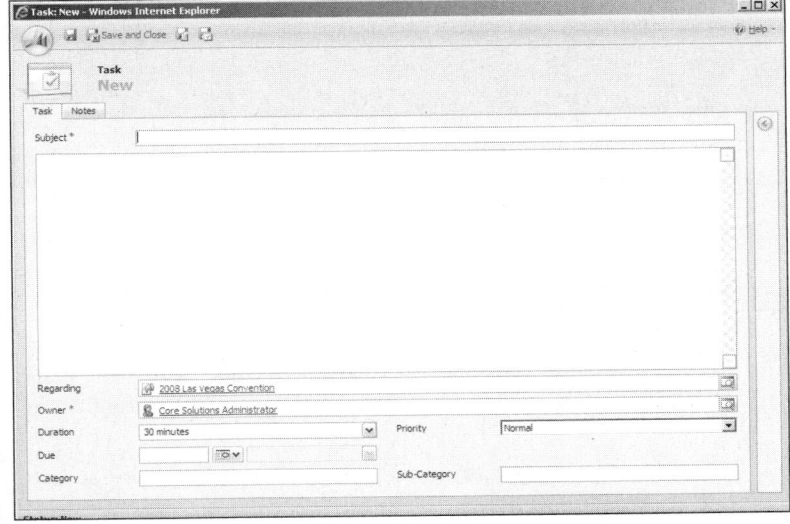

Figure 20-4: The Planning Task form — it looks exactly like the Schedule Task window!

6. **Fill in the Subject field.**

   The subject should be descriptive such as `Order Trade Show Booth Graphics`.

7. **Fill in the Description field (the large box below the Subject field).**

8. **(Optional) Change the owner from you to the person responsible for the task.**

   If you're the one responsible for the task, ignore this step.

9. **Ensure the Regarding field has the campaign entered.**

   It will be by default, but if you change it, the planning task will no longer be part of the campaign.

10. **If desired, fill in the remaining optional fields.**

    Remember, the more information you have, the better you can complete a task.

11. **To add notes to this task, click the Notes tab and enter away.**

    As with other note fields in Microsoft CRM, you can enter information free-form.

12. **Click the Save and Close button, which saves the task and returns you to the planning tasks workspace, or click Save and New and add more planning tasks.**

Defining Campaign Activities

Campaign activities are often referred to as *steps* or *waves*. This is where all the marketing takes place. The campaign responses are reactionary to the activities. Therefore, the better your message (the activity) is, the greater the responses. What's great about this is that you can assess those activities that generate the most response and improve future campaign responses.

To create a campaign activity, follow these steps:

1. **On the navigation pane, click the Marketing button.**

2. **At the top of the navigation pane, click Campaigns.**

   The Campaigns window appears. Most likely your view will be My Campaigns, but you can switch your view by clicking on the View drop-down list. (Refer to Figure 20-1.)

3. **Double-click a campaign to open it (or continue to use the campaign you created above).**

4. **From the campaign form, click Campaign Activities on the navigation bar.**

5. **Click the New button on the form toolbar.**

   The Campaign Activity: New window appears, as shown in Figure 20-5. Parent Campaign, Subject, and Owner are required fields, although Subject and Owner are the only fields you can edit.

   The Status Reason field is set to Proposed and grayed out. This will change later.

6. **Select the appropriate option from the Channel drop-down list.**

   This is where you tell the program how you want this phase carried out: phone, fax, letter, e-mail, appointment, and so on. To clarify, this isn't a marketing channel, such as direct marketing or distribution. By the way, you must make this selection to distribute campaign activities, a topic we cover later in this chapter in the Distributing Campaign section.

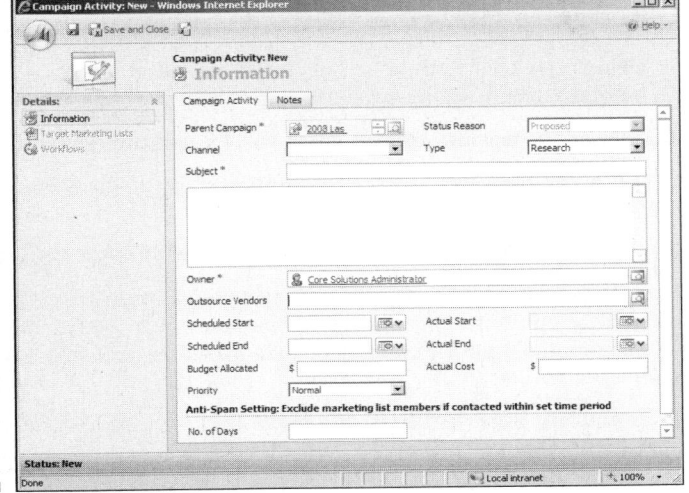

Figure 20-5:
Start by
creating
the first
wave of
your
campaign.

Channel Options:

- **Phone:** Schedule phone calls to marketing list members. These calls will be made by Microsoft CRM users.

- **Appointment:** Schedule appointments with marketing list members. These calls are made by Microsoft CRM users.

- **Letter:** Send letters to marketing list members. In reality, Microsoft CRM does not create a letter but an activity to send a letter. If you want to create an actual letter then use the Letter via Mail Merge option.

- **Letter via Mail Merge:** Send letters using the mail merge function. You can access letter templates that contain Microsoft CRM data. *Note:* You must use the Outlook Client to perform this step. See "Distributing Campaign Activities," later in this chapter.

- **Fax:** As with letters, Microsoft CRM does not create a fax but an activity to send a fax. If you want to create an actual fax then use the Fax via Mail Merge option.

- **Fax via Mail Merge:** Send Faxes using the mail merge function. As with letter via Mail Merge, this feature is available from the Outlook Client.

- **E-Mail:** Send e-mail directly to marketing list members from Microsoft CRM. E-mails can be sent immediately or scheduled for users to send. If scheduled, users will have to send them one at a time.

- **E-Mail via Mail Merge:** Send E-mails based on templates. This feature is available from the Outlook Client only.

- **Other:** Use this to indicate a type of campaign activity that will not be distributed, such as a Newspaper Advertisement.

7. **Choose the appropriate option from the Type drop-down list.**

    The type is the purpose of the campaign activity, such as research or lead qualification.

8. **In the Subject field, enter a subject for your campaign activity.**

    Although you can call the activity anything you want, we suggest that you keep the subject logical and self-explanatory. For example "first pre-conference e-mail to conference attendees" is preferable to "e-mail attendees."

9. **Add an activity description in the large text box below the Subject field.**

    If you'd like a label called Description associated with the box, speak to your dealer, or ask us how (http://www.consultcore.com/dummies.htm).

10. **(Optional) From the Owner drop-down list, choose an owner.**

    The Owner field automatically defaults to the user creating the campaign activity, but you can change it. If you want to delegate tasks in the campaign, this is where you do it. Assign the owner here, and the task appears in the owner's activities.

11. **In the Outsource Vendors field, assign an outsource vendor.**

    Use the magnifying glass to search for and select a vendor. For example, if the local printing company, Ink, Inc., is printing the invitations to your webinar, they are your outsource vendor.

12. **Choose a scheduled start and end date.**

    This is self-explanatory.

    To the right of these fields, you'll see Actual Start and End Dates, which aren't enabled. These are filled in automatically when you start the campaign.

13. **Fill in the Budget Allocated field with the cost of your budget.**

    This way, you can check your budget at a glance instead of having to e-mail folks or rifle through papers on your desk. The companion field to the right, Actual Cost, is just that — the actual tally of everything related to this campaign.

14. **Fill in the Priority field.**

15. **If desired, fill in the Anti-Spam No. (number) of Days field.**

    Microsoft CRM will scan the contact's record to make sure the contact hasn't received any other marketing materials within the time frame you specified. It prevents you from overloading the contact with multiple marketing messages. If done right, you can maintain the appropriate number of touches without spamming your customers and prospects.

16. **Click Save (the disk icon) or the Save and Close button.**

    Remember, if you want to do some more work on the campaign activity, just click Save. Your campaign activity will be saved and the option in the navigation pane will be enabled.

Prior to distributing this activity, we need to associate one or more marketing lists with the campaign. We'll do so later in the chapter; for now, save and close your campaign activity.

So let's take a look at target products and sales literature.

Often, marketing campaigns are designed to sell a product. If your campaign is designed around one or more products, you can associate those products with the marketing campaign (if not, skip this section). When the campaign is completed, you'll be able to analyze response rates and close rates and compare them by product as well as by campaign. A wonderful feature of Microsoft CRM is that it lets you analyze your data from many different perspectives.

To add a target product, follow these steps:

1. **With the campaign form open, click Target Products in the Sales area of the navigation pane.**

   The Target Products grid is displayed.

2. **Click Add Existing.**

   Look up the product(s) you want to associate with the campaign and click >> to add.

3. **Click OK.**

   The product(s) are associated with the campaign.

The process for adding literature to this campaign is very similar to adding products. Adding literature to a campaign is not required, however doing so let's you associate printed materials to the campaign:

1. **With the campaign form open, click Sales Literature in the Sales area of the navigation pane.**

   The Sales Literature grid is displayed.

2. **Click Add Existing.**

   Look up the literature you want to associate with the campaign and click >> to add.

3. **Click OK.**

   The literature is associated with the campaign.

Marketing lists are mechanisms used to determine the target audience for campaign activities. Every campaign needs at least one associated target marketing list to execute campaign activities. Without a target marketing list, you can't distribute campaign activities. If your campaign does not include personalized marketing or sending something to person, then you will not need to add a marketing list. However, most marketing done with Microsoft CRM is targeted to people, and therefore one or more marketing lists will be necessary. Adding one or more target marketing lists is similar to adding products and literature. Just follow these steps to add a target marketing list:

1. **With the campaign form open, click Target Marketing Lists in the Marketing area of the navigation pane.**

   The Target Marketing List grid is displayed.

2. **Click Add.**

   Look up the marketing list(s) you want to associate with the campaign and click >> to add.

3. **Click OK.**

   You're prompted with the Add Marketing Lists to Campaign dialog box shown in Figure 20-6. If you add the marketing list after you create campaign activities, you can add the list(s) to all existing activities. If you'd like to have more control over this, deselect the check box in the dialog box.

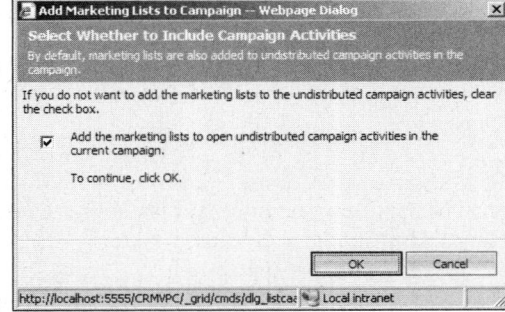

Figure 20-6:
Adding a marketing list to existing campaign activities.

If you add the marketing list before you add all of your campaign activities — and you'd like to distribute the list over all campaign activities — simply re-add the marketing list.

Distributing Campaign Activities

With at least one target marketing list assigned to the campaign, we can return to the campaign activity created earlier. Our activity is sitting dormant. It hasn't been associated to a single record in the database, nor has it been assigned to anyone on our team to carry out the activity. Microsoft CRM has a built-in mechanism called Distribute Campaign Activities to facilitate the association and assignment of individual campaigns.

Consider this scenario, which illustrates how and why campaign activities are distributed. Assume that the initial step or wave in our campaign calls for making outbound telephone calls. The marketing list we associated with the campaign has 3,500 prospects, and our inside sales team consists of 35 people responsible for making the calls. (They need not be sales people, simply users of Microsoft CRM.) Logistically, this task would be very difficult to do manually; however with Microsoft CRM, this task is quite manageable.

Here are the steps to take to distribute the campaign related calls to the sales team:

1. **On the navigation pane, click the Marketing button.**

2. **At the top of the navigation pane, click Campaigns.**

   The Campaigns window appears. Most likely your view will be My Campaigns, but you can switch your view by clicking on the View drop-down list. (Refer to Figure 20-1.)

3. **Double-click a campaign to open (or continue to use the campaign you created above).**

4. **Click Campaign Activities on the navigation menu.**

5. **Double-click the campaign activity to be distributed.**

   If you've already associated a Target Marketing list, skip to Step 11; otherwise, continue to Step 6.

6. **From the campaign activity form, click Target Marketing Lists on the campaign activity navigation pane.**

7. **Click Add from Campaign on the form toolbar.**

   The Lookup Marketing List Dialog box opens

8. **Click the magnifying glass on the upper-right to see all marketing lists or begin to type the marketing list name and click the magnifying glass icon.**

A list of all the marketing lists associated with the campaign appears. If the lookup dialog box is empty, you need to associate at least one marketing list with this campaign. To do so, cancel out of this dialog box and follow the steps to associate a marketing list above.

6. **Click the marketing list or Ctrl+click the marketing lists that you'd like to associate with the campaign.**

7. **Click OK.**

8. **On the Navigation Bar click Information. Ensure that the method of distribution from the Channel drop-down list is correct.**

   As you can see in Figure 20-7, we chose the Phone channel.

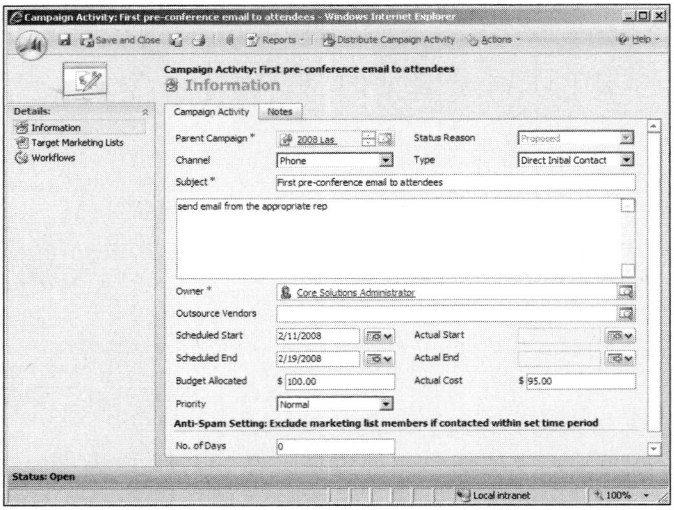

Figure 20-7:
The campaign activity before distribution.

9. **Click Distribute Campaign Activity on the toolbar at the top of the form.**

   The box that appears depends on the channel you selected. Because we selected Phone as the channel, the New Phone Calls dialog box appears, as shown in Figure 20-8.

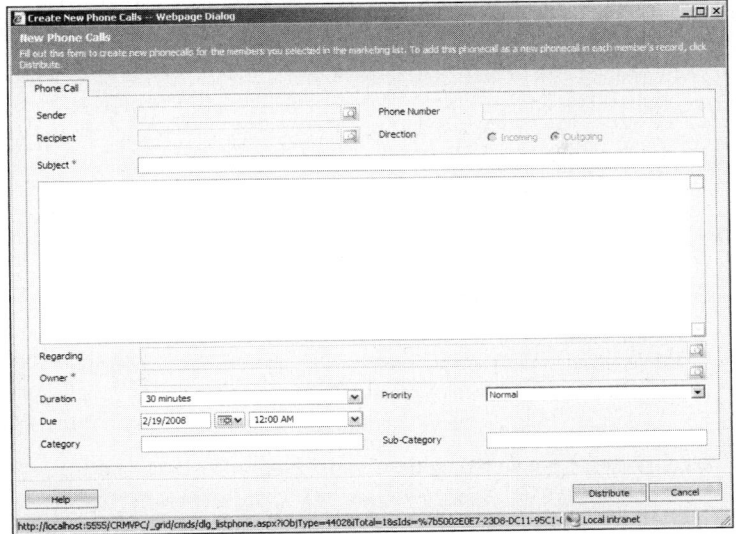

Figure 20-8:
Distributing
phone calls
as activities.

To distribute campaign activities where the channel option is Letter via
Mail Merge, Fax via Mail Merge, or E-mail via Mail Merge, follow these
steps from within the Outlook Client for Microsoft CRM. These activities
cannot be distributed from the Internet Explorer client.

10. Enter the subject.

Subject is a mandatory field. Basically, the subject is a description of the
activity you're distributing.

11. Enter a description in the large text box beneath the Subject field.

The description can be a short script for the person making the call.

12. On the bottom right corner, click Distribute.

Again, the dialog box that appears depends on the channel you chose to
deliver this activity. Because we're using a phone call as our channel,
the Distribute Phone Calls dialog box appears.

13. Select the appropriate options in the Confirm Distribution dialog box.

We have three options here to indicate the owner (the person the call is
being assigned to) of the phone call. Choose one of the following radio
buttons, as shown in Figure 20-9.

If your campaign activity is e-mail, you can choose the option to send
the e-mails automatically and close the activity. If you don't, you'll have
to send the campaign e-mails manually.

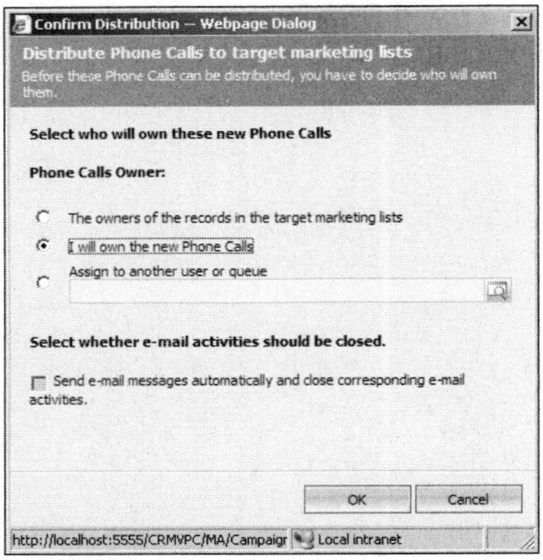

Figure 20-9:
Distributing
phone call
assign-
ments.

14. **Click OK.**

    You return to the campaign activity window. Take a look in the naviga-
    tion pane, where you'll see added options to help you track this
    distribution.

15. **Click Save (the disk icon) or the Save and Close button.**

    Voila! You're done!

The phone call option and channel will track where the phone calls went and
how many failed attempts were made. As you can see, Microsoft CRM makes
campaign scheduling especially easy for those in large companies and those
who handle a large number of activities for marketing campaigns.

The navigation bar on the campaign activity form now has two additional
items: Phone Calls Created and Failures. Figure 20-10 illustrates those changes.
Failures lists those activities that were not distributed. Usually, failures are
related to records where the contact method for the type of communication is
set to Do Not Allow. To learn more about Do Not Allow, refer to Chapter 19.

After an activity has been distributed, the next step is to close the activity.
This allows you to be able to distinguish between closed activities, completed activities, and pending campaign activities. To close an activity, follow
these steps:

1. **On the navigation pane, click the Marketing button.**

2. **At the top of the navigation pane, click Campaigns.**

The Campaigns window appears. Most likely your view will be My Campaigns, but you can switch your view by clicking on the View drop-down list. (Refer to Figure 20-1.)

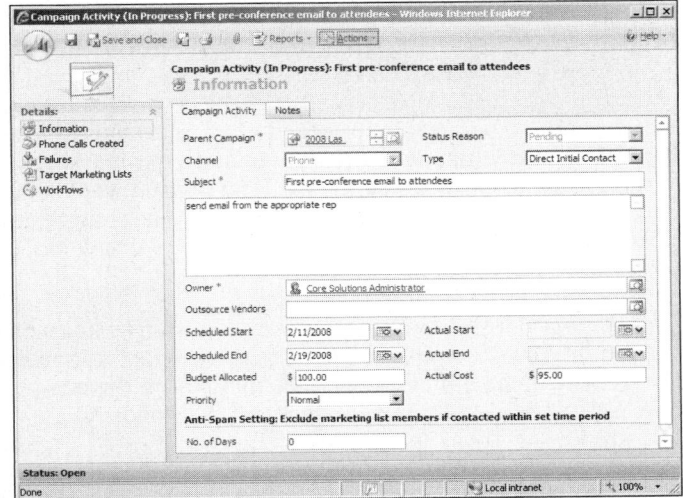

Figure 20-10:
The post-distribution activity form.

3. **Double-click a campaign to open (or continue to use the campaign you created above).**

4. **Choose Actions⇨Close Campaign Activity.**

   The Close Campaign Activity dialog box appears (as shown in Figure 20-11).

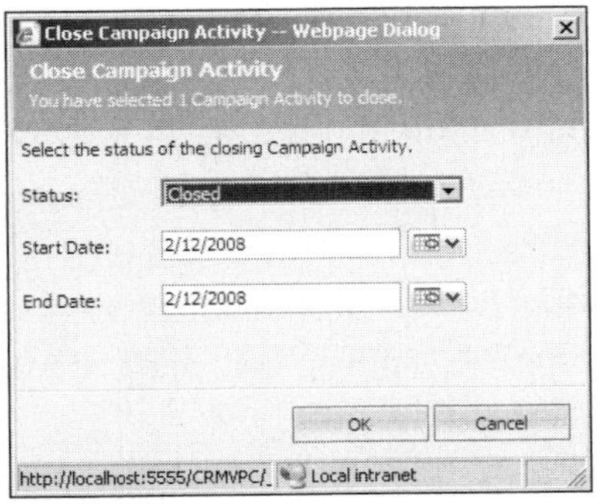

Figure 20-11:
The Close Campaign Activity dialog box.

5. **Indicate the Status, choose the dates, and click OK.**

Recording Campaign Responses

When you create a marketing campaign, you expect results or responses, whether they're negative or positive. There are even folks dedicated to determining response rates, filtering that information into percentages, and making little pie charts and bar graphs from those responses. Good news or bad, you can record it in Microsoft CRM.

Another little bonus to being able to record your responses in a central system like this is that your sales department and your marketing department can see the same information! Whoa! Who doesn't want their departments working together, in sync and in harmony? (Okay, maybe not in harmony, as the marketing department stomped the sales department last year in the softball game, but you get the picture.)

Excited now? Good. Here's how you (or your sales staff) can record those responses. Essentially, there are two ways to record campaign responses, from the activity form or from Campaign Responses on the campaign navigation bar. We explore both methods in the steps that follow.

Earlier in the chapter, we distributed phone calls to staff members. Presumably, an individual opens the activity and makes the call. If so, that person can convert the activity to a campaign response. Here's how to do it:

1. **On the navigation pane, click the Marketing button.**

2. **At the top of the navigation pane, click Campaigns.**

3. **In the Campaigns window, double-click your campaign.**

   The campaign window appears.

4. **On the navigation pane of the open campaign window, click Campaign Responses.**

5. **On the window's toolbar, click New.**

   The Campaign Response: New window appears, as shown in Figure 20-12.

   Another way to make this window appear? With the campaign activity open, just click Actions⇨Promote to Response.

   Most of the fields are self-evident, but we touch on some of them here.

   • *Response Code:* This indicates the response of the customer. You can choose from Interested, Not Interested, Do Not Send Marketing Materials, and Error.

   • *Promotion Code:* You can link the response to a particular promotion. If the customer is calling because of the free bunny slippers, for example, you can indicate that here. Several campaigns can have the same promotion, so this is just another way of grouping data for marketing analysis.

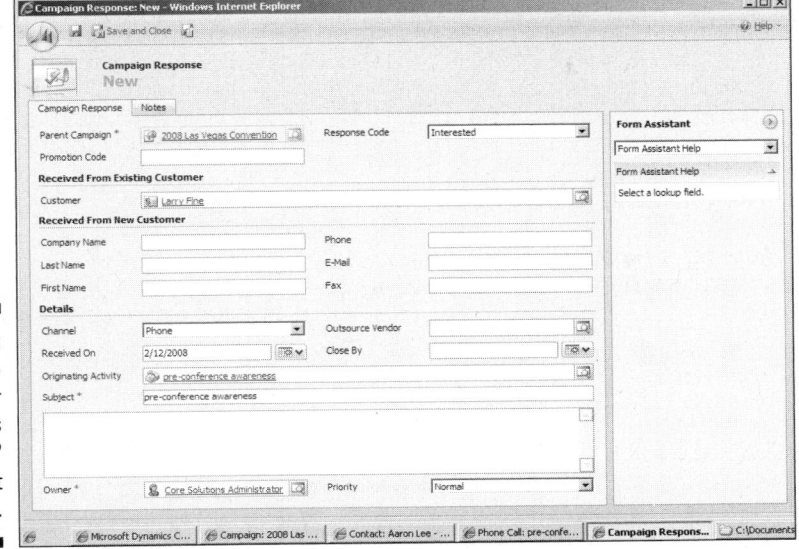

Figure 20-12:
Did the
customer
say yes
or no?
Record it
here.

- *Customer:* This can be an account, a contact, or a lead. If you arrived at the campaign response form via Step 1, the customer field will already be filled in.

6. **When you've completed the form, click the Save button.**

   After the form is saved, look at the toolbar. A new button has been added — the Convert Campaign Response button.

7. **Click the Convert Campaign Response button.**

   The Convert Campaign Response form opens. (See Figure 20-13.)

8. **Click OK.**

9. **When you've completed the form, click the Save and Close button.**

   The Campaign Response window closes, and you return to the open campaign window.

By recording campaign responses, you can easily check the status of each campaign throughout its lifespan. This is a great feature because you can see, for example, whether one promotion is taking off or a certain employee is having trouble making calls.

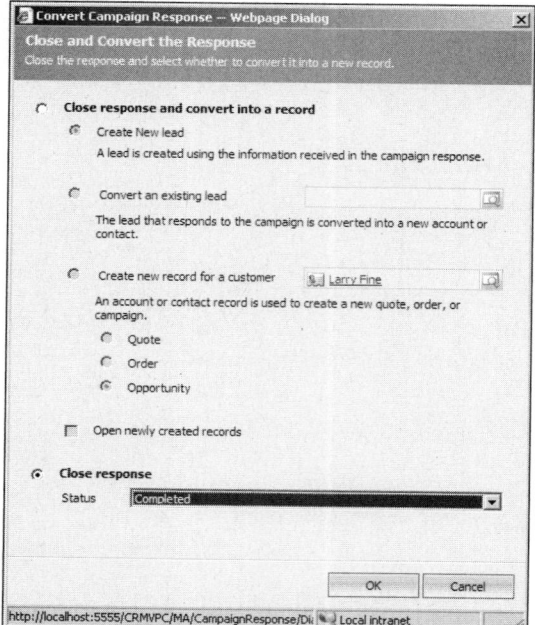

Figure 20-13:
The Convert
Campaign
Response
Button.

Relating Campaigns to Each Other

Now, say you're running two campaigns: one to identify interest by product category and one to reflect different marketing strategies for each product category. That's great. But what if you want to compare them? Easy! Just relate the campaigns to each other. Here's how:

1. **On the navigation pane of the open campaign window, click Related Campaigns.**

   The window switches to the Related Campaigns workspace, as shown in Figure 20-14.

2. **On the window's toolbar, click Add Existing.**

   Like the other options mentioned in this chapter, the Look Up Records dialog box appears.

3. **Search for the other campaign you want to relate to this one, select it, and click the right-pointing arrow to add it to the right-hand pane.**

4. **Click OK.**

   You return to the Related Campaigns workspace.

5. **Click Save (the disk icon) or the Save and Close button to save your work.**

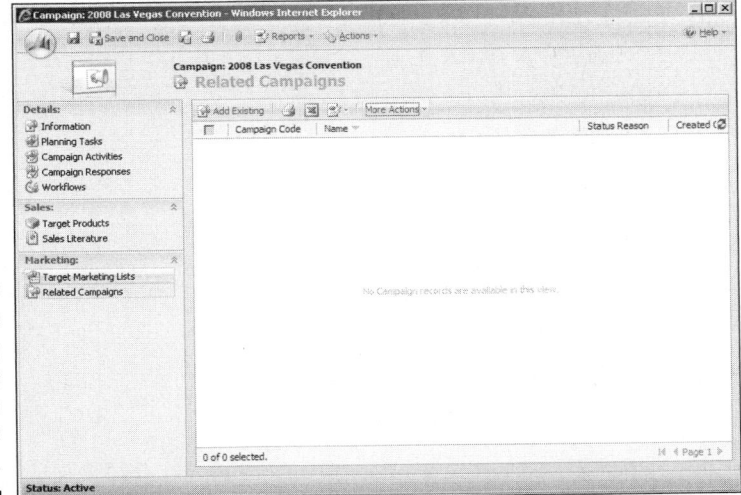

Figure 20-14:
Relating
campaigns
to each
other is also
a snap.

One of the great features of Microsoft CRM is that you can do a report on just about anything, including campaign performance, which you can check by clicking the Campaign Responses or Related Campaigns selection in the navigation pane of your campaign window. Then just click the Reports icon on the window's toolbar (or select a report from the drop-down box by clicking the arrow next to the Reports icon). You can print the report as a table or a graph. Either way, use the information to help you stay on top of what's going on in the campaign.

Working with Quick Campaigns

There are times when you'll want to create a single marketing touch and send it to a group of records. Quick campaigns are the answer. On the toolbar grid for Accounts, Contacts, Leads, and Marketing Lists, you can find a Create Quick Campaign button. Here, we explore this feature with contacts, but it's similar for other record types as well.

All you have to do to set up a quick campaign is follow these steps:

1. **On the navigation pane, click Contacts.**

   The window switches to the contact grid.

2. **On the grid toolbar, click Create Quick Campaign.**

   Figure 20-15 shows the three options available for a quick campaign:

   - *For Selected Records*
   - *For All Records on Current Page*
   - *For All Records on All Pages*

   If you want to select multiple records on the page, use Ctrl+click.

Figure 20-15:
Quick
Campaign
options.

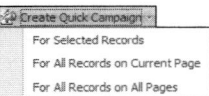

3. **Choose an option and click Next.**

4. **Provide a name for your campaign.**

   Make the name as descriptive as possible, keeping the 200-character limit in mind.

5. **Click Next.**

6. **Choose the activity type and the owner.**

   The next screen depends on what you choose for an activity. We're choosing Phone Call for this example.

7. **Enter a subject and a description.**

8. **Click Next.**

9. **Click Create.**

   Figure 20-16 shows the Create a Quick Campaign Wizard. It summarizes the number of records impacted by the quick create. If the summary looks good, click Create.

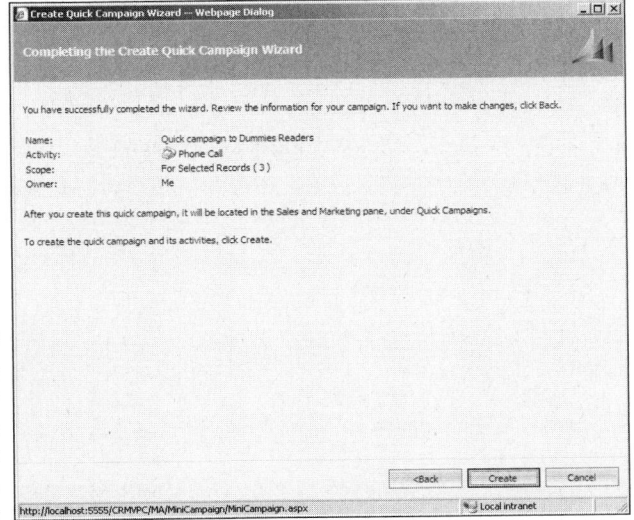

Figure 20-16:
We're ready
to launch
the quick
campaign.

To view all of the quick campaigns in the system:

1. **On the navigation pane, click the Marketing button.**

2. **At the top of the navigation pane, click Quick Campaigns.**

   The Quick Campaigns window appears.

3. **Double-click a quick campaign.**

4. **Figure 20-17 depicts the Quick Campaign grid.**

   From the grid, you can easily ascertain how many people were targeted (total members), the number of success and failures, and the status of the campaign.

5. **Double-click a quick campaign.**

   The Quick Campaign detail form opens. Figure 20-18 shows the quick campaign detail form. The items are self explanatory; however we want to point out that by clicking the Created item (Phone Calls Created, in our example) in the navigation pane, you open campaign activities and record responses as described in the "Recording Campaign Responses" section earlier in this chapter.

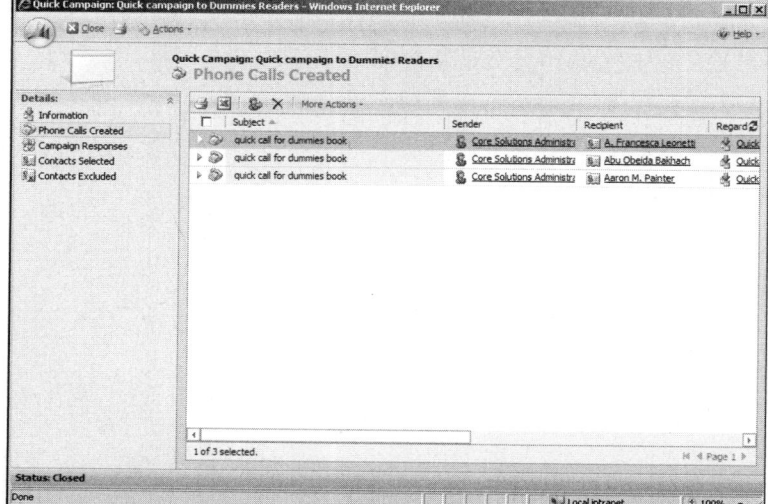

Figure 20-17:
The quick
campaign
shows key
results.

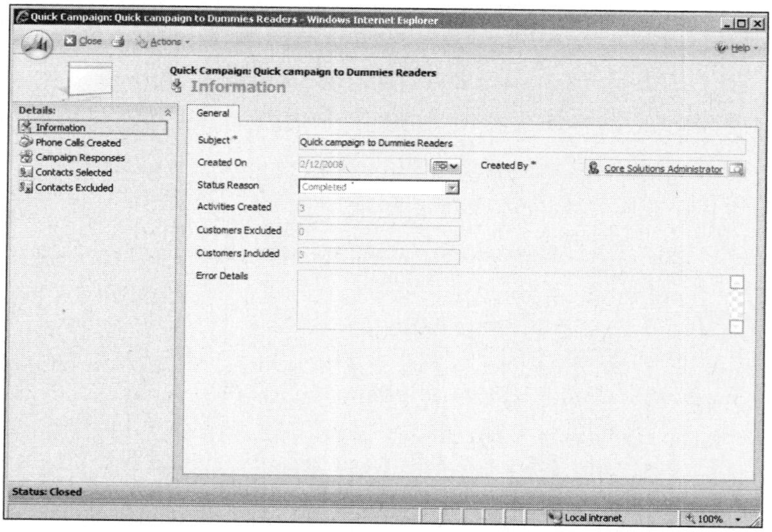

Figure 20-18:
The Quick
Campaign
results form.

Chapter 21

Integrating Your Web Site

So you've been successful in driving customers and prospects to your Web site. Now you want your Web site to integrate with your CRM system. The good news is that it can be done. The better news (admit it — you thought we were going to give you bad news) is that several integration options don't require much in the way of programming.

If your Web site has forms on it, say a lead form or a customer service help form, you can have the data from those forms (or others) entered into Microsoft CRM 4. After it's there, users can work directly with the data. You can also have workflow rules that further process the incoming data prior to any user interaction. There are also options for customer portals and data entered in — and perhaps retrieved directly from — your Microsoft CRM system.

In this chapter, we cover the items that don't require programming to integrate your Web site with Microsoft CRM. We also touch on some of the options that would require programming, as a means of introduction. Actual programming examples aren't part of the scope of this book.

Sending E-Mail to a Queue

In Microsoft CRM, you can set up a queue to handle incoming e-mail. For example, your organization might have a Web site with a support form on it. In that case, your customers can go to the Web site, fill out a support request, and an e-mail is generated from your Web site to a support e-mail box that in turn is monitored by an individual or team at your organization.

You don't need a support request form on your Web site. You could have customers e-mail to a support mailbox. The e-mail received into the support mailbox is then visible in a Microsoft CRM 4 queue. That way, an entire support team can monitor the queue for incoming customer service requests. A customer service representative can then take ownership of the support request and work with it. (To learn more about queues, see Chapter 25.)

A benefit of pointing a Microsoft CRM queue at a support e-mail box is that you can use CRM's Workflow to automatically create a case when an e-mail is received.

Microsoft CRM's workflow can associate a new case to a customer, based on the customer's e-mail address.

Should you choose to have an e-mail generated from a support form on your Web site and sent to a support box at your company, the e-mail's From address is the e-mail address your Web administrator created and not the From address of the person completing the form. In that case, you cannot directly link the incoming support request to an existing contact. This isn't a problem for companies that sell business-to-business (B2B), because those companies typically want to link cases to accounts and not to contacts. If your support organization focuses on B2B support we suggest you create a support account and link all cases created via workflow to that account. Then your support staff can re-link the cases when they've identified the company requesting support.

Ideally, you'd create a case from an e-mail sent to a queue and automatically link the e-mail to the newly created case. There's a wonderful blog post authored by Jagan Peri on the Microsoft CRM Team site with an example of a workflow that does just that. You can find that blog at `http://blogs.msdn.com/crm/archive/2008/02/19/e-mail-to-case-lead-using-crm-4-workflow.aspx`.

The general flow is as follows:

1. An e-mail is received into a Microsoft CRM 4 queue. (See Figure 21-1.)

2. Workflow creates a new case and relates the e-mail activity to the new case. The workflow that created the case assigns it to the Support Level 1 queue. (See Figure 21-2.)

   Figure 21-3 shows the newly created case, and Figure 21-4 shows the original e-mail saved as a related activity.

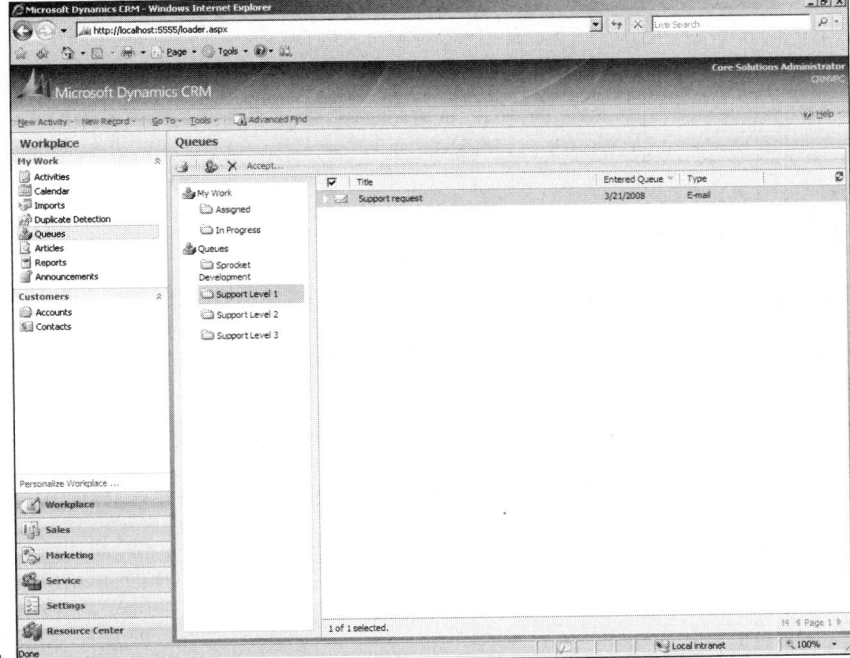

Figure 21-1:
A support
request is
received
into the
Support
Level 1
queue.

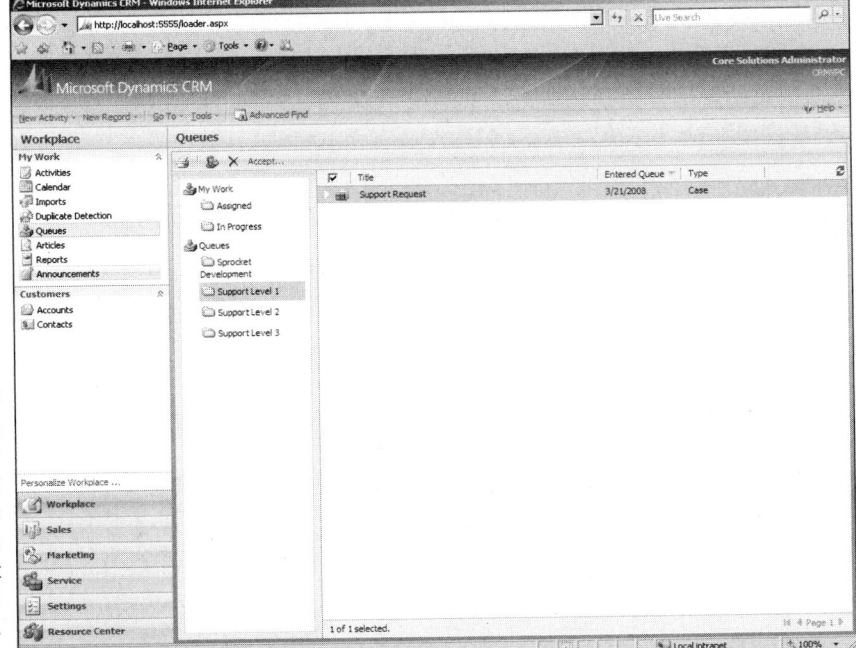

Figure 21-2:
The newly
created
case is
assigned to
the Support
Level 1
queue.

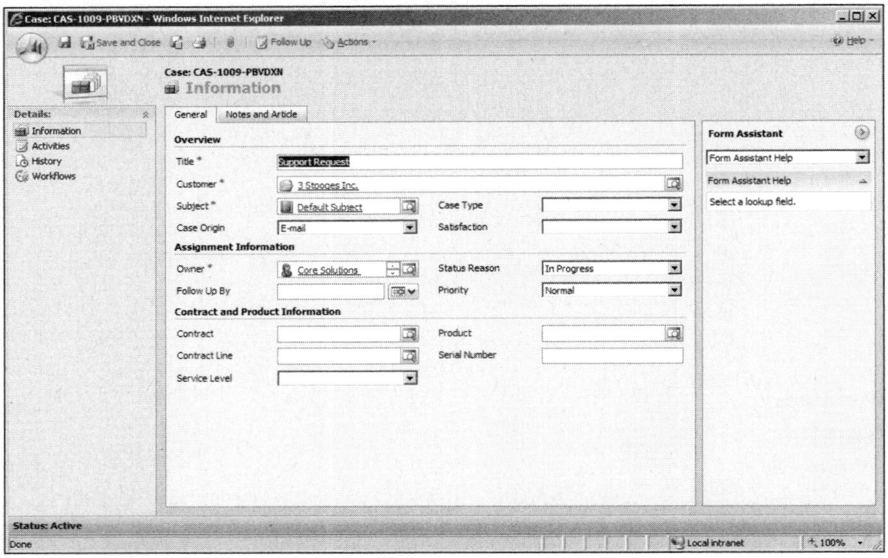

Figure 21-3:
The new
case details.

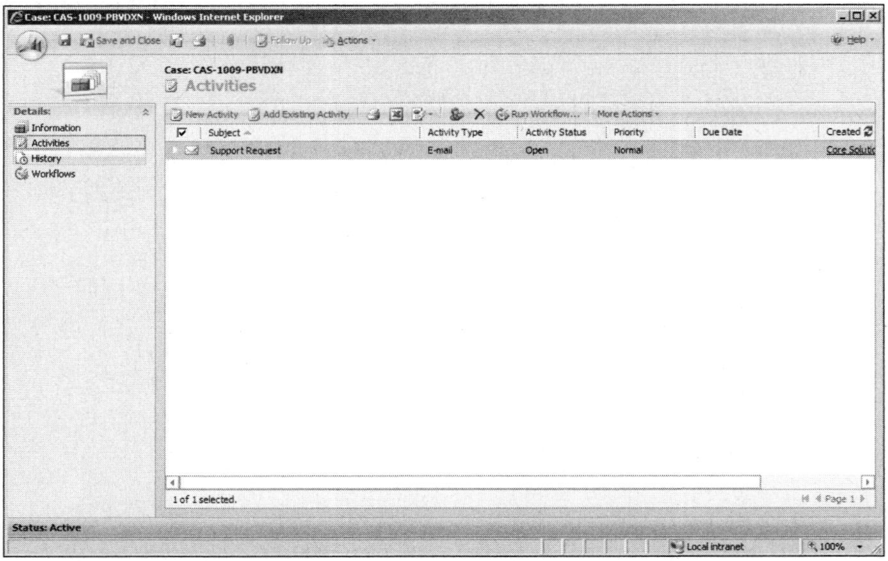

Figure 21-4:
The original
e-mail is
now related
to the case
as an
activity.

Creating leads works exactly as creating cases. A lead sends an e-mail to a specific e-mail account, such as sales@yourcompany.com, and from there, you can use workflow to create a new lead and associate the original e-mail to the lead.

Creating Records with Programming

We don't create code in this section, just simply discuss some options for creating leads, cases, contacts, accounts, or whatever type of record you'd like to create.

The Microsoft CRM SDK (Software Development Kit) is for programmers. The SDK allows programmers to extend the product beyond the built-in features. To help programmers or even beginners, the SDK provides several coding examples. The developers of Microsoft CRM recognize that they cannot anticipate how each organization will use Microsoft CRM and therefore cannot pre-create every feature that every end-user would want. The SDK goes a long way toward filling any gaps that exist between the built-in feature set and the features you will need.

The products listed in Chapter 21 use the SDK to interface with Microsoft CRM. In fact, it is usually more cost-effective to check for add-on products prior to creating custom solutions. Should you decide custom is the way to go, download the SDK. The SDK is available for free — yes we said free — from Microsoft at www.microsoft.com/downloads/details.aspx? FamilyID=82E632A7-FAF9-41E0-8EC1-A2662AAE9DFB&displaylang=en.

Creating a Web Portal

What is a Web portal? A *Web portal* is a Web site that provides users external to your organization access to certain Microsoft CRM data. We say *certain data* because an important aspect of a Web portal is that you control the data made available to people accessing your CRM database.

To allow for external users to access your Microsoft CRM database, Microsoft CRM has a special Web portal license. With it, companies can have unlimited user access to the Microsoft CRM database. The license provides access but doesn't allow for unlimited use of the Microsoft CRM application interface. A Web portal is a way for organizations to provide customers, prospects, and so on, read and write access to their Microsoft CRM implementation. The easiest way to put a Web portal in place is to purchase one from an ISV (independent software vendor). One such portal is available from c360 (www.c360.com), but there are others. We suggest you research the various options prior to purchasing.

Make sure you understand what you're purchasing when it comes to portal licenses. Most ISV portal software is purchased in addition to the Microsoft CRM license.

There are several aspects of the c360 portal we like, but one in particular is access to the CRM knowledge base. If your organization is diligent in creating CRM knowledge base articles, your clients can access that knowledge via a c360 portal. (For more on the knowledge base, see Chapter 24.) A robust knowledge base drives customers to your Web site, reduces calls to your support team, and is one element of providing superior customer service. You can learn more about the c360 portal at www.c360.com.

c360's Customer Support Portal focuses on providing external users access to cases and the knowledgebase. Through a configuration utility, you decide which case fields will be made available to the customer via the portal.

Once the portal is set up, customers are provided unique login information. They can then create new service cases, as shown in Figure 21-5. The customer uses this form to create a new case directly into your Microsoft CRM system.

Customers who have cases in the system can get a list of those cases via the c360 portal. Figure 21-6 is a list of cases for a particular customer. The customer can learn more details about the case status by drilling into the form from the list view.

Lastly, Figure 21-7 shows knowledge base articles. These articles are published in your CRM system and made available to your customers via the c360 portal.

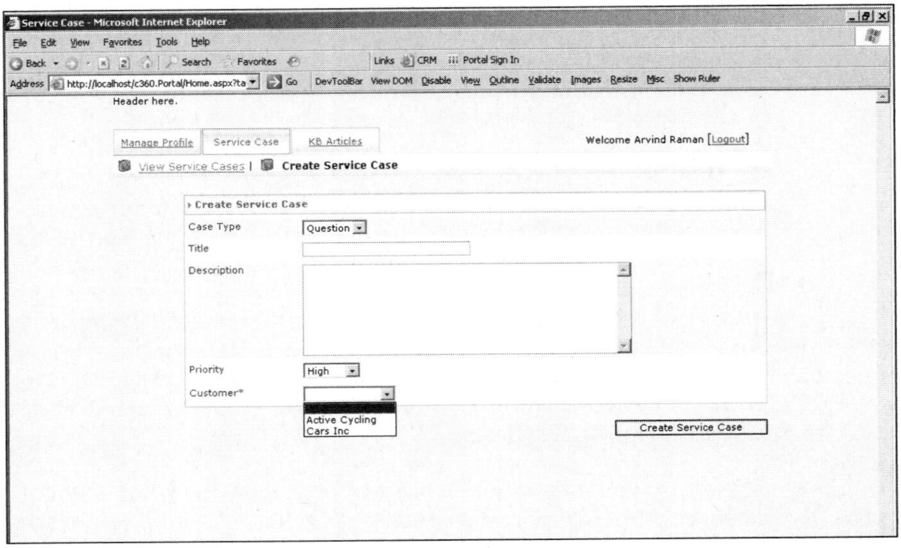

Figure 21-5:
The c360
new case
form.

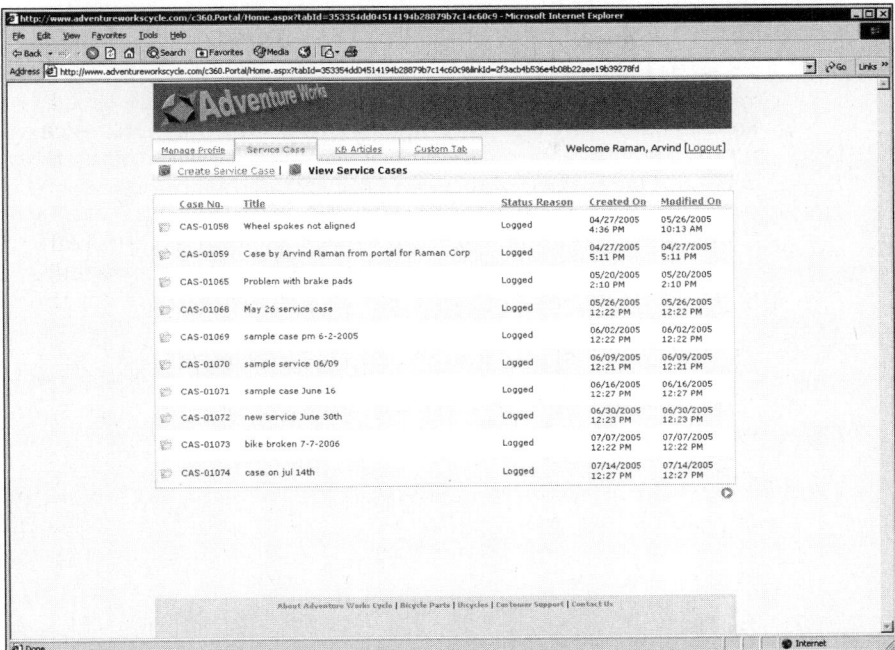

Figure 21-6:
A list of the customer's cases.

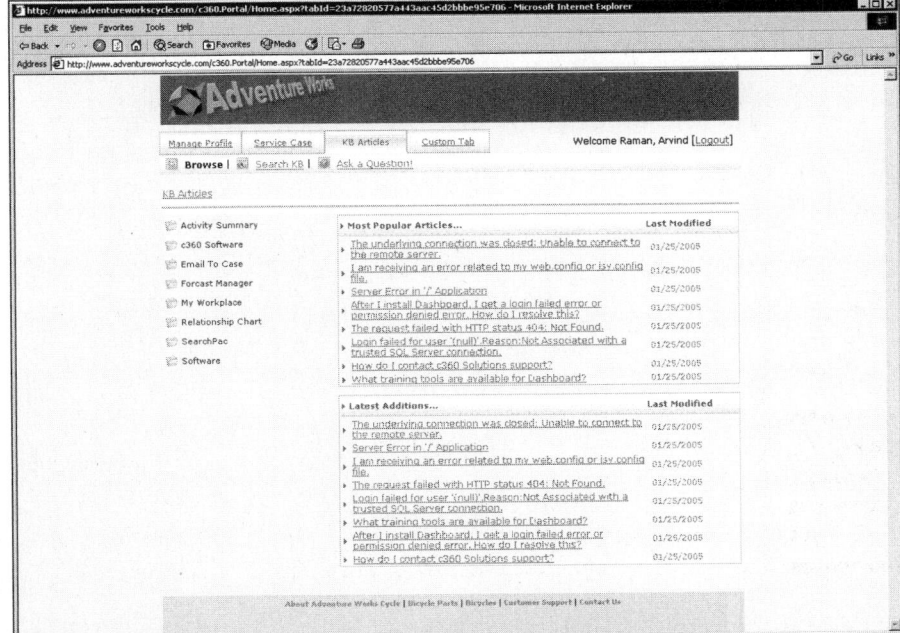

Figure 21-7:
The customer view of Microsoft CRM cases via the c360 portal.

Another commercially available Web portal is from Axonom. To learn more about their portal product go to `www.axonom.com/crm_solutions/ powertrak/pt_crm_partner_portal.html`.

You need not purchase a Web portal. You can build one — or have one built for you. Building one is easier than it sounds, but it requires programming skills and knowledge of the Microsoft CRM Software Developers Kit (SDK). We suggest you contact your Microsoft CRM reseller.

Part V
Taking Care of
Your Customers

The 5th Wave   By Rich Tennant

"Before the Internet, we were only bustin' chops locally. But now, with our Web site, we're bustin' chops all over the world."

In this part . . .

One of the beautiful parts of Microsoft CRM is that it handles sales *and* service. This integration enables your organization to coordinate activities from both sides of that fence. Salespeople, in the middle of trying to close a deal, won't be blindsided by some raging customer support issue, and customer service people will know enough to provide that little extra help when a major sale is about to go down.

Customer service is one of the hot buttons in CRM, and it's an area in which Microsoft CRM shines. When a customer calls with an issue, it's logged as a case (which we discuss in Chapter 22).

Managing your database of subjects is handled in Chapter 23. You can use CRM to manage your organizational knowledgebase, and that's discussed in Chapter 24. Cases and tasks are put into a queue for orderly disposition and management by staff members (which we discuss in Chapter 25).

Microsoft CRM even includes contract administration, so everyone can see what type of support a customer is entitled to and the software can properly decrement contracts and advise when renewals are in order (as we explain in Chapter 26).

Chapter 22

Working with Cases

*B*efore customer relationship management, or CRM, became a household term, organizations were focusing on something called *sales force automation* or *SFA,* which was essentially software that helped automate the sales process. Sales activities, opportunities, prospects, clients, and more were stored in the sales database. Salespeople would interact with the sales database either in the office or from a remote office. Remote office data was often synchronized back to the home office system. SFA was a great tool to help sales people win new business, but what about the rest of the organization?

Prior to the introduction of CRM software, customer service departments also recognized the need for effective case management software and often built or developed specific software for case or incident management. We think you're getting the picture: two products and two disparate databases. CRM solves the issue conceptually by treating the organization as a whole and recognizing that all customer-facing interactions should be stored in a single source or database.

A prime benefit of having sales and customer service share a single database is that customer interactions by both groups are captured in a central place. Sales people aren't blindsided by ongoing customer issues when calling on an existing customer. Customer service knows which customers or prospects to support, what the support requester's value is to the organization, and lots more. Management can report on *customer value* — the amount of revenue or margin attained from a specific customer minus the costs associated with sales and support.

In Microsoft CRM, the Service module (found in the navigation pane) has several entities, but the heart of the Service module is the Cases feature, where you can view, resolve, and reactivate cases in an easy and comprehensible manner.

A *case* (also known as an *incident)* is simply a record of customer interaction with the customer service department. When a customer has a question or a problem, the representative who interacts with the customer opens a case. The customer's issue can originate from a phone call, e-mail, or a support form on your Web site. (For more on this, see Chapter 21.) The customer service representative responsible for the incident opens a *case* to document the problem and its eventual solution. Cases need not be problems, but they should be a record of customer interaction with the customer service department.

Those of you without a customer service department need not skip this chapter. Cases still provide value to your organization if you view cases as important customer service follow-up. These can be items that — if they aren't attended to in a timely fashion — could alienate the customer. By using the Cases feature, you're elevating certain customer issues above simple calendar follow-ups or tasks. Even if you don't have a customer service department, we strongly recommend that you discuss how to use cases with your CRM dealer.

Some companies refer to cases as *tickets* or *issues.* Whatever they're called in your organization, active case management is the name of the game; the better you manage your cases, the better your customer service and customer satisfaction.

In this chapter, we show you how to create cases and assign them to someone on your team. You find out how to open an existing case and resolve it, scheduling activities related to gaining the solution along the way. We even explain how cases interact with queues and contracts. (For a refresher on queues, see Chapter 25; for contracts, see Chapter 26.) You also find out how to reactivate a case when necessary.

Case Management Overview

The case management path looks like this: A customer service representative (CSR) takes a call. Let's say the customer's having a problem with one of your time transporters. He dialed Camelot, A.D. 495 and ended up in Peoria, 1958.

The CSR creates a case and links it to the appropriate customer. The case is assigned to an engineer. The engineer sets about finding a solution, generating a few e-mails to the customer along the way. The engineer solves the problem and closes the case.

A week later, the customer calls back with the same problem. A CSR (not necessarily the same one as before) reactivates the case, and the solution process begins anew. A more thorough solution is developed and recorded, and the case is closed again. A month later, a different customer calls with the same problem. Any CSR can search the database for all cases related to the same problem. This is case management at its best.

Working in the Cases Window

Cases are listed in the main display area of the Cases window, like the one shown in Figure 22-1. You use this window to open cases, and then add notes and schedule activities, with the goal of resolving the case. The Cases window is also where you assign cases to other service representatives, share cases, or accept them yourself. The entire service team can use this window to collectively track the current status and ultimate disposition of cases.

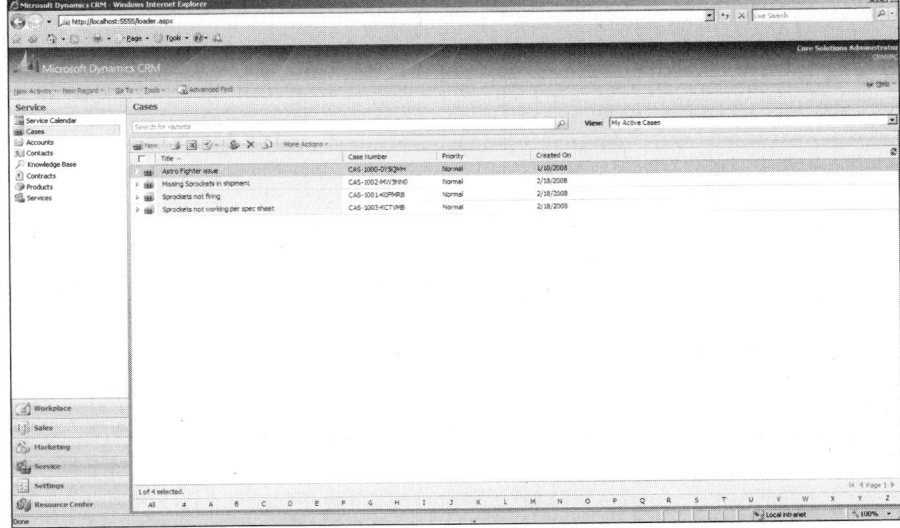

Figure 22-1:
The Cases window is where you can view and sort cases.

To open the Cases window, click the Service button at the bottom of the navigation pane. Then select Cases from the list of options at the top of the pane.

The main part of the window has a list of all your active cases. You can filter this list by choosing one of the following options from the View drop-down menu.

- ✔ **Active Cases:** All cases assigned to you or your fellow team members that haven't been resolved.

- ✔ **All Cases:** All cases assigned to you or your fellow team members that are open or have been resolved.

- ✔ **My Active Cases:** All cases assigned to you that haven't been resolved. During a Microsoft CRM session, when entering the Cases window for the first time or going back to it, the View option always reverts to My Active Cases (unless it's changed by the system administrator).

- ✔ **My Resolved Cases:** All cases assigned to you that have been resolved.

- ✔ **Resolved Cases:** All cases assigned to you or your fellow team members that have been resolved.

These are the views you get "out of the box." Your implementation partner or system administrator can add, rename, and delete views.

You can sort cases also by column headings. Just click a column heading to sort as follows:

- ✔ **Title** displays cases alphabetically.

- ✔ **Status** displays cases alphabetically by status (resolved or active). The status column is visible when choosing the All Cases view.

- ✔ **Case Number** displays cases in numerical order.

- ✔ **Priority** displays cases by level of importance.

- ✔ **Created On** displays cases in chronological order.

Again, note that your system administrator can add columns to this list or delete columns from this list.

Click a column header a second time to display the cases in reverse order.

You have two ways to find specific cases. The Look For field at the top of the Cases window lets you search active cases by title or case number. You may type the full title or any part of it. Click the Find button, and a list of matching cases appears. Use the wildcard character ***** to type only a portion of the text string you're looking for. For example, searching for _*porter_ returns _Porter_, _Transporter_, and _Exporter_.

You can also use the Advanced Find feature to search various fields. To do so, choose Tools⇨Advanced Find or click the Advanced Find button on the toolbar at the top of the screen. Microsoft CRM lets you define search criteria over several fields. Figure 22-2 shows just some of the case-related fields that you can use to perform a search.

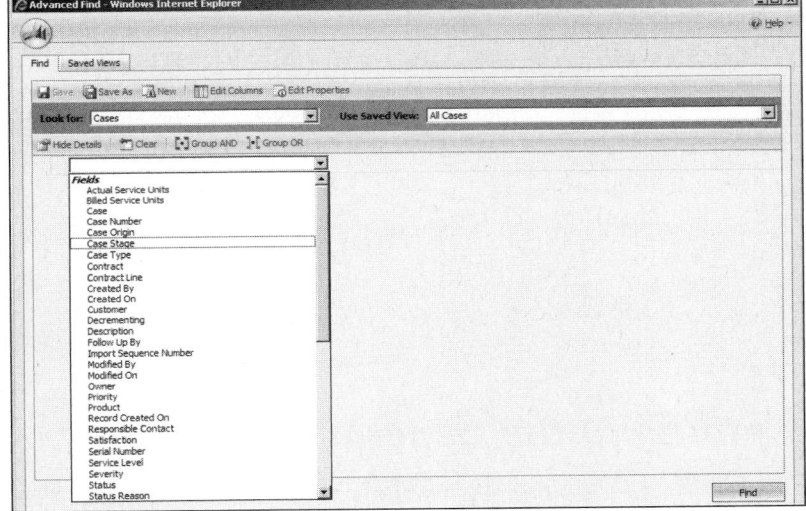

Figure 22-2:
The
Advanced
Find feature
enables you
to use
multiple
fields and
specific
definitions
to search
for cases.

Creating Cases

Anyone with create case rights can create or add a case to the Microsoft CRM system. Rights are assigned by your system administrator. Cases can be created in two places: from the main Cases navigation area or from an account or contact record. However you get to the new case window, the form is the same. To open a case from the Cases area in the service module, follow these steps:

1. **On the navigation pane, click the Service button.**

2. **At the top of the navigation pane, select Cases.**

   The Cases window appears on the right. (Refer to Figure 22-1.)

3. **On the Cases toolbar, click New.**

   The Case: New window appears, as shown in Figure 22-3.

Figure 22-3:
The General
tab of the
Case: New
window
contains
basic
information
about the
case.

Filling in the General tab

The Case: New window has two tabs: the General tab and the Notes and
Article tab. The General tab is divided into three sections: Overview, which
has six fields to further define the case; Assignment Information; and
Contract and Product Information.

Some fields (such as Subject) have a magnifying glass to the right of the field.
This means you must use the magnifying glass or the Form Assistant to fill in
the field. For more information on both options, see Chapter 3.

TIP

Lookup fields (magnifying glass icons) now has autocomplete. To enter the
"Sprocket Design" as the subject click in the subject field and begin typing
part of the word and tab out of the field. If auto-complete finds more than one
match, the various options will be displayed.

Remember, all fields with a red asterisk are required. Follow these steps to
complete the Overview area of the General tab:

1. In the Title box of the General tab, enter a title for the case.

    The title is a short description of the reported issue. The Title field can
    hold a maximum of 175 characters.

2. **Click in the Customer field and begin typing the customer name (account or contact). Before you complete the name, tab to the Subject field.**

   You can use the magnifying glass instead, or the Form Assistant, but we're going to explore the autocomplete feature. By leaving the Customer field — in our case, tabbing to the Subject field — we triggered auto-complete. The auto-complete options are:

   a. *If the customer name is unique in your database, it will show in the field blue in color and underlined (hyperlink). If so, skip to Step 3.*

   b. *If there is a yellow caution icon with the sequence of letters typed underlined in red, it means more than one possible match has been found.*

   The more you type, the less likely you'll find duplicate records.

   c. *Click the hyperlink field (Figure 22-4).*

   d. *Select the account or contact from the list.*

   The account is entered into the Customer field.

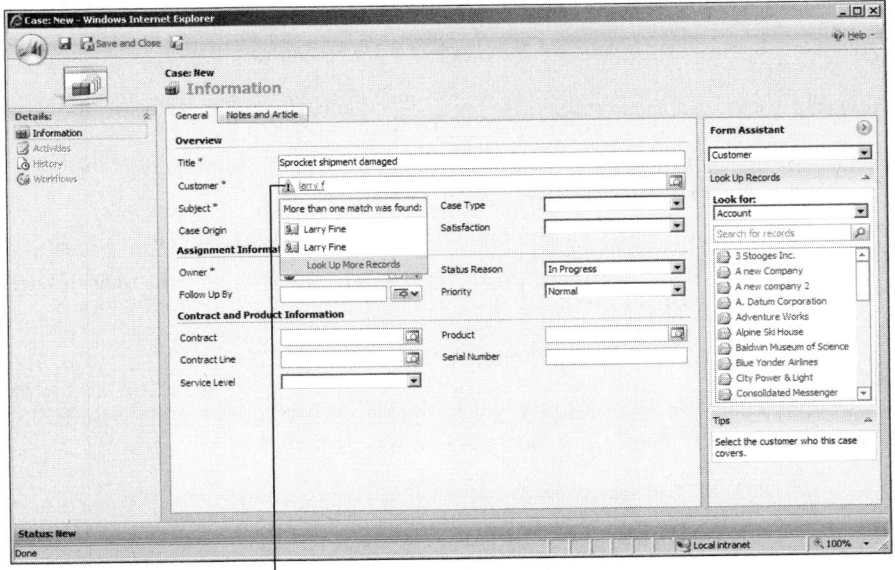

Figure 22-4:
A list of
possible
matching
records.

The hyperlink field

3. **Use the Form Assistant to fill in the Subject field.**

The Subject option categorizes your cases by subject, such as Sprocket Delivery Issues or Sprocket Quality. You can link the case to a subject in your subject tree. (For more on the subject tree, see Chapter 23.)

4. **Back on the General tab, in the Case Origin field, click the arrow and select how you received the case.**

Note: Your system administrator can edit this list.

5. **In the Case Type field, select a value from the drop-down list.**

The value categorizes the case as a question, problem, or request. (Your system administrator can also edit this list.)

6. **(Optional) In the Satisfaction field, select the option that best indicates the customer's level of satisfaction with your service.**

Typically, you fill out this field prior to closing the case, not when first opening the case.

The Assignment Information area of the General tab has four fields. Fill them in as follows:

1. **(Optional) Select the Owner field and choose who you want to assign the case to for resolution.**

This field defaults to you, the creator of the case. You can leave it as it is or reassign the case to another user.

2. **In the Follow Up By field, select the date on which the owner should follow up on the case.**

You can click the calendar or make a selection from the drop-down list.

3. **In the Status Reason field, select the option that best describes the current status of the case.**

4. **In the Priority box, set a priority for this case.**

The Contract and Product Information area offers five more fields to define your case:

1. **In the Form Assistant, select the Contract option.**

Select a contract to link this case to.

2. **In the Form Assistant, select the Contract Line option.**

Set the case to a contract line here.

3. **In the Service Level field, click the arrow and select the appropriate service level from the list.**

4. **In the Form Assistant, select the Product option.**

   This lets you link the case to a particular product.

5. **In the Serial Number field, enter a serial number associated with this case or with a product associated with this case.**

   If a serial number is associated with a contract line, you can fill it in from the Form Assistant.

Now you can move on to the Notes and Article tab.

Filling in the Notes and Article tab

The other tab of the Case: New window, Notes and Article, is much simpler than the General tab, as you can see in Figure 22-5. This is where you can enter any notes and articles pertaining to the case. For example, you can note your conversation with the customer in the Notes section and attach a knowledgebase article used to help the customer. You can also e-mail the knowledgebase article from here.

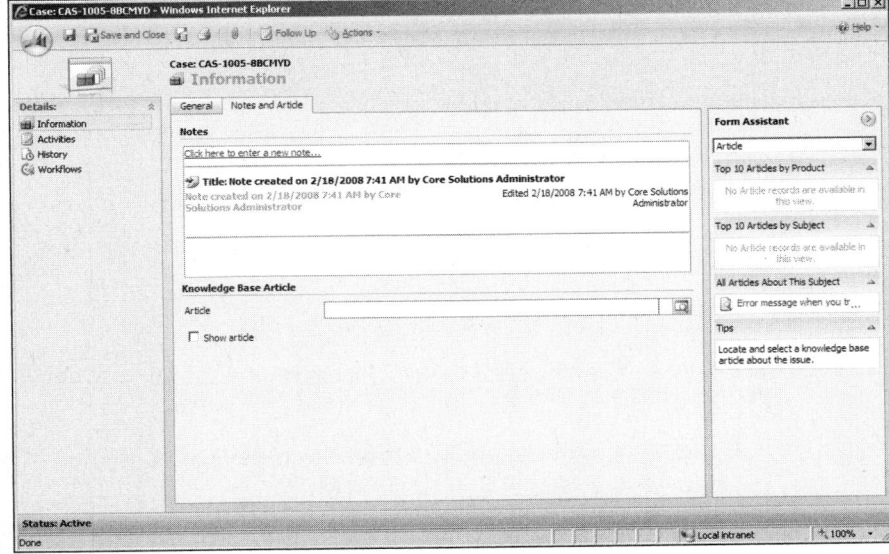

Figure 22-5: The second tab of the Case: New window shows the Notes and Knowledge Base Article areas.

To fill in the first area of the Notes and Article tab, follow the self-explanatory instruction to "Click here to enter a new note." A data entry area appears for you to manually enter a note. Enter as many notes as you like.

In the second area, you can link an article that ties into this particular case. If you use the Form Assistant and select the Article option, Microsoft CRM automatically displays your top ten article selections based on the links you defined in the knowledge base. (For more information on the knowledge base, see Chapter 24.) If this list doesn't show you the article you need, you can use the magnifying glass.

Click the Show Article check box to display the article you selected in the Notes and Article tab. After the article is displayed, you can e-mail it to a client from this tab by clicking E-Mail KB Article.

To look up a knowledge base article in your library and attach it to this case, do the following:

1. **Click the magnifying glass icon at the end of the Article field.**

   The Look Up Articles dialog box appears, as shown in Figure 22-6. You have a handful of ways for searching the knowledge base.

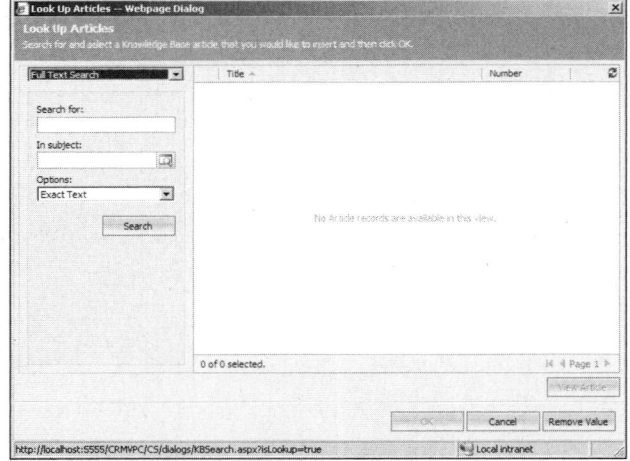

Figure 22-6:
Search the knowledge base for articles related to the case.

2. **Click the arrow in the top drop-down box to choose one of the following options to search for articles:**

   - *Full Text Search:* Search the full text of articles for specific words.

   - *Keyword Search:* Search by keyword.

   - *Title Search:* Search by article title.

- *Article Number Search:* Search for an article number.
- *Subject Browse:* Browse all the subjects to find what you want.

3. **In the Search For field, enter the word or words that you want to find.**

4. **In the In Subject field, make a selection:**

   a. *Click the magnifying glass to the right of the field.*

   The Look Up a Subject dialog box appears, listing your subjects organized by headings and subheadings. You can choose a specific subject for the program to search. For example, if you select the subject Marketing, the program won't look for your text in Sales, Service, or Thank You Letters.

   b. *Select a subject.*

   c. *Click OK.*

5. **In the Options field, make a selection from the drop-down list.**

   You have two options: Exact Text, which means the search looks for exact matches only, and Use Like Words, which searches for the string of text you entered. For example, enter the word *pro* and you'll get everything containing that sequence of letters.

6. **Click the Search button.**

   A list of articles meeting your search criteria appears on the right.

7. **When you find the article you want, double-click it (or select it and click OK) to attach it to the case.**

   You return to the Case: New dialog box, where you can continue adding articles or exit the case altogether. You can attach only one article per case.

   You can view the article prior to selecting it by clicking View Article on the bottom right.

8. **To e-mail the article, click the Show Article check box.**

   The article displays below the check box.

9. **In the knowledgebase article window, click E-Mail KB Article.**

   Fill out the e-mail form and send.

10. **To save your data, click the Save and Close button in the upper left corner of the Case form.**

The next step in working with a case is to assign it (if you're the assigner) or accept it (if you're the assignee).

Assigning and Accepting Cases

Often, cases are assigned to a queue that customer service representatives (CSRs) monitor. (For more on queues, see Chapter 25.) Of course, you can assign cases directly to an individual based on skill set, availability, or both. Microsoft CRM has provisions for assignment to either a queue or an individual. A case can be assigned to only one queue or one person at time. However, there is no limit to the number of times a case is assigned.

Through the use of workflow, case assignment can be automated based on the rules you establish. (For more on workflow, see Chapter 9.) For example, if a case has a subject of "Shipment Missing," a workflow rule could be employed that will assign it to the shipping department queue.

The first thing you want to do to start work on a case is to assign it to a queue or an individual. In the following steps, we assign a case to a queue. Here's all you need to do:

1. **On the navigation pane, click the Service button.**

2. **At the top of the navigation pane, select Cases.**

   The Cases window appears on the right.

3. **In the Cases window, select a case.**

   To select several records for an ensuing action, hold down the Ctrl key and click. Selecting the check box at the top of the first column (under the New button) selects all cases.

4. **Click the Assign icon on the toolbar above the list of cases.**

   The Assign to Queue or User dialog box appears, displaying two options for managing cases. Route Case is a powerful option after you establish workflow rules. Find out more about defining workflow rules and processes in Chapter 9.

5. **Click the Assign to Another User or Queue option and then click the magnifying glass icon to the right of the field.**

   The Look Up Records dialog box appears, as shown in Figure 22-7.

6. **In the Look For field, choose User or Queue.**

   By default, the field displays User. In this example, we're assigning the case to a queue, so we select Queue from the Look For drop-down box.

7. **Select a Queue.**

   When you change the Look For field to Queue, a list of all of the queues in the system are displayed. To limit the list, you can use the Search for Records field to the right of the Look For field. Type in all or part of the queue name and click the magnifying glass icon.

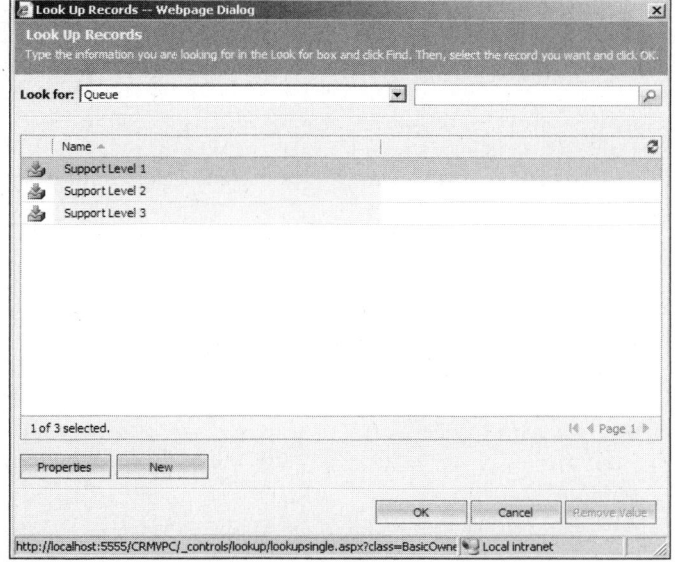

Figure 22-7:
You can
assign the
case to an
individual
CSR or
place it in
a service
queue.

8. **Select the Queue and click OK.**

   You must highlight the appropriate user or queue even if only one match is listed.

   When you click OK, you return to the Confirm Assignment dialog box, where the username appears.

9. **Click OK to close the Confirm Assignment dialog box.**

   You return to the window of the case you were assigning, and that case is assigned.

With this method, we assigned one or more cases to a queue without opening the individual case form.

Alternatively, case assignments can happen from the open case form by performing these steps:

1. **Open a case.**

2. **Click the magnifying glass to the right of the Owner field; or from the toolbar, choose Actions⇨Assign.**

3. **Follow Steps 4 through 8 in the preceding step list.**

For queues to work effectively, people need to monitor them. When someone responsible for monitoring a particular queue sees that a case has been assigned to the queue, he or she needs to take ownership of the case. In doing so, the case is removed from the queue and the owner is the CSR working on the case.

Follow these steps to monitor a queue and accept ownership of a case record:

1. **On the navigation pane, click the Workplace button.**

2. **At the top of the navigation pane, in the My Work section, select Queues.**

   If a plus sign appears next to My Work, click it first to open the list. The Queues window appears on the right, with its own navigation pane and a list of queues. (See Figure 22-8.)

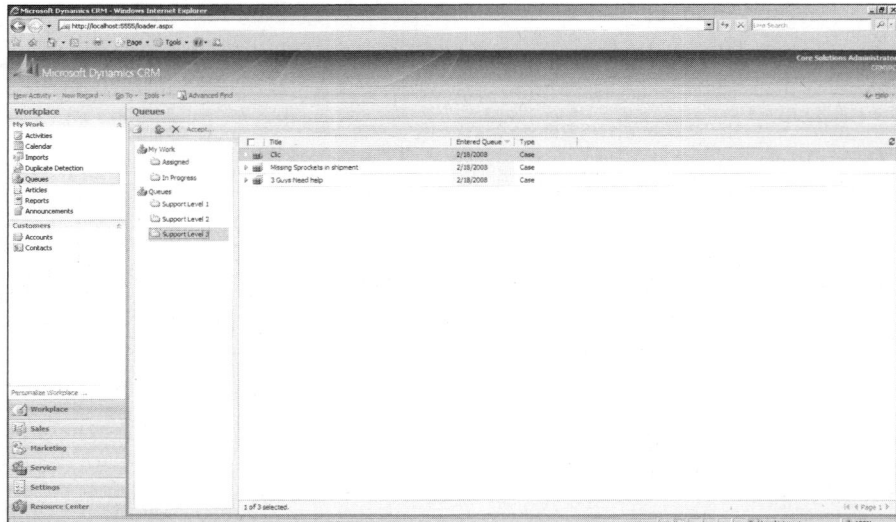

Figure 22-8: The pane in the Queues window enables you to view all cases assigned to a specific queue.

3. **In the Queues window, click a folder under My Work.**

   Each folder is a separate queue. All cases assigned to that queue appear in the main window.

   In Microsoft CRM, you can't reject a case or an activity. (By *activity,* we mean a task, a fax, a phone call, an e-mail, a letter, or an appointment.) If you don't want to accept a case or an activity that is assigned to you, you must reassign it to another user or queue.

4. **Click the Case you want to accept.**

   To select multiple cases, hold down the Ctrl key and click.

5. **At the top of the Queues window, click the Accept button.**

   The Confirm Assignment dialog box appears.

6. **Click OK.**

   The case is now removed from the queue and assigned to you in your In Progress queue.

Tending to Cases

As you work toward resolving a case, you typically have to perform certain activities to obtain a solution. For example, you might need to perform tests on the Spacely Sprocket to see whether it will repeat the problem your customer reported.

In this scenario, you'd perform the following steps to log your time and associate it with the case:

1. **On the navigation pane, click the Service button.**

2. **At the top of the navigation pane, select Cases.**

   The Cases window appears.

3. **In the Cases window, double-click the case you're working on.**

   To follow along with the example, we double-clicked the case for which we're scheduling a test.

4. **In the Case navigation pane, click the Activities option.**

   The window shows uncompleted activities associated with the case.

5. **On the toolbar, click the New Activity button.**

   The New Activity dialog box appears. Because we're performing a test on the equipment, we use Task.

6. **Highlight Task and then click OK.**

   The Task: New window appears.

7. **Enter a subject that describes the task you'll perform.**

   Note that the Regarding field already displays the case title, and your name should be in the Owner field. The Duration defaults to 30 minutes, but you can change this using the drop-down menu. If appropriate, you can also complete the Due date and time; Priority; Category; and Subcategory fields.

8. **Click the Save and Close icon.**

   The task now appears in the main display for the associated case.

To complete the task (and automatically accrue billable time against the case), follow these steps:

1. **In the Cases window, double-click the appropriate case.**

   The Case window appears, showing the case you selected. (The title of the window includes the name of the case.)

2. **In the navigation pane, click the Activities option.**

   You see a list of all activities associated with this case.

3. **Double-click the task you want to close.**

4. **Click the Save as Completed icon.**

In the Case window, you'll see that the task is no longer displayed under Activities in the navigation pane. But wait! Click History, which shows the completed task. If you had spent one hour performing the task, for example, the customer would now be on the hook for one hour of contract time.

You can close an activity as completed instead of saving and reopening. If the activity isn't a scheduled activity, but one you're entering in for historical purposes, simply click the Save as Completed icon.

You can associate existing activities with this case by clicking the Add Existing Activity button to the right of the New Activity button.

Resolving a case

Case resolution is the system's way of indicating that the problem is solved. (Many organizations like to set an intermediate status indicating that, from the technician's perspective, the case is resolved, but the customer has a period of time to indicate otherwise. This is a good topic to take up with your dealer.) You can resolve cases on the first call as they happen, or after extensive research.

In some cases, multiple activities are generated to help resolve a case. In Microsoft CRM, you can't mark a case as resolved if any activities associated with the case remain uncompleted. This might require completing phone calls, tasks, and appointments, sending e-mail messages, and more. This prevents a user from accidentally closing a case before completing all mandated workflow and activities.

After you determine a solution to a case and complete all associated activities, follow these steps to change a case's status to resolved:

1. In the Cases window, double-click the case you want to resolve.

You may find it helpful to first select My Active Cases from the View drop-down menu in the upper right corner of the window.

2. From the menu bar (at the top of the screen), choose Actions⇨ Resolve Case.

The Resolve Case dialog box appears, as shown in Figure 22-9. The dialog box has the following options:

- *Resolution Type:* A drop-down box in which you can indicate if the problem is solved.

- *Resolution:* A required field (see the red asterisk) for a brief description of how the case was resolved.

- *Total Time:* Microsoft CRM automatically calculates and fills in the Total Time field. *Total time* is defined as the sum of time spent on all activities associated with the resolution of the case. CRM recognizes the following activities in the total time calculation; task, fax, phone call, letter, e-mail, and appointment.

- *Billable Time:* A required field that defaults to total time, but you override it to adjust for the actual time to bill on the case. If this activity is linked to a contract, the billable time you indicate here is applied against the total time listed in the contract.

- *Description:* A note field to any case-related information not covered in the actual case. This is a good place to put the resolution results.

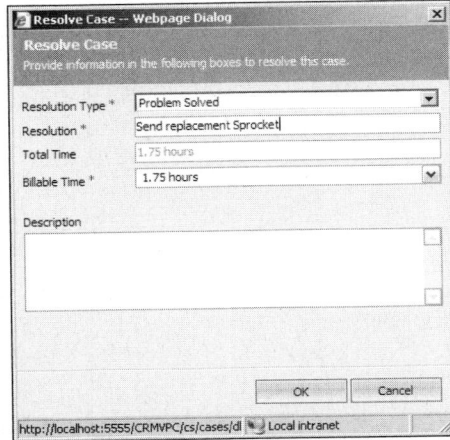

Figure 22-9:
Document the time you spent resolving a case.

3. **Click OK.**

   The Resolve Case dialog box closes. Note that the case status updates to Resolved in the lower left corner of the Case window.

Reactivating a case

If a customer calls with a recurrence of a previously resolved problem, you need to reopen or reactivate the case. Follow these steps:

1. **In the Cases window, select My Resolved Cases or All Resolved Cases from the View drop-down menu.**

   A list of all your resolved cases appears.

2. **Double-click the case you want to reactivate.**

3. **In the menu bar (at the top of the screen), choose Actions⇨Reactivate.**

   The Reactivate Confirmation dialog box appears.

4. **Click OK.**

   The case status in the lower left corner of the Case window appears as *Active*.

As you can see, Microsoft CRM offers extensive choices to help you better serve your customers, with almost everything just a few clicks away.

Chapter 23

Managing Your Subjects

*N*ow you can slice and dice your data without a Ginsu! Subjects are great way to organize and relate data. In Microsoft CRM, you can relate subjects to cases, products, and knowledge base articles. Subjects are like buckets. Associate a case, for example, with a subject, and it goes into that subject bucket. Over time as cases build, you can run reports based on subject bucket. For example, a computer laptop manufacturer may decide to create three subjects: Hard Drive, Screen, and Keyboard. When a customer calls and opens a case regarding her laptop's malfunctioning screen, the case is associated with the Screen subject.

By tracking the subject of a case, an organization's support manager can then report on the number of cases open by support technician by subject. Additionally, support organizations can route cases by subject, ensuring the most qualified support technician is assigned to the case.

If subjects are arranged in buckets, it's possible for buckets to contain other buckets. This is called *nesting*. Subject nesting allows one bucket to reside inside another bucket. For example, the hard drive bucket could be found in the laptop bucket. Another, hard drive bucket could be found inside the desktop computer bucket.

Also remember that Microsoft CRM subjects can not only be products but also services. For this chapter, we use Bikes, Clothing and Accessories, and Company Information as our subjects.

Structuring your subjects and their relationships to one another is important. We show you how to create your primary subjects and if required in your organization sub-subjects.

Tips for Defining Your Subjects

Microsoft CRM uses a collapsible tree system — trees, not buckets — much like the ones that Windows and Microsoft Outlook use. Creating a subject tree offers the following benefits:

- A consistent hierarchy for associating contacts with products, sales literature, and knowledge base information
- Easy access to information related to specific subjects
- Centralized management of subjects (including creating, editing, and removing subjects) and their relationships to one another in the subject tree

Building a subject tree is easy, but figuring out what to put on which branch can be difficult. We recommend scheduling a brainstorming session with different departments in your company. Divide your products and services into categories and topics. Then determine if you will need to further define one or all of your topics into sub-topics. Repeat this process until you're comfortable that your subject definition is detailed enough to aid in reporting, but not so detailed that you will have trouble differentiating one branch from the branch above it.

Brainstorming can become perplexing and lead to lengthy discussions. Don't worry — spending time on the subject tree at the beginning is far better than building the subject tree on the fly. And moving things around in the subject tree later isn't as easy as placing them at their appropriate level in the first place. Additionally, ad hoc subject design may not account for the needs of your entire organization. You can save yourself time and aggravation by having a blueprint in place first.

No hard-and-fast rules exist when defining the structure of a subject tree. Each company has its own priorities. But you might want to consider the following items when defining your subject tree structure:

- Price lists
- Sales literature
- Product specs
- Warranty information
- Service contracts
- Knowledge base articles

When is a subject not a subject?

If you open an activity form (task, appointment, phone call, and so on) in Microsoft CRM, you'll notice that there is a field called Subject. Under closer scrutiny, one would notice that the lookup magnifying glass icon is missing. What happened to our subject trees? Nothing, this subject field is a text field. In this case, *subject* refers to the subject of the activity and isn't related to Subjects, the object of this chapter.

Only users with the appropriate access rights can create subjects and add items to a subject tree. (See Chapter 8 for more information.)

You can also relate items such as product catalogs and sales literature to subjects.

Accessing the Subjects Window

After you create the outline or blueprint for your company's subject tree, be sure to save it where you can access it easily when you're ready to build it. A good idea is to have the administrative assistant (who as we all know, truly runs the company) create the outline in a Word document.

Before you can use subjects in CRM, you must create at least one subject. You add subjects, maintain them, and delete them from the subject management area, which you can find in Settings. Here's how you get to it:

1. **On the navigation pane, click the Settings button, which is second up from the bottom.**

   The Settings navigation options show at the top of the navigation pane.

2. **In the navigation pane, click the Business Management Link, which is second from the top.**

   Business Management options are now available on the right.

3. **In the Business Management pane, click the Subjects link on the bottom right.**

   The Subject Management area replaces Business Management on the right. See Figure 23-1.

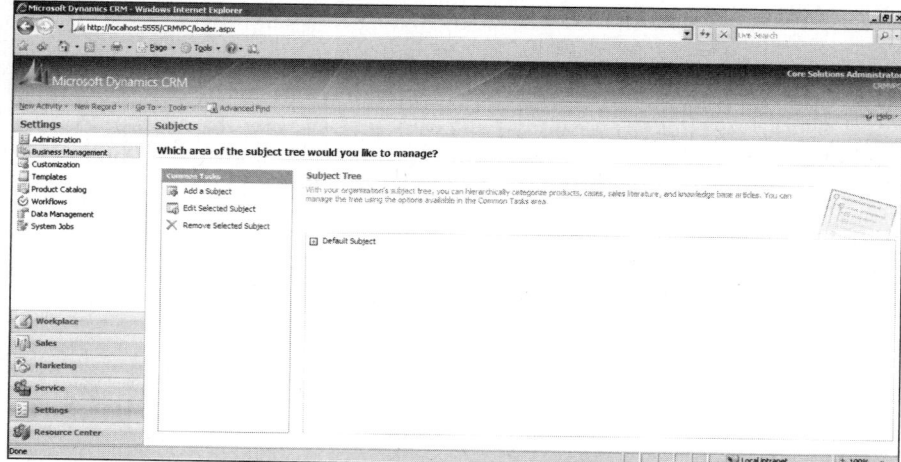

Figure 23-1:
Begin
managing
your
subjects
here.

Three options appear in the Common Tasks pane, which is to the left of the main display: Add a Subject, Edit Selected Subject, and Remove Selected Subject. We cover each of these in the following sections.

On the right is the Subject Tree. When accessing the Subject Management area for the first time, you'll find a single subject: Default Subject. A plus sign is located just to the left of the default subject, leading one to believe that additional subjects are available to cascade down. However, clicking the plus sign doesn't reveal any additional data; instead, the plus sign turns to a dot, indicating that this tree doesn't have children.

Adding a Subject

You've taken the time to create a subject hierarchy. Now it's time to add your subject tree to Microsoft CRM. Because you can nest subjects in a treelike format, we add a new subject at the root level (or the tree trunk, which is the same level as the default subject).

To add subjects, follow these steps:

1. **In the Common Tasks area of the Subjects window, click Add a Subject.**

   The Add Subject dialog box appears.

2. **Enter a title for the subject and (if desired) a description.**

   The title is required; you can't save the form without a title.

3. **To place the new subject under a previously created subject, click the magnifying glass icon next to the Parent Subject field, then click OK.**

   The Subject Lookup dialog box appears, as shown in Figure 23-2.

   If you navigate to the selected parent and child before you click Add a Subject, the Parent Subject field is automatically populated with your highlighted selection.

Subject Lookup
Select a subject.

Subjects

○ None

☐ Default Subject

| OK | Cancel |

http://localhost:5555/CRMVPC/_controls/lookup/lookupsubject.   Local intranet

Figure 23-2:
You can associate the new subject to a parent subject.

4. **Click the appropriate plus sign (+) to the left of a subject to open the subject tree, highlight the subject you want as the parent, and click OK.**

   The new subject is added to the subject tree. This design flexibility enables you to create a sophisticated hierarchy to match the blueprint you came up with at the brainstorming session.

   The desired parent can be the child of another subject.

5. **If you selected a parent subject and you want to display the subject you just added, you must click the plus sign to the left of the parent.**

   If you add the new subject as the child of a child, continue clicking plus signs until you drill down to the appropriate level.

Clicking the plus sign to the left of a subject displays its children (if any exist) and is the easiest way to drill down into a subject. If the plus sign turns into a dot, you know that you're at the end of the line for that subject.

Note: Whenever you make an addition or revision to the subject tree and click OK, Microsoft CRM saves the subject and refreshes the window. If you drill down several levels to add a new subject and click OK, the screen refresh takes you all the way back to the top-level view of the subject tree (arrgh!). It does this so that you'll always have an up-to-date view of your subject tree, but be prepared to spend a few extra mouse clicks when adding lots of branch subjects.

Editing a Subject

The Edit Selected Subject option is the second option in the Common Tasks pane. (Refer to Figure 23-1.) This option enables you to rename a subject or move it to another location in the subject tree.

Modifying and updating the subject tree is part of the evolutionary process of any business. Should you do so, all edits cascade through the system, meaning the new subject name changes anywhere the subject is in use. This includes historical data.

To edit a subject, follow these steps:

1. **In the Subject Tree area of the Subjects window, highlight the subject.**

2. **In the Common Tasks pane, click Edit Selected Subject.**

   The Edit Subject dialog box appears.

3. **Edit the subject's title, change the subject's parent/child relationship in the subject tree, or revise the description notes, all by entering text into the respective fields.**

   To change the parent subject, you must use the magnifying glass at the end of the field. You can modify the title and description by entering text.

Don't forget to change the Default subject to something that matches your business.

If you made a subject a child of another subject and would like to remove the parental relationship (would that be orphaning the subject?) click the magnifying glass icon and select the None button at the top of the dialog box.

Moving a subject to a new parent subject will move *all* of the selected subject's associated children. This action could lead to an unpleasant surprise for your co-workers the next time they look for a subject.

4. **Click OK.**

The Edit Subject dialog box closes, and your edits are saved.

Changing the subject title changes the title throughout the application. This means that historical records, such as cases, will have the new value as subject title and not the original value.

Removing a Subject

The Remove Selected Subject option, the last option in the Common Tasks pane, enables you to delete a subject from the subject tree. You might choose this option if a product line is discontinued or a service is no longer offered.

Microsoft CRM allows you to remove only subjects that aren't associated with existing records, such as Cases, Knowledgebase Articles, and Products. If you remove a subject from the subject tree, and that subject has child branches, child subjects move up a level.

To remove a subject, follow these steps:

1. **In the Subject Tree area of the Subjects window, highlight the subject you want to remove.**

2. **In the Common Tasks pane, click Remove Selected Subject.**

3. **When a window appears asking whether you're sure you want to delete the subject, click OK.**

The window closes and the subject tree refreshes, minus the subject you removed.

Relating Subjects to Other Entities

Now that you've built a rather complex subject tree, how do you use it? As we mention earlier, you can use subjects with knowledge base articles, cases, sales literature, and products.

For example, let's assume that Dick in the service department opens a new case pertaining to a software problem that Mr. Wayne is having with the Series 211 Transporter. Something about this case strikes him as familiar. Because other cases are associated to the subject "Series 211 Transporter," Dick can search for those cases and get a list of them almost instantly. Alfred, his cube neighbor, gets a request for sales literature on the Series 211 Transporter. He conducts a search for all sales literature linked to the subject "Series 211 Transporter" and gets a list of all related documents. Last but not least, there's Barbara, in the cube across the way. At a potential customer's request, she's researching the electrical requirements of all backup power supplies that your company sells. She performs a knowledge base search of all articles related to the subject "Power Supplies" and prints those articles.

Holy association, Batman! You mean by associating and organizing subject trees with logical, explanatory details, you can easily retrieve your company's data and information? Correct, Boy Wonder!

Relating subjects to cases

Subjects provide a mechanism to report on case issues. For example, the engineers responsible for developing future generations of The Series 211 Transporter may propose a redesign based on metrics learned from subjects.

Let's go back to Dick and the case he just opened with Mr. Wayne. He wants to make sure this case is linked to the Series 211 Transporter subject. Others might come across the same problem. Dick knows that this is important information for any of the customer service representatives in his company.

You can link new or existing cases to subjects by following these steps:

1. **Third from the bottom of the navigation pane, click the Service button.**

2. **At the top of the pane, click Cases (under Service).**

3. **To start a new case, click the New button in the upper-left corner of the form. Or to open an active case, double-click it.**

   Both options display the Case window.

4. **In the Case window, click the magnifying glass icon to the right of the Subject field.**

   The Subject Lookup window displays the subject tree. Although you may have only one subject tree for your company, you can design the subject tree with as much complexity as you need.

5. **Locate the subject to which you want to link the case.**

   You may need to click a plus sign or two to drill down to the appropriate subject.

6. **After you locate the subject you want, double-click it or highlight it and click OK.**

   The subject you select is displayed in the Subject field of the Case window.

The Form Assistant on the far right displays the subject tree when you enter the Subject field. You can locate the subject as in Step 5 above and skip Step 6 by simply selecting a subject from the form assistant.

7. **Click the Save and Close icon in the upper-left corner of the window.**

   Your case is now related to the subject you selected.

We recommend that you relate cases to subjects when you first create the cases. However, if you aren't sure of the best subject to link to, you can assign or change the subject later. Keep in mind that changing a subject related to a case may cause problems if a user has worked on the case and related information to the previous subject.

Subjects relate similar cases. Searching for cases with similar issues helps customer service representatives quickly find solutions to problems.

Putting the case link to work

Suppose a customer calls with a problem with one of your company's products — the Hop-n-Pop toaster just won't hop when it pops the bread out. Your customer service representatives can check to see whether any other cases are linked to the same product using the Advanced Find feature. This offers you the ability to conduct detailed searches in almost any searchable field in Microsoft CRM.

To view all cases linked to a specific subject, follow these steps:

1. **In the menu bar (at the top of the screen), choose Tools⇨Advanced Find.**

   The Advanced Find dialog box appears, as shown in Figure 23-3. The Look For field tells the program where to look for the parameters you're going to add later. The Use Saved View lists searches you've saved previously. The area below these fields is where you'll enter the data you want to search for.

2. **In the Look For field, verify that Cases is in the box; if it isn't, click the arrow to the right and choose Cases.**

   The look for box defaults to the entity you are on when you launch Advanced Find. It may not have cases in the box when the form first opens.

3. **If below the Look For drop-down box you see Show Details and perhaps certain field values such as Owner Equals Current User, click the Show Details button. If not, skip to step 5.**

   The Show Details button changes to Hide Details and now you can change the query options.

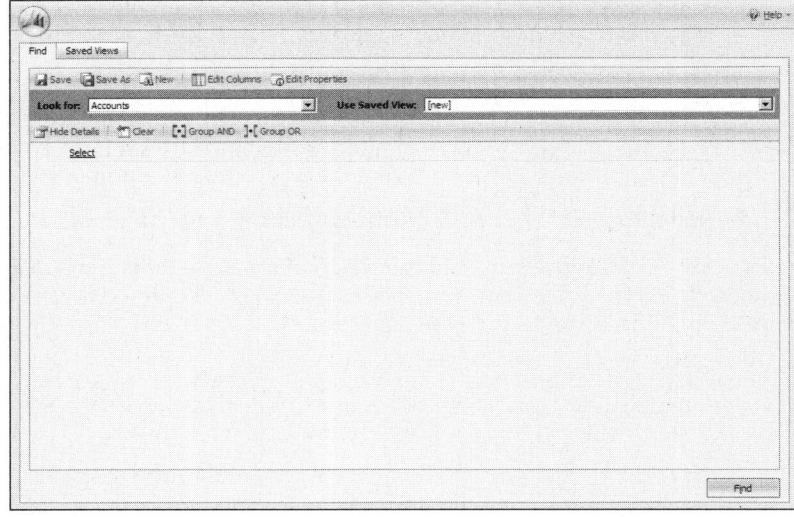

Figure 23-3:
You can
search for
records
based on
values you
define.

4. **Click the Clear button to clear out the current search parameters.**

   You can skip this step if there aren't any search parameters showing.

5. **Mouse over the Select option to activate the Select drop-down menu, and then click the arrow or in the box to open the menu.**

   The options in the Select drop-down box are related to the entity you're querying and vary based on the item selected in the Look For drop-down list. For example, if you chose (in Step 2) to look for Documents, your search options are File Size, Author Name, File Name, and so on. If you chose Facilities/Equipment, you can search for Name, Primary E-Mail, Business Unit, and so on.

   The list of items in the drop-down box have fields listed under two headers: Fields and Related. Fields represent the fields associated with the primary entity you are querying (in this instance Cases). Related, on the other hand, contains a list of entities related to the primary entity (again in our example, Cases).

   The options in the Select drop-down box are related to the entity you're querying and vary based on the item selected in the Look For drop-down list. For example, if you chose (in Step 2) to look for Documents, your search options are File Size, Author Name, File Name, and so on. If you chose Facilities/Equipment, you can search for Name, Primary E-Mail, Business Unit, and so on.

6. **Select a field to query.**

   In our case, Subject.

7. **Place your cursor over the word *Equals* and set the Condition for the search from the drop-down menu.**

Again, placing your cursor over the word *Equals* activates the drop-down menu. Click it to open the menu and make your selection.

8. **Under Enter Value, select or enter the appropriate value.**

   The value you enter depends on the field you chose in step 6. Because we chose Subject in our example, the value field is a Lookup. If we chose a field that is a textbox, you would type your selection in the box.

9. **Repeat steps 5-9 to add additional search criteria or skip to step 9.**

   The value you enter depends on the field you chose in step 6. Because we chose Subject in our example, the value field is a Lookup. If we chose a field that is a textbox, you would type your selection in the box.

10. **Click the Find button (in the lower left).**

    A new window appears with your search results, created from the choices you made in the main Advanced Find window.

11. **To open an entry in the search results list, double-click it.**

    Single-clicking in a hyperlink field brings you to that record. If you want to open a selection as per Step 9 above, double-click a non-hyperlinked field.

For more on Advanced Find, see Chapters 3 and 13.

Relating a subject to a knowledge base article

The process of linking a subject to a knowledge base article is the same as that for linking subjects to cases. (We discuss the knowledge base in detail in Chapter 24.) A *knowledge base article* is a record (stored in the knowledge base) that contains information. It may document a process, contain the history of the company, provide details on the company's health or retirement plan, or list employee addresses and phone numbers.

You can create a link between a knowledge base article and a subject when you create the article. You can also link existing articles to existing subjects. Linking knowledge base articles to specific subjects provides your customer service representatives with a quick and easy way to search for similar problems and solutions in a specific subject.

To link a new article to a subject, follow these steps:

1. **On the menu bar (at the top of the screen), choose New Record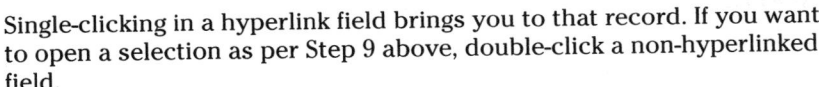 Article.**

   The Select a Template dialog box appears, as shown in Figure 23-4.

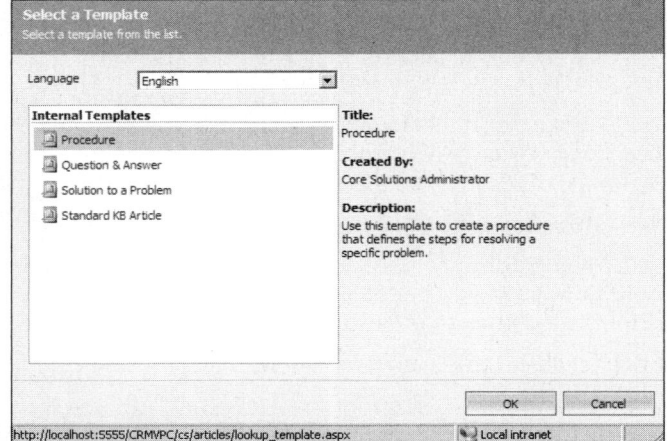

Figure 23-4:
The first
step to
creating an
article is
choosing
the
template.

2. **Select the appropriate language and template.**

   Templates help format your articles so that they're uniform in appearance, making them easier to read. (This is handy when you have a client on the phone.) Microsoft CRM has several predefined templates, and you can also create your own. (For more on templates, see Chapter 24.) Microsoft CRM also allows for multi-lingual templates. After you select your language in the Language drop-down box, click a template to highlight it and check the right side of the Select a Template window. You'll find basic information about the template you selected.

3. **Click OK.**

   The Article: New window appears, as shown in Figure 23-5. (You find out about creating and submitting articles in Chapter 24.)

4. **Enter a title for your new article.**

5. **Select the subject to which you want to link your article.**

   To do so, click the magnifying glass icon to the right of the Subject field. In the Subject Lookup window that appears, select the subject from the subject tree. You may need to click a plus sign or two to drill down to the appropriate subject.

6. **Add keywords.**

7. **In the body of the template, place your cursor over the reddish text and click it.**

   The predefined text is removed, and a free-form field appears so you can enter your Article question.

   You can edit text in this field just like in a Microsoft Word document.

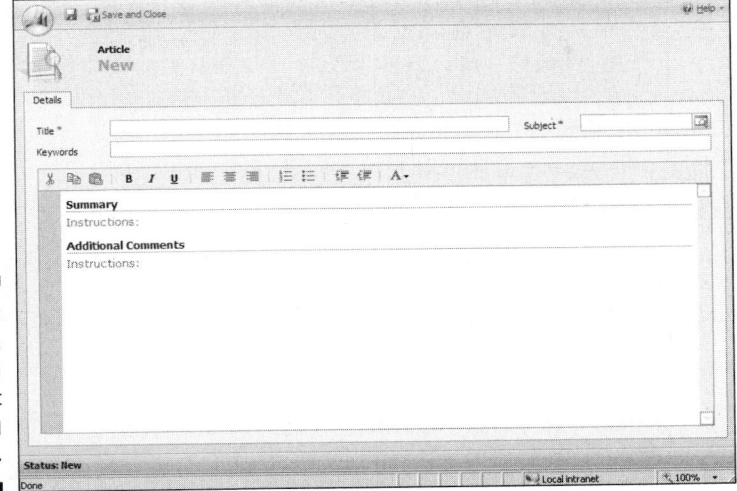

Figure 23-5:
From here,
you can
start
building
your article.

8. **Repeat step 7 as required by the template your chose.**

   Just like in Step 7, the predefined text is removed, and a free-form field appears so you can enter your answer.

9. **Click the Save or Save and Close icon.**

   Your article is now related to the subject you selected.

To link a previously created knowledge base article to a subject, follow these steps:

Only users with the appropriate security access can edit knowledge base articles.

1. **Click the Service button, which is third from the bottom of the navigation pane.**

2. **At the top of the pane, select Knowledge Base.**

   The Knowledge Base window appears.

3. **Under Article Queues: select Draft, Unapproved, or Published to find the knowledge base articles you'd like to select from.**

   All draft or unapproved articles are displayed in the main window.

   - *Draft articles* have been composed but haven't been submitted for approval by a user with editors' rights; consider them works in progress.

   - *Unapproved articles* have been submitted to a user who has been assigned the task of reviewing and approving articles.

- *Published articles* have been approved for the general population. After an article is published, the Subject link can't be altered. However, if you find you need to change a published article, you can un-publish the article to make the necessary changes.

4. **Click the desired article.**

   The Article window appears.

5. **Select the subject to which you want to link your article.**

   To do so, click the magnifying glass icon to the right of the Subject field. In the Subject Lookup window that appears, select the subject from the subject tree. You may need to click a plus sign or two to drill down to the appropriate subject.

6. **Click the Save and Close icon.**

   The article is now linked to the subject you selected.

Putting the article link to work

Let's say that another customer calls about the Hop-n-Pop toaster. She heard that an attachment is available that allows the user to toast hamburger buns. You can search the knowledge base for the article that talks specifically about the bun toaster option.

To view knowledge base articles linked to a specific subject, choose Go To⇨Workplace⇨Knowledge Base. The Workplace: Knowledge Base window appears. Change the drop-down box from Full Text Search to Subject Browse. Select the subject from the subject tree just below the drop-down box. The system automatically returns a list of related articles.

Relating a subject to the product catalog

As with cases and articles, you can link products listed in the product catalog to subjects. This is an efficient way to set up metrics for tracking sales by department, product type, sub-product type, and so on. And you can edit the Subject field related to a product catalog item at any time, as long as the product remains active. (See Chapter 7.)

To link a product to a subject, follow these steps:

1. **In the lower part of the navigation pane, click the Settings button.**

2. **In the upper part of the navigation pane, select Product Catalog.**

   The Product Catalog window appears. Detailed information on using the Product Catalog is in Chapter 7.

3. **In the Settings window, select Product Catalog.**

4. **Select Products.**

   The Products window appears, as shown in Figure 23-6.

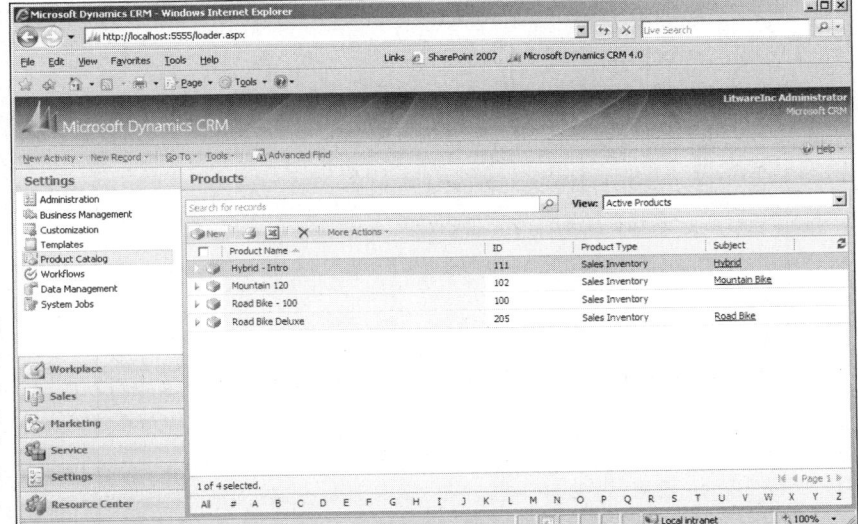

Figure 23-6:
This
window lists
all your
company's
products.

5. **In the window's toolbar, click the New button (or double-click an existing product to edit it).**

   The Product: New window appears. Chapter 7 contains detailed information about this window. For now, direct your attention to the Subject field.

6. **Select the subject you want to link your product to.**

   To do so, click the magnifying glass icon to the right of the Subject field. In the Subject Lookup window that appears, select the subject from the subject tree.

   or

   Use the form assistant to the right.

7. **Click the Save and Close icon.**

   Your product is now related to the subject you selected.

Searching for products linked to a subject requires using the Advanced Find feature, which is described earlier in this chapter in "Putting the case link to work."

Relating a subject to sales literature

You follow the same types of steps to link a piece of sales literature to a subject as you do to link cases and articles to a subject. What's the advantage? Here's an example: Suppose you have a training manual that you sell. Your marketing department has created a two-page advertisement for the manual in PDF format. It would be handy to be able to link the ad with the product using a subject relation.

When customers call to request training information related to a specific product, you can easily search for all the training materials associated with the product, including the spiffy ad slick. You can then e-mail those documents to your customers, and within minutes they can be perusing the information and deciding about training.

To link sales literature to a subject, follow these steps:

1. **On the navigation pane, click the Sales button.**

2. **At the top of the pane, select Sales Literature.**

   The Sales Literature window appears.

3. **On the Sales Literature window's toolbar, click the New button or double-click an existing sales literature item.**

   If you click New, the Sales Literature: New window appears. Otherwise, you see the window for the existing literature item. Chapter 17 contains detailed information about this window.

4. **Select the subject you want to link your sales literature to.**

   To do so, click the magnifying glass to the right of the Subject field. In the Subject Lookup window that appears, select the subject from the subject tree.

5. **Click the Save and Close icon.**

   Your sales literature is now related to the subject you selected.

Note that you can edit subjects related to sales literature at any time. Searching for sales literature linked to a subject requires using the Advanced Find feature, which we describe earlier in "Putting the case link to work."

Chapter 24

Creating and Using the Knowledge Base

In This Chapter

▶ Preparing your knowledge base

▶ Creating a knowledge base template

▶ Creating an article to add to the knowledge base

▶ Searching through the knowledge base

*B*ased on templates and articles, Microsoft CRM's library is called the *knowledge base* (also referred to as *KB)* and is a powerful tool for sharing information across your organization and with your customers. The knowledge base can house sales and technical literature as well as provide information to assist your customer service people with the thorniest customer issues.

Templates determine how information is formatted, found, and presented. *Articles* are the products created when information is stored in a template.

In this chapter, you find out how to create knowledge base templates and articles. You also discover how to search the knowledge base and associate relevant information with other sections of Microsoft CRM.

Organizing Information for Your Knowledge Base

The key to the knowledge base is organization. So announce a staff meeting and order pizza, the ultimate brainstorming food, because that's what this meeting is about — brainstorming and organizing your documentation and processes. If you have a whiteboard (complete with the permanent-marker line that can't be removed), make sure you use it to record ideas and thoughts for the stuff you want to put in the KB, so everyone can keep track of what's brought up. Your task is to organize all the sales and service documents your company uses. Ultimately, these topics become the building blocks for your knowledge base. You should also consider which people in your organization have access to each type of information and documents.

Your sales documents can include features and benefits of your products, pricing, system requirements, availability, delivery timelines, and fancy marketing advertisements.

On the service side, you have things like schematics, maintenance requirements, warranty information, and installation procedures. Also, on the service side of your business, you may want to consider stocking the knowledge base with a trouble-shooting guides to allow even rookie customer service people to sound like experts on the phone.

Remember to keep your topics and titles in plain, easily discernible language because, after you're finished here, you're going to put all your notes together in Microsoft CRM to create your company's knowledge base.

Creating Article Templates

The knowledge base contains articles built on templates. By using templates for the foundation of a new knowledge base article, all of your company's articles will be easy to enter and have a uniform layout, regardless of whether Accounting or Sales creates the article.

Microsoft CRM comes with a collection of default article templates: Procedure, Question & Answer, Solution to a Problem, and Standard KB Article, as shown in Figure 24-1. And those of you who like to think outside the box can create your own templates.

The Procedure template is laid out using a standard format of three sections: Purpose & Scope, Procedure, and Additional Comments.

Normally, you create a new article within an existing template. But we're going to walk you through creating a new template, just in case none of the standard ones fit what you're looking for. Later in the chapter, you create a new article based on an existing template.

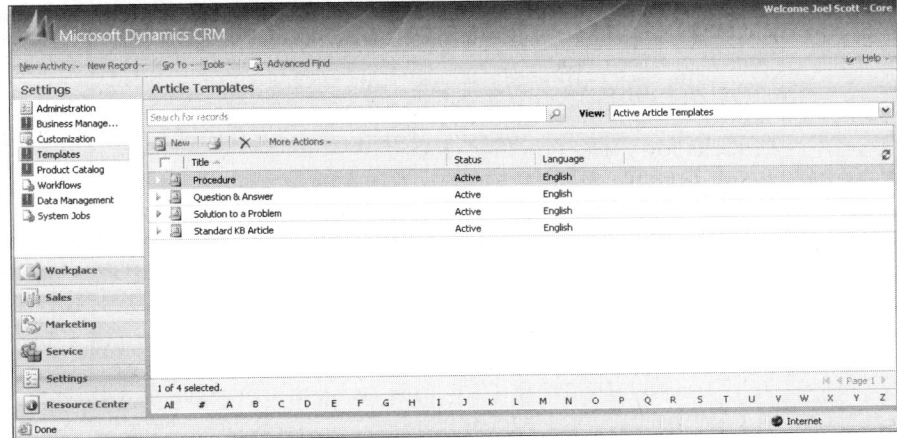

Figure 24-1:
The Article
Templates
window
displays a
list of all
current
article
templates.

To create a template, follow these steps:

1. **In the lower part of the navigation pane, click the Settings button.**

2. **In the Settings window, select the Templates option.**

3. **Select Article Templates.**

   The Article Templates window appears, displaying all available article templates. (Refer to Figure 24-1.)

4. **On the Article Templates window's toolbar, click the New button.**

   The Article Template: A new window opens and, right on top of that, the Article Template Properties dialog box appears, as shown in Figure 24-2.

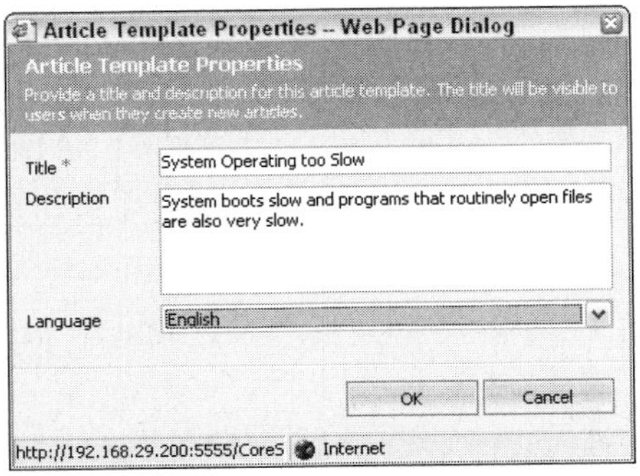

Figure 24-2:
This
window is
your first
step in
creating a
template.

5. **Enter a title and a description of the article template and then click OK.**

   The description is optional, but we suggest you include it because it offers one more way (in addition to the title) to describe the template you're creating. When you click OK, you return to the Article Template: New window to design the template.

6. **On the right of the Article Template: New window, in the Common Tasks pane, click Add a Section. A *section*, by the way, is just another level in the organizational structure of each template. You can scan ahead to Figure 24-4 to get a picture of some of this structure.**

7. **In the Add a New Section window, enter the title and a description or instructions for the section, and then click OK. The instructions, of course, are for those people in your organization who may be reading or modifying these articles.**

8. **If you want to add another section, repeat Step 7.**

   You can add as many sections as you want to the template. These sections will appear when you create articles (later in this chapter).

9. **Click the Save and Close icon in the upper-left corner of the Article Template: New window.**

   The window closes, the new template is saved, and you return to the Article Templates window.

Creating a Knowledge Base Article

The knowledge base acts as the staging area for all your company's articles. This is where you store, edit, and publish articles, and also where your staff finds the finished product.

Imagine that your company doesn't have an assigned editor and this happens: Bob from Sales adds an article regarding a quick blurb he heard on the news about the competitor's washing machine. Stan from Marketing adds a comic strip about computer repair guys. Jane from Accounting adds instructions on placing orders and taking credit cards. Thomas the CSR adds one about what to do with irate customers.

Microsoft takes another step in preventing chaos by enabling your company to choose who can add articles to and remove articles from the knowledge base. We recommend that you set up this person, or team, to also approve articles before they are published, checking for format, accuracy, and continuity.

The next few pages explain how to create and submit draft articles as well as approve and publish them. As shown in Figure 24-3, the knowledge base categorizes articles in three stages:

- **Draft:** Your works-in-progress, that is, composed articles that haven't been submitted for approval. Drafts are visible only to their respective authors, and users can't search for them in the knowledge base.

- **Unapproved:** Store your articles pending editor approval here. Users can't search for these in the knowledge base either.

- **Published:** Your finished, editor-approved articles, ready for the general public. Published articles are read-only (so your co-workers can't edit them), but users can search for them in the knowledge base.

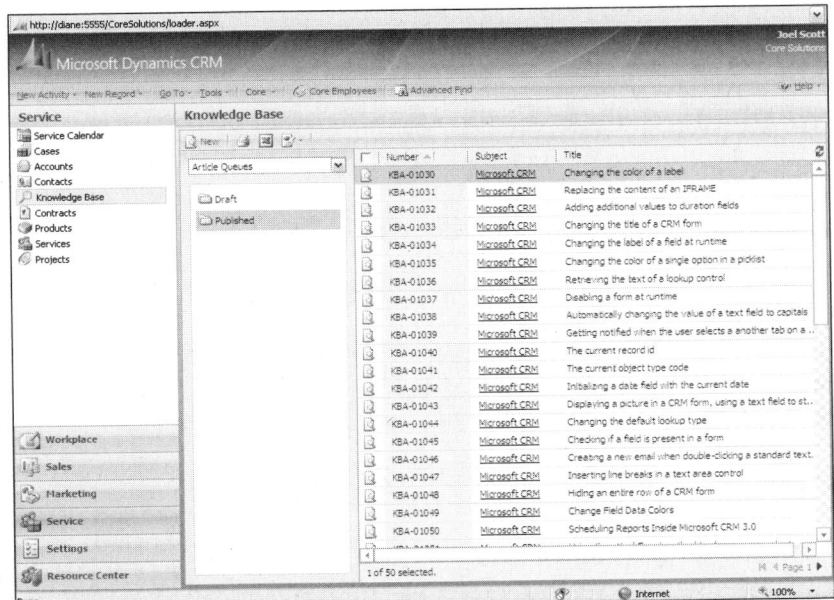

Figure 24-3:
The
Knowledge
Base
workspace.

Follow these steps to create a new article:

1. **In the lower part of the navigation pane, click the Service button.**

2. **Then, in the upper part of the pane, select Knowledge Base.**

   The Knowledge Base window appears (refer to Figure 24-3). You can view articles (based on their status and if any exist yet) in the main part of the window, on the right.

3. On the Knowledge Base window's toolbar, click the New button.

The KB Template window appears, listing all the templates currently available in your system. Find a template you would like to use. Template information (title and type, creator and description) appears on the right of the KB Template window as you highlight a template.

4. Highlight your template and click OK.

The Article: New window appears, as shown in Figure 24-4. The sections and instructions appear here.

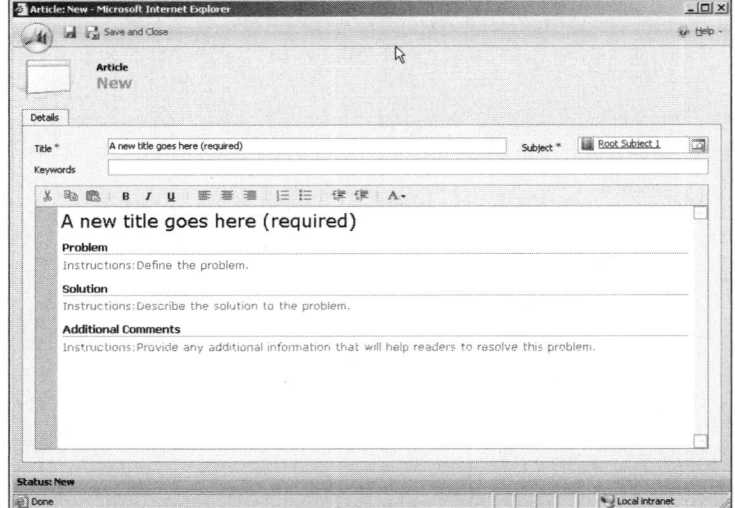

Figure 24-4:
This is
where you
build your
article.

5. Enter a title.

Required fields are Title and Subject; you must fill them in before you can save the article.

6. Link the article to a subject.

To do so, click the magnifying glass to the right of the Subject field. The Look Up a Subject window appears. Use the plus signs to open and collapse the subjects to specify a section within the subject. When you find your subject, highlight it and click OK. (The Subject field includes information that your organization can use to organize and track specific issues and items entered into CRM. If you need more information about using the Subject field in CRM, please see Chapter 23.)

7. In the Keywords field, enter words that will help your staff find this article.

Much like a search on the Internet, you can enter words here to search for articles pertaining to certain subjects. For example, if I were the CSR on the phone with Mrs. Reynolds concerning her air conditioner, I could search the knowledge base for *over-heating* and this article would show up in my search results — if the person who created the article tagged it with the term *over-heating* in the Keywords field.

Separate each of your keywords with a comma.

Another suggestion for your article keywords is the model number of your product.

8. **Click inside the text area and enter your information.**

The instructions disappear, and you're ready to type. Microsoft CRM's predefined templates are already formatted with specific information. For example, if we had chosen the Procedure template to create our article, the following section headings would be in the template, prompting the user to give all of the necessary information in the article: Purpose & Scope, Procedure, and Additional Comments.

The sections of the knowledge base article template allow you to create an easy-to-read, informative article for your customer service representatives and your customers. You can write step-by-step instructions, create question-and-answer scripts, or even make a Frequently Asked Questions (FAQ) section.

Use the toolbar under the Keywords field in the Article: A new window appears to do basic editing of your article and even add color text for emphasis.

9. **Click the Save and Close icon.**

The article goes into your Draft folder for further editing and, ultimately, submission for approval.

Although this publishing process may seem overwhelming and (in some cases) unnecessary, maintaining the process is important. Carefully managing information stored in the knowledge base guarantees that you're providing the latest, most accurate information to your sales and service staff and, even more importantly, your customers.

Submitting a draft article

Now is the moment every writer dreads: time to hand over your masterpiece to the person your company designated as editor (when your business units were defined in Chapter 6).

To submit a draft article for approval, follow these steps:

1. **In the navigation pane, click the Service button.**

2. **Then in the upper part of the navigation pane, select Knowledge Base.**

   The Knowledge Base window appears on the right.

3. **On the left side of the Knowledge Base window, click the Draft folder to access your drafts.**

4. **On the right side of the window, highlight the article you want to submit.**

5. **In the Knowledge Base window toolbar, click the Submit button.**

   The Confirm Submittal dialog box shown in Figure 24-5 appears.

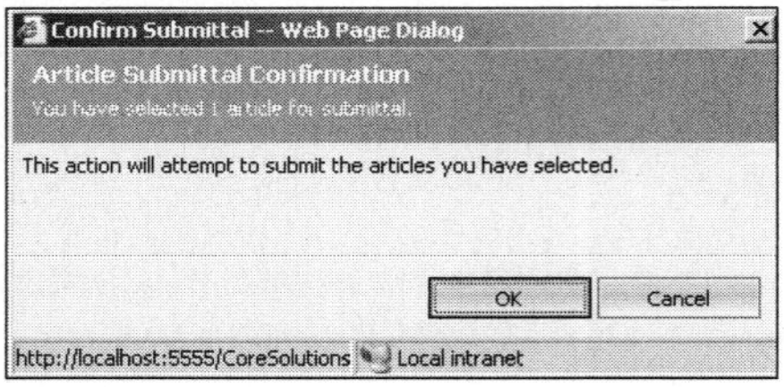

Figure 24-5:
This appears when you're submitting an article for approval.

6. **Click OK.**

   The article you submitted moves from the Draft folder to the Unapproved folder.

You can check that your article has been moved by clicking the Unapproved folder on the left side of the Knowledge Base window. All the articles pending editor approval are here. Just a reminder: These aren't searchable.

Approving an article

All those articles in the Unapproved folder are yours (if you have editing rights, that is) to check, edit, correct, and otherwise make your high school English teacher proud (or cry).

Anyone with editing rights can open and edit articles in the Unapproved folder. After all appropriate changes have been made, the editor can approve the article and add it to your company's knowledge base.

Follow these steps to approve an article:

1. **In the navigation pane, click the Service button.**

2. **Then in the upper part of the navigation pane, select Knowledge Base.**

3. **On the left side of the Knowledge Base window, click the Unapproved folder.**

   All the articles awaiting approval are displayed.

4. **On the right side of the window, find your article, highlight it, and double-click to open it.**

   This opens the article so that you can make changes. If you make changes, make sure to click Save (the disk icon) in the upper-left corner of the screen.

5. **On the Knowledge Base window toolbar, click Approve.**

   In the event that you have to reject the article, click Reject instead of Approve. You're given the option to add comments explaining your rejection in the Provide a Reason dialog box, as shown in Figure 24-6.

6. **In the confirmation window that appears, click OK.**

   The Article is automatically moved to the Published folder and is now searchable in the knowledge base.

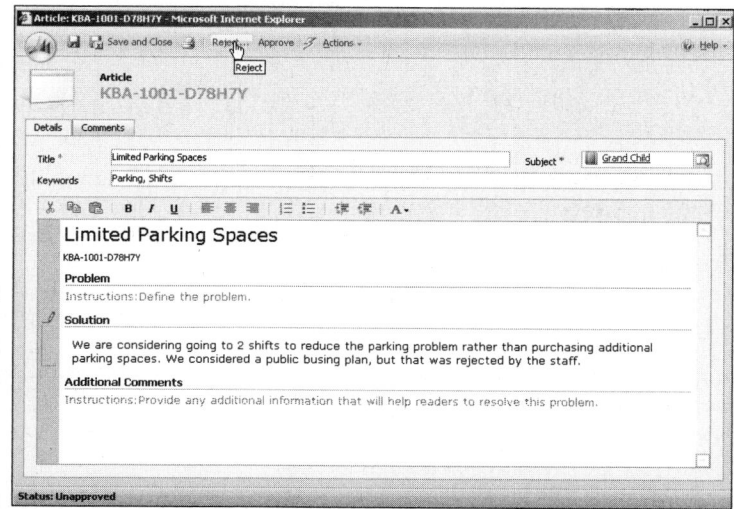

Figure 24-6:
Enter your suggestions and reasons for rejecting an article.

Let's say you've approved the article, but a week later, someone finds an error in it. For example, the company logo's reddish color isn't called Cinnamon. It's called Beauty Red. In this situation, you (with the appropriate rights) can unpublish an article. To do so, follow these steps:

1. **Click the Published folder in the Knowledge Base window.**

2. **Click the article you want to unpublish.**

3. **Click the Unpublish button.**

    The article is automatically moved to the Unapproved folder for revisions.

Now let's say that you've found an article that is out of date and you need to delete it. Again, you'll need the appropriate rights to complete this two-step process: Unpublish the article first and then delete it.

1. **Click the Published folder in the Knowledge Base window.**

    All published articles are displayed.

2. **Click the article you want to unpublish.**

3. **Click the Unpublish button and then click OK.**

    Your article is moved to the Unapproved folder. When you return to the Published folder, the list is refreshed automatically.

4. **Click the Unapproved folder.**

5. **Highlight the article you want to delete and then click the Delete button.**

    The Delete Confirmation dialog box appears.

6. **Click OK.**

    Goodbye out-of-date article. The Unapproved folder refreshes automatically.

Because all articles and subjects in Microsoft CRM are related, you're warned that deleting an article will also cause Microsoft CRM to remove any files attached to the article. Normally, this isn't a problem because the only attachment an article can have is to a subject, but we recommend that you and your staff use the delete feature sparingly. For those of you who don't want to delete the article and start over, you can simply add a comment to it on the Comments tab in the open article window.

Searching the Knowledge Base

Mrs. Reynolds is on the phone again, and you need to find the article you read aloud to her last week. Problem is, you don't remember the article's name. That's right, retreat to your trusty knowledge base and take advantage of the search function. Like a card catalog in a library, the knowledge base is the warehouse of information for your company.

With Mrs. Reynolds in one ear, here's how you search the knowledge base:

1. **At the bottom of the navigation pane, click the Workplace button.**

2. **In the upper part of the navigation pane, select Service and then select Knowledge Base.**

   All of your company's published articles are displayed. You can reach this section also by clicking the Service button at the bottom of the navigation pane and then selecting Knowledge Base at the top of the pane.

3. **On the left side of the Knowledge Base window, click the down arrow to the right of Article Queues and then select the appropriate search option.**

   The Search pane appears, as shown in Figure 24-7.

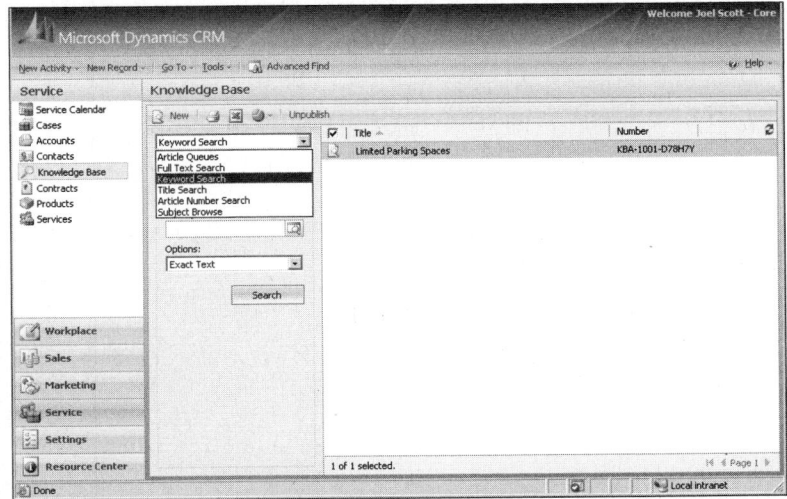

Figure 24-7:
Use the Search pane to zero in on the article you want.

4. **Fill in the following fields to define your search criteria:**

   • *Unlabeled Field:* Use the drop-down menu in the first field to tell your search engine which fields to search. Full Text searches the title, case number, and body of every article. It doesn't search for keywords. Keyword Search goes through only the keyword field of every article. Title Search looks at the title field of every article. Article Number Search can find a specific article number. Similarly, Subject Browse helps you find all the articles with a particular subject, and Article Queues show all the articles in the system in their various stages of being published.

- *Search For:* This is where you enter your search words. For our example with Mrs. Reynolds, you might enter *air conditioner* and the model number. If you remember only part of the model number, you can use a wildcard character. For example, entering ***1138*** returns every article with the numbers 1138 in the field you search.

- *In Subject:* Narrow your search even more by selecting the subject you want to search. This is especially helpful if you have, say, several hundred articles.

- *Options:* Another drill-down feature, this option allows you to search for the exact text you enter in Search For, or you can choose a broader search with Use Like Words. An Exact Text search is quicker but less forgiving; you'll need the exact wording to ping the articles you want. Use Like Words takes longer but allows you some freedom if you can't remember whether Mrs. Reynolds has, say, the Model 1138 or the Model 1138A.

In the Options field, you can use the * wildcard only with Options: Exact Text. Using the wildcard character with the Use Like Words option results in an error message.

5. **Click the Search button.**

   All articles that match your search criteria appear on the right side of the window.

Just a note on searching for articles: When you add a new article to the knowledge base, you can view it from the Published folder, but you can't search for it until the catalog's index is updated. Microsoft CRM does this automatically every 15 minutes (unless your administrator changes this value).

Chapter 25

Managing Queues

• •

• •

*A*ccording to the dictionary, a *queue* is a line of people waiting. *Queues* in Microsoft CRM are collections of information waiting for action, such as activities and cases waiting for processing. *Activities* are tasks, appointments, calls, and e-mails. (See Chapter 14 for more about creating and managing activities.) *Cases* are service support tickets. (See Chapter 22 for more about working with cases.) *Processing* means assigning and accepting activities and cases. Queues are handy not only for providing centralized lists of outstanding activities and cases, but also for sorting tasks by subject matter or assignment.

Queues are ways to route issues and cases to departments without having to assign them directly to individuals. Issues requiring third-level support (that is, the people in your organization who know how to fix anything) can simply be assigned as such to the queue. The people responsible for providing third-level support monitor their queue and, when they're available, take over the case. In some organizations, an individual has the responsibility for issue routing monitoring the various queues and assigning the cases to people based on skill sets.

Cases or issues can be assigned to more than one queue but not at the same time. Perhaps a customer calls with an issue that is handled by a level 1 customer service representative (CSR). If that person can't solve the problem, the level 1 CSR escalates the issue to a level 2 CSR. That CSR does most of the legwork and reassigns the case back to the first CSR to ensure that the client is informed of the solution. Soon after, the case is closed.

Queues can also be used as e-mail inboxes. In Microsoft CRM 4, a queue can be associated with an e-mail inbox, and all incoming e-mail to that mailbox will show in the queue.

Queues are a valuable tool for your company. You can examine them for up-to-the-minute information on how many customers have a specific issue or how many CSRs are engaged with issues relating to a specific product. This information can go a long way toward optimizing the efficiency of the service department and helping identify issues in other departments as well.

Before associating a queue with an inbox, ensure that the e-mail associated with that inbox should be seen by everyone with access to the queue.

In this chapter, we discuss the various queues defined by Microsoft CRM, and we tell you how to use them. You'll also discover how to create, modify, and manage your own queues.

Queue Overview

Your company probably has a person who acts as a human router, directing service calls and e-mails to the appropriate CSRs or taking care of an escalated situation when the CSR can't handle it. You may call these people customer service managers, quality attention retainers, or what have you, but for this book, we call them *service managers*. They are the optimal choice for creating and defining your queues because they manage the front lines of your customer service department. Your service managers also know the strengths and weaknesses of your CSRs and can assign them to the proper queues; in this way, your best washing machine guy isn't dealing with refrigerator issues.

When you assign your CSRs to queues and then assign activities and cases to those queues, you're giving your people (and your company) an effective and efficient means of solving problems and making customers happy.

How many queues should your company have? Queues should be as numerous as it makes sense logistically in your company. An organization with only a few CSRs should not have a large number of queues, when one or two would do the trick. Larger organizations should decide on queue design based on the types of products or services sold. Queues could be set up based on product line, such as one for coffee beans, one for coffee brewers, and one for coffee grinders. Another approach is to set up queues based on department, such as engineering, billing, and shipping departments. Then if you need a department involved in a case, you can assign an activity or the entire case to that departmental queue.

Looking at Personal and Public Queues

Microsoft CRM comes with two predefined queue areas, which you can see in the Queues window's navigation pane: the My Work queue, listing folders for the activities and cases assigned to you, and the Queues area. The Queues area displays all the queues that you have access to.

When you look into a public queue, you see all activities and cases associated with that queue, whether they're assigned to you or not. Everyone who is a member of that queue can see these activities and cases.

The My Work queue, shown in Figure 25-1, has two folders:

✔ **Assigned:** You'll find all the cases that are assigned to you. These are cases that you haven't accepted yet. We cover accepting cases in the section called "Working with Cases and Activities Assigned to Queues," later in this chapter.

✔ **In Progress:** These are all the cases you've accepted, and you're currently working on them.

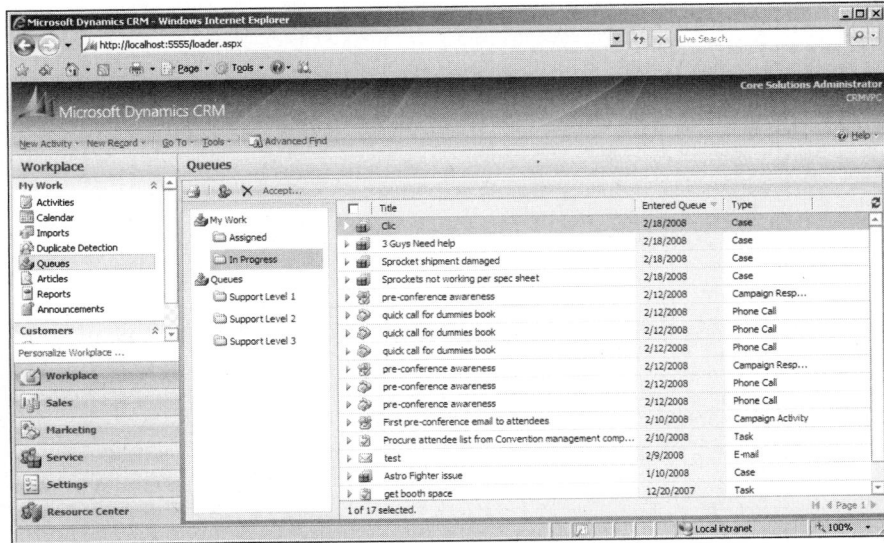

Figure 25-1:
Your folders in the My Work queue.

Creating a Queue

Users who are assigned the appropriate rights can create queues. Because you can create many queues in Microsoft CRM, we recommend that you plan your queues around your company's workflow. Create a master plan of all your services and products and determine how you want to handle customer service scenarios before building your queues.

For example, a chocolate chip cookie manufacturer could have a queue for shipping-related issues: freshness or breakage. Whereas a bank may create queues based on the depositor: ordinary depositors, wealthy depositors, small business accounts, and large corporate accounts. Cases can be assigned based on the person or organization initiating the issue.

Follow these steps to add your new queues:

1. **On the navigation pane, click the Settings button.**

2. **At the top of the navigation pane, click Business Management.**

   The Business Management window appears on the right.

3. **Click Queues.**

   The Queues window appears, as shown in Figure 25-2. All queues are listed here.

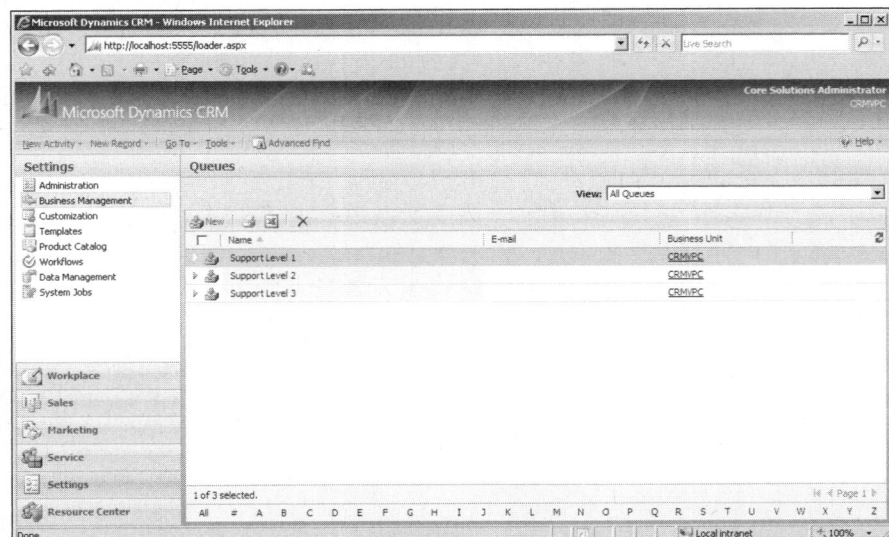

Figure 25-2: All current queues are displayed here.

4. **In the window's toolbar, click the New button.**

   The Queue: New window appears, as shown in Figure 25-3. Three fields are required: Queue Name, Business Unit, and Owner.

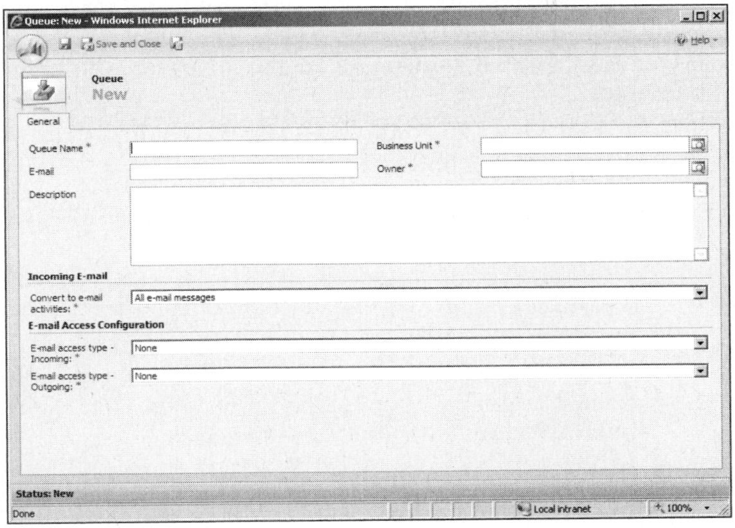

Figure 25-3:
Create your queues in this window.

5. **In the Queue Name field, enter a name for this queue.**

   Remember to keep it simple and descriptive. This is the only way your users will know which queue a case belongs to.

6. **In the Business Unit field, click the magnifying glass to display the Look Up Records window and select the appropriate business unit.**

   Business units are similar to departments or regions. For example, if you're in the Customer Care department or a regional center, and you want to create a queue for your staff, you would select Customer Care or the name of your regional center here. See Chapter 6 more on creating business units.

7. **In the Owner field, choose an owner for the group.**

   Clicking the magnifying glass opens a Look Up Records window with all your users. Choose one and click OK. You're returned to the Queue: New window. The owner essentially monitors the queue — assigning cases, shifting workloads, and so on.

8. **Indicate the e-mail account associated with the queue.**

   This step is optional. However, if you have an e-mail support box such as support@yourcompany.com, add the e-mail address here. All e-mail sent to support@yourcompany.com can be seen in the queue. See your system administrator for help with setting up the routing of e-mail to a queue.

9. **If you want, enter a description for the queue, as well as any important notes.**

10. **Make a choice from the Convert to E-Mail Activities drop-down list. The choices are as follows:**

    • *All E-Mail Messages:* All e-mail sent to the inbox listed above will be sent to the queue.

    • *E-Mail Messages in Response to CRM E-Mail:* Only e-mail sent by people outside of your organization in response to your e-mail will be sent to the queue.

    • *E-Mail Messages from CRM Leads, Contacts, and Accounts:* All sent e-mail that can be associated with existing Lead, Account, or Contact records will be sent to the queue.

11. **Make choices from the E-Mail Access Type - Incoming and E-Mail Access Type - Outgoing drop-down lists.**

    This pertains to the setup of the e-mail router, which is beyond the scope of this book. Ask your system administrator what values you should enter in these fields.

12. **Click the Save and Close button.**

    The Queue: New window closes, and you return to the main Queues display, where your newly created queue is listed along with the other queues. The e-mail address and business unit for each queue is also displayed.

Working with Cases and Activities Assigned to Queues

In Chapter 22, we discuss cases and how to assign them to queues. In some organizations, case-related activities — and not entire cases — are assigned to queues. For example, a CSR logs an issue with a Spacely Sprocket that needs to be reviewed by a technical designer. The CSR retains ownership of the case but assigns a review and comment task to the new VP of Development, Mr. Jetson.

We already mentioned that when a new activity (a task, a phone call, an e-mail, an appointment, and so on) is created, it can be found in the In Progress queue of the person who created the activity. This is true unless the creator of the activity changes the owner, in which case the activity will be in the Assigned queue of the assignee or the queue *Assigned*. Microsoft CRM doesn't automatically assign it to a queue except as mentioned above.

Your service manager isn't going to monitor all activities created by every CRM user, only those assigned to a queue. Service-related activities created by workflow and assigned to a queue are easily monitored by the service manager. (See Chapter 9 for more on workflow.)

Here's where your service manager ensures his job security. He looks at the activity and assesses the situation: Simple issues can go to the level 1 support queue but advanced issues can jump all the way to the level 3 support queue. This efficient utilization of your company's resources (that is, the service manager's training and fancy computer equipment) saves time, prevents redundancy, and most importantly, makes the customer happy. This is CRM working as all managers envision.

Activities should be created first and then assigned to a queue. You can't create an activity from within a queue. (See Chapter 14 for details about creating an activity.)

Assigning an activity to a queue

As we mention earlier in the chapter, activities can be assigned to queues or to users. The difference? Queues can have a number of users assigned to them, and a user is just that: a single individual.

Keeping that in mind, as the service manager, when should you assign activities to an individual CSR or manager and when should you drop an activity into a queue for the next available CSR to pick it up?

A good service manager determines the answer to these questions based on the situation. He then determines the best course of action and assigns activities accordingly. If the assignment process is the same all the time, workflow rules can be created to automate the functions of assignments and escalation. (See Chapter 9 for details on rules and workflow.)

As we discussed earlier, most likely case activities are assigned to a queue but other activities can be assigned to users. Because this chapter is all about queues, we're going to assign an activity to a queue. Activity assignment can happen regardless of how you get to the activity form — we're going to get there from the Activities window, but you can do so from the In Progress queue, case, contact, account, opportunity, or any entity associated with activities. Follow these steps to assign an activity to a queue or a user:

1. **On the navigation bar on the left, click Workplace.**

2. **At the top of the navigation pane, click Activities.**

   You can sort the activities by clicking the column headers or filter the activities according to date, type, or status (under the View drop-down list).

3. **Double-click the activity to open it.**

4. **On the menu bar, choose Actions⇨Assign or click the magnifying glass to the right of the owner field.**

   The Confirm Assignment dialog box appears.

5. **Select the queue to which you want to assign this activity:**

   a. *Click the magnifying glass icon.*

   A Look Up Records dialog box appears, as shown in Figure 25-4.

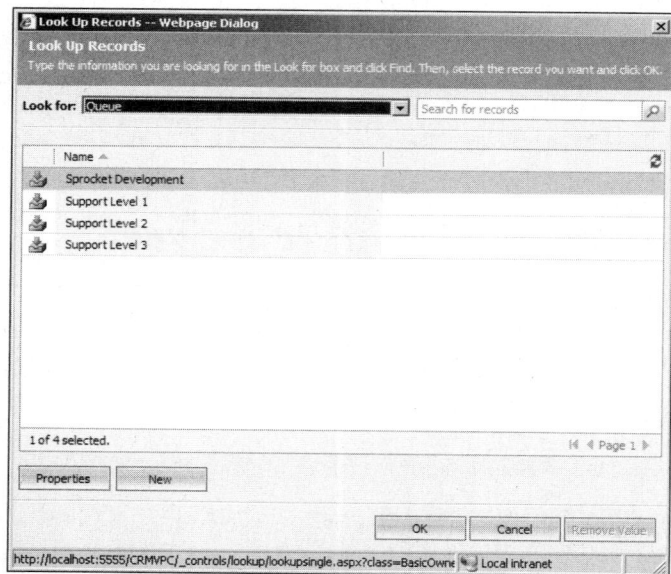

Figure 25-4:
Search for a
queue and
assign the
activity to it.

   b. *In the Look For field, click the arrow and select Queue from the list.*

   A list of all current queues is displayed in the lower part of the screen. You can also assign activities to users from this window.

   Queues don't accept assignments, but users do! (We show you how to do that in the next section, "Accepting activities.")

    c. Double-click the queue or highlight the queue and click OK.

    You return to the Confirm Assignment dialog box.

You can also search for queues using the Find box or alphabetize the queues by clicking the Name column header.

6. In the Confirm Assignment dialog box, click OK.

You're back in the Activity window.

7. Click the Save and Close icon.

Note that the task is still displayed in the Workplace: Activities window. It's still a legitimate activity. However, you can see the task also in the Queues display because you've assigned the task to a queue.

8. Under My Work in the navigation pane, select Queues and find the queue to which you assigned the activity. Click that queue to open it.

The Queues window appears (refer to Figure 25-1). You now see the activity assigned to that queue.

Remember to save, Save, SAVE! Always click the Save and Close button, even if you're reassigning a previously created activity. This way, you guarantee that all changes will be saved.

Accepting Queue Assignments

For this section, let's become the CSR. We need to picture ourselves in a cubicle with a bunch of information attached to the cubicle walls by push pins. Our cube mates are also CSRs, so when you understand this section, yell EUREKA! And perhaps you can teach them. Better yet, have them buy their own copies of this book.

There are two types of activities:

- ✔ Activities or Cases assigned directly to you (which are in the Assigned folder under My Work: Queues).
- ✔ Activities or Cases assigned to a queue that you monitor (which are found in the public queue in the Queues window).

In either case, you have to accept the activity or case before you can begin work on it. If no workflow rules are in place, it's up to you to monitor your queues for outstanding activities or cases.

You need to find the queues you are monitoring before you can accept an assignment. To find queues:

1. **On the navigation pane, click the Workplace button. In the upper part of the pane, select Queues (under My Work).**

2. **In the pane on the right, click the Assigned folder under My Work or click a folder under Queues to display any pending activities or cases.**

3. **Click an item to highlight it.**

4. **Click the Accept button on the toolbar.**

    The Confirm Assignment dialog box appears, asking you to verify that you want to move the selected activity to your In Progress folder.

5. **Click OK.**

    Queue windows don't automatically refresh, you can click the refresh icon on the top right of the grid or click the queue on and off and then on again.

    You've now accepted the activity or case.

After the activity or case moves to your In Progress folder, you can open it, create associated activities, and ultimately complete it. You may also reassign the activity or case. When completed, it will no longer be in your In Progress folder. It will be found in the history of the case, contact, account or whatever entity you related to it.

Chapter 26

Working with Contracts

*W*hat are contracts? In Microsoft CRM contracts aren't legal documents, they're an indication that the person requesting support is under a support plan.

Essentially, a contract is defined in Microsoft CRM as an agreement or plan that depreciates with time or use. For instance, say a customer purchases an extended warranty. That warranty expires over time, perhaps over the next three years. That's a contract. Or say your customer purchases a support plan based on a number of incidents or cases. His contract will expire when he's used up the number of incidents. Microsoft CRM also allows you to combine the two options. This means that customers can purchase number-of-incident plans that expire either when they use all of the incidents or when the contract expires.

The best part about contracts is that you don't have to do anything after they're executed. Contracts are tracked by the system. Better yet, if you define some workflow rules, contract renewal can be handled in an automated function as well. (See Chapter 9 for more on workflow rules.)

When creating contracts in Microsoft CRM you first create a contract template. Templates are a great way to quickly execute contracts, as most organizations have a few standard contracts.

After you create them, you can associate contracts with cases. If per-incident contracts are associated with cases, they'll automatically decrement when you use them.

This chapter is all about creating and using contracts. Getting started with contracts is simple. You first need to create a new contract template.

Creating a Contract Template

Why contract templates? As we discussed, Microsoft CRM contracts are based on duration or the total number of cases. When they're based on the total number of cases, contracts can also have an expiration date. This creates a "whatever comes first" scenario. Defining a template aids in the creation of contracts by simplifying data entry later. And of course, we create contract templates because we have to. All new contracts are based on contract templates.

In this chapter, we look at how Bob's Building Blocks (BBB) uses contracts in Microsoft CRM. BBB sells building blocks that children the world over love. Often, the children (or most likely their parents), need help building the intricate block models. A few years ago, BBB had the inventive idea of selling support access at a discounted rate. The support plans are prepaid and allow members to call 10 times at a deeply discounted rate. To track the status of a client's support plan, BBB uses Microsoft CRM. (If not, what would be the point of this chapter?)

You need to create contract template before creating the actual customer contract.

The first step in creating a Microsoft CRM contract is to create a contract template. First, follow these steps to create a contract template:

1. **Click the Settings button, which is the second button from the bottom of the navigation pane.**

2. **At the top of the navigation pane, click Templates.**

3. **Click the Contract Templates option.**

   The Contract Templates window appears, listing all current contract templates.

4. **On the Contract Templates window's toolbar, click the New button.**

   The Contract Template: New window appears, as shown in Figure 26-1.

5. **Fill in the Name and Abbreviation fields.**

   The name can be anything you want. For the abbreviation, use something that you think logically abbreviates your contract name. The abbreviation is an alternate way to refer to the contract.

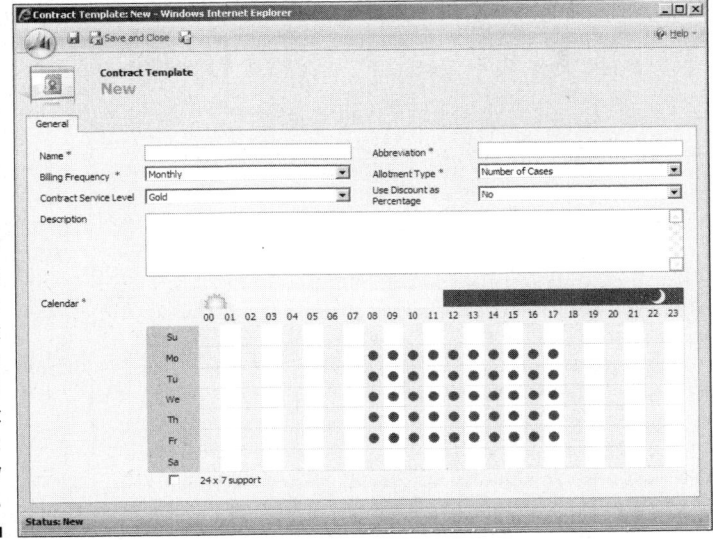

6. **Choose a billing frequency from the Billing Frequency drop-down list.**

   Choose a billing cycle, whether it's monthly, bimonthly, quarterly, semiannually, or annually.

7. **Select an Allotment Type.**

   The three options for providing support are Number of Cases, Time, and Coverage Dates.

   - *Number of Cases:* Offer your services by the case or call. For example, you might offer a five-call service package in which Bob's Building Blocks allows five support calls.

   - *Time:* You can provide your services for an amount of time, whether it's hours, days, and so on. For example, Bob's Building Blocks might offer their support contract for 5 hours of time.

   - *Coverage Dates:* Set a time frame for your services. For example, Bob's Building Blocks may offer unlimited support 12 months from the date of purchase.

8. **If you want, select a service level and discount, and fill in the Description field.**

   Use the Service Level field to designate the contract's status.

9. **Fill in the Calendar grid.**

   Set the days and hours of support this contract offers by clicking in the appropriate box. A green dot appears in each box you click. In our example, Mr. Wayne provides his services from 8 a.m. to 5 p.m., Monday through Friday.

If you provide an option for clients to purchase a support contract with extended support hours (weekends or after 5 p.m. in our example), you must create additional contract templates to reflect those options.

Here's a quick trick to save clicks: Assume Bob's Building Blocks offers 24-hour support on weekdays. Their support is closed on weekends. Click the 24x7 check box at the bottom and then click the Sunday label (Su) at the top of the grid. The green dots in the Sunday row disappear. Repeat for the Saturday (Sa) row.

10. **Click the Save and Close icon in the upper left corner.**

    The Contract Template: New window closes, and your new contract appears in the Contract Templates window.

After you save a contract template, you can't edit it.

Understanding Contract Status

Before we get into showing you how to create your contracts, let's go over the different levels of contract status: draft, invoiced, active, on hold, cancelled, and expired. Because everyone can see contracts, the status allows your sales and service staff to be consistent with their answers and support.

Each contract starts out as a draft and automatically moves to active status once the beginning date has been reached, regardless of whether it's still a draft or has been invoiced. Contracts expire on the end date specified in the contract. Your sales and service staff can place contracts on hold or cancel them.

Here's the list of contract status types:

- ✔ **Draft:** After a contract is created, it automatically has draft status. This is the default option and allows your staff full access to it for modifications or updates.

- ✔ **Invoiced:** After the contract is ready for use, it can be invoiced (from the Actions menu). We show you how to do this later in the "Adding Contract Lines to a New Contract" section. After you invoice the contract, you can't edit the dates, contract names, and contract ID.

- ✔ **Active:** A contract still in draft status moves to active status automatically after the beginning date set in the contract is reached. For example, if your beginning date is June 18, 2009, the contract will go to active status on that date. As with invoiced contracts, you can't edit the dates, contract names, and contract ID after the contract becomes active.

✔ **Expired:** A contract expires automatically on the end date set in the contract. After this happens, you can't open new cases against it. (Although you can close existing cases.) You can renew expired contracts. When renewing you can edit the Contract Start and End dates, the Contract Name, as well as billing information on the General tab. On the details tab, you can change the Service Level, the Contract Template, and the Owner. For more information, see the section, "Renewing Contracts," later in this chapter.

✔ **Cancelled:** You can cancel (from the Actions menu) a contract that is active or invoiced, but you can't edit cancelled contracts.

✔ **On Hold:** You can place a contract on hold (from the Actions menu). While it's on hold, you can't log cases against it. To take it off hold, choose Release Hold from the Actions menu.

Creating a Contract

As we mentioned earlier, you'll need to create a contract template before creating a contract. If you haven't, please see the section, "Creating a Contract Template," earlier in this chapter. With at least one contract template, the Bob's Building Blocks team is ready to sell contracts to customers. That's a good thing because little Timmy is on the phone and wants his block set built . . . NOW! After your support specialist has determined that Timmy needs to purchase a set of five support cases — and Timmy's mom has provided a valid credit card number — you're ready to create a contract.

Here's how to create a contract:

1. **In the lower part of the navigation pane, click the Service button.**

2. **In the upper part of the navigation pane, select Contracts.**

3. **In the Contracts window's toolbar, click the New button.**

   The Template Explorer dialog box appears.

4. **Double-click the contract template you'd like to use.**

   The Contract: New window appears, as shown in Figure 26-2. For our example, we'll choose the B5P Template to create the contract for Timmy.

   We'd like to point out two things about this Contract: New window. First, as with most of Microsoft CRM, the fields with the red asterisks (on your screen) are required. Second, you can't modify the Contract ID field. The contract ID is generated automatically when you click the Save and Close button to create the contract. However, your system administrator can specify some of the characteristics of the contract ID.

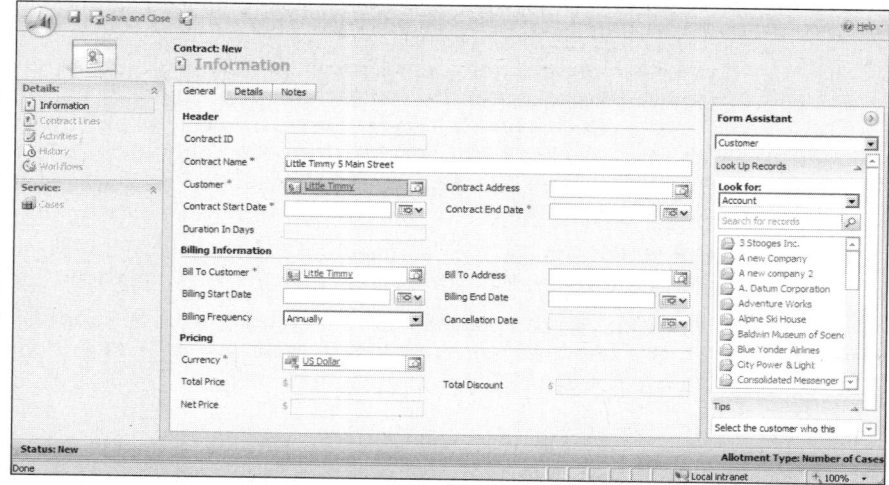

Figure 26-2:
The
Contract:
New
window.

5. **In the Contract Name field, enter a name for the contract.**

   For our example, we've used Little Timmy and his street address

6. **Fill in the Customer field.**

   To do so, click the magnifying glass and select the customer from the Look Up Records window. You can also open the Form Assistant on the right of the screen and select Customer from the drop-down list. When you do, a list of customers appears.

7. **Enter the contract start and end dates.**

   You can use the calendars or enter the dates manually.

8. **Use the magnifying glass to select the Contract Address.**

   The contract address Look Up shows the address on hand for the customer. Select the appropriate address. In our example, we have only one address for Little Timmy. (See Figure 26-3.)

   The Bill To Address automatically fills in to reflect the contract address; change it if necessary.

   When creating a contact address, make sure to enter an address name. Without it, the address won't show in the contract address field.

   It's worth taking the time to add these addresses now because you need them later when you change the contract's status.

9. **Click Save (the disk icon) to record these addresses.**

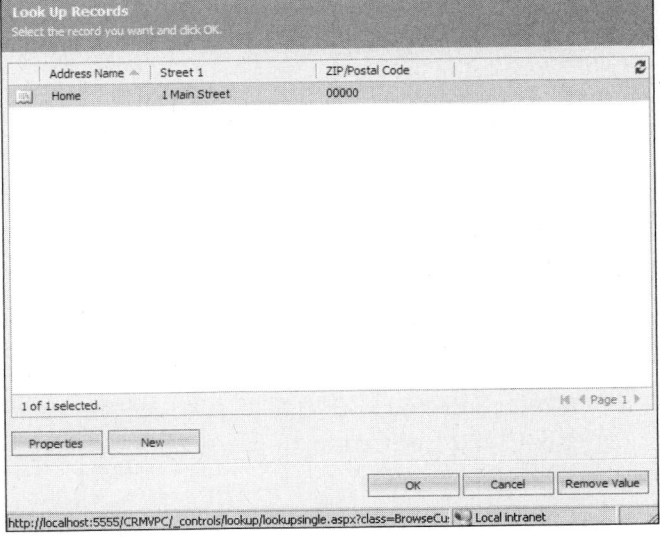

Figure 26-3:
Add a
customer
billing
address.

10. **Click the Details tab in the Contract: New window and fill it in as necessary.**

    The only required fields (Contract Template and Owner) are already filled in. You can choose the type of discount you want the customer to have (percentage or amount) and enter a description for the contract. You can also indicate the service level agreement.

11. **To add a note, do so on the Notes tab.**

12. **Click Save (the disk icon).**

    Your contract is now a draft. Keep this in mind for the rest of the chapter. We will move it out of draft status later, in the "Adding Contract Lines to a New Contract" section.

Now that you've saved the contract, the following options are live. These options allow you to enter or view information relative to the contract during its life:

- ✓ **Information:** You entered the initial information for the contract here.

- ✓ **Contract Lines:** This option outlines what the contract covers. You can associate several contract lines (for example, hardware, software, parts, and maintenance) with a single contract.

✔ **Activities:** This is where you find every activity scheduled as part of the support in the contract, such as phone calls, e-mails, tasks, and appointments.

✔ **History:** All completed or closed activities go here.

✔ **Cases:** All cases related to this contract are visible here.

Shortcut alert! For the most part, your contracts will contain a lot of the same information (such as billing frequency or pricing). Instead of creating a contract from the template, you can open a contract similar to the one you want to create and copy it.

Follow these steps to copy a contract:

1. **In the lower part of the navigation pane, click the Service button.**

2. **In the upper part of the navigation pane, select Contracts.**

3. **Double-click the contract you want to copy.**

We recommend that you write down the current contract ID number. When you get to Step 4, the contract is copied with all the same information except the contract ID. The program generates a new contract ID for the new contract you're creating. The only way you can distinguish your new contract from the old one is by the contract ID.

4. **On the main menu (at the top of the screen), choose Actions⇨Copy Contract.**

The Create from Existing Contract dialog box appears. You can choose to copy over cancelled contract lines as well, just by selecting the box in this window. (For more on contract lines, see the next section.)

5. **Click OK.**

You return to the open contract window. The new contract usually takes a minute to pop up, so be sure to keep an eye on that contract ID.

6. **Check the contract ID to make sure you're using the new contract.**

7. **Go ahead and change the new contract information.**

For our example, we made a new contract for Little Timmy's neighbor, Little Suzie, by copying her contract and giving it a new name, as shown in Figure 26-4.

When changing the information, make sure that that you change both the Bill to Customer and the Bill to Address in the Billing Information section.

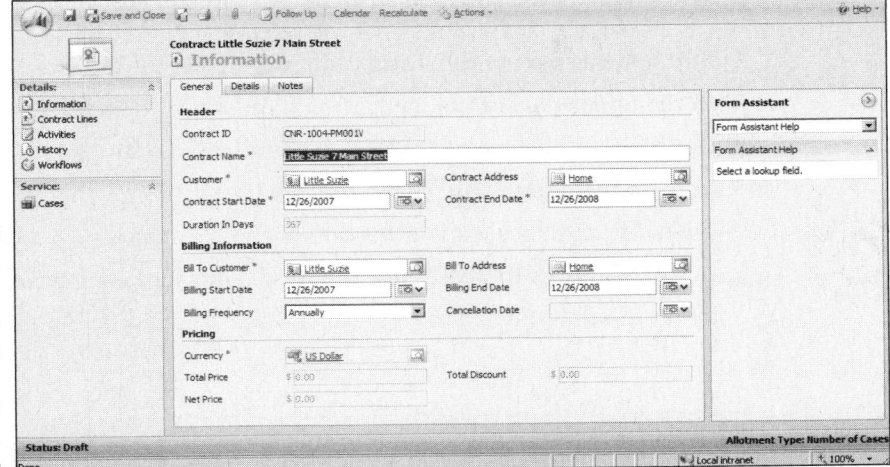

Figure 26-4:
The
Contracts
window
with a
copied
contract.

Adding Contract Lines to a New Contract

Now that you have your new contract for Little Suzie set up, it's time to create one or more contract lines. A *contract line* is a description of what the contract is covering. For example, you might offer an in-home building block inspection. Once a month, your team of Bob's Building Blocks Building Block Inspectors will visit the customer's home to check on the stability and overall structural safety of the building blocks. Or you may want to indicate that the contract is covering Little Timmy's new purchase, the Astro Wars Space Station. That would mean that this contract will not cover his purchase of the Astro Wars Moon Station. Of course, you could have more than one contract line associated with a contract, so if it is appropriate you could add the Moon Station as one of the products covered by the contract.

Contracts need not be associated with products. If you're simply allowing Little Suzie to call for support, then a single contract line is all that is needed.

The Contract Line: New window has three tabs: General, Administration, and Notes. The General tab has areas for the following:

- ✔ **General Information:** This includes the name of the contract line and the product.
- ✔ **Allotment Details:** These details show the total minutes or cases, how many have been used, how many remain, and pricing.
- ✔ **Total Price:** This shows the price for the product for this contract.

To add a contract line, follow these steps:

1. **In the lower part of the navigation pane, click the Service button.**
2. **In the upper part of the navigation pane, select Contracts.**
3. **Double-click the contract that you want to add a line to.**
4. **In the navigation pane, click Contract Lines.**

   The Contract Lines window for that contract appears.

5. **In the window's toolbar, click the New Contract Line button.**

   In our example, shown in Figure 26-5, we're using Little Timmy's Astro Fighter.

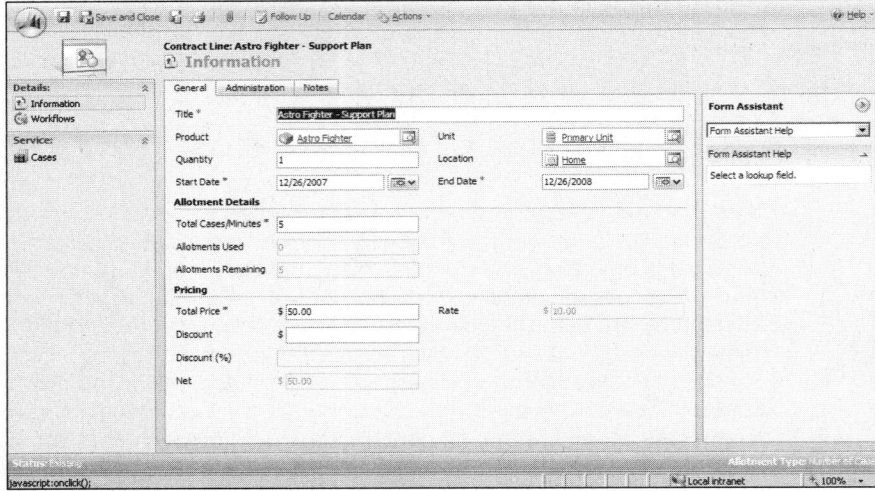

Figure 26-5:
Establish
Service
terms that
your ser-
vice staff
members
can track
as they
support the
customer.

6. **In the first section, type a title for this contract line and choose the start and end dates.**

   These three fields are required, but the others in the top section aren't. The start and end dates default to the contract start and end dates but can be changed.

7. **In the Allotment Details section, enter the number of minutes or cases you want to specify for this contract.**

   The other two fields are optional and show how much the customer has used and how much is left.

8. **In the Pricing section, enter the total price for this product for this contract.**

   Of the remaining fields under Pricing, Discount is the only one you can fill in. Keep in mind that the amount or percentage of the discount is determined by what was entered for this product on the product list. The other two fields are filled in automatically based on the discount you enter. Net is the total after the discount is applied.

9. **Click Save (the disk icon).**

10. **Click the Administration tab and check your customer. Enter a serial number if necessary.**

    The customer field is required and should already be filled in. The serial number field is optional and is a good place to track product serial numbers against the contract (say for inventory or quality assurance, for instance).

11. **On the Notes tab, enter information important to this contract.**

    The Notes tab, like the other Notes areas in Microsoft CRM, offers a free-form place to enter data.

12. **Click the Save and Close icon.**

    The new contract line appears in the Contract window's main display. You see the contract line's title, product, allotments remaining, and net (a dollar amount).

Clicking any column heading sorts the list of contract lines by that criterion.

Now that you've added a contract and the contract lines, you can see how Microsoft CRM tracks things such as time, available cases, or remaining minutes. In just a few clicks and a glance, you can easily see the status and details of a contract. We know what that translates to: getting information to the customer quickly, which means happy customers.

As we mentioned, you can move a contract from draft to invoiced status, if the start date hasn't yet been reached.

Follow these steps to move a contract from draft to invoiced status:

1. **In the lower part of the navigation pane, click the Service button.**

2. **In the upper part of the navigation pane, select Contracts.**

   The Contracts window appears.

3. **Double-click the contract you created earlier.**

4. **On the menu bar (at the top of the screen), choose Actions⇨ Invoice Contract.**

   The status of the contract, displayed in the lower left corner of the window, is updated to Invoiced (if the start date has not yet been reached) or Active (if the start date has been reached).

Expired contracts are automatically updated to expired status on their end dates. The other status levels — cancelled, on hold, and renew — can be updated.

Renewing a Contract

As we mentioned, you can renew cancelled or expired contracts in a few short steps:

1. **In the lower part of the navigation pane, click the Service button.**

2. **In the upper part of the navigation pane, select Contracts.**

   The Contracts window appears.

3. **Double-click the contract you want to renew.**

4. **From the menu bar (at the top of the screen), choose Actions⇨ Renew Contract.**

   The Renew Contract dialog box appears, asking for verification and whether you want to copy the cancelled contract lines as well.

5. **Click OK.**

   Keep an eye on the status in the lower left corner. When you renew a contract, its status is changed automatically to draft.

Creating a Case and Linking It to a Contract

Little Timmy needs help completing his Astro Fighter. He calls Bob's Building Blocks for help. The Bob's support agent takes his call and, prior to beginning the session, she opens a case. She wants to associate Little Timmy's support contract with the case. (You can learn how to create a case in Chapter 22.) Here we show you how to associate that case to the contract.

See the instructions in Chapter 22 for opening a new case. Then follow these steps to link the new case to Little Timmy's contract.

1. **In the newly created case, go to the Form Assistant and select Contract from the first drop-down menu.**

   Available contracts associated with the customer are listed in the Form Assistant under the lookup field. Only active and invoiced contracts appear.

2. **Find and select the contract.**

   The Contract field under Contract and Product Information in the main window should now be filled in. (See Figure 26-6.) Now that you've assigned the contract, you have to assign the contract line associated with this call.

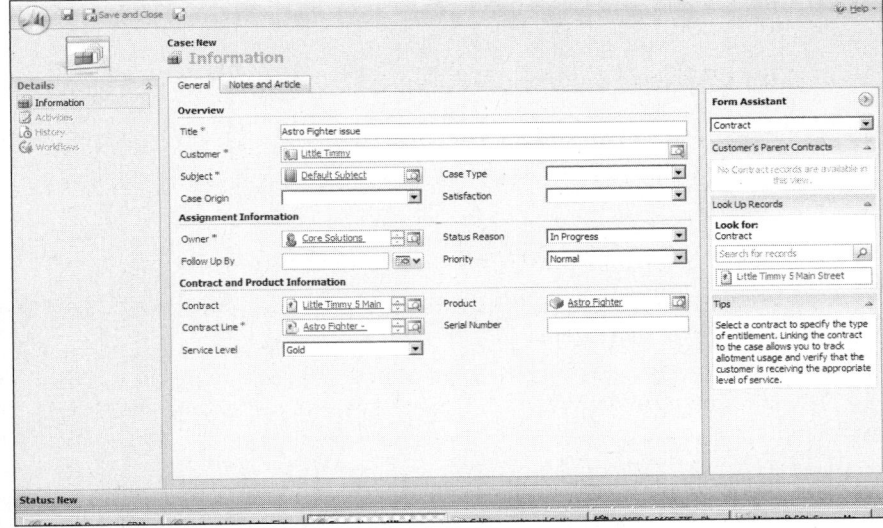

Figure 26-6: Your case assigned to the customer's contract.

3. **Click the magnifying glass icon to the right of the Contract Lines field.**

   The Look Up Records dialog box appears, listing all the contract lines associated with this contract.

4. **Find the contract line, highlight it, and click OK.**

   The case is now properly linked to the contract, and any work performed while resolving the case will be tracked against the active contract.

5. **Click the Save and Close button.**

Remember the cardinal rule of computers: save, Save, SAVE!

Part VI
The Part of Tens

The 5th Wave

By Rich Tennant

"We monitor our entire operation from one central location. We know what the 'Wax Lips' people are doing, we know what the 'Whoopee Cushion' people are doing, we know what the 'Fly-in-the-Ice Cube' people are doing. But we don't know what the 'Plastic Vomit' people are doing. We don't want to know what the 'Plastic Vomit' people are doing."

In this part . . .

You can find many official and unofficial independent software vendors (ISVs), all madly developing add-on products for Microsoft CRM. We review what we think are the best products and present the top ten in Chapter 27.

Everyone needs a little help once in a while. In Chapter 28, we describe the best places for getting an essential tip, training, or consulting.

Chapter 27

The Top 10 (Or So) Add-on Products for Microsoft CRM 4

*I*t's surprising that now, even after several years in the marketplace, there are so few add-on products for Microsoft CRM. There's a crying need for more. We're still looking for a good expense reporting system that works with CRM, for example. Now that the Enterprise version supports multi-currency, how about a real-time, automated system to update exchange rates? How about an automated way to check and update zip codes and postal codes? Maybe we've missed these. Certainly, there are good add-ons under development and still under our radar.

There is no one, good consolidated place to find all the CRM add-ons, so in conjunction with the release of *Microsoft Dynamics CRM 4 For Dummies*, we've created a site to review the contenders and the pretenders. Check out `www.consultcore\add-ons.html`. To cull the list in this chapter to approximately ten (depending on how you count), we established several criteria for making selections, including the following:

> ✔ **General applicability:** CRM is about managing prospect and client data. And it's about making it easier for a team of users to work together. If an add-on module didn't address one or both of these issues, it didn't make the cut.

- ✔ **Integration with Microsoft CRM:** Many vendors advertise their products as Microsoft CRM add-ons even when little, if any, integration exists. If there's little integration or no apparent reason for the integration, the product didn't make the cut.

- ✔ **History of and support from a vendor:** The CRM dealer industry is still a bit of a cottage industry, with dealers coming and going. Often, a vendor writes a custom application for one client and then decides to offer it as a general product to an unsuspecting public. We've tried to check out the vendors and their motivations as well. Evaluating motivation, of course, is much more subjective than the first two criteria.

- ✔ **Updated for Version 4:** Some of the less popular add-ons for versions 1 or 3 haven't been overhauled for version 4. Any add-on we mention here works with version 4.

Just because a product doesn't appear in this chapter doesn't mean that you shouldn't be interested in it. The product may not have been available for review at the time of this writing, or it may be of special interest to your company but not of more general interest. And, conversely, just because a product appears in this chapter doesn't mean that you should buy it without further evaluation.

Many developers put out advertising materials on products that they're thinking about developing. That is known as *vaporware*. Before plunking down your hard-earned money, make sure that the product exists and has documentation and support — maybe even a reference site or two. The consultcore site referenced previously attempts to separate the wheat from the chaff for you.

Checking Spelling with Google Toolbar

Microsoft CRM doesn't include any spell-checking or grammar-checking features, and these are among the most asked-for applications. Google comes to the rescue, and the price is right — free. Because almost everyone likes "free," Google's spell-checker tops our list.

The Google Toolbar's spell-checker feature can correct most spelling mistakes you make when you type into a Web form, including Web-based e-mail, discussion forums, and even intranet Web applications. Of course, if you type "to" instead of "too," there's still no help for you. And, if your notion of grammar has always prevented you from writing something as complex and sophisticated as a For Dummies book, this tool won't help you either.

To run Google spell-checker, go to www.google.com, install the Google Toolbar, and click the Check button on your toolbar. Spell-checker sends text for review to Google's servers, so it catches and highlights any incorrect spellings.

Google's spell-checker feature automatically corrects your spelling if you click the arrow to the right of the Check button and select click AutoFix. Don't worry; if Google spell-checker isn't sure, it highlights the words it's unsure of and allows you to correct them yourself.

Automating Processes and Generating Alerts

Workflow and escalation (also known as automated processes) functionality is built into Microsoft CRM. And it has even been enhanced for version 4. With workflow, you can automate a variety of business rules, processes, and alerts. However, Microsoft's workflow integrates only with the files (entities) that are part of Microsoft CRM. Workflow can't trigger activity based on data that might be in an accounting system or in an HR system.

Sometimes it's important to base your automated decisions on data outside CRM. If you want your salespeople to be notified when one of their accounts is overdue with its payments, for example, you'll want one of the add-on products cited in this section. If you want to focus on client retention, one of these add-ons may also be on your short list of add-ons.

There are two add-on packages that provide this additional functionality and, in fact, go well beyond the features and functions that come out of the box with Microsoft CRM. KnowledgeSync, from Vineyardsoft (which you can find online at www.vineyardsoft.com), has been around for many years integrating with many earlier CRM systems. TaskCentre (can you tell from the spelling?) is a more recent entrant from the U.K. (Go to www.orbis-software.com for more information on TaskCentre.) Both require some self-paced or Web-based training before you can expect to become proficient.

KnowledgeSync v7 is a business-activity monitoring application that detects and responds to critical, time-sensitive data in Microsoft CRM, in incoming e-mail, and in many other applications. KnowledgeSync v7 updates Microsoft CRM, other databases, and users (through e-mail, faxes, pagers, and the Web) with critical information. KnowledgeSync comes with many *canned* alerts (called EventPaks). To develop a customized alert, you may want to find a specialist — probably a Vineyardsoft partner.

KnowledgeSync can easily alert you to a variety of conditions within your database. Here are a few examples:

- A forecasted sale is suddenly overdue.

- A lead distributed to an outside salesperson hasn't been pursued.

- Money has come in (or has not come in) from a client.

✔ A request was made from your Web site by a prospect and the system has responded by sending literature and scheduling you to follow up.

✔ A deal was closed.

TaskCentre, from Orbis Software, is functionally similar to KnowledgeSync, but it's a bit more graphical.

Increasing Your Productivity with c360

According to Microsoft, c360's productivity packs are included in about half of Microsoft CRM implementations. c360 packages groups of utilities into three productivity packs: a Core Productivity Pack, a Sales Productivity Pack, and a Service Productivity Pack.

The Core Productivity Pack includes the following:

✔ A utility for combining multiple screen views into one screen to reduce the number of clicks to get from one screen to another.

✔ Duplicate record detection across multiple record types. For example, if you enter a new lead record for ABC Corp., it can check to make sure that ABC Corp. doesn't already exist as an account record.

✔ Alerts that trigger pop-up windows based on any type of record.

✔ Roll-up summaries for all record types. A *roll-up summary*, by the way, compiles results from separate but related records.

✔ Relationship charting to see how various records in the database relate to each other.

✔ E-mail linking that simplifies connecting an e-mail to a CRM record.

The Sales Productivity Pack includes:

✔ An enhancement to CRM's forecasting.

✔ A connection to your Web site to automate creating and updating records. This is particularly useful if you combine this automation with workflow to automatically respond to inquiries.

The Service Productivity Pack includes:

✔ The ability to link e-mails to cases.

✔ A workplace configuration that enhances the use of queues.

In particular, if you want to integrate your Web site with your CRM system, c360 has a Web connector for you. This is traditionally one of the most compelling integrations for any CRM package. You want your clients and prospects to go to your Web site and make inquiries and request downloads. And, just as important, you want to know about it. c360's Web site (www.c360.com, (678) 781-3189) provides a nice tour of all features of their Web Connector and all their other products.

Increasing Your Productivity with Axonom's Powertrak

Several Microsoft competitors have positioned themselves against Microsoft CRM by claiming that Microsoft's product isn't *vertically oriented,* meaning that it has no solutions for particular industries. And in most cases, they're right — as long as you don't look at all the rapidly developing third-party products.

Powertrak, from Axonom {www.axonom.com, (952) 653-0351}, for example, provides industry-specific templates extending the range of Microsoft CRM. They have modules for advanced marketing, technical case management, call centers, multichannel portals, e-commerce, and time and billing. The real news here may be the templates for retail and financial organizations, non-profit associations, and high-tech manufacturing. In particular, the wealth management system (which features *house-holding,* a method of rolling related peoples' accounts into one view) is of interest.

Migrating and Manipulating Your Data

Scribe's main claim to fame is its ability to gather data from other applications and get it into CRM. In versions 1 and 3 of CRM, Microsoft's built-in utility was almost too weak to be useful. Scribe answered that call.

If the truth is to be told, Microsoft has strengthened its own import utility, but many migrations still need more.

And Scribe (you can find their Web site at www.scribesoftware.com) is still there providing that additional strength that seems to be needed in the majority of implementations. Although Microsoft has addressed the duplicate-record issue, we still almost alway need the ability to reformat data or apply some kind of math to incoming data fields.

Scribe is available as a short-term (60-day) license, if all you need is some initial assistance with data migration. If your requirements are of an ongoing nature, Scribe offers a permanent license as well.

Accessing Instant Advice, Tips, and Tricks

Every once in a while, it's nice to have a coach sitting on your shoulder whispering advice in your ear just when you want it. That's what CanDoGo (at www.candogo.com) does. They've assembled a world-renowned team of sales, marketing, and business experts who've written and recorded snippets of advice. So, when you get stuck or frustrated, you can press a button and search for just the snippet you may need.

This really comes under the heading of training, but it's so task-specific that we hesitate to call it training — although it could be.

Displaying Data in Graphical Formats

Microsoft CRM allows you to relate contacts to accounts and, in fact, records in nearly every entity to records in other entities: one-to-one and many-to-one and even many-to-many. The problem is that sometimes you want to see graphically how various records relate to one another. A good example is an organizational chart: If you want a traditional org chart, SalesCentric (at www.salescentric.com) provides that functionality.

On the other hand, if you'd like a full set of dashboard displays, FusionCharts (at www.fusioncharts.com) fits that bill. With FusionCharts, you (or your dealer) can develop a series of realtime pie and line charts that show critical CRM or other data. A useful example might be the display of your sales pipeline showing upcoming sales in various categories.

Upgrading Your Service Area

We haven't used the Neocase add-on ourselves, but according to Neocase (at www.neocase.com), their customer service module is an on-demand or an on-premise customer service solution that maximizes the productivity and quality of customer service through collaboration, self service, knowledge management, partner centers, and advanced workflow management with strict adherence to service level agreements (SLAs).

What we particularly like is the self-service component of the system. In self-service systems, clients can use the Web to look up the status of their orders or their customer service issues. Each client doesn't have to have a CRM license in order to do so. If you have a large number of clients often making inquiries about their order status, or if you just need a more sophisticated approach to Microsoft's Customer Service module, Neocase might be your ticket.

Chapter 28

Ten Ways to Get Help

*I*n this chapter, we show you ten ways to get help. There are other ways to get help, of course, and we're sure you'll stumble across them as you investigate the various features described here. But here, we explore some free options (our favorite) and some paid-for services. The paid-for services are usually worth the investment. However, we leave it up to you to decide how much you're willing to pay for the help you need. Free help is available through Microsoft CRM's online help system, blogs, the Resource Center, and from the newsgroups. Then there's paid help from dealers, developers, and Microsoft itself.

It seems that most dynamic help options are blogs and newsgroups. Often, newsgroup articles point to blogs. Blogging has become so popular that the number of Microsoft CRM blogs grows almost daily. With newsgroups, you can simply read posts or, as you become more comfortable with them, you can post your own questions. Subscribing to a newsgroup now and getting comfortable with the posting process is a good idea. As time goes by, more and more users will be sharing information, best practices, and the inevitable workarounds.

You can find Microsoft partners all over the world, and they serve as your best — and often local — support. Beyond that group is a cadre of independent software vendors (ISVs), ready to sell you their custom CRM add-on products. (See Chapter 27 for more on CRM add-ons.) Don't overlook ISVs as resources, too. They have a lot of experience dealing with the substance of CRM's programming code and can offer insights into problems you may encounter. These developers can also help you design custom enhancements to the program. After all, that's their business.

Using Microsoft CRM's Built-in Help

Microsoft CRM's help is available from any and all screens. To access help, you simply click the Help button on the top right of the screen you're on. From there, you're provided a few options, but most likely you'll choose the Help on this Page option. The depth of help provided depends on the page you're on.

Figure 28-1 shows the Microsoft CRM help menu. When you need help with a particular form — such as the Account form — the Help on this Page feature is quite handy.

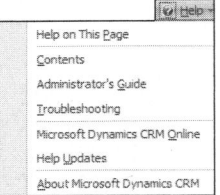

Figure 28-1:
The Microsoft CRM Help menu.

To use the Help on This Page feature, follow these steps:

1. **Click the Help button at the top right of the form.**

2. **Select Help on This Page from the drop-down box.**

   An option list appears. (See Figure 28-2.)

3. **Choose the best option for your needs by clicking the appropriate radio button.**

   The help text appears at the bottom of the pane.

4. **When you've finished exploring everything that the built-in help feature has to offer, click the X in the upper-right corner to close the window and return to Microsoft CRM.**

Figure 28-2:
An example
of contextual
help from
the Account
form.

Reading the Blog

The Microsoft CRM blogosphere has grown significantly since the release of version 3. Our favorite blogs are those written by the Microsoft CRM developers. In fact, there is a single blog maintained by the Microsoft CRM developers called (have you guessed?) The Microsoft CRM Team Blog. You can find it at `http://blogs.msdn.com/crm`.

Accessing the Resource Center

New to Microsoft CRM 4 is the Resource Center. It's a collection of CRM knowledge that's maintained by Microsoft. There are links to the Microsoft CRM Team Blog (which we discuss in the previous section) and the newsgroups (see the next section) as well as lots of general CRM knowledge. You can't update the content that is handled directly by Microsoft, however. To access the Resource Center, here's what you need to do:

1. **At the bottom of the navigation pane, click Resource Center.**

   The Resource Center appears. (See Figure 28-3.)

Figure 28-3:
The
Microsoft
CRM
Resource
Center.

2. **At the top of the navigation pane, select one of the following:**

- *Highlights:* Topics that transcend the other options below. Often the items listed here are interesting ways to use Microsoft CRM or some interesting tips.

- *Sales:* Sales related information, such as articles suggesting ways Microsoft CRM can benefit your sales team.

- *Marketing:* Marketing-related content is found here. Often you'll find interesting suggestions on how to get more out of the Marketing module in Microsoft CRM.

- *Service:* Suggestions on how to use Microsoft CRM to its fullest in your support organization.

- *Settings:* Links to content on how to customize or configure your Microsoft CRM system.

The content changes to reflect what is selected in the navigation pane.

Getting the Straight Story from Newsgroups or Forums

The newsgroups contain a wealth of knowledge. Microsoft has an MVP program where frequent contributors to the newsgroups are nominated and awarded MVP status. Microsoft CRM MVPs are people who frequently provide useful responses on the CRM newsgroup.

Within the newsgroup threads (a *thread* is a chain of related responses), you can find input from users, dealers, developers, and an occasional response from someone at Microsoft. Mostly, the tone is polite and professional. Usually, the information is correct — but not always.

Often, your issue has already been posted to the newsgroup, so we suggest you start by searching existing newsgroup posts. If you post or choose to take the free help provided in the newsgroup, do so with caution. If you're unsure as to the proper course of action and the newsgroup post suggests something that you're unfamiliar with, we suggest you find help in more traditional ways (read on).

To access the newsgroups, follow these steps:

1. **At the bottom of the navigation pane, click Resource Center.**

   The Resource Center appears.

2. **Click the Newsgroup hyperlink in the rightmost column (near the top).**

   Figure 28-4 shows the Newsgroup window. You can read, search, and add your own threads. You can also reply to an existing thread. Note the following elements of this window:

   - On the left is a display of many different newsgroups. There are three Microsoft CRM-specific newsgroups: Microsoft Dynamics CRM, Microsoft Dynamics CRM Deployment, and Microsoft CRM Dynamics CRM Developer.

   - The top contains a search field.

   - The center column contains the newsgroup threads. Click the + to expand and read the entire thread.

   - When a newsgroup article is highlighted, the right panel displays the text.

3. **To search for case-related threads, type** case **in the Search For field.**

4. **Click the Go button or press Enter.**

   All existing threads related to your keywords appear. Figure 28-5 shows many threads that relate to the search criteria of *email to case*.

5. **Click whichever thread seems most relevant and interesting.**

6. **You can then browse through the conversations everyone is having.**

If you don't find an answer to your question on an existing thread, you can start your own thread instead. Just follow these steps:

1. **From the Newsgroup window's toolbar, click the New button. (Refer to Figure 28-5.)**

2. **When asked whether you want to submit a question or a comment, make a selection.**

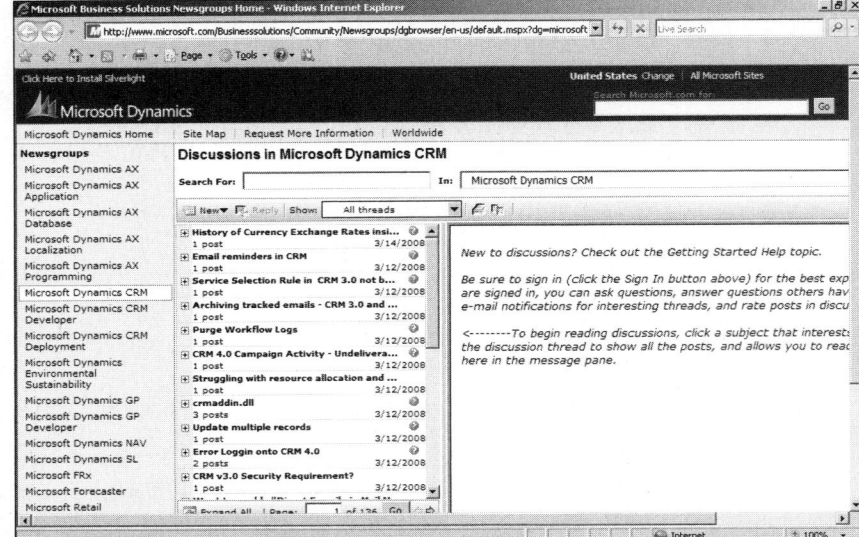

Figure 28-4:
There are
three
Microsoft
CRM
newsgroups
to choose
from.

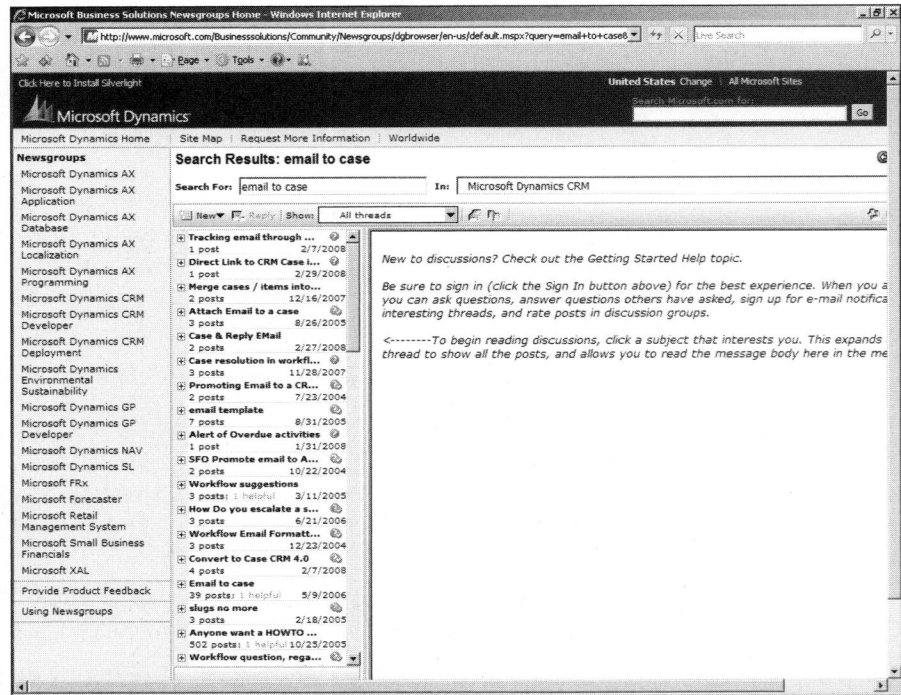

Figure 28-5:
Newsgroup
threads
regarding
*email to
case*.

You're prompted for your Windows Live ID. (If you don't have a Windows Live ID, you can sign up for one to the left of the logon boxes.) You now see a screen where you can begin your new thread. You may also need to create a profile before you can create your first message.

3. **Enter as much as you can about your issue and then click Post (at the bottom of the window).**

   This submits your issue to the world.

4. **Go about the rest of your business for a while.**

   Please note that "a while" might be minutes, hours, or days.

5. **Return to the newsgroup area occasionally to see whether anyone has responded.**

   Chances are that within a day, various people will have replied with helpful advice.

The Microsoft CRM forums are much like the newsgroups in that they're monitored by Microsoft CRM experts and allow for searching and posting of questions and comments. To reach the forums, click Resource Center at the bottom of the navigation pane, then click the Forums hyperlink. (Refer to Figure 28-3 for a view of the Resource Center.)

Finding an Expert

Microsoft products are typically implemented by Microsoft *partners*. The partner community consists of companies that have passed certain certification exams and met other Microsoft criteria. The Microsoft CRM partner community is vast, but not all partners are the same. A certification in Microsoft CRM doesn't necessarily translate into strong CRM knowledge. We suggest you do your due diligence prior to engaging a partner.

A partner is often the best place to get help. Sure you'll pay for the advice, but your implementation cycle will often be shorter and your use of the product will be better. The partner community is a prime place to go for serious help. If you need assistance with installation, customization, training, integration with other software, importing data, or just routine support, there's no better place to go. In the United States, rates range from $140 to $200 per hour.

Microsoft doesn't publish a comprehensive list of all their CRM dealers. One way to get a few names, however, is to go to the following Web address:

```
http://www.microsoft.com/dynamics/crm/purchase/default.mspx#EDAA
```

Using Technical Sites for Developers

If you're interested in learning how to write custom code for Microsoft CRM, there are two sites of interest:

✔ **Microsoft Dynamics Code Gallery:** The Microsoft Dynamics Code Gallery is housed on the MSDN code gallery site. There are interesting code examples posted to this site. This is a fluid site, with code being posted often. If you want to develop custom code for Microsoft CRM and you're a developer, you should check this site out.

```
http://code.msdn.microsoft.com/Project/ProjectDirectory.aspx?ProjectSearch
        Text=crm
```

✔ **Microsoft Dynamics CRM Dev Center:** The Microsoft Dynamics CRM Dev Center provides links to the Microsoft CRM SDK (Solution Developers Kit) as well as some links found in the Resource Center. As with the Code Gallery, this is a valuable site to developers. It can be reached via this Web address:

```
http://msdn2.microsoft.com/en-us/dynamics/crm/default.aspx
```

Investing in Training

A key ingredient to a successful implementation of Microsoft CRM is training — end-user training and administrative training. Overlook these and your implementation won't be a success. New training materials and companies are appearing so rapidly that a list printed here will quickly become outdated. Again, surfing the Web (using the keywords *Microsoft CRM training*) or asking your dealer is probably the best approach to finding the right training.

Training is a tradeoff in time, budget, and commitment. In the following list, we itemize the best training at the top, with a gradual descent toward barely useful:

✔ Send all your users to a training facility away from your office and daily distractions. Maui is good.

✔ Bring an experienced Microsoft CRM trainer to the facility and make sure it really is a training facility.

✔ Have your own in-house trainer trained and come back to train all of your users. This is almost never as good as having an experienced CRM trainer do the job, but it's less expensive.

- Find some live Web-based training that each of your users can access.
- Find a Web-based or CD-based tutorial for your users.
- Attend free webinars.
- Just tell each user to use the new software. Some of them will probably get it.

Microsoft offers many types of training, not only for their CRM product but also for many of their other business software products. A good starting point to find out about all these options is

```
www.microsoft.com/learning/training/default.asp
```

And, of course, buy each user a copy of this *For Dummies* book. Give each one a raise after they've read it.

Selecting Microsoft Packaged Service and Support

Microsoft offers several levels of decision-making, design, and support services. They each cost real money, but it may be money well spent. Design and planning always pay off in the end. You can access the details of Microsoft's programs by going to

```
www.microsoft.com/dynamics/crm/support/serviceplans.mspx
```

Microsoft offers different support plan options. They range from Flex Per-Incident Support, where you can pay on a per-incident basis, to a deluxe support service that provides faster response times and a host of other benefits. These plans are offered by Microsoft directly, so we suggest you check out the link above.

Microsoft offers software assurance as means of keeping you current on the latest product versions. Software assurance is usually renewed on an annual or semiannual basis, but longer terms can be purchased. Customers current on software assurance also have access to CustomerSource, which is a Web portal that allows you access to a considerable amount of information about each of your Microsoft products. CustomerSource also provides you with detailed information about various types of training that are available. In addition, you can search the official Microsoft knowledge base, submit support incidents, and much more.

Getting in Touch with Us

We use Microsoft CRM. We write about Microsoft CRM. We sell and support it. We have a team of experts who do nothing but CRM consulting. We can even help you find additional resources, if that's what's needed. You can get in touch with us at the following address:

```
www.consultcore.com/dummies.htm
```

Accessing General CRM Resources Online

Not to be confusing, but the CRM that we talk about in this section isn't related specifically to Microsoft CRM. These CRM resources are dedicated to client relationship management in general. Much of the information on the Web sites we list here doesn't deal with software. Instead, it's about the philosophy and concepts behind more actively managing your customer base.

A solid understanding of CRM concepts can enhance your Microsoft CRM investment. Here are a few resources to get you started:

- ✔ **www.crmguru.com:** Membership is free. Newsletters arrive directly in your e-mail inbox. This site has a Community Forum link and a Guru Panel link. The site also features a searchable GuruBase.

- ✔ **www.crmdaily.com:** The site's self-proclaimed description is Real-Time CRM Industry News from Around the World, but we think it's best described as an online newspaper. Articles are fresh, and the layout is great. Each article has a brief overview on the front page with a link to the details. This site also has a searchable archive.

- ✔ **www.crm2day.com:** Excellent articles and a concise design make this page easy to read. It features an Experts Corner and a searchable library, which puts a lot of great CRM information only a few clicks away. And the free company listing is great for networking!

We hope this chapter provides you with a good start. Everyone needs a little help when they're first starting, or even later when digging a little deeper into a new feature.

Appendix A

Converting to Microsoft CRM

. . . .

In This Chapter

▶ Planning the conversion

▶ Designing a system that meets your needs

▶ Establishing the new system and testing it

▶ Cleaning and importing the data

▶ Showing co-workers how to use the new installation

. . . .

*A*lthough the end results can dramatically increase effectiveness, for most sales organizations, the prospect of migrating to a different CRM system is a harrowing prospect. Most sales managers would rather donate a kidney . . . without anesthesia!

It can be technically challenging, but the key to an effective migration is in management. It's important to get everybody on board and excited. Of course, if in the end everything goes wrong, if all of your contacts have the first and last names switched and billing information is mismatched, the challenge will be having enough lifeboats for everyone jumping ship. But the best advice before the migration is to keep morale high and keep people participating in the process.

We recommend working with a Microsoft CRM professional who has done this hundreds or even thousands of times. Let her handle the technical stuff while you keep everyone excited.

If you're committed to Microsoft CRM, it's a good idea to order the hardware and software early in the process so that when you get to the point of installation there won't be a delay. Obviously, there are financial considerations to be made, but there is no reason that the hardware and software installation can't proceed in parallel with the system design.

In this appendix, we discuss the best, most efficient way to migrate your system to CRM.

Developing a Process for the Conversion

Whether you work with a CRM professional or with in-house talent, the process should be similar to the one outlined in this chapter. Here it is in a nutshell:

1. Evaluate the current system.
2. Define expectations.
3. Design the system.
4. Implement the design.
5. Test the system.
6. Clean the data.
7. Migrate the data.
8. Train the staff.

The following sections discuss all of these steps in greater detail.

Evaluating the Current System

The first step in converting your existing CRM system is to take a critical look at it. You know what I mean: Take a look at it with your head tilted sideways and one eye squinted shut, like the way your dog responds to the strange sounds your stomach makes after a *muy grande* burrito for dinner.

You may think that you don't have an existing CRM system, but if you're doing business with people and organizations, you must be keeping track of them somewhere. Maybe it's all in your accounting system. Maybe in a little black book. There are some professions where the little black book *is* the de facto method of CRM.

You need to take a good look at your current method for tracking your customers and consider its strengths, its weaknesses. Find out what kind of data you're tracking. Try to write it all down, or document it somehow, maybe in a spreadsheet. Note features that you *need* to keep, features you want to keep, and features you'd like to add with the new system. This is a good thing to do even before you start shopping for a new CRM solution.

Keep in mind how the data relates to itself. In the strange and mysterious world of relational data, there are only three basic types of relationships: one-to-one, one-to-many, and many-to-many. (Actually, there are four, but the many-to-one relationship is just a one-to-many turned around.) Let's look at these in a little more detail. They are as follows:

- **One-to-one:** This one is simple. It's like your social security number. Unless you're a spy or someone doing some very interesting tax reporting, you have only one, and it belongs to you only.

- **One-to-many:** This is a little more complex. An example might be credit cards. You have many, but each belongs to you only.

- **Many-to-one:** Yeah, I said I wasn't going mention it, but I have twice already. A good example of a many-to-one relationship is your birthday. You have only one (hopefully), but it isn't just yours. Many people share that birthday with you.

- **Many-to-many:** Ah yes, the granddaddy of them all. This relationship will allow you to make a bigger mess of your data faster than all the others. Use with caution. However, it's also the most flexible. An everyday illustration might be the relationship between a household and its vehicles. A household may have many drivers and many cars, and any driver can use any car. The thing is that with this kind of relationship the relationship generally goes through an intermediate entity, with this intermediate having a one-to-many relationship with the other two entities. In the preceding example, the intermediate entity is actually the household, and it has one-to-many relationships with both vehicles and drivers.

Okay, enough with the ugly data details.

Defining Expectations

Whether you're working with a CRM professional or your own in-house talent, this is the point where you really need to nail down your expectations. Clearly understood expectations are critical to effective system design, implementation, and ultimately end user adoption. Don't take anything for granted and document everything. *Everybody* needs to be on the same page!

Start with the data. What do you need to track in the system and how is the data related? Don't look only at your current CRM solution, which might just be Outlook or a series of Excel spreadsheets. Look at your paper forms. How much of that data can you enter and track in CRM? Even if you scan and link the document to a client record in CRM, you can't effectively search on it or report against it. Think how much easier it would be to fill out that form online or to be able to print a nice typed copy of it instead of having to decipher someone's handwritten interpretation of our Latin alphabet every time.

Keep in mind also that most CRM systems track much more than just clients. They might also track employees, vendors, competitors, suppliers, strategic allies, possibly even personal contacts, and more. In fact, with the release of CRM 4, Microsoft has billed Dynamics as an *XRM system*, meaning that you can use it as a general relationship management system in addition to the typical client or contact management system.

After fully exploring the specific information that you want to track for each of your customers and any other relationships that you decide to keep track of in CRM, you should look at process. If you have clearly defined business processes, it will be easier to automate them using CRM than if you don't. For instance, you might have a business rule that states this: After a lead is qualified, we send the lead an information packet. Then one week later, the sales representative calls or follows up with an e-mail to the lead, . . . and so on. In Microsoft Dynamics CRM, you can automate most of this process. For automation of your sales representative, on the other hand, look for the upcoming *Mind Control For Dummies.*

Different installations have different priorities. Some companies have very strict security policies and complex organizational structures, and others have a very flat org chart and allow nearly everyone full access to the system. Some may make extensive use of the product catalog and workflow, and another might work mostly through a customized add-on.

For some organizations, help-desk support is a main part of their business; these businesses can benefit from using cases. Cases are a way to track support requests, who handled them, and whether they need to be escalated to senior technician.

For some organizations, reports are the ultimate end product of CRM. They show them who is producing and who isn't. What kind of marketing is working and what isn't. Reporting also tends to be very dynamic. People like to say, "We'll just run a report on it." As stated previously, you can't run a report on widget sales by color if you aren't tracking the color.

Very few installations are actually comprehensive and make extensive use of all the features of CRM.

A Word on Reports

As important as they are, not much has been said about reports. In fact, reporting is probably one of the major reasons that organizations try to standardize their contact management.

Reporting can be a very enigmatic element of data management. More times than not, a system is meticulously designed, implemented, tested, and then rolled out, and users find out later that important information necessary to key reports isn't being tracked effectively.

The point is that even if you have an in-house report writer who creates and updates reports, you still need to keep the reports in the conversation for the entire process. The project manager needs to know what kind of reporting you'll expect to be doing, even if the reports aren't part of the project.

Some items to consider as part of the process of your business:

- ✔ Templates
- ✔ Territories
- ✔ Business units
- ✔ Workflow
- ✔ Product catalog
- ✔ Cases
- ✔ Reports
- ✔ Security
- ✔ Customization

Designing the System

After you have all of your expectations hammered out, it's time to design the system. The design will be mostly on paper or, more likely, Excel, and will generally be performed by a project manager if you're working with a CRM professional. If you're doing this in-house, it will most likely be done by you.

The design process will include such mundane tasks as naming and labeling all the attributes and possibly new entities with unique names. For instance, you'll most likely have a spreadsheet that lists all the entities and attributes along with their system names, their "friendly" label names, as well as where they will appear on forms and in relationships in CRM.

It will also include mappings for the data migration. There will be a list of every discrete piece of information that will be coming from the old system along with where it will be going in the new system — as well as the relational information, so all of the linkages will remain intact.

It will also describe in great detail all of the elements in "defining expectations" above.

The design will result in several documents, which you'll then send to the engineer(s), who will implement the design and bring the data in; these engineers may be the same person or they may be two or more individuals that will work in parallel setting up the system and migrating the data.

Implementing the Design

Okay, now that you have a highly defined design to work from, it's time to start implementation. Hopefully, you're already working with a CRM professional at this point, but if you aren't, this is the time to start.

At this point, it's a good idea to stand up a demo or test system to begin designing on. This might vary depending on how your CRM professional or in-house IT staff works. Your CRM professional might set up a development system at his site and give you remote access to it, or you might set one up at your location. You might even just start developing on your production system if your CRM professional or IT staff doesn't expect the configuration to be too complex. Regardless, there should be a system with demo data that the developers can start configuring based on your design.

Testing the System

At some point, or more likely, several points, you or your staff will log in to the system to test and sign off on certain functionality. It's very important to test as extensively as you can. One excellent, albeit time-consuming, way to test is to spend a day using the new system and your existing system in parallel. That is, enter all of your activities, clients you work with, and so on in the new system just as you're entering them in the old system. You'll be surprised how much you'll learn through this exercise. Much of it will be minutia, but it will most likely be a real eye opener. Eventually, after several test runs, the system will be complete. Well, complete for now. CRM systems seem to continuously evolve.

Cleaning the Data

Data cleanup is a touchy subject. Qualified data experts can do nearly anything with the data, as long as they understand what the expected result is. Unfortunately, they speak an entirely different language than most other humans. Well, that's not entirely true, but it can be difficult and frustrating for someone from the sales world and someone from the data world to find common ground. "Assign all clients in Atlanta to the Southeastern region" means nothing to the data guy. He needs to know to insert a value of 7 into a field named *region* when the date in the field named *state* is equal to *GA* and the data in the field named *city* is equal to *Atlanta, Alpharetta,* . . . or a half dozen other suburbs. This is why the project manager and the documents that come out of the design process are so important.

The rules for any data cleaning need to be very specific. "Delete all the old unimportant stuff" will generally result in the data expert making no changes because there isn't enough information to work with. Part of the design process should've been to decide which data isn't being migrated to the new system, as well as which is being migrated. Again, it's important that expectations are clearly understood.

As well as removing the old unimportant stuff, this is an ideal time to finally correct all the inconsistencies in your data, such as converting all of those records where the city was entered as *atl* instead of *Atlanta*.

The process of cleaning the data will be tied to the entire data migration process, and the experienced engineer will use the best tools he has at his disposal. It might be best to perform some cleaning while the data is on the existing system. Many engineers prefer to work with data in the SQL world (*SQL* is a programming language commonly used for databases) and won't even bother looking at it on the existing system. They simply find a way to export it, import it into a SQL database, and then go to work on it with the tools they're most familiar and skilled with. If you have this kind of skill in-house, you may want your SQL expert to work on the data before turning it over to the migration team.

Migrating the Data

After the design of the system is fully implemented and signed off on and the data has been fully cleansed, the data will be imported. In many cases, the data import will run in parallel with the design implementation. The import engineer will probably work on a separate system that cleans, converts, and maps the data.

It's possible, especially on complex systems, that the data import overlaps with the design implementation where small samples of data aren't enough to effectively test the system.

Your migration might take several, import, review, revise, and re-import cycles. Hopefully, this has been accounted for in time and budget. The better that communication is in the beginning, the smoother the process should be. Don't despair if the first time you log in to review the import, some data is missing or misplaced.

It is, however, another area where it's important to scrutinize heavily. It can be much more difficult to correct an import issue after the system has been used for a few weeks or even a few days. You may also be billed for the work if you've already signed off on the original import.

Your team will have many options on the data import. There is the built-in import tool mentioned in Appendix B, as well as several third-party tools that can be used for more complex importing.

Training the Staff

So you've completed the harrowing task of migrating your CRM system to Microsoft CRM. You've tested the new installation heavily and gone through all the data with a fine-toothed comb. Everything is perfect, but . . . you're really only half way there! Training your staff to effectively use the new system is at least as important as all the technical work required to actually migrate the data and processes to the new system.

How you train your staff will depend on a number of factors, with size, culture, and geographic dispersion being just a few.

Training can be done all at once in a room large enough to hold everyone or online. For larger organizations, it can be done as part of a roll-out where different subsets of the organization are trained and go online with the new installation on different dates.

For very large organizations, a train-the-trainer model can be used, where regional or departmental representatives are trained first and then sent back out into the field to train others.

Appendix B

Managing Your Data

. . . .

In This Chapter

▶ Defining and creating duplicate detection rules

▶ Editing duplicate detection rules

▶ Publishing and unpublishing detection rules

▶ Importing and exporting data

. . . .

*W*hile the cloning debate rages in political circles, database users have already decided, no clones, no duplicates!

In version 4, Microsoft CRM lets the system administrator determine the rules an organization will use to determine what constitutes a duplicate record. Microsoft CRM calls this Duplicate Detection.. The administrator can add duplicate detection rules to any entity in the system, even custom entities. Duplicate detection rules are run behind the scenes when creating or updating a record, going online with the Outlook client, or during data import.

This chapter discusses CRM's ability to implement duplicate detection rules and how to use those rules to manage your data.

Tips for Creating Duplicate Detection Rules

Microsoft CRM uses the concept of match codes to determine duplicate records. For example, if the duplicate detection rule for your contact consists of the first four letters of the last name and the first three digits of the zip code, the match code for John Smith, 123 Main Street Boston, MA 02111 would be SMIT021. Meaning, Sally Smith of 999 Tremont Street, Boston, MA 02111 would also be SMIT021. The records would match. Therefore, we suggest the following rules when setting up your match codes:

✔ **Use a unique identifier whenever possible.** This can be the e-mail address of a contact or the account number of an account.

✔ **Keep your detection rules as simple as possible, or you'll end up detecting too many duplicates, slowing down data entry.**

✔ **You can have more than one rule per entity, but do so sparingly.**

✔ **After your rules are established, try not to change them.** Changing duplicate detection rules means match codes will be regenerated. This could be slow when done against large entities.

Creating duplicate detection rules isn't easy. You need to consider many variables when creating the match code. Remember, you're creating a string of data to match on. Should your rules be too strict, every record will match, causing continuous duplicate detection prompts. (See Figure B-1.) If your rules are too loose, many duplicates won't be detectect and your database will be full of duplicates.

Create rules that match your business best practices. For example, determine how your users should import the account name. Should the account name be: Department of Usually Micro Managed Important Executive Secretaries, or DUMMIES, or D.U.M.M.I.E.S? Now imagine what your match code would be.

For the record: A best practice for account names is to use the organization's full name in the account name field — such as, Department of Usually Micro Managed Important Executive Secretaries.

To Dot or Not to Dot, That Is the Question

The administrator can add a second field to the account form for the shorter, abbreviated name. A second duplicate detection rule could monitor the short name field. What's next? Decide upon and create a best practice around abbreviations. Should the short name be DUMMIES or D.U.M.M.I.E.S? Decide at design time and have your users follow this best practice.

What do you do with Inc, Incorporated, Company, Co, LTD, and so on? Don't ask us — it's up to you. It is your job to establish a corporate best practice.

You can have more than one rule per entity.

An on-change event that with the help of regular expressions helps to enforce your corporate standards, however, is beyond the scope of this book. To learn more about both on-change events and regular expressions, contact your Microsoft CRM professional.

Defining Duplicate Detection Rules

So you and your users are ready to establish duplicate detection rules. Let's stop cloning around!

Before your duplicate detection rules can run, you need to enable duplicate detection and define when the rules will fire. To do so, just follow these steps:

1. **On the navigation pane, click the Settings button second up from the bottom.**

   The Settings navigation options appear at the top of the navigation pane.

2. **In the navigation pane, click the Data Management button.**

   Data Management options are now available on the right.

3. **In the Data Management pane, click the Duplicate Detection Settings link on the top left.**

   The Enable Duplicate Detection Settings dialog box opens. (Refer to Figure B-1.)

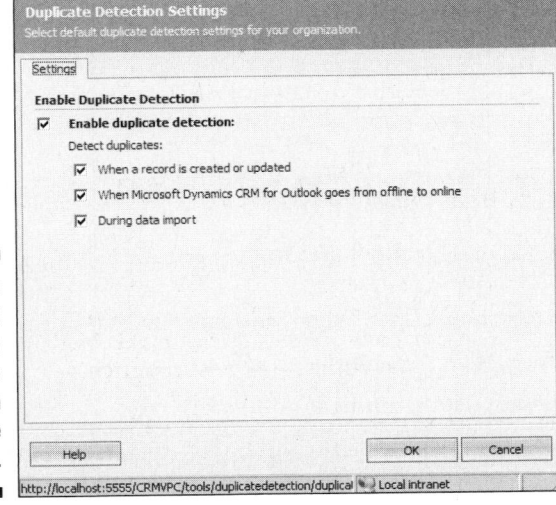

Figure B-1:
Enable and define when duplicate detection rules will be applied.

This dialog box includes a primary check box to enable duplicate detection.

4. **Select the Enable Duplicate Detection check box.**

   These three additional options activate:

   - *When a Record Is Created or Updated:* This option turns duplicate detection on when records are created or updated. However, only entities with detection rules active will actually be evaluated. See the section, "Creating a Duplicate Detection Rule," later in this chapter to learn more.

- *When Microsoft Dynamics CRM for Outlook Goes from Offline to Online:* If you don't have any users using CRM in offline mode, don't select this option.

- *During Data Import:* Select this check box if you regularly import external data such as trade show attendees or purchased marketing lists. If your initial import doesn't contain duplicates, don't select this option.

5. **Select any of the check boxes that apply.**

6. **Click OK.**

You still need to create the actual duplicate detection rules. This step simply enables duplicate detection.

Creating a Duplicate Detection Rule

Because matching on a unique identifier is a great way to establish your rule, we will create a contact rule based on the contact's e-mail address. The wrinkle here is that your database will probably contain more than one e-mail address. Microsoft CRM ships with three e-mail address fields for the contact. Our rule will need to address all contact e-mail addresses.

Duplicate detection rules are created in a similar fashion to Advanced Find. (See Chapter 26 for more on Advanced Find.)

To create a duplicate detection rule for the Contact entity, follow these steps:

1. **In the Data Management area, click Duplicate Detection Rules.**

   The Duplicate Detection Area replaces data management.

2. **Click New to create a new duplicate detection rule.**

   The Duplicate Detection Rule: New form opens. (See Figure B-2.) This form has three tabs: General, Administration, and Notes.

   All the action happens on the General tab, but you can explore the Administration and Notes tabs on your own.

3. **Fill out the required Name field.**

   We're calling our rule "Contacts with the same e-mail addresses."

   Status Reason is a system field; you can skip it.

4. **From the Base Record Type drop-down list, select Contact.**

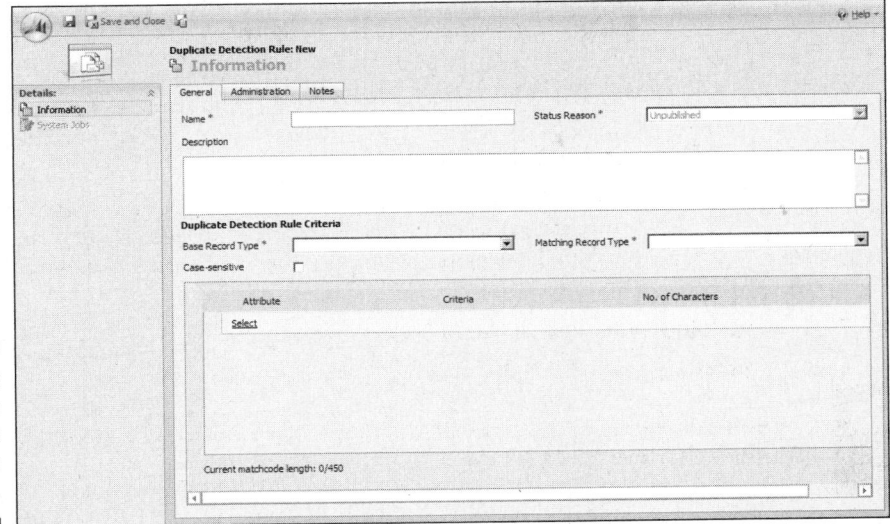

Figure B-2:
Create a
duplicate
detection
rule form.

5. **From the Matching Record Type drop-down box, select Contact.**

6. **Mouse over Select in the Attribute area.**

   A list of contact attributes is displayed.

7. **Select the E-mail Address option.**

8. **For Criteria, select Exact Match.**

   We want the e-mail addresses to match exactly. The other two choices are Same First Characters and Same Last Characters. If either of these is selected, the third box, No. of Characters, becomes available.

9. **Repeat Steps 6-8 two more times with E-mail Address2 and E-mail Address3.**

   You only have to add E-mail Address2 and E-mail address3 if those fields are on the contact form, ergo you're using those fields.

10. **Click Save.**

The matchcode that your rule generates can not exceed 450 characters. Plan your rules accordingly. The bottom left of the Duplicate Detection Rule form keeps a count for you. (Refer to Figure B-2.)

To publish a rule, follow these steps:

1. **Click on the rule you want to publish**

   The rule is highlighted.

2. **Click the Publish button on the menu bar.**

3. **Click OK to begin the match code generation.**

   A prompt indicating that the rule is going to generate the match codes while running in the background appears. (See Figure B-3.)

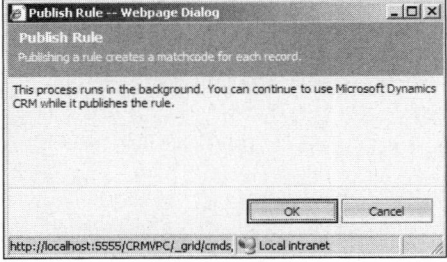

Figure B-3:
Publishing a duplication rule.

Should you decide that a published duplicate detection rule is not working as you'd like, you can *un-publish* the rule. In doing so, the rule will not be run. To unpublish a rule, follow these steps:

1. **Click on a rule to be un-published.**

2. **On the toolbar, click More Actions.**

3. **Click Unpublish.**

   The Status Reason will remain Publishing until the match codes are generated. The Status Reason field changes to Published when the match codes are generated.

Editing a Duplicate Detection Rule

To edit a duplicate detection rule for a contact (or any other entity), follow these steps:

1. **On the Navigation Bar, click Settings.**

   The settings menu is displayed in the top of the Navigation Bar.

2. **In the top portion of the Navigation Bar, click Data Management.**

   The data management options are displayed.

3. **In the Data Management area, click Duplicate Detection Rules.**

   The Duplicate Detection Area replaces Data Management.

4. **Double Click on a duplicate detection rule to edit.**

   The Duplicate Detection Rule form opens.

5. **Edit your rule as necessary.**

6. Click the Save icon (The Blue Disk) or the Save and Close Icon.

You'll be prompted with a message indicating that modifying the rule necessitates a regeneration of match codes. The match codes will be removed and the rule will be unpublished. (See Figure B-4.)

Figure B-4:
The unpublish prompt when editing a Duplicate Detection rule.

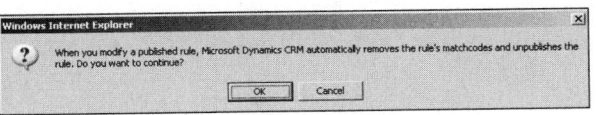

7. Click OK.

8. On the Menu Bar click Publish.

New match codes will be generated for the rule.

Only changes to the rule's match code rules will result in unpublishing and clearing of existing match codes. You can edit the Description or other fields such as a the rule name, without regenerating the match code.

Putting the Rule to Work

If you've followed our instructions in the "Creating a Duplicate Detection Rule" section, you can test out the new rule. To do that, create a contact with a test e-mail address, such as `test@test.com`. Save and close the record. Then create another contact with the same e-mail address. You'll be prompted with the Duplicate Detection dialog box. (See Figure B-5.)

The Duplicate Detection dialog box is split into two areas. The top is the record you're trying to create. The bottom half of the dialog box lists the potential duplicate records.

The drop-down box at the top of the second portion shows the duplicate detection rule or rules that triggered the dialog box. Below that are the potential duplicate records.

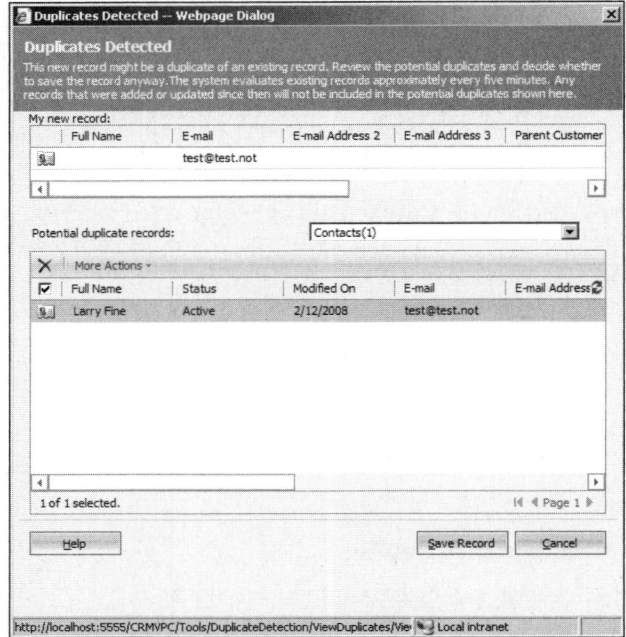

Here are some tips about manipulating records:

- ✔ **To open a possible duplicate record:** Double-click the record or select Edit from the Action button on the menu bar.

- ✔ **To activate or deactivate records:** Click the More Actions button and select Activate or Deactivate.

- ✔ **To activate or deactivate multiple records:** Ctrl+click all the appropriate records' rows in the grid and select Activate or Deactivate.

- ✔ **To affect all the records in the grid:** Click the check box on the top left of the grid first.

- ✔ **To delete a record:** Highlight the record and click the X icon on the menu bar.

Importing and Exporting

With the duplicate detection rules in place, you're now ready to import records into Microsoft CRM. Microsoft CRM 4 Import/Export Wizard allows importation to any and all entities in the system. This is an enhancement over prior versions. To import data, keep in mind the following:

✔ The file to import must be a CSV file.

✔ When mapping to a drop-down list, the source values need to be mapped to drop-down list items.

✔ When the import has finished, you have the option of receiving an auto-mated e-mail indicating that the import has finished.

For our example, we import sample data collected at a trade show. The trade show data was collected by the marketing team working the trade show booth. When they returned to the office they provided us with a file called `tradeshow.csv`.

Because the data is coming from a trade show, we will import the records into the Lead entity. You can import into other entities, but the process is the same.

The trade show list import is subject to the duplicate detection rules you create earlier in this chapter.

Creating data maps

Microsoft CRM uses data maps to translate the incoming data to the proper fields in Microsoft CRM. A *data map* is simply the mapping of the source fields (the data you wish to import) with the target fields (the fields in Microsoft CRM where the data will be going). The Import Wizard is based on a data map. So the first step is to create a data map. To create a data map for an account, follow these steps:

1. **In the Navigation Bar Click Settings.**

   The Settings options show at the top of the Navigation Bar.

2. **Click Data Management on the top of Navigation Bar.**

   The Data Map area replaces Data Management.

3. **In the Data Management area, click Data Maps.**

   The Data Map area replaces Data Management.

4. **Click New in the upper left corner.**

   The Data Map: New form opens. (See Figure B-6.)

5. **Give the map a name in the Name field.**

   In this example, we use ABC Trade Show Leads.

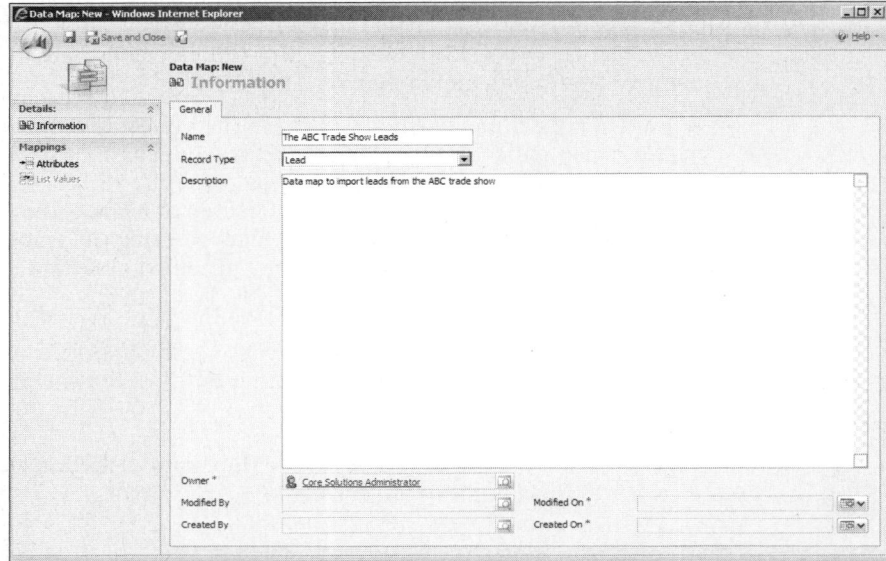

6. **Make sure that the value in the Record Type drop-down list is Lead.**

   You use the drop-down list to select the target entity — the entity where the data will reside., such as Contact.

7. **Provide a description in the Description field.**

8. **Click Save at the top left of the form.**

9. **On the left navigation pane, click Attributes.**

   The Attributes form is displayed on the right.

10. **On the bottom left, click the Load Sample Data button.**

    Browse to the CSV file that you're importing. (In our case, it's called ABC Trade Show Leads.csv.)

    The Attributes section is now split into two sections: Source on the left and Target on the right. (See Figure B-7.)

    Source is further split into two columns: Column Headings and Mapped Target Attributes.

11. **On the Source side, map the items under Column Headings with the appropriate fields in the Target column. Highlight the source row to map, find the appropriate target row item, and click the Map button on the bottom right.**

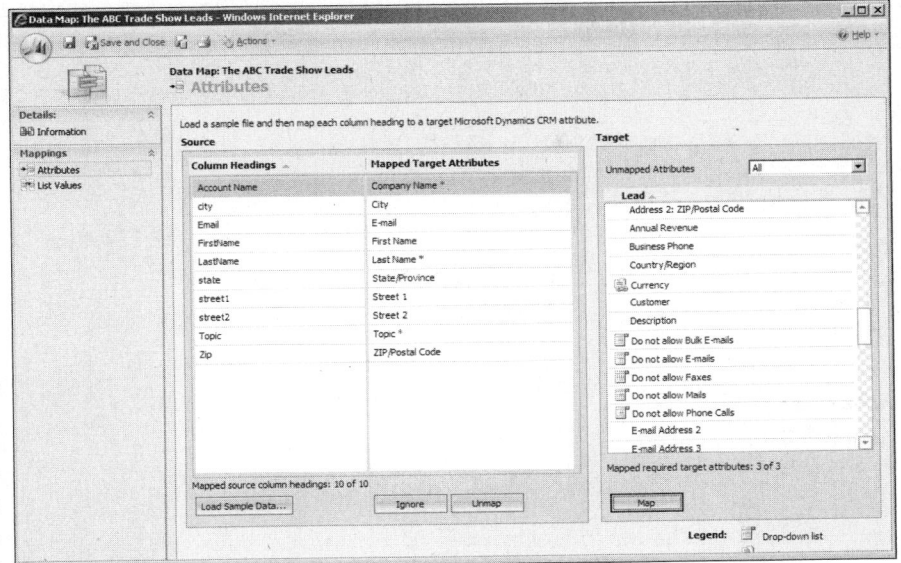

Figure B-7:
Detailed
view of
attribute
mapping.

The required fields in the Microsoft CRM have a red asterisk to the right of the field name.

Double-clicking the target item also maps it to the highlighted source row.

If you're importing to the Lead entity, Topic is a required field. Add a Topic column to your import CSV file and add copy a topic to each record.

If your source data has fields being mapped to drop-down list fields, the source values need to be mapped to the values in Microsoft CRM.

12. **Click List Values on the left navigation pane.**

    The List Attributes form appears.

    The left panel lists the drop-down fields that were mapped in Step 11. On the right, there are two boxes. The top box lists the distinct values in the source file. The box on the bottom lists the options in Microsoft CRM.

13. **Highlight a source value in the top box and a corresponding value in the bottom box and click Map below. Repeat for all fields on the left.**

14. **When all attributes and list values are mapped, click Save and Close on the menu bar at the top of the form.**

    The data map is completed.

Editing data maps

If your data map needs to be updated or edited, follow these steps:

1. **In the Navigation Bar Click Settings.**

   The Settings options show at the top of the Navigation Bar.

2. **Click Data Management on the top of Navigation Bar.**

   The Data Map area replaces Data Management.

3. **In the Data Management area, click Data Maps.**

   The Data Map area replaces Data Management.

4. **Find the Data Map in the grid and double-click.**

   The data map form opens.

5. **Double Click a Data Map.**

The data map form opens.

Edit the items in in much the same way you created the map. Refer to steps 9–14 in the section, "Creating Data Maps," above.

Importing records

To import records you first need a data map. The data map created earlier maps where the source data will go in Microsoft CRM, but until you actually import the data, it remains in the CSV file where it currently resides. To import records, follow these steps:

1. **From the menu bar at the top of the screen, choose Tools⇨Import Data.**

   The Import Records Wizard launches. (See Figure B-8.)

2. **Click the Browse button and browse to the file containing the data to be imported.**

3. **Click Next.**

4. **In the Record Type drop-down list, select the target source.**

   In our example, you'll select Account.

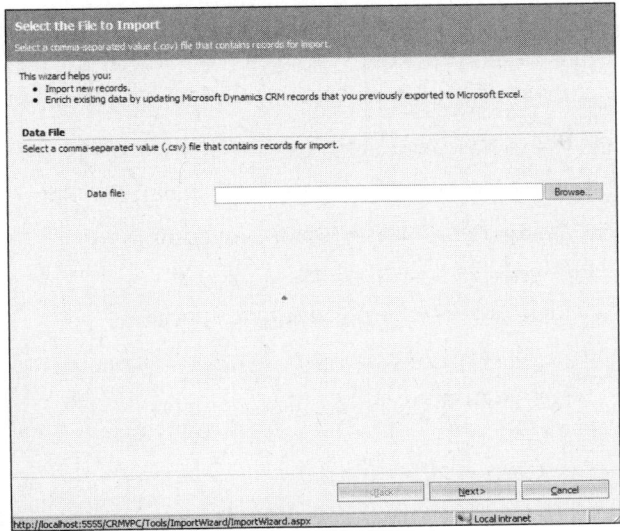

Figure B-8:
Importing
data with
the wizard.

5. **In the data map box, select your map from the lookup box.**

   Clicking New from the data map lookup form is another way to add a new data map. For details see the section, "Creating a New Data Map," earlier in this chapter.

   It's best if the field headings in the source file match the field names in the target columns. If not, there's a chance the import will fail.

6. **Click Next.**

7. **Determine who the record owner will be.**

   The assign to lookup will set the owner of the imported records. By default it is set to the importing user, but can be changed here.

8. **Choose Do Not Duplicate if you've created a duplicate detection rule (if not, and you want a rule, review the beginning of this chapter) or if you're interested in duplicate records, choose Import Duplicates.**

9. **Name the import rule and select the Notification check box if you'd like an e-mail notification when the job is completed.**

10. **Click Import.**

To review the import job status, just follow these steps:

1. **On the navigation bar, click Settings.**

2. **In the Settings area, click Data Management.**

   The data management options are displayed on the right.

3. **Click Imports.**

4. **Double Click an Import.**

   The Import Source form opens. (See Figure B-9.)

5. **On the left navigation pane, Click <<Entity>> Created.**

   A list of records created is displayed (Leads in our example).

6. **On the navigation bar Click Failures.**

   A list of failed records is displayed.

7. **If desired, Click Export Error Rows on the toolbar.**

   The failed records will be exported to Excel.

8. **Close the form when done.**

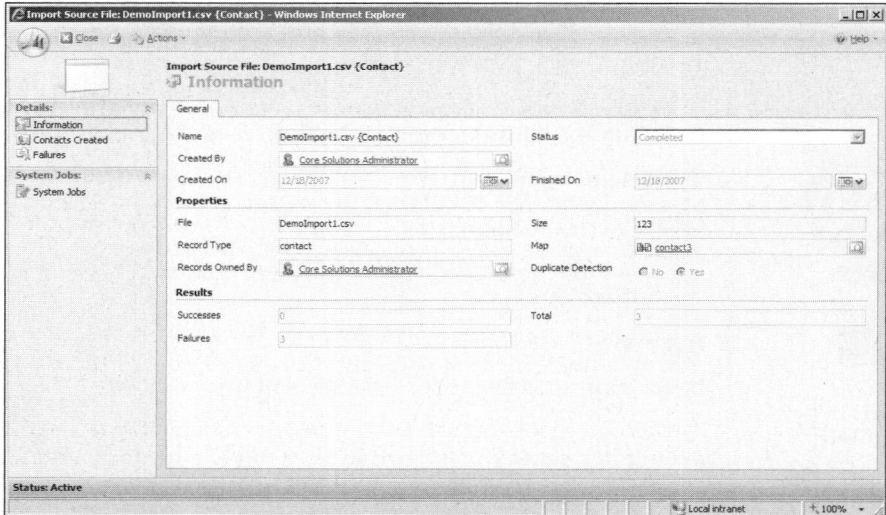

Figure B-9:
System Job
Information.

Exporting and re-importing data

There are several reasons to export data from Microsoft CRM. A common request is to export certain data from Microsoft CRM to further manipulate in Excel, which is covered in Chapter 10.

However, a new feature in Microsoft CRM is the ability to export data, update the data, and re-import the changed data. This feature has been added to the Export to Excel function. The fields that are available to update are those that are in the grid view. To export, update, and re-import, follow these steps:

1. **When viewing a grid of data, click the Excel icon on the toolbar.**

   The Export to Excel dialog box opens.

2. **At the top of the box, select Static Worksheet with Records from this Page.**

3. **At the bottom of the form, select the Make this Data Available for Re-Import by Including Required Columns check box.**

4. **Click Open when prompted.**

5. **Edit the Excel spreadsheet and Save it as a CSV file.**

6. **From the menu bar at the top of the screen, choose Tools⇨Import Data.**

   The Import Records Wizard launches. (See Figure B-6.)

7. **Click the Browse button and browse to the file containing the data to be imported.**

8. **Click Next.**

9. **Ensure that the Enrich Data by Updating Existing Records Rather Than Creating New Records check box is selected.**

10. **Click Next twice.**

11. **Name the import rule and select the Notification check box if you'd like an e-mail notification when the job is completed.**

12. **Click Import.**

   Fields not contained in the grid can't be updated. To update these fields, ask your system administrator to add those fields.

Index

Notes

Notes

BUSINESS, CAREERS & PERSONAL FINANCE

0-7645-9847-3   0-7645-2431-3

Also available:
- Business Plans Kit For Dummies
  0-7645-9794-9
- Economics For Dummies
  0-7645-5726-2
- Grant Writing For Dummies
  0-7645-8416-2
- Home Buying For Dummies
  0-7645-5331-3
- Managing For Dummies
  0-7645-1771-6
- Marketing For Dummies
  0-7645-5600-2

- Personal Finance For Dummies
  0-7645-2590-5*
- Resumes For Dummies
  0-7645-5471-9
- Selling For Dummies
  0-7645-5363-1
- Six Sigma For Dummies
  0-7645-6798-5
- Small Business Kit For Dummies
  0-7645-5984-2
- Starting an eBay Business For Dummies
  0-7645-6924-4
- Your Dream Career For Dummies
  0-7645-9795-7

HOME & BUSINESS COMPUTER BASICS

0-470-05432-8   0-471-75421-8

Also available:
- Cleaning Windows Vista For Dummies
  0-471-78293-9
- Excel 2007 For Dummies
  0-470-03737-7
- Mac OS X Tiger For Dummies
  0-7645-7675-5
- MacBook For Dummies
  0-470-04859-X
- Macs For Dummies
  0-470-04849-2
- Office 2007 For Dummies
  0-470-00923-3

- Outlook 2007 For Dummies
  0-470-03830-6
- PCs For Dummies
  0-7645-8958-X
- Salesforce.com For Dummies
  0-470-04893-X
- Upgrading & Fixing Laptops For Dummies
  0-7645-8959-8
- Word 2007 For Dummies
  0-470-03658-3
- Quicken 2007 For Dummies
  0-470-04600-7

FOOD, HOME, GARDEN, HOBBIES, MUSIC & PETS

0-7645-8404-9   0-7645-9904-6

Also available:
- Candy Making For Dummies
  0-7645-9734-5
- Card Games For Dummies
  0-7645-9910-0
- Crocheting For Dummies
  0-7645-4151-X
- Dog Training For Dummies
  0-7645-8418-9
- Healthy Carb Cookbook For Dummies
  0-7645-8476-6
- Home Maintenance For Dummies
  0-7645-5215-5

- Horses For Dummies
  0-7645-9797-3
- Jewelry Making & Beading For Dummies
  0-7645-2571-9
- Orchids For Dummies
  0-7645-6759-4
- Puppies For Dummies
  0-7645-5255-4
- Rock Guitar For Dummies
  0-7645-5356-9
- Sewing For Dummies
  0-7645-6847-7
- Singing For Dummies
  0-7645-2475-5

INTERNET & DIGITAL MEDIA

0-470-04529-9   0-470-04894-8

Also available:
- Blogging For Dummies
  0-471-77084-1
- Digital Photography For Dummies
  0-7645-9802-3
- Digital Photography All-in-One Desk Reference For Dummies
  0-470-03743-1
- Digital SLR Cameras and Photography For Dummies
  0-7645-9803-1
- eBay Business All-in-One Desk Reference For Dummies
  0-7645-8438-3
- HDTV For Dummies
  0-470-09673-X

- Home Entertainment PCs For Dummies
  0-470-05523-5
- MySpace For Dummies
  0-470-09529-6
- Search Engine Optimization For Dummies
  0-471-97998-8
- Skype For Dummies
  0-470-04891-3
- The Internet For Dummies
  0-7645-8996-2
- Wiring Your Digital Home For Dummies
  0-471-91830-X

SPORTS, FITNESS, PARENTING, RELIGION & SPIRITUALITY

0-471-76871-5

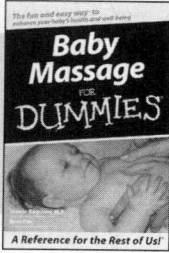
0-7645-7841-3

Also available:
- Catholicism For Dummies
  0-7645-5391-7
- Exercise Balls For Dummies
  0-7645-5623-1
- Fitness For Dummies
  0-7645-7851-0
- Football For Dummies
  0-7645-3936-1
- Judaism For Dummies
  0-7645-5299-6
- Potty Training For Dummies
  0-7645-5417-4
- Buddhism For Dummies
  0-7645-5359-3

- Pregnancy For Dummies
  0-7645-4483-7 †
- Ten Minute Tone-Ups For Dummies
  0-7645-7207-5
- NASCAR For Dummies
  0-7645-7681-X
- Religion For Dummies
  0-7645-5264-3
- Soccer For Dummies
  0-7645-5229-5
- Women in the Bible For Dummies
  0-7645-8475-8

TRAVEL

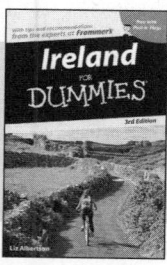
0-7645-7749-2

0-7645-6945-7

Also available:
- Alaska For Dummies
  0-7645-7746-8
- Cruise Vacations For Dummies
  0-7645-6941-4
- England For Dummies
  0-7645-4276-1
- Europe For Dummies
  0-7645-7529-5
- Germany For Dummies
  0-7645-7823-5
- Hawaii For Dummies
  0-7645-7402-7

- Italy For Dummies
  0-7645-7386-1
- Las Vegas For Dummies
  0-7645-7382-9
- London For Dummies
  0-7645-4277-X
- Paris For Dummies
  0-7645-7630-5
- RV Vacations For Dummies
  0-7645-4442-X
- Walt Disney World & Orlando
  For Dummies
  0-7645-9660-8

GRAPHICS, DESIGN & WEB DEVELOPMENT

0-7645-8815-X

0-7645-9571-7

Also available:
- 3D Game Animation For Dummies
  0-7645-8789-7
- AutoCAD 2006 For Dummies
  0-7645-8925-3
- Building a Web Site For Dummies
  0-7645-7144-3
- Creating Web Pages For Dummies
  0-470-08030-2
- Creating Web Pages All-in-One Desk
  Reference For Dummies
  0-7645-4345-8
- Dreamweaver 8 For Dummies
  0-7645-9649-7

- InDesign CS2 For Dummies
  0-7645-9572-5
- Macromedia Flash 8 For Dummies
  0-7645-9691-8
- Photoshop CS2 and Digital
  Photography For Dummies
  0-7645-9580-6
- Photoshop Elements 4 For Dummies
  0-471-77483-9
- Syndicating Web Sites with RSS Feeds
  For Dummies
  0-7645-8848-6
- Yahoo! SiteBuilder For Dummies
  0-7645-9800-7

NETWORKING, SECURITY, PROGRAMMING & DATABASES

0-7645-7728-X

0-471-74940-0

Also available:
- Access 2007 For Dummies
  0-470-04612-0
- ASP.NET 2 For Dummies
  0-7645-7907-X
- C# 2005 For Dummies
  0-7645-9704-3
- Hacking For Dummies
  0-470-05235-X
- Hacking Wireless Networks
  For Dummies
  0-7645-9730-2
- Java For Dummies
  0-470-08716-1

- Microsoft SQL Server 2005 For Dummies
  0-7645-7755-7
- Networking All-in-One Desk Reference
  For Dummies
  0-7645-9939-9
- Preventing Identity Theft For Dummies
  0-7645-7336-5
- Telecom For Dummies
  0-471-77085-X
- Visual Studio 2005 All-in-One Desk
  Reference For Dummies
  0-7645-9775-2
- XML For Dummies
  0-7645-8845-1

HEALTH & SELF-HELP

0-7645-8450-2

0-7645-4149-8

Also available:
- Bipolar Disorder For Dummies
  0-7645-8451-0
- Chemotherapy and Radiation
  For Dummies
  0-7645-7832-4
- Controlling Cholesterol For Dummies
  0-7645-5440-9
- Diabetes For Dummies
  0-7645-6820-5* †
- Divorce For Dummies
  0-7645-8417-0 †

- Fibromyalgia For Dummies
  0-7645-5441-7
- Low-Calorie Dieting For Dummies
  0-7645-9905-4
- Meditation For Dummies
  0-471-77774-9
- Osteoporosis For Dummies
  0-7645-7621-6
- Overcoming Anxiety For Dummies
  0-7645-5447-6
- Reiki For Dummies
  0-7645-9907-0
- Stress Management For Dummies
  0-7645-5144-2

EDUCATION, HISTORY, REFERENCE & TEST PREPARATION

0-7645-8381-6

0-7645-9554-7

Also available:
- The ACT For Dummies
  0-7645-9652-7
- Algebra For Dummies
  0-7645-5325-9
- Algebra Workbook For Dummies
  0-7645-8467-7
- Astronomy For Dummies
  0-7645-8465-0
- Calculus For Dummies
  0-7645-2498-4
- Chemistry For Dummies
  0-7645-5430-1
- Forensics For Dummies
  0-7645-5580-4

- Freemasons For Dummies
  0-7645-9796-5
- French For Dummies
  0-7645-5193-0
- Geometry For Dummies
  0-7645-5324-0
- Organic Chemistry I For Dummies
  0-7645-6902-3
- The SAT I For Dummies
  0-7645-7193-1
- Spanish For Dummies
  0-7645-5194-9
- Statistics For Dummies
  0-7645-5423-9

Get smart @ dummies.com®

- **Find a full list of Dummies titles**
- **Look into loads of FREE on-site articles**
- **Sign up for FREE eTips e-mailed to you weekly**
- **See what other products carry the Dummies name**
- **Shop directly from the Dummies bookstore**
- **Enter to win new prizes every month!**

* **Separate Canadian edition also available**
† **Separate U.K. edition also available**

Available wherever books are sold. For more information or to order direct: U.S. customers visit www.dummies.com or call 1-877-762-2974.
U.K. customers visit www.wileyeurope.com or call 0800 243407. Canadian customers visit www.wiley.ca or call 1-800-567-4797.